JUNGIAN
CRITICISM

JUNGIAN LITERARY CRITICISM

Edited by
Richard P. Sugg

Northwestern University Press
Evanston, Illinois

Northwestern University Press
Evanston, Illinois 60201-2807

Copyright © 1992 by Northwestern University Press
All rights reserved. Published 1992
Printed in the United States of America

ISBN cloth 0-8101-1017-2
    paper 0-8101-1042-3

Library of Congress Cataloging-in-Publication Data

Jungian literary criticism / edited by Richard P. Sugg.
    p.   cm.
    Includes bibliographical references and index.
    ISBN 0-8101-1017-2 (cloth). — ISBN 0-8101-1042-3 (paper)
    1. Criticism.   2. Psychoanalysis and literature.
3. Psychoanalysis in literature.   4. Jung, C. G. (Carl Gustav),
1875–1961.   I. Sugg, Richard P.
PN98.P75J8   1992
801′.92—dc20   92-3557
                                                                     CIP

CONTENTS

PREFACE

This book intends to honor a tradition of Jungian literary criticism, nearly as old as the century itself, that continues to offer much of value to the current understanding of both literature and the life of the psyche. Jung-and-literature is a shorthand term the book will use occasionally to express the mutuality of the two disciplines operative in all Jungian literary studies; it provides a convenient name for an interdisciplinary subject characterized by the explicit application of C. G. Jung's psychology to the understanding of matters appropriate to literature and literary criticism.

Although the subject has enjoyed a long and substantial history, including something of a boom in scholarly interest during the past fifteen years, today it lacks a focal point. I believe it can gain both a broader audience and a salutary clarification of its enduring interests and feasible objectives if the full range of its accomplishments is made visible in one coherent shape. Further, an increased awareness of and respect for the psychology that underlies it will encourage a more informed level of discourse than sometimes obtains in studies proclaiming themselves to be Jungian.

Psychological literary critics have tended to bring to their work the discipline's sense of the traditional tasks of literary criticism, and then to ask how psychology might help. But recently an increasing number have begun their work with an education in psychology (whether drawn from extensive reading, formal training, analysis, or some other form of clinical practice) that more nearly matches their study of literature. Thus they have felt more confident in bringing into their literary studies a critical sensibility informed by psychology's ongoing investigations, and then asking how literature reflects or furthers it. The two different starting points produce two different models of the critic's task, and sometimes widely divergent results. Nevertheless, both models have proven capable of providing valuable and mutually informing perspectives on both literature and psychology. By gathering and arranging a selection of the excellent work generated by both approaches to Jungian literary studies, this book hopes to demonstrate, not only the many uses of the field, but also its possibilities and its power.

The book begins by surveying representative moments in the interdisciplinary history of Jung-and-literature and then develops the major

topics of the field. Part 1's selections from such writers as Elizabeth
Drew, Northrop Frye, Joseph Campbell, Albert Gelpi, James Olney,
James Hillman, Annis Pratt, and Kathleen Raine not only epitomize important, enduring issues and summon up something of the intellectual
milieu from which they first emerged, but remind the reader of the value
of understanding critical issues in terms of their historical development.
The historical then gives way to the topical approach of Parts 2 and 3,
where selections have been chosen to identify and display the most
significant subjects of Jungian literary studies. Throughout, the book
presents extensive editorial matter, including Preface, Introduction,
headnotes to all selections, Appendixes, Glossary, and Index, to aid the
book's intended audience—everyone interested in understanding the
dynamic interaction of Jung-and-literature.

The ultimate strength of this book resides in its selections from
original sources. The combined impact of these essays on literature and
psychology, excerpted from more than thirty authors, does far more to
define and substantiate the book's subject than any argument or sum-
mary here could do. Further, the intelligence and information that shine
through both old and new selections, and their synergistic revitalization
when gathered in one place, I hope will inspire the reader not only to new
discoveries beyond this book but also to new ideas about the nature and
direction of the field itself.

The variety and liveliness of the work typically done in Jungian
literary studies may be limned here by citing a few of the relevant selections for illustration. An initial overview of critical issues central to the
field can be gleaned from reading Jacoby the analyst/artist and then Baird
the critic; but these are amplified later by the whole of Part 2, "Jung and
Critical Theory." The practice of Jungian literary criticism takes many
forms, from discovering and explaining recurring, archetypal patterns (of
symbols, character, theme, and genre) and myths—whether found in the
traditional literary canon (Willeford on the Fool/Trickster, or Gelpi on
H.D.'s later poetry) or in an area of more recent prominence, such as
women's popular genre fiction (Pratt)—to describing a literary pattern's
psychological relationship to the spirit of a specific culture and period
(Gelpi on Emily Dickinson, both selections by Hinz and Teunissen).

A second important activity of Jungian literary studies, work that
needs to be done more often, is the conscious use by literary critics of the
new discoveries psychology can contribute toward rethinking the assumptions of critical theory (Philipson, Willeford, Adams, Boer, and
Pratt). In this same vein, Jungians have made important contributions to

the understanding of the psychological contexts bearing upon literature's reception by its readers, whether by teachers and students in the developmental group typically found in a classroom (Maud), or by psychologists and patients in a clinical setting (Hillman), or by a group delimited by gender, such as women reading women's fiction (Pratt, in Part III). For scholars who are interested in reader-response, Jungian analyses of personality type (Atkinson and Beebe), validated by a storehouse of statistical data gathered over four decades by several widely used Jungian type-indicator personality assessment tests, have great but largely untapped potential both for criticism and for pedagogy.

Finally, at the other end of the interdisciplinary spectrum conjoining Jung with literature, a Jungian approach can become transposed into a literary re-visioning of Jungian psychology itself: a trained analyst may invoke literature and critical theory for models to revise the theoretical assumptions of his own discipline of psychology. For instance, the psychologist may re-vision the significance of the dream symbol, or the fiction of the case history, in the analytic context; indeed, he may argue for modifying the traditional Jungian hermeneutic by studying the powerful, universal phenomenon of imaginative response to literature and the arts by the human psyche (Hillman, Willeford, et al.).

The interdisciplinary nature of the book's subject, as well as the great number of books and essays available, have dictated several principles governing the selection of material. First, each essay should contribute to exploring and defining Jung-and-literature from an interdisciplinary perspective. It should argue in some way for the validity of Jungian literary studies by satisfying the pragmatic criterion: one discipline must prove useful in shedding light on the other.

Second, each selection should add to knowledge of individual works of literature, or of issues concerning the theory of literature—whether centered on the artist, the artwork, or the audience. Several selections by analysts present statements that clarify Jungian concepts (Samuels, and Maduro and Wheelwright define key terms; Jacoby identifies central issues of Jung and literary criticism). But, as a rule, essays directed exclusively toward psychologists, though they make use of literature, are not included.

Finally, for reasons of space, the book's scope had to be delimited. Although many worthy essays using a Jungian approach to understand literature from every historical period do exist, this book focuses primarily on twentieth-century American and British literature and criticism; indeed, several selections treat the work of authors who have spoken at length of the influence of Jung's psychology on their art and life—for example, Robert Bly, Charles Olson, and Robertson Davies.

These general principles are supplemented by the specific information and editorial comment in each selection's introductory headnote, intended to suggest some relevant contexts for the respective essay. Selections not infrequently refer to other essays in the book, though of course each was written independently. When selections have been excerpted from books and essays, short omissions from the original text are indicated by three ellipses dots (. . .) separating passages; longer omissions are indicated by four squares (■ ■ ■ ■) placed alone on a line between one block of text and the next. Citations for the original texts may be found in the Source Acknowledgments at the end of the book.

The Introduction presents an overview of the relationship of each selection to the book's subject. Further, it explains the rationale for the arrangement of the selections into three major parts, with various subsections. The design of the book is intended to offer an accurate representation of the broad field of Jung-and-literature to those who already know it, while enlightening others who are coming to it for the first time.

Besides the headnotes, the Preface, and the Introduction, a Chronology of Jung's life and works, compiled by Aniela Jaffé, his longtime friend, relates his writings on literature to the *Collected Works,* and to Jung's life and times. The editorial matter of the book also includes two appendixes. Appendix A begins by tracing the historical development of Jung's thought in terms of the publication, with dates, of his writings relevant to the study of literature. His theory of psychology was developed over fifty years, with many significant changes and additions. Also, since Jung wrote primarily in German, the history of when his works became available to the English-speaking world must be considered. Appendix A should demonstrate the importance of asking the writers and critics who have invoked Jung's psychology two elementary questions: what Jung have they read, and when was it written?

Appendix B comprises a list of bibliographies whose range covers virtually all aspects of Jung-and-literature. It also includes a brief guide to material in the book that offers useful explanations of Jungian concepts, not only as Jung used them, but also as they have been employed by later psychologists and critics. A glossary of Jungian terms follows the Notes section.

ACKNOWLEDGMENTS

Many people deserve acknowledgment for their help in creating this book. I am grateful to the authors of the original material from which the selections were made, and to their publishers and agents for permission to reprint. Thanks also to the editors at Northwestern University Press, especially Amy Schroeder, Lee Prater Yost, and Susan Harris.

The project was begun with the support of a National Endowment for the Humanities fellowship, and later was helped by a sabbatical award from Florida's State University System.

The Ann and Erlo Van Waveren Foundation, under the direction of Olivier Bernier, must be cited here for its early and continuing financial support—first with a grant for a summer of research at the Library of Congress, and lately with another grant to underwrite the completion of the book.

Equally important contributions came from the numerous dedicated and ingenious professionals who made the research system work in the various libraries to which this book sent me, but especially those at Princeton University and the Library of Congress.

Since the beginning this project has benefitted in myriad ways from the interest and suggestions of two scholar-editors. A. Walton Litz has been unfailingly generous with his advice and encouragement. William McGuire has made himself available continually to share, through conversation and unflagging correspondence, his encyclopedic knowledge of the Jung world. By exemplifying the scholar's vocation as a shared and generous pursuit, as much as by the excellence of their own works, these two have served as models during the past five years.

Finally, thanks to those who made this book possible by creating supportive environments: colleagues and students at the university; fellow members of the Washington Society for Jungian Psychology; and most important of all, the family at home—Ellen, Pete, and Buttons.

Chronology of C. G. Jung
Aniela Jaffé

1875	Born July 26.
1895–1900	Medical training and qualification, Basel University.
1900	Assistant physician under Bleuler at the Burghölzli, the insane asylum of Canton Zurich and psychiatric clinic of Zurich University.
1902	M.D. dissertation, *On the Psychology and Pathology of So-Called Occult Phenomena, CW*, 1; Winter semester (1902–3) with Pierre Janet at the Salpêtrière, in Paris, for the study of theoretical psychopathology.
1903–5	Experimental researches on word associations and complexes, later associated with archetypes, *Studies in Word-Association, CW*, 2.
1905–9	Senior staff physician at Burghölzli; conducts policlinical courses on hypnotic therapy. Research on dementia praecox (schizophrenia), *CW*, 3.
1905–13	Lecturer on medical faculty of Zurich University; lectures on psychoneuroses and psychology.
1906	April: Correspondence with Freud begins.
1907	March: First meeting with Freud, in Vienna.
1908	First International Psychoanalytic Congress.
1909	September: First visit to U.S.A., with Freud and Ferenczi; lectures on association experiment at Clark University, receives honorary degree of LL.D.
1909–13	Editor of *Jahrbuch für psychoanalytische und psychopathologische Forschungen*, published by Freud and Bleuler.
1910–14	March: First president of the International Psychoanalytic Association (to 1914).
1910	Reading and lectures on mythology, leading to 1911–12 *Wandlungen und Symbole der Libido* (*Psychology of the Uncon-*

scious, 1916), extensively revised in 1952 as *CW,* 5, *Symbols of Transformation.*

1912   September: Lectures at Fordham University, New York, on "The Theory of Psychoanalysis," *CW,* 4.

1913   Break with Freud; Jung designates his psychology as "Analytical Psychology" (later also as "Complex Psychology").

1913–19   Period of intense introversion and confrontation with the unconscious.

1916   "Seven Sermons to the Dead," text resulting from his encounter with unconscious; first mandala painting; first description of process of "active imagination" in "The Transcendent Function," *CW,* 8; first use of terms "personal unconscious," "collective/suprapersonal unconscious," "individuation," "animus/anima," and "persona" in "The Structure of the Unconscious," *CW,* 7.

1918–19   Medical Corps doctor and commandant of camp for interned British soldiers in Switzerland; first use of the term "archetype" in "Instinct and the Unconscious," *CW,* 8.

1920   Journey to Algeria and Tunisia; first summer seminar in England at Cornwall.

1921   *Psychological Types, CW,* 6 (pub. in English, 1923); first use of term "self."

1923   First Tower built in Bollingen; death of mother; Richard Wilhelm's lecture on the *I Ching* at the Psychological Club, Zurich; summer seminar at Polzeath, Cornwall, on "Technique of Analysis."

1924–25   Trip to U.S.A., visits Pueblo Indians in New Mexico; also New Orleans and New York.

1925   First English seminar at the Psychological Club, Zurich; visits the Wembley Exhibition, London; summer seminar at Swanage, England, on "Dreams and Symbolism."

1925–26   Trip to Kenya, Uganda, and the Nile; visit with the Elgonyi on Mount Elgon.

1928   Beginning of encounter with alchemy; *Two Essays on Analytical Psychology, CW,* 7.

1928–30   English seminars on "Dream Analysis" at the Psychological Club, Zurich.

1929   Publication, with commentary, of *The Secret of the Golden Flower*, trans. Richard Wilhelm, ancient Chinese text on yoga and alchemy.

1930   Vice-President of General Medical Society for Psychotherapy, under Ernst Kretschmer as president.

1930–34   English seminars on "Interpretations of Visions" at the Psychological Club, Zurich.

1932   Awarded Literature Prize of the City of Zurich.

1933   *Modern Man in Search of a Soul* published, a widely read introduction to Jung's ideas; beginning of annual *Eranos* conferences, where Jung lectured until 1951; first lecture, "A Study in the Process of Individuation," *CW*, 9, pt. 1.

1934   Second lecture, "Archetypes of the Collective Unconscious," *CW*, 9, pt. 1.

1934–39   English seminars on "Psychological Aspects of Nietzsche's *Zarathustra*" at the Psychological Club, Zurich.

1934–39   Editor of *Zentralblatt für Psychotherapie und ihre Grenzgebiete* (Leipzig).

1935   Appointed titular professor at the Eidgenössiche Technische Hochschule (E.T.H.), Zurich; gives Tavistock Lectures at the Institute of Medical Psychology, London (not published until 1968, as *Analytical Psychology; Its Theory and Practice, CW*, 18).

1936   Receives honorary doctorate from Harvard University; Eranos lecture on "Ideas of Redemption in Alchemy," expanded as part 3 of *Psychology and Alchemy, CW*, 12.

1937   Gives Terry Lectures on "Psychology and Religion" (*CW*, 11) at Yale University.

1938   Invitation to India on the twenty-fifth anniversary of the Indian Science Congress, Calcutta; honorary doctorates from the universities of Calcutta, Benares, and Allahabad; International Congress for Psychotherapy at Oxford with Jung as president; he receives honorary doctorate from Oxford University; appointed Honorable Fellow of the Royal Society of

Medicine, London; Eranos lecture on "Psychological Aspects of the Mother Archetype," *CW,* 9, pt. 1.

1941   With Karl Kerényi, published *Essays on a Science of Mythology.*

1943   Honorable member of the Swiss Academy of Sciences; appointed to the chair of Medical Psychology at Basel University.

1944   Resigns Basel chair on account of critical illness. *Psychology and Alchemy, CW,* 12.

1945   Honorary doctorate at University of Geneva on the occasion of his seventieth birthday; Eranos lecture on "The Psychology of the Spirit," expanded as "The Phenomenology of the Spirit in Fairy Tales," *CW,* 9, pt. 1.

1946   Eranos lecture on "The Spirit of Psychology" (expanded as "On the Nature of the Psyche," *CW,* 8); "The Psychology of the Transference," *CW,* 16.

1948   Eranos lecture "On the Self" (expanded to chap. 4 of *Aion, CW,* 9, pt. 11); Inauguration of the C. G. Jung Institute, Zurich, the first training institute for Jungian analysts.

1951   *Aion, CW,* 9, pt. 11; Jung's last Eranos lecture, "On Synchronicity," in *CW,* 8, expanded as "Synchronicity: An Acausal Connecting Principle."

1952   *Symbols of Transformation, CW,* 5: 4th, greatly revised, edition of *Psychology of the Unconscious*; "Answer to Job," *CW,* 11.

1953   Publication of the first volume of the American/British edition of the *Collected Works* (trans. R. F. C. Hull): *Psychology and Alchemy, CW,* 12.

1955   Honorary doctorate from the E. T. H., Zurich, on the occasion of his eightieth birthday; November 27: Death of his wife, Emma.

1955–56   *Mysterium Coniunctionis, CW,* 14, the final work on the psychological significance of alchemy.

1957   *The Undiscovered Self, CW,* 10; starts work on *Memories, Dreams, Reflections,* with the collaboration of Aniela Jaffé (publ. 1962); BBC television interview.

1958   "Flying Saucers: A Modern Myth," *CW,* 10.

1960   Made Honorary Citizen of Kusnacht on the occasion of his eighty-fifth birthday.

1961   Finishes his last work ten days before his death: "Approaching the Unconscious," in *Man and His Symbols* (publ. 1964). Dies after short illness on 6 June in his house at Kusnacht.

1964   Inauguration of the Clinic and Research Center for Jungian Psychology, Zurich.

INTRODUCTION TO THE SELECTIONS

Richard P. Sugg

The essays in this book address topics both historically and currently important to Jungian literary criticism. But the reader will reach a more complete understanding of the book's interdisciplinary project, as well as the significance of each essay, by taking into account also the stance of the critics themselves toward their subjects. What degree of familiarity with Jung's psychology do they have, and what do they believe to be the range of possibilities and the limitations of the interdisciplinary approach of Jung-and-literature? Of course, the book's selections can speak for themselves, and the introductory headnotes discuss both essay and author. But it is useful to consider here, using the authors of selections in Part 1 for reference, three groups of literary critics and the different attitudes they hold toward Jung-and-literature. Among these, a few would deny that they are Jungian critics, much less members of a Jungian school of literary criticism, though a discerning reader may judge otherwise. Nevertheless, all have acknowledged at some point the useful influence of Jung-oriented ideas in their work; and many have developed a pervasively Jungian approach over a long career. Certainly, all have written literary criticism that has furthered the exploration of the interdisciplinary possibilities of Jung-and-literature.

The first of the three groups consists of literary critics evincing certain shared affinities with the investigations and interests of those more committed to Jung's psychology. The second group is the myth critics. In

1

the third group are the demonstrably Jungian literary critics, whose writing shows evidence of a substantial understanding and use of Jung's psychology; these include the analyst-critics. The work of a number of critics could fit into more than one group, and of course critics vary from essay to essay in their reliance on Jung, so these categories are not restrictive. But they can serve to draw broad distinctions, regarding both the nature of the approach and the degree of sophistication of the involvement, among those who have found Jung's psychology useful.

Part 1 of the book, "Jung and Literary Criticism: A Historical Sampling," offers several selections representative of the best of those critics whose work reveals shared affinities with Jung's psychology. In the first category are Elizabeth Drew's 1949 work on T. S. Eliot's mythical vision; Northrop Frye's three essays, spanning twenty-five years, on the affinities of his archetypes of literature with Jung's archetypes of psychology; James Baird's preface to his 1956 book on Melville, coupled with his lengthy analysis in 1976 of the possibilities and limitations of Jung's psychology for literary critics of his persuasion; and Evelyn Hinz and John Teunissen's 1985 essay on D. H. Lawrence's archetype-driven rewritings of *Lady Chatterley's Lover.*

James Baird's essay illustrates some of the possibilities and problems of the approach to Jungian criticism typical of the shared affinities group. Baird speaks well of Jung, uses his writings extensively, develops a central argument based on several of his key ideas (e.g., refashioning Jung's "archetype" into his own concept of the "autotype"), yet he never assents outright to the validity of Jung's work. Like many mid-century critics, Baird is scrupulous in honoring, first of all, what he considers to be the boundaries of his discipline, and in carefully separating it from the discipline of psychology. He sees no need for a school of critics who might extend, critique, and renew Jungian literary criticism through reference to Jung's psychology (nor a need for any of the other critical schools based on extraliterary knowledge that have recently emerged, such as feminism or new historicism). Rather, Baird acknowledges Jung merely as one influence among several whose work has contributed importantly to the "climate" of literary criticism in this century.

But this position raises several questions. Does Baird mean that Jung is relevant only insofar as he has been absorbed into our intellectual climate? Or that the literary critic can learn all one needs of Jung's psychology from the texts of literature and literary criticism? If Baird's allegiance to his discipline saves the literary critic from reductionism or other New Critical fallacies, it also sometimes leaves the reader feeling that he has failed to respond fully to the call from the literature itself, the reading experience that first led the critic to adopt an archetypal-psychological approach. Even the best work from the shared-affinities-but-no-more group of Jungian critics, including Baird, occasionally makes the reader wish that the critic had been more curious.

However, in spite of its self-imposed limitations, the work of Baird and the best of the critics of this first group constitutes an important part of Jungian literary criticism. Their writing is frequently doubly interesting because it is necessarily engaged in rethinking the possible boundaries of literary criticism even as it applies Jung's psychology to a specific literary work or theory. For example, it is instructive to compare the rules of evidence governing their arguments, and the kinds of conclusions they are able to arrive at under rules admitting evidence only from the text, with the rather different guidelines used by critics who were trained also to be analysts, such as Henderson, Jacoby, and Hillman (or, later, Willeford and Beebe), or by critics using ideological approaches such as feminism (Pratt) or something akin to the New Historicism's poetics of culture (Gelpi on Dickinson, Hinz and Teunissen on Lawrence).

A second important group, whose work has a significant and in many cases essential relationship to Jung's psychology, are the myth critics. Selections in Part 1 from this second group include: Elizabeth Drew's 1949 "The Mythical Vision," exploring the relationship of myth, psychology, and literary criticism; Northrop Frye's 1951 seminal essay "The Archetypes of Literature," in conjunction with "Forming Fours," his 1954 review-essay of two books of Jung that Frye deemed especially relevant for literary criticism, as well as his retrospective view in "Expanding Eyes," written twenty years later; Joseph Campbell, whose Jungian affinities are especially evident in "The Fashioning of Living Myths"; Baird, especially in his book *Ishmael*; and Hinz and Teunissen's special use of the term "mythic literature" to apply to D. H. Lawrence.

Myth criticism was a broad-based movement rivaling in importance the New Criticism throughout the 1950s; Leitch's recent *American Literary Criticism* characterizes Jung's influence on all elements of that movement as "profound and pervasive from the 1930's onwards." Jung was especially influential among those critics who, applying the philosophy of Ernst Cassirer and others to literary criticism, saw myth as a mode of apprehension, a way of thinking about and of envisioning the world (hence Drew's essay on Eliot's mythic vision), and consequently considered literature informed by a mythic vision (as Eliot had praised *Ulysses* in 1923 for its mythic method) as carrying a significance of archetypal and collective importance (see Jung's 1922 essay "On the Relation of Analytical Psychology to Poetry"). Thus, though many literary critics who use myth would not call themselves Jungian, a large number first discovered Jung's psychology through their interest in myth and have used his extensive work in that field to good effect. Certainly, over the past seventy-five years a great deal of Jung-oriented criticism has involved work with myth.

Some myth critics, often following the lead of anthropology, have preferred to dissociate myth and archetypes from any psychological base in the individual, viewing them instead as universal cultural patterns generated by sociological factors (see Hinz and Teunissen, and Willeford, in Part 2). Such critics downplay myth's origin and emphasize instead its effects on readers: myths and the mythic elements in literature can touch a reader powerfully, they can communicate a complex of ideas and feelings in a symbolic way, and over time myths can develop a tradition of meanings and emotions that readers respond to because, somehow (conditioning? heredity?—does the answer matter for literary criticism?), they are imbued with this cultural legacy.

In practice, the work of many myth critics is congenial with Jungian ideas, whether or not they stop short of making the leap from myth as universal idea to myth as product of, and related importantly to, the individual psyche. It is not uncommon for non-Jungian myth critics to use Jungian terms and ideas with virtually the same meaning that Jung himself gave them. Some myth critics have argued, as James Olney and Kathleen Raine do, that the terms and ideas were not specifically Jung's but part of a perennial philosophy going back to the pre-Socratics. But whether or not every myth critic acknowledges Jung as a source, the fact remains that many readers and critics have felt that, to understand most fully the mythic, archetypal approach to literature (particularly, how that approach related literature to an individual psyche, a specific culture, and to history), the best source to draw upon is Jung's psychology.

Selections from Part 1 that illustrate the third group, those acknowledging a strong Jungian influence (some of these were cited in group two as well), include the following: Joseph Henderson's 1968 "The Artist's Relationship to the Unconscious"; Mario Jacoby's 1969 "The Analytical Psychology of C. G. Jung and the Problem of Literary Evaluation"; Michael Atkinson's 1976 piece on individuation and the shadow in Robert Bly's *Sleepers Joining Hands*; Albert Gelpi's 1977 essay on Emily Dickinson's most difficult poem; James Olney's 1980 book on Yeats, Jung, and the perennial philosophy; James Hillman's 1983 book, *Healing Fiction*; Annis V. Pratt's 1985 essay relating Jung to a feminist criticism, "Spinning Among Fields"; and Kathleen Raine's 1988 essay-memoir on her own and her generation's debt to Jung.

This third group is comprised only of those who identify an important aspect of their critical approach to literature as Jungian. They have written powerful literary criticism, and in it have demonstrated the usefulness of a serious study of both Jung's psychology and the history and practice of approaches to literature that stem from it. Many have proclaimed an interest in the subject ranging beyond the usual bounds of criticism; their reading in Jung is declared relevant to their life as well as to their literary criticism. Typically, such critics begin to work in both directions (thereby emulating both Freud and Jung), using literature to clarify psychology, as well as the other way round. They may find in literature a source of new therapeutic practices for the clinic (Hillman and the imaginal analyst-critics) and in psychology a source not only of powerful literary interpretation but also of effective pedagogical practices for the classroom. They frequently discover a desire to further their education by entering into a Jungian analysis. As Jungian literary critics, their goal is to enhance their own and their discipline's evolving sense of a literary work as situated in a more comprehensive human context than formalism admitted, one where an evolving Jungian psychology may be useful.

Part 2, "Jung and Critical Theory," is intended to suggest something of the range of Jung-oriented critical theory, and to highlight several topics that are central to all of it. The selections begin with subsection A, " 'Myth' and 'Archetype': Critics and Analysts," which presents statements from a range of sources focused solely on the key, interrelated topics of myth and archetype. In the first, analysts Maduro and Wheelwright give an authoritative psychological account of these fundamental concepts. Samuels, also an analyst, offers a very recent Jungian definition of "Archetype," "Myth," and the related "Numinosum." Hinz and Teunissen, both literature professors, discuss how myth and archetype can be related to culture. Finally, Willeford, as professor of literature and practicing Jungian analyst, discusses the definitions of myth and its relationship to psyche and experience.

Part 2 continues with its selections relating Jung's psychology to the critical theory of literature. Philipson, trained as a philosopher, discusses the key Jungian concept of the symbol for its value to aesthetics. In subsection B, "Imaginal Archetypal Criticism," are three selections concerning the recent Hillman-inspired revision of Jungian psychology and its application to current literary criticism. Adams provides an extended theoretical analysis of current Jungian psychology in terms of the similarities between Hillman's archetypal theory and the work of Derrida and other continental thinkers; Boer discusses the history of the image in twentieth-century poetry and relates it to Hillman's revisioning of Jung's archetypal image; and Maud's essay works out some of the ideas of Hillman's critical theory in terms of practical criticism and pedagogical technique.

Part 3, "Jungian Concepts in Critical Practice," presents three groups (A through C) of selections concentrated on applications of an important Jungian concept to literary criticism. The concept itself, as well as each individual selection in the group, is introduced by an explanatory headnote.

Group A, "Archetypes and Literature: The Trickster," presents selections demonstrating the variety of ways in which literary criticism can make use of the psychological concept of the archetype. This subsection looks specifically at the trickster, though it illustrates approaches that have been used with other major archetypes—such as the anima, animus, hero, wise old man, and the quest.

Group B, "Jung's Individuation Process and Literary Character," focuses on Jung's theory of personality, especially his description of the developmental stages a person's psyche passes through during a complete life-cycle. The first selection discusses its effect on various twentieth-century authors' depiction of literary character. Another essay shows how Jung's theory of psychological types and their relationships can be used to elucidate the archetypal pattern of the Sherlock Holmes mystery novel. The last selection describes how a novelist relates the individuation process to the symbols and stages of the alchemical process, as Jung himself had done. Also, the headnote directs the reader to other essays on this topic.

Group C centers on the currently prominent topic of Jung and gender criticism. Three selections illustrate the range of applications of Jung's psychology to this approach to literature, as well as some of the controversy surrounding the broader discussion of how to relate Jung to feminism. The headnote indicates other essays in the book on this subject.

JUNG AND LITERARY CRITICISM: A HISTORICAL SAMPLING

Part I

1   T. S. ELIOT: THE MYTHICAL VISION

Elizabeth Drew

Elizabeth Drew taught literature both in England and America, publishing widely on the subject. In her seventh decade she wrote "The Mythical Vision" to introduce her Jungian study T. S. Eliot: The Design of His Poetry *(1949), extending a phrase that Eliot himself had used in 1923 to describe Joyce's "mythical method" in* Ulysses. *Drew's straightforward presentation of the origins and meanings of myth for modern literature would have been acceptable to any of the myth critics of her day; but her emphasis on the psychological basis of the mythical vision, more pronounced in this essay than in her readings of the poetry, is specifically Jungian and reflects a wide reading in his works. Drew links a subject often invoked in myth criticism—death and rebirth—with Jung's individuation process (she calls it the "archetype of transformation"). Further, Drew premises her reading of Eliot not merely on an archetypal reading of symbols in his individual works but on an interpretation of the sequence of symbols during his career. This approach leads to a psychobiographical reading. Every work casts light upon those before and after it, insofar as all relate to the author's continuing individuation and transformation of psyche, as reflected in the symbolic design of his poetry.*

In looking at objects of Nature, I seem rather to be seeking, as it were asking for, a symbolical language for something within me that already and for ever exists, than observing anything new.

S. T. Coleridge

I hold this book to be the most important expression which the present age has found. . . . In using the myth, in manipulating a continuous parallel between contemporaneity and antiquity, Mr. Joyce is pursuing a method which others must pursue after him. They will not be imitators, any more than the scientist who uses the discoveries of an Einstein in pursuing his own, independent, further investigations. It is simply a way of controlling, of ordering, of giving a shape and a significance to the immense panorama of futility and anarchy which is contemporary history. . . . It is a method for which the horoscope is auspicious. Psychology (such as it is, and whether our reaction to it be comic or serious), ethnology and *The Golden Bough* have concurred to make possible what was impossible even a few years ago. Instead of narrative method, we may now use the mythical method. It is, I seriously believe, a step towards making the modern world possible for art, towards . . . order and form. And only those who have won their own discipline in secret and without aid, in a world which offers very little assistance to that end, can be of any use in furthering this advance.[1]

The whole tone of this passage from Eliot's review of *Ulysses* suggests that in it he is not merely commenting on an interesting and original work by a fellow literary artist, but that there is something in the method of the creation of that work which has excited him profoundly; that it contains some revelation of wide and deep significance for himself and for others. He likens its importance to that of the most revolutionary discoveries in the physical universe, and his mind jumps for an analogy to the ancient belief that linked man's fate with the courses of the stars. As an astrologer of old plotted the encompassing position of the constellations to discover the controlling forces of a particular future, and rejoiced to find them favorable, so Eliot sees the happiest future for art under the influence of a new controlling factor. He calls this "the mythical method," and he sees it as a way by which the artist can give shape and significance to the chaotic material of contemporary life. He can set the "immense panorama of futility and anarchy" in opposition to the pattern of a different vision; he can "manipulate a parallel" with the world of myth.

But the stories of ancient mythology have always been a source of inspiration to the literary artist, as their use in every age has amply shown. What, then, does Eliot mean when he says that recent discoveries in anthropology and psychology have made the mythical method possible, and that it is the most important expression the present age has found?

He means that modern explorations of myth have changed completely the conceptions of its origins, its nature, and its function. Myth (the etymological root is the same as that of *mystery*) leads us back to ultimate mysteries, not only the mystery of life itself, but of that element in life by which man differentiated himself from the rest of the animal creation: speech. *Mythos* meant "word," and the development of man's use of the term from *mythos* to *epos* to *logos* is itself the story of his developing use of language: from the word meaning a symbolic reflection of his earliest consciousness, to the word meaning a structure of events in time, to the word meaning a pattern of rational values.

Modern scholarship now recognizes that myth is no dead form, a relic of antiquity, an empty survival. It is true that the ancient stories we call "myths" are primitive legends expressing man's first response to his world, but the *manner* of that response springs from a faculty alive in all ages of man's existence. The mythical method is the presentation of experience in symbolic form, the earliest and still the most direct and immediate form of human expression. Long before man developed the power of logical discourse and intellectual interpretation, the material transmitted to his mind through his senses molded itself into meaning in myth. The outer worlds of physical nature, of human character, action, and endeavor, and the inner world of his own conscious and unconscious response to these things, formed themselves in him, and were in turn formed and developed *by* him into symbolic configurations, into metaphorical conceptions and expressions. It was the first step of primitive man "towards order and form"; the giving of imaginative shape and significance to the totality of his experience.

And since its aim was to encompass his experience in its wholeness, to communicate his sense of the revelation of its meaning, primitive myth always creates a pattern in which man brings himself into significant relationship with mysterious forces outside the actualities of his daily life. He senses himself as part of a symbolic drama extending far beyond himself. Anthropologists now trace all the symbolic formulations of primitive myth and religion, and of the ritual inseparable from them, to the primeval consciousness of a magic or *mana* potency indwelling in the physical universe and accessible to man, though forever evading his practical understanding:

In the case of any important magic we invariably find the story
accounting for its existence. Such a story tells when and where it
entered the possession of man. But it is not the story of its origins.
Magic has never been made or invented. All magic simply 'was' from
the beginning an essential adjunct of all such things and processes as
vitally interest man and yet elude his normal rational efforts.[2]

Myth, therefore, was the symbolic presentation of primitive man's
instinct that his workaday world was interpenetrated with a superrational
or extrarational activity in which he himself could and did share. There
was an anonymous source of vitality diffused throughout the universe and
in himself, which he objectified in dramatic symbols and so made operative in human experience. His myths were fabulous fictions that revealed
psychic facts: they were images that intensified and expanded and gave
grandeur of design to his existence. Through them he became part of a
unity composed of two activities. On the one hand he appeared to be
merely a social unit in the common round of diurnal enterprise, but he
apprehended, too, a symbolic drama where that apparently planless flux
of being and becoming related itself to changeless patterns of creative
and destructive forces—patterns of value, existing on a different plane of
living, and requiring a language of their own.

He created this symbolic drama in that language, the language of
myth and ritual, which thus became the heritage of the race handed on
from generation to generation. Through it the individual and the tribe
alike were united with the indestructible potencies symbolized, and
brought into close and purposive relation with them. Thus the function of
myth and ritual in the primitive community was the creation of expressive forms that satisfied man's primeval need of spiritual reassurance and
social stability. The myth vouched for the "magic" that was alive in the
universe, while the ritual associated with the sacred tradition defeated
the destructive aspects of the "magic" and transmitted its beneficent
powers into the life of the individual and the tribe. The formal rite concentrated and channeled the cosmic energies, disposing their strength
and value directly upon the affairs of men.

Modern anthropology sees all religion and all art as springing and
growing from this primitive root of symbolic transformation. By his symbol-
making instinct, man's knowledge and experience of the outer and inner
world were projected into direct sensuous embodiment, giving them life
and outline and meaning, turning force into form. And it was the juxtaposition of the "shape and significance" of life given expression in these sym-

bolic terms with "the immense panorama of futility and anarchy which is contemporary history" in which Eliot saw a hope for a new advance towards order and form.

The contribution of psychology to that possibility has been to explore behind the *results* of man's symbol-making instincts and needs to their source in his own being. Though psychology has come to no verifiable conclusions about the origins or the nature of the source, it has done much to clarify both its workings and its functions. It has also given it a name and called it "the unconscious," that part of the psyche which Jung describes as "the eternally creative mother of consciousness; the never failing source of all art and of all human productivity." To the psychologist, the "magic" which, to the primitive, just "was," originates in the unconscious, whence man projects it upon the external world, endowing physical objects or his self-made symbolic figures with properties and behavior from its own reality; giving psychic life from its own energies to the objects of its wonder, fear, love, hate, reverence, or contempt.

Freud, at his seventieth birthday celebration, refused credit for the discovery of the unconscious. That, he said, properly belonged to the masters of literature, who had always been aware of its presence, its pressures, and its powers. Jung would agree with him. But the two great psychological pioneers of the contemporary world parted company over the question of the derivation of myth. Though both agreed it has its root in the unconscious and the strange phenomenon of the dream image, they differed radically in their theories and interpretations of its genesis.

To Freud, the scientific positivist, the unconscious contents of the human psyche consist solely of material suppressed by the conscious. To him the unconscious is a pathological or infantile activity of the mind and the disguised symbols of mythological situation that arise in it mere symptoms of these all-prevailing but basically unhealthy suppressions. He sees all myth, all religion, and all art as originating in such suppressions. Moreover, although the resulting symbolic manifestations are so complex and so varied, their originating cause is simple: "the beginnings of religion, ethics, society and art meet in the Oedipus complex."[3] He interprets all unconscious drives exclusively in sexual and familial terms, and their emergence into myth and ritual as illustrating various aspects of the ambivalent emotions of love and hate, admiration and fear, attraction and repulsion, inherent in the parent-child relationship. "In the beginning was the deed,"[4] the original murder (whether in imagination or in actuality) of the primal father, springing from the incest motive, and all further developments of mythical legend and religious ritual are transpositions and releases into acceptable terms of the repressed emotional forces occasioned by that ever-recurring central situation in the life of the individual.

To Jung, however, this theory very early appeared inadequate. He could not square the tremendous dynamic effects of mythic-religious concepts on man's history, art, and behavior with a belief that their symbolic origin was morbid or that they derived solely from experience in the single individual life. He felt that such psychic happenings could not be explained *away* in other terms, but must be explained as psychic events with an independent nature of their own. He became convinced that the symbols generated in dream from the unconscious sprang not only from man as a disordered object, but also from a level of his psychic activity where his faculty of symbolic transformation made him a self-creating subject.

It is clear that such a conception of the activities of the human psyche would be more congenial to Eliot as a contribution to the "mythical method" than the theories of Freud. In his remarks on *Ulysses,* however, Eliot injects parentheses after his mention of psychology—"(such as it is and whether our reaction to it be comic or serious)." In *The Dry Salvages* he appears to class it with fortune-telling, palmistry, and astrology as "pastimes and drugs." He is, however, kinder elsewhere:

> Psychology has very great utility in two ways. It can revive, and has already to some extent revived, truths long since known to Christianity, but mostly forgotten and ignored, and it can put them in a form and a language understandable by modern people to whom the language of Christianity is not only dead but undecipherable. . . . But I must add that I think psychology can do more than this, in discovering more about the human soul still; for I do not pretend that there is nothing more to know; the possibilities of knowledge are practically endless. Psychology is an indispensable handmaid to theology; but I think a very poor housekeeper.[5]

But in spite of this "serious" reaction to the subject, the core of the criticism is in the last sentence, and it is obvious that it was not through psychology that Eliot reached his own conclusions about the nature of reality. Yet apart from such ultimate problems, the development of his poetry contains an interesting parallel to some of the materials cited by Jung, and a confirmation of his belief that certain archetypal patterns of imagery that recur and interfuse in the myths of the human race are of great significance in the problem of the nature of the symbolizing process, as well as that of the nature of life in general.

To Jung these archetypal patterns inhabit a psychic territory which he has called the "collective unconscious," an area beyond the personal unconscious first defined scientifically by Freud, and much vaster. It is not altogether clear in what terms Jung regards the collective unconscious. He speaks of it sometimes as a working hypothesis, sometimes as a kind of mighty metaphor (similar to Yeats's "Great Memory") which images the permanent sameness of man's deepest psychic patterns. It would surely seem as if it belongs in this category, where it could be generally accepted as of very great interest and enlightenment in the exploration of all the great recurring themes of myth and literature. But Jung, while admitting that evidences of it are to be found only in particular individuals, seems often to accept it as having universal scope as fact.

> There is no reason for believing that the psyche, with its peculiar structure, is the only thing in the world that has no history behind its individual manifestations. Even the conscious mind cannot be denied a history extending over at least five thousand years. It is only individual ego-consciousness that has forever a new beginning and an early end. But the unconscious psyche is not only immensely old, it is also able to grow unceasingly into an equally remote future. It forms, and is part of, the human species just as much as the body, which is also individually ephemeral, yet collectively of immeasurable duration.[6]

Just as tradition is the inherited wisdom of the race consciously expressed, so Jung envisages the collective unconscious as the *un*conscious inherited wisdom of the race. As such he sees it as accounting not only for the striking analogies between the themes and patterns of myth in many different cultures, but also for the presence of recurring mythological and archaic symbols in dreams, even in the dreams of those who have no knowledge of the traditional and literary sources which perpetuate them.

It is to these symbols that Jung has given the name of *archetypes* or *primordial images,* and he sees them, not only as the raw materials from which the myths and religions of the race have been consciously elaborated, but as constantly recurring revelations of creative and destructive potentialities in the individual. They appear as symbols in man's deepest inner conflicts, in which his most vital energies are brought into play and "they become accessible to consciousness only in the presence of that degree of self-awareness and power of understanding which enables a man to think what he experiences instead of just living it blindly."[7] In fact, just as tradition is meaningless unless its continuity is also a process of continual recreation in society and in the individual, so with this racial memory. Its images, to be of any value, must be recreated in collaboration with the conscious intelligence into a process of ordered growth. Just as the language of myth and ritual gave significant pattern to tribal tradition and so satisfied the needs of primitive man for inner communal security, so Jung sees the same process accomplished for modern man through the conscious adaptation of these symbolic messages from the unconscious into richer patterns of individual living.

Moreover, not only do they make him aware of the character of the eternally recurring conflicts to be resolved, but they are actual instruments of the resolution. Jung not only postulates the *presence* of the racial memory, of these deposits of inherited psychic experience which in certain circumstances and in certain temperaments can become stirred and active, but his experience has led him to detect in them not only a peculiarly powerful dynamism, but a *purposive* quality of their own. At the other extreme from Freud's belief that such dream images are relics of primitive and infantile modes of reaction, blocking the way to the mature development of the ego, Jung regards them as revelations of psychic potentialities, "the mighty spiritual inheritance of human development, reborn in every individual." When particular circumstances are encountered in the life of the individual that bring him into touch with some aspect of this universal collective experience, the images appear, modified by the personal circumstances and sensibilities of the dreamer, but bringing with them always the peculiarly stirring and energizing sense of involvement in larger and more impersonal forces.

> Each of these images contains a piece of human psychology and human destiny, a relic of suffering or delight that has happened countless times in our ancestral story, and on the average follows ever in the same course. It is like a deeply graven river-bed in the soul, in which the waters of life, that had spread hitherto with groping and uncertain course over wide but shallow surfaces, suddenly become a mighty river. This happens when that particular chain of circumstances is encountered which from immemorial time has contributed to the laying down of the primordial image. The moment

when the mythological situation appears is always characterized by a peculiar emotional intensity; it is as though chords in us were touched that had never resounded before, or as though forces were unloosed, the existence of which we had never dreamed.[8]

And to Jung, not only are the forces unloosed, but the symbols through which they reveal themselves have a peculiarly compelling power. It is as if the individual were agent and interpreter of something which, is as it were, shaping *him* and being shaped *by* him in a reciprocal action. For, in the incessant flux of lively antagonisms and perpetual oppositions which sustain the energies of psychic vitality, Jung detects an inner ordering principle, a purposive process, as compulsive as that of physical growth itself. Though he does not pretend to know what "spirit," is, he insists on it as a force in its own right. He will not accept the "spiritual" as a derivative of sex, even in the widest application of that term. "The spiritual appears in the psyche likewise as a drive, indeed as a true passion. It is no derivative of another drive, but the indispensable formative power in the world of drives." To those who become aware of this drive, this true passion, the archetypes and primordial images can act in the nature of energy transformers. They absorb and resolve the opposing charges on which the purposive use of psychic force depend, and the fresh energy thus released can be directed toward future development.

In such cases it is as if the individual were himself caught up into the world of myth, made living instead of legendary, and with the content of its conscious and unconscious dramatic material revealed gradually as a creative process. And, being in a sense artist too as well as a character in the drama, controlling as well as being controlled by the symbolic forms, being able "to think what he experiences instead of just living it blindly," the individual has the power to collaborate consciously in the design. He waits for those moments when fabulous fiction explodes into psychic fact; when seemingly unrelated and ambiguous symbols constellate into pattern; when many-faceted "meaning" resolves itself from apparently irreconcilable paradox. Thus the material from the conscious and the unconscious situation "given" symbolically in the dream image is reduced by the conscious formative process to new contours and compounds of thought and action. The *mythos* of the symbol itself is united to the *epos* of action and to the *logos* of constructive thought.

There are as many archetypes as there are figures and situations in myth, for to Jung the psyche contains all the images that have ever given rise to myths. He has analyzed a great number of them in his own terms of interpretation,[9] but there is one particular "constellation of primordial images" to which he repeatedly returns in his writings, and which he regards as the accompaniment of the central psychic adventure of mature human life. He refers to the whole experience under the general title of "the archetype of transformation" and, in nonsymbolic language, as the Process of Individuation or the Integration of the Personality. It is the experience of detachment from the world of objective reality as the center of existence and the finding of "a new dimension" in which it can and must be contemplated and lived. Detachment, too, from the ego as the center of interest and the discovery of a different center. As such, it involves the process of the death of an old life and the birth of a new, the process traced back by Frazer and other scholars as the inner meaning of the symbolism of the oldest fertility rituals and the basis of their development into tragic drama. It is the paradox expressed in the pattern of *Oedipus Rex*. There, in the scene where Oedipus begins that exploration of the truth which will shatter his whole framework of temporal prosperity, the seer Tiresias says: "This day shall give you birth and death." It appears in innumerable forms in myth and legend, and is, of course, inseparably intertwined with the whole symbolic content of Christianity. "Except a corn of wheat fall into the ground and die, it abideth alone: but if it die, it bringeth forth much fruit"; "Except a man be born of water and of the spirit he cannot enter into the Kingdom of God"; "Whosoever will save his life shall lose it."

During the process of "transformation," as observed psychologically by Jung, certain archetypal images regularly occur, forming a continuity and interaction of symbols expressing the disintegration and death of the old pattern and the gradual emergence of a new order. When this has established itself, the center of the personality has been shifted from the ego to a hypothetical point of equilibrium between the individual consciousness and the collective psyche. Rather confusingly, Jung calls this point the "Self," and he says it is

> Sensed as an indefinable state of being to which the ego is neither
> opposed nor subjected, but is in a relation of dependence and
> around which it revolves, very much as the earth rotates about the
> sun. I use the word "sensed" in order to indicate the apperceptive
> character of the relation between the ego and the Self. In this rela-
> tion there is nothing knowable in the intellectual sense, because we

can say nothing of the contents of the Self. The ego is the only content of the Self that we know. The individuated ego experiences the
fact that it is object of an unknown and superordinated subject. . . .
Visualizations are never more than awkward attempts of a fumbling
mind to give some kind of form to the inexpressible psychological
facts.[10]

Of the whole progression he concludes: "As to what these processes consist in, I have no theory to offer. One would first have to know what the
psyche is." And he thinks that the natural history of the mind is no further advanced today than was the natural science of the thirteenth century.

The central experience that informs most of the poetry of Eliot is
this same age-old pattern of symbolic death and birth, lived through as an
intense personal experience and accepted as the central truth of a religious faith. The Anglican church to which he belongs has its own historic
archetypes and rituals, containing in themselves a complete symbolic ordering of the theme and, by abstraction in theology, the whole conceptual ordering of the psychic material involved. But Eliot in his poetry does
not often use traditional Catholic symbolism. His "transformations" are
all his own in his reliving of the inner reality of the myth. It is, of course,
obvious that without any hypothesis of a collective unconscious, the "primordial" character of many of his dominating symbols can be accounted
for very easily by his saturation in literary tradition. But the *sequence* in
which the archetypal images arise in the course of his poetry, their interrelationships, and their final resolution into the design of *Four Quartets*,
reflects in a strange way the succession in the appearance of the symbols
which Jung has described as the archetype of transformation. The final
development of the images, too, is in a "sensing" of a pattern of vital
relationships between the ego and a larger order, which arranges itself
into the same kind of symbolic design. In this design "reality" is felt to
inhere, though apprehended only through "hints and guesses."

This is interesting psychologically; though, if the parallel be valid,
it is only a confirming of Jung's hypothesis and not a "discovering more
about the human soul still." The symbols will be discussed more fully
when they begin to emerge in the poems themselves. Meanwhile, to get
back to Eliot's review of *Ulysses*, it was not any special symbolic *content*
that he was discussing there, but the mythical *method*; myth as illustrating the direct presentation of experience in symbolic form. He was em-

phasizing Joyce's use of this to manipulate a parallel between past and present. Eliot himself does that specifically in *The Waste Land*, but he had been using the method in its general meaning long before. The recognition of sensuous symbolism as the richest form of human perception, and its ordering into pattern as the basis of poetic technique, had been from the beginning his whole theory and practice of poetry.

(1949)

2 THE ARCHETYPES OF LITERATURE "FORMING FOURS" "EXPANDING EYES"

Northrop Frye

Northrop Frye, perhaps the most prominent literary critic of the past half-century, presented in The Anatomy of Criticism *(1957) an elaborate critical theory based on archetypal literary genres, whose origin he had traced, in "The Archetypes of Literature" (1951), back to primitive rituals and nature myths patterned on the seasonal cycle. In this seminal essay Frye denies that the archetypes of literature are explained—let alone caused—by the archetypes of Jung's psychology. However, Frye's repeated praise of Jung's work as important for literary criticism encouraged other critics to push the relationship between the two perhaps beyond the "interpenetration" to which Frye would restrict such interdisciplinary instincts.*

"Forming Fours" displays the range and depth of Frye's familiarity with Jung and links key elements of his literary criticism with Jung's psychology and Frazer's anthropology, declaring both "cornerstones in archetypal criticism."

"Expanding Eyes," written twenty years later, addresses more directly the relationship between Jung's and Frye's system. Again, though, Frye resists confusing the two kinds of archetypes—literary and psychological—while displaying a thorough familiarity with, and interest in, such Jungian touchstones as mandalas and alchemy. As Frye acknowledges, "If spiritual seeker and poet share a common language, perhaps we cannot fully understand either without some reference to the other."

THE ARCHETYPES OF LITERATURE

. . . We say that every poet has his own peculiar formation of images. But when so many poets use so many of the same images, surely there are much bigger critical problems involved than biographical ones. As Mr. Auden's brilliant essay *The Enchafèd Flood* shows, an important symbol like the sea cannot remain within the poetry of Shelley or Keats or Coleridge: it is bound to expand over many poets into an archetypal symbol of literature. And if the genre has a historical origin, why does the genre of drama emerge from medieval religion in a way so strikingly similar to the way it emerged from Greek religion centuries before? This is a problem of structure rather than origin, and suggests that there may be archetypes of genres as well as of images.

It is clear that criticism cannot be systematic unless there is a quality in literature which enables it to be so, an order of words corresponding to the order of nature in the natural sciences. An archetype should be not only a unifying category of criticism, but itself a part of a total form, and it leads us at once to the question of what sort of total form criticism can see in literature. . . .

■   ■   ■   ■

. . . We may call the rhythm of literature the narrative, and the pattern, the simultaneous mental grasp of the verbal structure, the meaning or significance. We hear or listen to a narrative, but when we grasp a writer's total pattern, we "see" what he means.

The criticism of literature is much more hampered by the representational fallacy than even the criticism of painting. That is why we are apt to think of narrative as a sequential representation of events in an outside "life," and of meaning as a reflection of some external "idea." Properly used as critical terms, an author's narrative is his linear movement; his meaning is the integrity of his completed form. Similarly, an image is not merely a verbal replica of an external object, but any unit of a verbal structure seen as part of a total pattern or rhythm. Even the letters an author spells his words with form part of his imagery, though only in special cases (such as alliteration) would they call for critical notice. Narrative and meaning thus become, respectively, to borrow musical terms, the melodic and harmonic contexts of the imagery.

Rhythm, or recurrent movement, is deeply founded on the natural cycle, and everything in nature that we think of as having some analogy with works of art, like the flower or the bird's song, grows out of a profound synchronization between an organism and the rhythms of its environment, especially that of the solar year. With animals some expressions of synchronization, like the mating dances of birds, could almost be called rituals. But in human life a ritual seems to be something of a voluntary effort (hence the magical element in it) to recapture a lost rapport with the natural cycle. A farmer must harvest his crop at a certain time of year, but because this is involuntary, harvesting itself is not precisely a ritual. It is the deliberate expression of a will to synchronize human and natural energies at that time which produces the harvest songs, harvest sacrifices, and harvest folk customs that we call rituals. In ritual, then, we may find the origin of narrative, a ritual being a temporal sequence of acts in which the conscious meaning or significance is latent: it can be seen by an observer, but is largely concealed from the participators themselves. The pull of ritual is toward pure narrative, which, if there could be such a thing, would be automatic and unconscious repetition. We should notice, too, the regular tendency of ritual to become encyclopedic. All the important recurrences in nature, the day, the phases of the moon, the seasons and solstices of the year, the crises of existence from birth to death, get rituals attached to them, and most of the higher religions are equipped with a definitive total body of rituals suggestive, if we may put it so, of the entire range of potentially significant actions in human life.

Patterns of imagery, on the other hand, or fragments of significance, are oracular in origin, and derive from the epiphanic moment, the flash of instantaneous comprehension with no direct reference to time, the importance of which is indicated by Cassirer in *Myth and Language*. By the time we get them, in the form of proverbs, riddles, commandments, and etiological folktales, there is already a considerable element of narrative in them. They, too, are encyclopedic in tendency, building up a total structure of significance, or doctrine, from random and empiric fragments. And just as pure narrative would be unconscious act, so pure significance would be an incommunicable state of consciousness, for communication begins by constructing narrative.

The myth is the central informing power that gives archetypal significance to the ritual and archetypal narrative to the oracle. Hence the myth *is* the archetype, though it might be convenient to say "myth" only when referring to narrative, and "archetype" when speaking of significance. In the solar cycle of the day, the seasonal cycle of the year, and the organic cycle of human life, there is a single pattern of significance, out of which myth constructs a central narrative around a figure who is partly the sun, partly vegetative fertility, and partly a god or archetypal human being. The crucial importance of this myth has been forced on literary critics by Jung and Frazer in particular. . . .

■ ■ ■ ■

. . . Again, because psychology and anthropology are more highly developed sciences, the critic who deals with this kind of material is bound to appear, for some time, a dilettante of those subjects. These two phases of criticism are largely undeveloped in comparison with literary history and rhetoric, the reason being the later development of the sciences they are related to. But the fascination which *The Golden Bough* and Jung's book on libido symbols have for literary critics is not based on dilettantism, but on the fact that these books are primarily studies in literary criticism, and very important ones.

In any case, the critic who is studying the principles of literary form has a quite different interest from the psychologist's concern with states of mind or the anthropologist's with social institutions. For instance: the mental response to narrative is mainly passive; to significance, mainly active. From this fact Ruth Benedict's *Patterns of Culture* develops a distinction between "Apollonian" cultures based on obedience to ritual and "Dionysiac" ones based on a tense exposure of the prophetic mind to epiphany. The critic would tend rather to note how popular literature which appeals to the inertia of the untrained mind puts a heavy emphasis on narrative values, whereas a sophisticated attempt to disrupt the connection between the poet and his environment products the Rimbaud type of *illumination*, Joyce's solitary epiphanies, and Baudelaire's conception of nature as a source of oracles; also, how literature, as it develops from the primitive to the self-conscious, shows a gradual shift of the poet's attention from narrative to significant values, this shift of attention being the basis of Schiller's distinction between naive and sentimental poetry.

The relation of criticism to religion, when they deal with the same documents, is more complicated. In criticism, as in history, the divine is always treated as a human artifact. God, for the critic, whether he finds him in *Paradise Lost* or the Bible, is a character in a human story; and for the critic all epiphanies are explained, not in terms of the riddle of a possessing god or devil, but as mental phenomena closely associated in their origin with dreams. This once established, it is then necessary to say that nothing in criticism or art compels the critic to take the attitude of ordinary waking consciousness towards the dream or the god. Art deals not with the real but with the conceivable; and criticism, though it will

eventually have to have some theory of conceivability, can never be justified in trying to develop, much less assume, any theory of actuality. It is
necessary to understand this before our next and final point can be made.

We have identified the central myth of literature, in its narrative
aspect, with the quest-myth. Now if we wish to see this central myth as a
pattern of meaning also, we have to start with the workings of the subconscious where the epiphany originates, in other words, in the dream. The
human cycle of waking and dreaming corresponds closely to the natural
cycle of light and darkness, and it is perhaps in this correspondence that
all imaginative life begins. . . .
(1951)

FORMING FOURS

For some time now the Bollingen Foundation has been producing a series
of books on symbolism, the unifying theme of which would have puzzled
anyone who did not realize that they were mostly Jungian documents.
Now, as number 20 in the series, a complete English translation of Jung
in eighteen volumes is announced, and the first two, volumes 7 and 12,
have just appeared. One is a revision of *Two Essays on Analytical Psychology*
(the phrase "analytical psychology" means Jung, just as "psychoanalysis" means Freud), and the other, *Psychology and Alchemy,* is a more systematic and erudite version, with a tremendous bibliography, of the
desultory work previously known in English as *The Integration of the Personality.* . . .

. . . The four "archetypes," or semiautonomous personalities
which the psyche has partly created and partly evoked, now settle into
the four functions of psychic life: thought, feeling, intuition, and sensation. (At least I think they do, but this point comes somewhere in between the two books, and Jung's argument here may be less symmetrical
than my account of it.) The self is now the center of a circle with four
cardinal points, and this fourfold circle appears everywhere in religion,
art, and private dreams as the diagram called the "mandala." A simple
Western example is a picture of Christ as the fourfold Word of God, surrounded by the four "beasts" of Revelation, later identified with the four
Gospel narrators. The whole process of shifting the center to the true self
Jung calls "individuation," or, sometimes, "transformation."

Of the differences between Jung's thought and Freud's, there are
two that concern us just now. All modern scientific analysis of the psyche
must of course be rooted in therapeutic techniques for helping the men-

tally ill to function at least normally, whatever normally means. Jung believes, however, that the ordinary medical analogies of diagnosis,
treatment, and cure are not adequate for the psychologist. The physical
body nearly always matures in about twenty years, but in most people the
psyche remains largely undeveloped throughout life, though possessing
within it a force of growth towards the "individuation" which is its peculiar maturity. This growing force within the psyche is what Jung, in contrast to Freud, means by libido, and, being a biological force, it behaves
teleologically, just as an acorn behaves as though it intended to become
an oak tree. When a psychologist tries to help a neurotic, he is helping to
release this power of growth, and he ought to realize that any "cure" is
only one stage in the process he has started going.

Secondly, the drama of individuation does not take place entirely
within the individual. The archetypes come into the individual from a
"collective unconscious," inherited from our ancestors and extending
over present-day society. Hence the dreams and fantasies of the individual should not be interpreted solely in relation to his personal life: they
are also individual manifestations of a mythopoeic activity found in everybody; and private analysis should be supplemented by an objective study
of the analogies between the patient's mythopoeia and that of the art,
folklore, mythology, and romance of human beings generally. In Jung, as
in Proust, the study of the psychology of the mind leads to the discovery
that men are "titans in time," and that their creative powers rise from an
essentially timeless world.

■   ■   ■   ■

When Jung began to supplement the purely analytical interpretation of dreams with a hermeneutic study of the analogies to dreams in
myth and romance, the result was a most important study, soon to be
republished in this series as volume 5, *Symbols of Transformation*. It was
previously known in English as *The Psychology of the Unconscious*, although
its original title, *Wandlungen und Symbole der Libido,* gives a much better
idea of its contents. Just as the "individuation process" became the informing principle of his psychology, so the mythopoeic counterpart to it,
the hero's quest, became the informing principle that Jung, with some
help from Frobenius, perceived in myth, folklore, and literature. The
heroic quest has the general shape of a descent into darkness and peril
followed by a renewal of life. The hero is confronted by a dragon or power
of darkness who guards a treasure or threatens a virgin. He is often accompanied by a shadowy companion who seems to be a double of him-

self, and is given counsel by a magician, an old woman, or a faithful
animal, the last being a regular symbol of unconscious powers. The hero
kills the dragon, or sometimes, as in the story of Jonah and the Harrowing
of Hell, disappears into its body and returns, often finding, as Beowulf
does, that the most dangerous aspect of his enemy is a sinister female
principle, whom Jung calls the "terrible mother" and links with the fear
of incest and other erotic regressions.

In any case, the accomplishing of his quest gains him his bride, the
dragon's hoard, or both. The double-edged power of the archetypes for
good or evil is reflected in the stock black-and-white patterns of romantic
characters: there is a wise old man and an evil magician, a solicitous
mother and a wicked stepmother, a heroine and a siren or temptress, a
hero and a traitorous companion. One can see in the quest-myth, too, not
simply a psychic allegory but a kind of geotropism as well, as the heroic
quest catches the cyclic rhythm of nature, the sun setting and reappearing from the body of a dark monstrous underworld the next day, and,
every year, transforming the sterility of winter and raising new life from
underground. Thus the salvation of the individual soul, the religious
myth of a Messiah or redeeming God, and the renewal of energy in nature all seem to be contained in a single mythopoeic framework. At the
same time there is a dialectic in the quest, not a passage from death to
revival but a transformation to a new and timeless life, which means that
in the final analysis the dragon or enemy of the quest is the cycle of time
and nature itself, symbolized by the uroboros, or serpent with his tail in
his mouth.

The themes and patterns of this book are strikingly similar to those
of Frazer's *Golden Bough*. I think there is an explanation for the similarity,
but I have first to explain my explanation. Literary criticism, as a science,
is obviously a social science, but the social sciences are so recent in their
development that they have not been clearly separated even yet. Thus
The Golden Bough was intended to be a book on anthropology, but it was
also a book on literary criticism, and seems to have had far more influence
in literature than in its alleged field. Perhaps the reason is that, in extracting a single type of ritual from a great variety of cultures, Frazer has
done what the anthropologist, with his primary interest in cultural pattern, cannot do—if I may speak under correction of a science I know very
little about—but he has also done precisely what the literary critic, with
his interest in ritual pattern, wants to see done. Similarly, Jung's book on
libido symbols extracts a single dream type from a great variety of individuals, all except one unanalyzed and many of them not even identified.

Again, he has done something that may be largely meaningless to most therapeutic psychologists, but places the book squarely within the orbit of literary criticism. It has thus become, along with *The Golden Bough*, a cornerstone of archetypal criticism, and it appears to have made more stir among the literary critics who happen to be, like the girls in *Finnegans Wake*, "jung and easily freudened," than among psychologists—though again I speak under correction. At any rate, Jung seems to be leading Freud's great discoveries in the direction of a first-hand study of literature, whereas Freudian criticism itself, even Freud's own brilliant essay on Leonardo, tends to take us away from the works of art into the biography of the artist, and so, like many other forms of research, to neglect real criticism in favor of the peripheral darkness of "more light."

Archetypal criticism is that mode of criticism which treats the poem, not as an imitation of nature, but as an imitation of other poems. It studies conventions and genres, and the kind of recurrent imagery that connects one poem with another. The archetype is thus primarily the *communicable* symbol, and archetypal criticism deals with literature as a social fact and as a technique of communication. To an Aristotelian critic, poetry exists, as Sidney says, between the example and the precept. The events of a poem are exemplary and general, hence there is a strong element of recurrence in them. The ideas are precepts, or statements of what might be or ought to be, hence there is a strong element of desire in them. These elements of recurrence and desire come into the foreground with archetypal criticism. From this point of view, the narrative aspect of literature is a recurrent act of symbolic communication: in other words, a ritual. The narrative content of a poem is studied by the archetypal critic as ritual or imitation of action, and not simply as a *mimesis praxeos* or imitation of *an* action. Similarly, the significant content is the conflict of desire and reality that has for its basis the work of the dream. Hence it is inevitable that the archetypal critic would find much of interest in the work done by contemporary anthropology in ritual, and by contemporary psychology in dreams.

Archetypes are most easily studied in highly conventionalized literature, which means, for the most part, naive, primitive, or popular literature. It attempts to extend the kind of comparative study now made of folktales and ballads into the rest of literature, and seizes on the primitive and popular formulas in great art: the formulas of Shakespeare's last period, or the Book of Revelation with its fairy tale about a damsel in distress, a hero killing dragons, a wicked witch, and a wonderful city glittering with jewels. We may distinguish two kinds of archetypes: structural or narrative archetypes with a ritual content, and modal or emblematic archetypes with a dream content. The former are most easily studied in drama: not, as a rule, in the drama of the educated audience and the settled theater, but in naive or spectacular drama: the folk play, the puppet show, the pantomime, the farce, the pageant, and their descendants in masque, comic opera, and commercial movie. Modal archetypes are best studied first in naive romance, which includes the folktales and fairy tales that are so closely related to dreams of wonderful wishes coming true, and to nightmares of ogres and witches.

Frazer's *Golden Bough* is, as literary criticism, an essay on the ritual content of naive drama: that is, it reconstructs an archetypal ritual from which the structural and generic principles of drama may be logically derived. It does not matter two pins to the critic whether this ritual ever had any *historical* evidence or not. Frazer's hypothetical ritual would inevitably have many and striking analogies to actual rituals, and such analogies are part of his argument. But the relation of ritual to drama is a relation of content to form, not of source to derivation. Similarly, the dream content of naive romance is the communicable dream content. It has no relation to psychoanalyzing dead poets, but it would have striking analogies to the fantasies dredged up during psychoanalysis. Jung's book on libido symbols, is, as criticism, an essay on the dream content of naive romance, and Jungian criticism is always most illuminating when it deals with romance, like Zimmer's *The King and the Corpse*, an earlier volume in the Bollingen series. And the central dream in Jung is essentially identical with the central ritual in Frazer, though the hero is individual libido in one and social fertility in the other, and his enemies parental regressions in one and the waste land in the other.

Soon after the publication of *Wandlungen und Symbole der Libido*, an associate in Jung's field, Herbert Silberer, made a study (known in English as *Problems of Mysticism and Its Symbolism*) of an alchemical tract in the Rosicrucian tradition, which he analyzed first psychologically and then in terms of its own cosmological, or, as he called it, anagogic, meaning, and showed that the two interpretations ran parallel. Jung also soon discovered in alchemy another mythical parallel to his individuation process and plunged into a study of alchemical symbolism, both Oriental and European, which has borne fruit in his lavishly illustrated, exhaustively documented study of *Psychology and Alchemy*. The structure and symbolism of alchemy is here compared, not simply with Jung's own psychological system, but with the archetypes of the heroic quest as well. It should be said at once that most of its readers will want to hold it up to a mirror,

like Jabberwocky. That is, the way that Jung has approached myth, working outward from his own practice as a doctor, has had the result of turning every mythopoeic structure he has studied into a vast allegory of his
own techniques of psychotherapy. It is doubtful that anyone not a hundred percent Jungian can take the whole of myth, including alchemy, in
quite that form, but the parallel mythopoeic structures that emerge from
his study are not less rewarding in themselves. Some of these parallels
are suggested by the admirably chosen illustrations, even when they are
not explicitly dealt with in the text.

Alchemy, at least in its fully developed Christian form, was based
on the idea of a correspondence between Scripture and Nature, the *verbum scriptum* and the *verbum factum*. Its religious basis is biblical commentary (*not* the "Church," as Jung keeps saying). Repeating classical
experiments is a normal part of scientific training, and the idea of alchemy was to repeat the original divine experiment of creation: "Lapidis
generatio fit ad exemplum generationis mundi," as one alchemist quoted
by Jung remarks. One isolated, first of all, a *prima materia,* corresponding
to the chaos of Genesis; then one extracted from this a spirit of life, called
Mercurius and asssociated with the *anima mundi,* which contained within
itself the potency of all life and was consequently hermaphroditic. This
hermaphrodite then became the substance that had to be redeemed or
transformed; it changed from the chemical analogy of the Holy Spirit to
the analogy of the old Adam or fallen nature (not Adam as first man,
which would be the homunculus). As such; this hermaphrodite corresponds to the antagonist of the heroic quest: the dragon or monster, the
leviathan, the old man, the serpent or uroboros, and it is represented by
these symbols.

From this the principle of complementary opposition was next
evolved, associated with various symbolic pairings, male and female, sun
and moon, odd and even numbers, red and white. It was often called the
marriage of the red king and the white queen. The union or *coniunctio* of
these (often thought of as some form of incest, because they sprang from
a common parent) shifted the theater of operations from a hermaphroditic to a female principle, just as in the Bible it is shifted from fallen
nature to the Church or Bride of Christ. At this stage a third principle, a
son or divine child, regularly made his appearance. The final stages are
full of associations with the number four, especially the four elements, as
the final work of redemption brings with it the power of living in water
and fire as well as earth and air—a symbolism familiar to us from a late
and not over-profound Masonic treatment of it in *The Magic Flute*.

The philosopher's stone itself was the chemical or demiurgical analogy (or perhaps rather *aspect)* of Christ, the elixir being to nature what his blood is to man. The fourfold symbolism is based on the fact that both man and nature have an inside and an outside, a subject and a object. The center of nature (the gold and jewels hidden in the earth) is eventually to be united to its circumference in the sun, moon, and stars of the heavens; the center of the spiritual world, the soul of man, is united to its circumference in God. Hence there is a close association between the purifying of the human soul and the transmuting of earth to gold, not literal gold but the fiery quintessential gold of which the heavenly bodies are made. The human body and the *vas* or alembic vessel of the laboratory thus experience parallel phenomena. The power of Christ, is, in Scripture, the teaching that gives man immortality, the fountain of eternal youth; in Nature, it is the healing power or panacea that will restore nature to its original innocence, or the golden age.

The relation of all this to the actual attempt to transmute base metals into gold was, and still is, the great mystery about alchemy. The unifying conception soon died out, presumably because the alchemists got nowhere with their experiment (although, as we really don't know what they were trying to do, many of them may, for all we know, have done it), and alchemists broke into straight chemical experimenters on the one hand, and occult philosophers on the other, each group regarding the other as a rabble of self-deluded charlatans. The associations of alchemy were apocalyptic and visionary, but not necessarily heretical, as Jung tends to think: the notion of a redeeming principle of nature as an aspect of Christ is a quite possible inference from the conception of substance that underlies the doctrine of transubstantiation. The parallels between alchemy and the mass, worked out by some of the more zealous allegorists, are perfectly logical granted their premises, and there is no occasion for Jung's speaking of their "bad taste." The rejection of transubstantiation by Protestants, however, along with the Protestant minimizing of the value of works (which would of course include the alchemical *opus*), had a lot to do with hastening the decay of alchemy. The essential point to remember is that when alchemy loses its chemical connections, it becomes purely a species of typology or allegorical commentary on the Bible.

In Jung's book the symbolic structures of alchemy and the heroic quest are united on the Euclidean principle that things equal to the same thing are equal to one another. The "same thing" is Jung's own individuation process, whose general resemblance to the *great work* of alchemy, on its psychological side, is not difficult to demonstrate. But, centuries before Jung was born, the "same thing" to which alchemy and romance were equal was biblical typology. For the Bible was not only the definitive alchemical myth for alchemists, but the definitive grammar of allegory for allegorical poets. Its central structure is that of quest-romance: it tells the story of a progress from creation to recreation through the heroism of Christ in killing the dragon of death and hell and rescuing his bride, the Church. Jung would perhaps have made this point clearer if his own literary experience, being German, had not given so central a place to Goethe.

For Goethe's Faust is already a chemist, ready to believe that Saint John's *in principio* means "nothing but" (one of Jung's most effective phrases) "Im Anfang war die That." And Goethe himself does not follow the central structure of biblical typology: hence his treatment of symbolism, while it is brilliant, varied, and ingenious, is not scholarly, as Dante, Spenser, and Blake are scholarly. When we read the quest-myth in the first book of *The Faerie Queene*, with its elaborate red and white imagery, it seems loaded down with alchemical symbolism, but we don't need to assume that Spenser knew about alchemy, because we can derive all the symbolism from the biblical tradition anyway. True, when we meet the hermaphrodite and uroboros in the temple of Venus in the fourth book, we realize that Spenser *did* know about alchemy, but by that time we have a better idea of the context of such symbols. As for Blake, there is hardly a page of *Psychology and Alchemy* without close analogies in the Prophecies. But that does not prove that Blake knew alchemy; it proves that he knew the Bible and how to use it in poetry. With this additional connecting link, we can see that Jung's book is not a mere specious paralleling of a defunct science and one of several Viennese schools of psychology, but a grammar of literary symbolism which for all serious students of literature is as important as it is endlessly fascinating. (1954)

EXPANDING EYES

We have long since weathered the Newtonian crisis of separating mythological from natural space, and the Darwinian crisis of separating mythological from natural time. A third crisis, more difficult and subtle, is succeeding it: the distinguishing of the ordinary waking consciousness of external reality from the creative and transforming aspects of the mind. Here the distinction between the scientific and the mythological ceases to operate, for science is a creative construct like the arts. And it seems clear that there is nothing on the rising side of human life except what is, in the largest sense, creative. The question therefore resolves itself into the question of the relation of ordinary life, which begins at birth and ends at death and is lived within the ordinary categories of linear time and extended space, to other possible perspectives on that life which our various creative powers reveal.

This is a question that the great religions have tended to dodge, except in special areas. Marxism deliberately excludes it, and the traditional religious myths project it, pushing it into an "afterlife" in heaven or hell or purgatory or this world, conceptions which, to say nothing of their inherent crudity, betray an obvious political motivation. The area to be explored is thus reduced to methods of intensifying imaginative experience. Hence, today, the drug cults; hence the vogue for techniques of meditation, including yoga, magic, and various kinds of divination like astrology. I had noticed, ever since working on Blake, how large a part, after the decline of the "discarded model" of the Ptolemaic universe, occult schematisms had played in literature, so large as to make it clear that something more than a temporary fashion is involved now.

The current interest in such matters brings a third figure into focus within the area of cultural criticism, and that is Jung. Without belittling Jung's achievements in psychology, it is possible that he too, like Spengler and Frazer, is of greatest significance as a critical and cultural theorist. At the center of his vision of life is a progress from the "ego," ordinary life with its haphazard and involuntary perceptions of time and space, to the "individual," who works with far more coordinated and schematic modes of perception. In Jung the symbol of the "individual" perception is the "mandala," as he calls it (perhaps he should have called it a "yantra"), a symmetrical diagram recalling the geometrical cosmologies so common in the Middle Ages and the Renaissance. The view of literature set out in *Anatomy of Criticism* has many points in common with a mandala vision, so much so that many people have drawn up mandalas based on the book and have sent them to me, asking if this was what I really had in mind. I generally reply, with complete truth as far as I am concerned, that they have shown much more ingenuity in constructing their models than I could achieve myself. A mandala is not, of course, something to look at, except incidentally: it is or should become a projection of the way one sees.

I am continually asked also about my relation to Jung, and especially about the relation of my use of the word "archetype" to his. So far I

have tended to resist the association because, in my experience, whenever anyone mentions it, his next sentence is almost certain to be nonsense. But this may actually be a reason for welcoming it. When one finds
that very perceptive people are describing one as the exact opposite of
what one is, one may feel that one has hit a fairly central area of social
resistance. And when I, who have fought the iniquity of mystery in criticism all my life, am called a neo-Gnostic and a successor of Proclus and
Iamblichus, who were pagans, initiates of mystery cults, and very cloudy
writers, perhaps I should feel that I am well on the road to identification.
Even granting the human tendency to look in every direction except the
obviously right one, it seems strange to overlook the possibility that arts,
including literature, might just conceivably be what they have always
been taken to be, possible techniques of meditation, in the strictest sense
of the word, ways of cultivating, focusing, and ordering one's mental processes on a basis of symbol rather than concept. Certainly that was what
Blake thought they were: his own art was a product of his power of meditation, and he addresses his readers in terms which indicate that he was
presenting his illuminated works to them also, not as icons, but as mandalas, things to contemplate to the point at which they might reflect,
"Yes, we too could see things that way."

One of the central principles in *Anatomy of Criticism* is founded on
an analogy with music, though the usual objections to mixing up the arts,
formulated in Lessing's *Laocoön* and elsewhere, do not apply to it. I am
by no means the first critic to regard music as the typical art, the one
where the impact of structure is not weakened, as it has been in painting
and still is in literature, by false issues derived from representation. For
centuries the theory of music included a good deal of cosmological speculation, and the symmetrical grammar of classical music, with its circle of
fifths, its twelve-tone chromatic and seven-tone diatonic scales, its duple
and triple rhythms, its concords and cadences and formulaic progres-
sions, makes it something of a mandala of the ear. We hear the resonance
of this mandala of musical possibilities in every piece of music we listen
to. Occasionally we feel that what we are listening to epitomizes, so to
speak, our whole musical experience with special clarity: our profoundest
response to the B Minor Mass or the Jupiter Symphony is not "This is
beautiful music" but something more like "This is the voice of music"—
this is what music is all about. Such a sense of authority, an authority that
is part of one's own dignity and is not imposed from outside, comes
mainly from the resonance of all our aural experience within that piece of
music. I am sorry if this sounds obscure, but such a response does hap-

pen, and words like "classic" and "masterpiece" really mean very little except the fact that it does happen. One difficulty here is that the response itself may come from anywhere at any time, even from a bird asserting his territorial rights. The classic or masterpiece is a source of such a response that won't go away and will not elude us if we return to it.

Anatomy of Criticism presents a vision of literature as forming a total schematic order, interconnected by recurring or conventional myths and metaphors, which I call "archetypes." The vision has an objective pole: it is based on a study of literary genres and conventions and on certain elements in Western cultural history. The order of words is there, and it is no good trying to write it off as a hallucination of my own. The fact that literature is based on unifying principles as schematic as those of music is concealed by many things, most of them psychological blocks, but the unity exists and can be shown and taught to others, including children. But, of course, my version of that vision also has a subjective pole: it is a model only, colored by my preferences and limited by my ignorance. Others will have different versions, and as they continue to put them forth the objective reality will emerge more clearly.

One prevailing assumption in criticism is that the work of literature is an object set over against us, as something to be admired and studied. So it is, and if criticism ended there, there would be little point in trying to substitute a vast schematic abstraction, however impressive, as the end of literary experience, instead of actual plays and poems and novels. But, first, I am not suggesting that all works of literature are much the same work, or fit into the same general scheme. I am providing a kind of resonance for literary experience, a third dimension, so to speak, in which the work we are experiencing draws strength and power from everything else we have read or may still read. And, second, the strength and power do not stop with the work out there, but pass into us. When students complain that it will kill a poem to analyze it, they think (because they have been told so) that the poem ought to remain out there, as an object to be contemplated and enjoyed. But the poem is also a power of speech to be possessed in his own way by the reader, and some death and rebirth has to be gone through before the poem revives within him, as something now uniquely his, though still also itself.

Jung being a psychologist, he is concerned with existential archetypes, not imaginative ones: with the recurring characters and images that turn up on the way to "individuation." His most significant book, from our present point of view, is *Psychology and Alchemy,* in which he treats the "great work" of the alchemists as an allegory of self-transformation, a process of bringing an immortal body (the stone) to birth within the ordinary one (the *materia prima*). Such a work of transformation is the work specifically of saints, mystics, and yogis. However the alchemists managed, it seems to require teachers, oral instruction, and joining a school, and it is so unimaginably difficult that very few get far along the way, though they undoubtedly make a big difference to the world when they do. The transmission of such teaching, however, is often accompanied, especially in the East, by a total unconcern for society as a whole, or else, especially in the West, by an overconcern with the preserving of the unity of the transmitting body. In any case, some powerful force of social entropy seems to affect it wherever it appears.

One of the most impressive figures in this tradition in our own century, Gurdjieff, distinguishes two elements in man: the essence and the persona, what a man really is and what he has taken on through his social relationships. Gurdjieff clearly thought of the kind of training that he could give as essentially a developing and educating of the essence. Perhaps there is also a way to development through the persona, through transforming oneself into a focus of a community. This includes all the activity that we ordinarily call creative and is shown at its clearest in the production of the arts. What is particularly interesting about alchemy is the way in which it uses the same kind of symbolism that we find in literature to describe the "great work" of the mystic. If spiritual seeker and poet share a common language, perhaps we cannot fully understand either without some reference to the other.

Here we return to the point we started from: the nature of the commitment to literature. We remember Yeats:

> The intellect of man is forced to choose
> Perfection of the life, or of the work,
> And if it take the second must refuse
> A heavenly mansion, raging in the dark.

It seems to me that the first two lines express a profound insight and that the next two are self-dramatizing nonsense. Those who seek perfection of the work, though called creators, are really, as they keep telling us, more like receptors: they are nursing mothers (the female metaphor we began with has, we see, a proper application), bringing to birth something not themselves, yet more genuinely themselves than they are. The something, call it a poem, is made out of both conscious and unconscious materials: the unconscious is something that nobody short of a bodhisattva can control, but in certain mental places it can find its own mode of expression. When it does so, it forms a kind of transformer of mental power, sending its voltage into its readers until, as Blake says, the expanding eyes of man behold the depth of wondrous worlds.

It is at this point that the question of the social function of the arts becomes so important. Some people find it a shock to discover that, say, the commandant of a Nazi death camp can also be someone with a highly developed taste in music. If he had a thorough knowledge of organic chemistry, there would be no shock, but—well, the arts are supposed to have or be based on values, aren't they? But that is precisely the trouble. We find it hard to escape from the notion that the arts are a secondary social luxury, something to turn to after the real standards of living have been met. On that basis they become subject to evaluation, like jewels: they are enjoyed and possessed by what Jung calls the "ego," and something even analogous to price develops. The arts approached in that way can add pleasure and refinement and cultivation and even some serenity to life, but they have no power to transform it, and the notion that they have is for the birds.

It would be better to think of the arts as, like physical exercise, a primary human need that has been smothered under false priorities. If we look at any culture that has reduced its standard of living to the barest essentials, like that of the Eskimos, we see at once how poetry leaps into the foreground as one of those essentials. Not only so, but the kind of poetry that emerges has precisely the quality of primitive simplicity that keeps eluding the poets of a more complex society, however earnestly they seek it. One might start drawing morals here about what kind of society we should reconstruct or return to in order to achieve such simplicity, but most of them would be pretty silly. I merely stress the possibility, importance, and genuineness of a response to the arts in which we can no longer separate that response from our social context and personal commitments. As for the danger of poetry becoming a "substitute" for religion, that again is merely bad metaphor: if both poetry and religion are functioning properly, their interpenetration will take care of itself. (1975–76)

3 "PREFACE" TO *ISHMAEL*

JUNGIAN PSYCHOLOGY IN CRITICISM: SOME THEORETICAL PROBLEMS

James Baird

James Baird, a professor and critic contemporaneous with Frye, wrote books on Herman Melville and Wallace Stevens. In his preface to the Melville book, Ishmael, *he carefully limns the principles governing his critical use of Jung in 1956. To honor the primacy of the individual auteur in the creative act, and to ward against the reductive tendencies in so much psychological criticism, Baird accepts the challenge of devising a new critical terminology, replacing Jung's archetype with his own term, "autotype."*

After twenty years of further thinking upon the matter, Baird directly addressed the problems and the possibilities facing the Jungian literary critic in "Jungian Psychology in Criticism." Baird begins by declaring that "Jung did not found a school of criticism," and concludes by saying that there has as yet been no purely Jungian literary criticism. However, he acknowledges the usefulness of Jung's psychology in twentieth-century criticism, especially for confronting "the problem of the anagogic," both in the work of art and in the reader's response to it. Baird insists that the "unnameable vision" of certain kinds of art, found in so many cultures and historical periods, cannot be ignored merely because it does not conform to the biases of the prevailing critical system. The reason Jung's psychology remains attractive to literary critics is because it honors that unnameable but felt vision which underlies humankind's enduring spiritual impulses. In this context, Baird takes up important topics in Jung's psychology and evaluates their relevance for modern criti-

cism: the collective unconscious, the libido, the archetypes, the archetypal symbols, the genesis of art and the artist, and the relationship of archetypal art to social periods.

"PREFACE" TO *ISHMAEL*

There is no law which requires the study of literature to take all or nothing of psychology. It may take what it pleases. For it so happens that much of what Jung said of archetypes is more common sense than particularized psychological theory for the specialist. . . .

But in justice to both Freud and Jung it should be remembered that neither is concerned solely with the processes or the objectives of art criticism. It is their critical followers who have established criteria, and methods of analysis.

The interpretation and the judgment of art must rest finally upon individuated form, that form which is singularly achieved by the artist who shapes his symbol from multiple feeling. It is critically dishonest to read symbols through Freud unless the artist by his own confession intended to project the Freudian method; it is critically dishonest to read symbols through the archetypes of Jung *without concern for any other genetic factor.* To reduce art to evidence for psychology is to deny the authority of the artist as creator. The authority of individuated form is potentially within the grasp of the artist through the particular autotype that gives both locus and singularity to feeling. Thus Melville's savages aboard the *Pequod* are singular symbolic forms. As autotypically wrought symbols, they are exclusively his. They were not made of "dream content" alone. Yet the fact that they all refer to an archetype defines a misfortune in the vocabulary of criticism. It happens that no one other than Jung has yet offered a terminology of the collective unconscious, and in its use of Jung's language, criticism may find itself misread as psychoanalysis. Let some critic devise a new terminology, and the study of literature may be freed from professional psychology as a source of vocabulary. The bases of feeling antecedent to the shaping of a symbol are archetypes for want of another term. They are the "drives" in the sentience of the primitivist which elicit individuated forms and authorize the purpose of genuine artistic construction. The allegiances of an artist discover the substructure of his symbols. It is of the greatest importance for the ends of this study that the *partial* dependence upon Jung's terminology evident here should be understood for what it is. . . .

Melville may be thoroughly studied through Jung, of course, if one wishes to examine archetypes without attention to the nature of the unique symbol of the artist.

(1956)

JUNGIAN PSYCHOLOGY IN CRITICISM: SOME THEORETICAL PROBLEMS

The presence of Carl Gustav Jung in criticism has endured for half a century. Yet this presence, however commanding or repellent to scholars, is essentially indistinct. Clinical psychology, with which I am unconcerned, has no doubt reached certain categorical assessments qualifying the admissibility of Jung to scientific method. For the scholar-critic who studies and evaluates the work of art, the perseverance of Jung is cloudy and obscure at the edges. The modern interpreter of art knows of the gulf between Jung and Freud. He may have in mind Jung's own insistence upon the *visionary* as the distinctive attribute of art: "It is essential that we give serious consideration to the basic experience that underlies it— namely, to the vision." In the same statement Jung names the Freudian opposite: "The psychologist who follows Freud will of course be inclined to take the writings in question as a problem in pathology . . . to account for the curious images of the vision by calling them cover-figures and by supposing that they represent an attempted concealment of the basic experience."[1] The critic may recognize this "basic experience" as the common inheritance of humankind, a vision rising from the mysterious depths of the unconscious and given form through the medium of the artist. He may assume his critical task to be an explication of the symbol in art as evidence of the primary, basic experience shared by all humankind. Or he may be hostile to this basic experience because it is unnameable. He will resist the persuasions of the anagogic. He may then choose to follow a Freudian problem in pathology as he conducts his reading. Or perhaps he rebels against all psychological method and turns to the anthropological premises of Frazer. In the end, he may declare the work under study an artifact, created through the sovereign choice of the artist, a making fully open to empirical inspection of its unique character. But the problem of the anagogic in the genesis of art will continue to disturb him. He cannot totally escape Jung's insistence on the unnameable vision. The perseverance of Jung is indistinct simply because the vast stores of the unconscious cannot be defined. They can be known only through the aperture of the work of art as a symbol suggesting the vision.

Certain critics who have written handbooks of modern criticism may have disavowed concerns with the basic experience. But the unanswerable

questions remain. Let us assume that such questions pertain to a multiplicity of works of art, in a variety of cultures, displaying a basic impulse toward
the creating of a cosmos. What commonly held basic experience is revealed,
for example, by symbols in quite disparate modes of landscape architecture? The first of these, for present illustration, may be Japanese, the classic Shugakuin, in the vicinity of Kyoto. When the sensibility and the taste of
its time and its evidence of Buddhist aesthetic have been analyzed, the
power of the vision has still to be encountered. This garden, in its symbols
of rock, flowing water, and figuratively shaped trees, manifests a deep
thrust toward the creation of a man-fashioned cosmos. The same thrust
necessitated the symbols of the gardens in the Alhambra—polished espla-
nades, fountains, beasts of stone, grand allées—all fashioned through the
strict geometry of sovereigns with a passion for mathematics, yet all realizing a human vision of cosmic order. There is no name for the basic experience, Japanese and Moorish. But there is a major difference in expression:
in the first, a cosmos is shaped in conformity with Japanese insistence upon
occult balance; in the second, a cosmos is shaped with axial exactitude. But
the unanswerable question remains: what is the nature of the material in
the unconscious that impels these aspirations toward the making of cosmic
symbols, gardens for the magisterial seclusion of princes, and gardens, now
in the public domain, which elicit unnameable responses of satisfaction and
reverence? The viewer's response transcends a simple sensuous delight.
The problem of the anagogic is there. What is the significance of the kinship he feels with the creators of these enclosures?

The same questions arise when the viewer turns to examples of
disparate temple complexes. The distance between Delphi and Isphahan
is immense. Yet the temples of each are treasuries erected in praise of
gods. Each is a man-made cosmos, imperiously insisting upon a human
knowledge of divine order. The ruins of Delphi are a celebration of the
human mind, its strength displayed in columns thrusting toward the
power of Zeus. The domes of Isphahan speak of the sun; and every lu-
nette in every mosque symbolically admits light into the shadowy vault of
human existence. Beyond Delphi stands the cosmos once realized in the
Acropolis. Beyond Isphahan lies Persepolis, where every remaining symbol speaks of the convergence of the known world upon Darius, master
and cosmic king. What does one name in these monumental evidences of
vision? The visitor open to the power of these disparate symbols will experience a mysterious recognition. Yet he will remain inarticulate, since
his recognition is closed to discourse.

The questions posed by these examples are appropriate to the basic premises of Jung. It must be stated initially that the major theories of

Jung are primarily intuitive. They are founded upon what he believed to be a human sharing, common from culture to culture, in the visionary. I propose that architecture for Jung is an art of manifesting the basic experience, the vision, through symbols, varying from culture to culture, of the human impulse to reflect, or to rival, a suprahuman cosmic order. If he is an artist and not a mere utilitarian designer, the architect functions beyond the problems relating to his willed arrangement of weight, volume, and space. Architecture acts as a medium for the "flowing through" of the basic experience. His symbol is his claim upon the vision.

Some critics will be content to live with the anagogic implications of the questions just stated. Others will dismiss them as wholly unrelated to the criticism of art. But it is probably true that both groups will reject Jung as a literary critic when he turns to a long discourse upon the basic experience common to Longfellow's *Hiawatha* and the Gilgamesh epic.[2] Jung at no point in his work intended to associate himself with the profession of literary criticism. He intended to use literature only as evidence of a commonly held vision. To the professional critic, Jung's alignment of Hiawatha and Gilgamesh as manifestations of an archetypal hero-reborn-from-nature will seem preposterous; and perhaps his conjoining of Longfellow's Nokomis and Hiawatha with the mythic Hera and Hercules will seem more preposterous. Obviously, such chosen affinities seem to have no place in literary criticism. But Jung was not interested in *Hiawatha* as a *form* in poetry. He was probably indifferent to the certainty of Longfellow's minor stature. Nor could he have been much concerned with the difference between an American fabricated epic and a genuine folk epic. He was in search only of evidence of the visionary as an attribute relating two examples separated by cultural difference as vast as he could discover. The foregoing questions proposed with respect to architecture in widely separated examples are again insistent as Jung himself chooses from literature. Jung is not the critic. He wishes to be the expositor of the basic experience. By this act he becomes a presence in criticism rather amorphous than distinct. He did not found a school of criticism. He created an attribute of the climate in which criticism of the last fifty years has flourished.

The purpose of the following comment is to review that portion of Jungian theory which has exerted a force in modern criticism. The problems created by the theory may be clarified. It is not assumed that the presence of Jung can be comparably and clearly identified. A possibility cannot be dismissed: the next fifty years may judge Jung to have been more the mystic than the clinician in an age anticipating a regimen of criticism as an exact science.

JUNG AND THE UNCONSCIOUS

. . . The time is appropriate for new summaries of that portion of Jung's thought inviting to criticism. In restating Jung's views of the unconscious, I shall limit the discussion to literary criticism and suggest some problems from literary analysis to which the theory might be applied.

"We mean by collective unconscious a certain psychic disposition shaped by the forces of heredity; from it consciousness has developed."[3] The disposition named cannot be defined, but it is qualified as an inheritance. . . .

Disposition means the potentiality of a mental function in an inheritance contemporaneous with the inheritance of physical, organic function. The collective unconscious is "all the contents of the psychic experience of mankind." These contents acquire value and position through confrontation with consciousness,[4] of which reason is a function. The most striking aspect of the theory then emerges: individual consciousness is born mysteriously of the hereditary psychic disposition, from the totality of the experience of the race. The true genesis of consciousness is not in experience but in the inheritance of disposition. If the literary critic wishes to be faithful to Jung, he must recognize the disposition of the unconscious as it urges consciousness toward the making of images and symbols to represent its material. The content of the material will, then, inevitably refer to a large province of mind apart from the artist's individual ability to create. Reason in the conscious mind governs in the making of images and symbols. But these are empty and superficial—invalid as art—if they do not reflect the content of the unconscious.

The unnameable in the deep content engenders an absolute blockage of empirical method for the critic, whose inspection must be intuitive. He can do no more than Jung did with *Hiawatha*. Comparative readings of other material enable him to say: here and here is a likeness of content, even though image and symbol differ from consciousness to consciousness. The critic is unwilling to surrender his task as interpreter to an evidence of multifarious and singular states of consciousness as paramount in the genesis of art. At this point the presence of Jung becomes indistinct. . . .

The Libido   One must go to Jung's theory of energy from the unconscious. He assigns this energy to the concept of the *libido* (at total variance with Freud's clinical concept of sexual urgency): "Libido as an energy concept is a quantitative formula for the phenomena of life. Its laws are the laws of vital energy. . . . "[5]

How, then, can libido as a concept of energy apply to the work of the critic? Presumably he can study the waxing and waning of the individual poet's energy, and name certain symbols and images as evidence of the life force and of its diminution in prospect of death. But he has no means of analysis. He responds intuitively. He cannot even say that the life force of the artist is greater than that of other men surrounding him. As will be noted later in the theory of Jung, the artist is the person who opens his consciousness to a free flowing of the libido from the unconscious. His work is his symbol of the pulse of life. But the critic, as we have known the critic through history and as we name him now, will scarcely abdicate his position by an entrance into that "transcendental territory" predicted by Jung. He has not, and he will not be prepared to, equate libidinal energy with the primal energy in the structure of matter.

The Archetype   The nature of the unconscious, as associated with the theory of Jung, is recognized in the *archetype*. Jung employs his term in the radical Greek sense: the primal image, the original form, the model. Hence the material of the collective unconscious is a collection of archetypes. But it must be understood that the archetype cannot be named until it is represented by a symbol. . . .

. . . The archetype is inherited, but *not* the representation of it. We may take as statements ignored by certain of Jung's misinterpreters the following:

> The archetypes are . . . the hidden foundations of the conscious mind. . . . They are systems of readiness for action, and at the same time images and emotions. They are inherited with the brain structure—indeed, they are its psychic aspect.[6]

> I mean forms or images of a collective nature which occur practically all over the earth as constituents of myths and at the same time as autochthonous, individual products of unconscious origin.[7]

> You cannot explain one archetype by another, that is, it is impossible to say where the archetype comes from, because there is no Archimedean point outside the *a priori* conditions it represents.[8]

Thus, to return to initial proposals in this essay, it may be said that the garden-cosmos in each instance cited comes of a master system of "readiness for action," from "forms of a collective nature"; that the same is true for the origin of the temple-complex-as-cosmos in each instance; that the archetype genetic in the garden symbols will not explain the archetype genetic in the temple symbols; that the diverse *representations* of the two archetypes are in no sense inherited. The impossibility of inherited representations is perhaps best expressed in this contention of Jung:

> The archetype as such is a psychoid factor that belongs, as it were, to the invisible, ultraviolet end of the psychic spectrum. . . . We must . . . constantly bear in mind that what we mean by "archetype" is in itself irrepresentable, but it has effects which make visualizations of it possible, namely, the archetypal images.[9]

This question of "archetypal images" leads to confusion unless it is understood that Jung is speaking of a pattern from the unconscious rather than of an image figuring in the consciously designed metaphor, for example, of a poem or a painting.

The God-Imago   . . . The critic who follows Jung will not be concerned with "passages" in the history of thought, that is, with "influences."[10] No doubt there may be "reflections" of Eckhart in Rilke, just as, by another passage, there is a "reappearance" of Plato in Shelley. And to place Jung momentarily at the center, it may be argued that Wallace Stevens, among poets in the twentieth century, most closely approximates Jung's concept of "a split-off sum of the libido, which has activated the God-*imago*."[11] But the theory of Jung cannot be applied to a critical method devoted to chronologies in literary history. *This* poetry does not grow from *that* poetry preceding it. Tradition, in the usual sense of the term, is meaningless. Affinities between writers are not incidental to "influence." They are affirmed by similar thrusts from the unconscious; the nomenclature of thinkers and of schools of thought is irrelevant; and centuries may separate the likenesses.

Jung's insistence upon God as a psychodynamic state proposes that the critic be concerned with Romanticism. To this premise must be added Jung's notion that this God-in-man is a function reconciling opposites. Jung is the chief Western interpreter in this century of Brahmanical doctrines propounding a union of opposites through the governance of the unconscious. He finds in the concept Brahman a realization of oneness which only the archetypes can effect. "Brahman is *sat* and *asat*, the existing and the non-existing, *satyam* and *asatyam*, reality and unreality." New studies of the phenomenon of Orientalism in Romantic poetry of the nineteenth century are overdue, for Orientalism in the Jungian sense must claim its own validity. This is not evidence of an artist's reading in Vedic literature, or of the critic's lists of the artist's references. It is the emergence of an unconscious content as the Romantic artist seeks new symbols when the symbols of his society have ceased to command him. Of special interest is the decline of Christian orthodoxy in the United States and the resultant struggle to dismiss the absolute God and to celebrate the reconciliation of opposites. In the Jungian sense, the Orientalism of Emerson and Whitman, for example, is archetypal. A reading of "Uriel" or "Brahma" or "Chanting the Square Deific" suggests affinities with Jung's explorations of archetypal material in Indian thought. Yet neither poet had a wide acquaintance with Indian metaphysics. Furthermore, to speak of them as "anticipating" Jung is idle if the critic is faithful to the principle advanced above, that archetypal "instances" are not susceptible to arrangement in sequences. Romanticism, as an epoch, seems to have been essentially a liberation of the unconscious, and this liberation made American Orientalism possible.

■   ■   ■   ■

The Archetype Symbolized . . . The raw symbols of dream must be considered apart from the symbols formed by the conscious mind, which are beyond the nonsensical and open to rational inspection. Both groups are reflections of archetypes, but there could be no conscious artistry if the symbol were simply automatic. . . .

I regard the raw symbols of the dream state, in Jung's theory, as evidence of the genesis of myth. Joseph Campbell is right when he assesses Jung's interpretation of mythology: it is "a group dream, symptomatic of archetypal urges within the depths of the human psyche."[12] Mythology as the raw representation of this group dream can be an area of investigation for the Jungian critic.

The critic may investigate, for example, mythic manifestations of the sea monster: the leviathan-reincarnation of Vishnu bringing the sacred Vedas from the floor of the sea; the Teutonic *middengeardes* sea serpent; the albino leviathan in the American mariners' whaling lore. But this critic is merely the explorer of raw material. He is not the reader of the consciously wrought symbol. When he becomes the critic of the symbol in art, he may confront Melville's renowned chapter on whiteness in *Moby Dick*.[13] The raw archetypal material related to mythology is to be found in the substrata of the chapter: the mystical properties of whiteness. The symbol-making power of the conscious mind, that of the artist, is revealed in Melville's choices of illustration from various provinces of human history, his "throwing together," in the sense of the Greek *symballein,* of this chosen content into a symbol of radial significance.

The critic is scarcely the critic of art if he limits himself to the raw materials of mythology. When Jung deals with problems inherent in an assessment of the art of poetry, he speaks of "the saving factor . . . the symbol, which is able to reconcile the conscious with the unconscious and embrace them both. . . . "[14]

Jung's theory about polarities may be applied to *Moby Dick.* "The whale, as a denizen of the sea, is the universal symbol of the devouring unconscious. The bird, as a citizen of the luminous kingdom of the air, is a symbol of conscious thought."[15] Ahab is then the Prometheus of Melville's total symbol, the full novel. He is the victim of the inner world, of the devouring unconscious. He surrenders the "middle ground" and denies the outer reality. The sea hawk, impaled on the masthead of the sinking *Pequod,* is the conscious mind annihilated. W. H. Auden, whose early psychological allegiances turned to Freud, appears to follow Jung when he writes of Melville's novel: "The hawk in *Moby Dick* is the messenger bird of Zeus who warns Prometheus-Ahab of his hybris when he cheats the lookout by snatching away his hat, i.e., his heroic crown, but whom in its last death-defiance the *Pequod* drags down with it."[16] Jung's principle applies: the symbol reconciles Prometheus and Epimetheus, the unconscious and the conscious.

■　■　■　■

The symbol representing the archetype is interpreted by Jung with attention to the time span of the individual's life. Joseph Campbell has noted precisely the differences between Freud and Jung with respect to the time span. "Sigmund Freud stresses . . . the passages and difficulties of the first half of the human cycle of life—those of our infancy and adolescence, when our sun is mounting toward its zenith. C. G. Jung, on the other hand, has emphasized the crises of the second position—when, in order to advance, the shining sphere must submit to descend and disappear, at last, into the night-womb of the grave. The normal symbols of our desires and fears become converted, in this afternoon of the biography, into their opposites; for it is then no longer life but death that is the challenge. What is difficult to leave, then, is not the womb but the phallus."[17]

The individual's life describes a circle. Jung thinks of childhood as the beginning in the life cycle of a reenactment of the sexual habitudes

preserved in the unconscious, "a period in which the impulses toward
these archaic inclinations appear again and again." There is a youthful
correspondence "to the thought of the centuries of antiquity and barba-
rism."[18] Of the shift in the function of the libido from youth to age Jung
writes: "In the first half of life its will [of the libido] is for growth, in the
second half of life it hints, softly at first, and then audibly, at its will for
death."[19] With Freud infantile sexuality will account for the "passages"
of the first half of the cycle, but Jung, advancing the libido as the primal
life force, then meets the second half, left relatively unexplored by
Freud, and names the passages in terms of archetypes ordering, through
a shift in libidinal energy, the wish for death. The wish will be marked by
the conscious mind with fears. Nonetheless, it is an archetypal inevitability; and the archetypes *symbolized* appear to Jung to be persevering in the
endless transmission of the unconscious: "The serpent . . . represents
the fear, the fear of death, and is thought of as the antithesis to the
phallus."[20]

■   ■   ■   ■

Whether Wallace Stevens had read intently in Jung I cannot say.
The published letters and the prose provide implications but not firm
evidence. Yet the range of the total poetry provides a brilliant opportunity for the critic who is fully committed to Jungian theory. The complete
poetic record of Stevens describes the circle. The carefully disciplined
"evidences" of spring and summer seem to be lyrical namings, symbols,
of the thrust of phallic vitality in the libido. The seasonal passages of the
poetry to autumn and winter describe the shift of libidinal energy to the
will toward, and the fear of, death. The Jungian critic will find his evidence as Stevens opens "The Auroras of Autumn" with the arresting
line: "This is where the serpent lives."[21] Jung would have found the passage to the threshold of death thereafter symbolized through the late
poetry of Stevens a clear archetypal representation. A Jungian commitment to a reading of Stevens will, of course, require rigid exclusions of
other qualities in this poet's art.

The Genesis of Art and the Artist   "Creative man is a riddle that we may
try to answer in various ways, but always in vain."[22] Here is Jung's full
admission of the mystery. The soul in its inner world (Prometheus) and
in its expression of the unconscious is a mystery; the "strange something" of modern man "derives its existence from the hinterland of man's
mind—[and] suggests the abyss of time separating us from pre-human

ages." The "something" is "a primordial experience which surpasses man's understanding. . . . It arises from timeless depths."[23] For Jung it may be proposed that these beliefs amount to a Kierkegaardian leap into faith. Since the "strange something" must be reckoned with by the literary critic who accepts Jung, the work of that critic will be judged inadmissible as criticism by his adversaries, those who argue for a rational and total knowledge of works of art. The intrusion of Jung upon the field of full critical authority has been answered to in our time by indifference, and more often by fury.

All that has thus far been said in this essay leads to the question: Who is the artist? For Jung there is little possibility of middle ground for traditional criticism and its empirical schools. Traditional criticism, in any hypothetical judgment of a purely Jungian critic, must either accept, and remake itself, or reject. Jung's contention is absolutely unyielding:

> Every creative person is a duality or a synthesis of contradictory aptitudes. On the one side he is a human being with a personal life, while on the other side he is an impersonal, creative process. . . .
>
> Art is a kind of innate drive that seizes a human being and makes him its instrument. The artist is not a person endowed with free will who seeks his own ends, but one who allows art to realize its purposes through him . . . he is "collective man"—one who carries and shapes the unconscious, psychic life of mankind.[24]

To this Jung adds his definition of the artist in his public function:

> The work of the poet comes to meet the spiritual need of the society in which he lives, and for this reason his work means more to him than his personal fate, whether he is aware of this or not. Being essentially the instrument for his work, he is subordinate to it, and we have no reason for expecting him to interpret it for us.[25]

And elsewhere, as Jung discusses the problem of types in poetry, one reads: "[Poets] voice rather more clearly and resoundingly what all know. . . . The mass does not understand it although unconsciously living what it expresses; not because the poet proclaims it, but because its life issues from the collective unconscious into which he has peered."[26]

Jung concedes that the public function of the great artist is not admitted by the society. "The reading public for the most part repudiates this kind of writing—unless, indeed, it is coarsely sensational—and even the literary critic feels embarrassed by it."[27] Emerson defines the poet as the *namer*, in his essay "The Poet." When he writes fully as poet, the artist names existence as of the moment he writes, not for himself alone but for all his contemporaries. And yet how many of Whitman's American contemporaries tolerated *Leaves of Grass?* (Whittier said, "This will never do!" as he threw the volume into the hearth fire.) How many Americans judged Herman Melville, after the Polynesian romances and *Redburn* and *White-Jacket,* to be other than a madman? Or, for that matter, how many French readers, apart from the academicians, were disposed to "receive" the poetry of Valéry, for example, the "Ebauche d'un Serpent"? But what is the good of art if it is the artist's transcription of the truth of the unconscious and yet is publicly rejected? The artist does not impart knowledge of the soul to contemporaneous masses. Jungian and traditional criticism must recognize that art is received exclusively by the elite, though it might be guidance and revelation for the masses. It is better to follow the judgment of Wallace Stevens in his notebook, the "Adagia." It reads: "Poetry is the scholar's art."

Shifts in Symbolic Systems . . . I have seen no instances of Jung illustrating his theory from literary texts of anti-Romantic writers, apart from his citations of myth and of epic poetry. I suppose his predilection for Romantic art marks him as a Romantic in the brief history of psychology. But Jung's arguments centering on Romanticism as a phenomenon in recent cultural history cannot be ignored. He gives us his psychologist's reasons for the inception and the perseverance of the Romantic. Harry Levin has proposed that the mythopoeic revival of the Romantic movement came from the German "transcendental world view." "It is no mere historic accident that this impetus originated in Germany, or that it found itself pitted against the more classicized culture of France."[28] Certainly these judgments must hold. We all know that French neoclassicism flowed from the Continent into the theory and the practice of such poets as Dryden and Pope; and we know that the Romanticism of Coleridge in the *Biographia Literaria* derived deeply from German transcendentalism. But Levin, as I understand him, did not purpose to explore the origins of these "movements." Jung asks his questions at their thresholds. He directs his major attention to the beginnings and the endurance of Romanticism with, as we should expect, primary dependence upon the reassertion of archetypes.

Jung posits a theory of "extinct symbols." He studies the waning power of traditional Christian symbolic forms. These symbols, originally representations of contents of the unconscious, exerted a sovereign power over art. With their extinction, there occurred unconscious thrusts toward consciousness from other archetypes that have preserved their power throughout a long period of "blockage" by the commanding symbols inherited by consciousness. Thus Jung is prepared to write of the "paganism" which marks Romantic art.[29]

> A general attitude corresponds with a religion, and changes of religion belong to the most painful moments in the world's history. . . . The religion of the last two thousand years [the Judaeo-Christian] is a psychological attitude. . . . But the deeper levels of the psyche continue . . . to operate in the former attitude, in accordance with psychic inertia. In this way the unconscious has preserved paganism alive. . . . The readiness with which the vastly older primitive spirit reappears can be seen in our own time, even better perhaps than in any other historically known epoch.[30]

It is clear that, for Jung, shifts in symbolic systems come about because of losses in libidinal vitality authorizing the perseverance of symbols. When the system is on the threshold of inertia, on the same threshold archetypes in the unconscious (in those "systems of readiness" earlier discussed) lead to the beginnings of new symbols. Yet the new symbols are representative of material long preserved in the unconscious; and in the instance of a reappearing "paganism" the material is indeed old. Modern paganism, in Jung's view, and few even among his adversaries will dispute him, arose at the end of the eighteenth century in the West. Contents of the unconscious from pre-Christian "holdings" reappeared. Expression came about "in every possible way, in aesthetics, philosophy, morals, even politics (philhellenism)." "It was the Paganism of antiquity, glorified as 'freedom', 'naiveté', 'beauty' . . . which responded to the yearnings of that time."[31] Thus the poet-priest, in contradistinction to the artisan, the colorist, the clothier of design in neoclassicism, arose, a "romantic" reincarnation of pagan archetypes. Here it must be understood that neoclassicism and Romantic paganism are distinctly unlike. The reincarnation of the pagan priest, or sacerdos, is related to the God-imago function of the libido; for a sacerdos, in his most primitive role, is the sayer of the arcane. Before he becomes surrounded by complex creed and ritual, he is the purveyor of the God-imago.

The claims made by the early Wordsworth of the "pagan" period as recorded in *The Prelude*, by Whitman in the 1855 Preface and in "Song of Myself," and by Mallarmé in *Igitur*, have in common a sacerdotal mode. As three disparate exemplars of the priestly role attendant upon Romanticism, their affinities must somewhere be encountered by the critic, Jungian or non-Jungian. It seems to me that the critic must confront these manifestations of the anagogic in the poet's role or not concern himself with the Romantic. The question must be asked whether it is possible for the anti-Jungian fully to criticize Romantic literature. When it comes to poetic speech bearing the marks of sacerdotal "aspiration," this problem should be recognized. I have to conclude this review of Jung and the Unconscious with this assertion: since Jung insisted upon the superior evidence, for his own purposes, of Romanticism, and since he found the release of paganism still massive,[32] it must follow that the critic who examines the literature of the West from the end of the eighteenth century onward must at least recognize the Jungian problems. If he is serious, he will yet be unable to name the archetypes represented in the symbols before him. The presence of Jung will remain for him indistinct. But he will proceed toward explorations of genesis—how the last two centuries of expression in the forms of Western art came to be—as he turns in retrospect or confronts the present. For in this procedure he will think and work in the climate in which modern criticism flourishes. Jung was one of the makers of this climate, whether the critic is prepared to accept him or not.

VARIABLES WITHIN CRITICAL RESPONSIBILITY

The chief value of Northrop Frye for criticism derives from his insistence upon postulates of criticism growing out of art. Frye attacks all determinisms in criticism, for example, Marxist, Thomist, liberal-humanist, neoclassical, Freudian, Jungian, or existentialist.[33] The critic's job is to allow his critical principles to be shaped by his encounter with literature. "Critical principles cannot be taken over ready-made from theology, philosophy, politics, science, or any combination of these. . . ."[34]

■   ■   ■   ■

The variables in critical responsibility endure because of the unique set of problems exposed by each critic's reading. No purely Jungian literary criticism has yet appeared. But why should it be desired, or even expected? Conceivably, a critic might suppose that he follows Jung faithfully in reading, for example, two works from American literature.

He might contend that Willa Cather's symbols in *Death Comes for the Archbishop* are representations of archetypes: the Southwest Indians' sacred cavern and the rock of Acoma; the Bishop's cathedral pushing its towers heavenward in the raw settlement of Santa Fe; the emergence of human greed as the new American frontier seeks the gold under Pike's Peak. He might argue that William Carlos Williams's *Paterson*, with its symbolic patterns of descent into the dark underworld of despair and of ascent into the light of affirmation, is a reenactment throughout of the archetypes represented in the classic Persephone-Kora myth. Presumably, the critic would begin with Williams's deliberate adherence to the myth, a Jungian openness of himself to permit passage of material from the unconscious, as he, the poet, begins to frame the poem. But apart from other questions posed by the poem, an answer to a Jungian mandate will negate the act of the critic. In the same vein the Jungian critic will fail in his reading of Cather's novel.

I return to the perseverance of questions of the anagogic, of the visionary in the sense of Jung, with which this essay opened. If questions of the anagogic are present in the critic's final and thorough reading, why should they not be recognized along with all the other questions? And why should the critic assume, as he establishes his postulates, that he has escaped the play of his own imagination on the material? The state of criticism to be hoped for is a liberation from determinisms, which, in particular, this century has produced. The vitality of any genuine work of art comes out of the complex interplay of the artist's own variables within his intent. Until the critic admits this variety as his governance, his conclusions will inevitably miss the mark, for the density and the complexity of great art will never yield to a full critical exposition when the critic himself has initially yielded to a theory constructed apart from the work to be examined. The conclusion is that critical theory cannot be equated with the authority of art.

(1976)

4 THE ARTIST'S RELATION TO THE UNCONSCIOUS

Joseph L. Henderson

The analyst Joseph L. Henderson has been associated with Jungian psychology since the 1920s, and is one of the founders of the C. G. Jung Institute of San Francisco. His writings, including Cultural Attitudes in Psychological Perspective *and his many essays for the journal* Psychological Perspectives, *continually provide fruitful interdisciplinary links between psychology and the arts, especially literature and film.*

This selection explores the important aspect of the relation of the artist to the unconscious. Henderson discusses and critiques Jung's developing views on the topic, as well as those of Jung's disciple Erich Neumann. Henderson speaks from experience (he has analyzed many artists, including Jackson Pollack) when he warns against the dangers inherent in confusing artistic development with psychological development, whether in criticizing art or in treating the artist-patient. In a memorable line, Henderson declares that "the artist is not merely a mouthpiece for the unconscious."

When Jung first approached the subject of artistic creativity he defined it as a form of sensibility that denies the experience of reality. The artist may be an introvert who creates an abstraction or an extrovert who pours himself into an object that becomes a work of art. The first attitude stands aside from the creation of an image that "has the magical importance of a defense against the chaotic change of experience . . . and therewith life which might disturb the enjoyment of abstract beauty is wholly suppressed." The second attitude, that of the extrovert artist, "feels his activity, his life, into the object. . . . He becomes the object and in this way gets rid of himself, he desubjectifies himself."[1] In this view, the artist is not so much concerned with exposing or exploring the unconscious as with protecting himself against it.

Later in his life, Jung changed these earlier notions about art (influenced by Lipps-Worringer) and believed that art is concerned with expressing the unconscious, but not the personal unconscious. Neumann restated this conception and carried it further:

> Not the ego and consciousness but the collective unconscious and the self are the determining forces; the development of man and his consciousness is dependent on the spontaneity and inner order of the unconscious and remains so even after consciousness and unconsciousness have entered into a fruitful dialectical relation to each other.
>
> There is a continuous interchange between the collective unconscious, the cultural canon, and the creative individuals of the group.[2]

There are three different stages in the relation of the artist to his epoch:

> The first stage presupposes a greater or lesser degree of unity, whether conscious or not, in the creative man's personality: that he must be embedded in his group . . . (and) the product is an art integrated with the group as a whole.[3]

The second stage is represented by the artist who still accepts the validity of the cultural canon of the group but who must, out of the need of his epoch, "operate underground" and so transform the known images into new versions.

> The third stage is the stage of compensation for the cultural canon (the point especially emphasized by Jung). It is grounded in the vitality of the collective unconscious of the group. Compensation for the cultural canon means opposition to it. The creative artist, whose mission it is to compensate for consciousness and the cultural canon, is usually an isolated individual, a hero who must destroy the old in order to make possible the dawn of the new.[4]

In the course of this development "the artist becomes constantly more individualized and loses his original anonymity." Increasingly, ego-consciousness develops and "the physiognomy of the individual artist is liberated from the anonymity of the current style. This . . . is the beginning of his individuation—that is, of the last form of relation between art and its epoch." Accordingly, the great artist, who is capable of this step, may ultimately become "the Great Individual who, precisely, transcends his bond with the collective both outwardly and inwardly. . . . It is no longer his function to express the creative will of the unconscious or to regenerate or compensate for the existing culture out of the depths of the collective unconscious . . . the artist here attains the level of timelessness. . . . "[5]

Neumann then asks whether we can speak of a transcendent art in which art and nature may be synthesized. Wherever this has happened, he says: "The creative impulse seems to have liberated itself. United on the plane of artistic creation, the Self which man experiences within him, and the world-creative self which is manifested outwardly, achieve the transparency of symbolic reality."[6]

Neumann modestly restricts the achievement of this type of individuation to a very few artists, great old men such as Leonardo, Titian, Goethe, or Beethoven, recognizing that even very important artists may not be any more individuated, possibly even less, than the rest of us. In fact, we know the artist to be as much a victim of his art as its master.[7] No such modesty is apparent, however, in Otto Rank's similar formulation.[8] He speaks of two steps beyond psychology. Projecting the idea of rebirth into the future, he "envisages 'a new type of human being,' coming to the forefront of history with 'a new structure of personality.' " This is a point "beyond psychology where art and religion meet, join and transform each other."[9]

Rank had originally been the aesthetician of psychoanalysis, and in his last period, having separated fully from the influence of Freud, he proclaimed that man could become a kind of artist-hero of the future. We know the danger of this kind of doctrine of the superman, and I hope to show that the artist can be understood as he is, not as he ought to become, and that we do not have to go beyond psychology to do so. (I do, however, admit that, insofar as Rank does in spots define the nature of individuation in the artist's experience, his viewpoint is valid.)

The whole development of modern art as a vehicle for archetypal imagery has, in addition to Neumann's work, been carried further in Aniela Jaffé's excellent contribution to *Man and His Symbols*.[10] This type of study, not only of the visual arts, brings us back to the subject of aesthetics as a whole, which was, as I have said, Jung's own starting point.

The urge toward individuation is not peculiar to the artist, and if we are to speak of the artist as a subject for psychological investigation, we have to limit ourselves to what really defines him as an artist and not as a scientific, religious, or philosophic, or social, or some other kind of being. I think the artist is one whose aesthetic attitude gives him his specific form of cultural identity. We see this in autobiographical writings and from individual case studies of artists in analysis. Here we find the true evidence for Jung's having changed his original view that an aesthetic experience leads only to "self divestiture." While this formulation was valid at the time when the collective canon of taste was expressed by the principle of "Art for Art's sake," we are more likely to find today that a true artist, far from seeking self-divestiture, discovers his identity, that which makes him most real to himself and to others, by means of an aesthetic attitude which has all the continuity and consistency of a conscious vocational commitment. From this point of view, the artist is not merely a mouthpiece for the unconscious; he functions as a craftsman or artificer whose actual technique is just as important to his work as its content.

■   ■   ■   ■

The emotion by which any form of artistic creativity is engendered is like falling in love, but in no transitory or worldly sense. Yet a real object for that love is as necessary to the whole creation as Dante's love was for Beatrice or Petrarch's for Laura.

Joseph Campbell has referred to this as "the moment of aesthetic arrest," and I think it is this experience which makes an artist cling so strenuously to his belief that the creation of beauty is a conscious, not an unconscious, process. Joyce in his early work had called it an enchantment of the heart and also recalled Shelley's image of this as a fading coal. The moment of aesthetic arrest is like "an awakening to love, an object apparently without passes (in the words of Joyce) into the soul forever. . . . And the soul leaps to the call. To live, to err, to fall, to triumph, to recreate life out of life."[11] Such an experience of the anima or animus reflected in and through an encounter with a real person and a corresponding real fantasy (Campbell's term is "that outward innermost object") creates a feeling of absolute loyalty by which the artist then devotes himself and his life without question to the work he has to do.

When this occurs in a person under our observation, we analysts are tempted to classify it as a delusional transference. Instead of falling into this temptation, Rosemary Gordon, in her paper "Symbols: Content and

Process," urges us to adopt a term from H. Segal called "symbolic equivalence":

> Here two separate objects are related to each other in such a way
> that the reality and the characteristics of one of them is denied because
> it has become completely absorbed in and identified with the
> other. . . . Symbolic equivalence and its correlative projective identification
> should not be regarded as necessarily pathological phenomena;
> certainly in any analysis their presence must be accepted
> with respect and openness. . . . I wonder if artistic creation does not
> in fact depend on the artist being able, during certain stages of his
> work, to experience at the level of symbolic equivalence. The normality
> or pathology of a process, so Jung has taught, must be assessed
> by examining whether it serves or whether it obstructs the
> development of a person. . . . [12]

This strikes me as a useful, even necessary, formulation, if we are
to treat the artist's experience as being normal for him, even when it may
contain obvious pathological features from a psychiatric viewpoint.
(Joyce's writings provide an excellent example of this.) But I must question
that last statement as being perhaps biased in favoring the therapeutic
process at the expense of the creative process. What would be true of
the nonartist in this respect is perhaps not true for the artist or for the
person who is identified consciously with an aesthetic attitude. The criterion
of the validity or normality of the process is then not whether it
promotes the development of a person, but whether or not the product of
the process really is a work of art; whether the response to this work on
the part of the beholder, as well as the creator, affirms its "truth" as well
as its beauty. Any interpretation of an artist's vision, or his choice of a
living model for his muse, is in danger of destroying rather than encouraging
his talent. Fortunately, most true artists successfully avoid allowing
an analytical interpretation to unsettle them. However delusional or symbolic
or projected may be the image they think they see, they will continue
to regard it as their "outward innermost" source of inspiration.
(1968)

5   THE ANALYTICAL PSYCHOLOGY OF C. G. JUNG AND THE PROBLEM OF LITERARY EVALUATION

Mario Jacoby

Mario Jacoby, once a concert violinist, is a trainer of analysts and member of the board of directors of the C. G. Jung Institute in Zurich. His books available in English include Longing for Paradise and The Analytic Encounter. This selection, then, is an authoritative, scholarly presentation of Jung's psychological approach to an important question of literary criticism.

Part 1 begins by comparing and contrasting the views of Freud and Jung on art. Laying the groundwork for his later discussion, Jacoby reviews five key aspects of Jung's psychology: the personal and collective unconscious, the archetype and archetypal symbol, the compensation by the unconscious, via art and dreams, of the individual's conscious attitudes, individuation as a natural drive for every person's psyche, and amplification as a method of interpreting dreams.

Part 2 reviews two of Jung's most important writings on psychology and literature: "On the Relations between Analytical Psychology and Literature" (1922) and "Psychology and Literature" (1930). Jacoby reminds the reader that Jung prized literary works for psychological, not literary, values.

Part 3 of the essay addresses directly the possibilities of a psychological contribution to literary criticism's task of literary evaluation. Jacoby cites the criteria established by three literary critics; he discusses how these "literary value criteria . . . correspond to general human archetypal value ideas" as described in Jung's psychology.

I

When a psychologist is invited to discuss a problem in the field of literary criticism, he must ask himself first of all what points of contact exist between that discipline and his own. What do psychology and the study of literature have in common? Literary criticism analyzes, interprets, and evaluates works of art; psychology tries to throw light on the nature of the human mind and its functions. But every literary composition owes its existence to the creative effort of a human being with special gifts for this particular endeavor. Thus, the poet's human qualities—as far as they affect the creation of his work—become part and parcel of the literary researcher's concern.

Conversely, the literary product itself provides insights into the basic human condition and its problems, which do lie in the psychologist's field of interest. Therefore, no serious attempt at understanding literature can be made without an examination of certain psychological aspects. Psychology, for its part, has, since the beginning of our century, received some completely new impulses toward the exploration of man's creative imagination.

■　■　■　■

One of the main reasons why Freud's collaborator, C. G. Jung, soon decided to go his own way was Freud's narrow view of the human imagination, his assumption that it was nothing more than an expression of unconscious instinctual wishes. . . . And so Freud circumscribed the workings of man's imagination, so rich in images and ideas, with scientific models and theorems to which—with little variation—he clung all his life. Jung reports that Freud said to him one day: "My dear Jung, promise me never to abandon the sexual theory. That is the most essential thing of all. You see, we must make a dogma of it, an unshakable bulwark."[1] For Jung, this remark was "the thing that struck at the heart of our friendship."[2] Scientific truth was for him "a hypothesis which might be adequate for the moment but was not to be preserved as an article of faith for all time."[3]

■　■　■　■

Both Freud and Jung had noticed how often dreams and spontaneous fantasies resemble motifs from mythology, from fairy tales, and from folklore. Both began to study mythology around 1910. Freud, however, warned Jung, in one of his letters, not to stay away too long in those tropical regions of the occult; it was necessary to govern at home.[4] To his coworker, Sándor Ferenczi, Freud wrote: "his own investigations have carried him far into the realm of mythology, which he wants to open up with the key of the libido theory. However agreeable all that may be, I nevertheless bade him to return in good time to the neuroses. There is the motherland where we have first to fortify our dominion against everything and everybody."[5]

But Jung's main concern was not the interpretation of myths by means of established theories that derived from the treatment of neuroses. He wanted to penetrate more deeply and without preconceived ideas into the unconscious life of the mind. The unconscious mind is, by definition, hidden from our consciousness; there is no direct access to it. Myths, fairy tales, and visions are spontaneous manifestations from which we can deduce unconscious psychic activity. Jung does not see them as epiphenomena of the realm of impulse, but as original, intrinsically human creations of the unconscious. . . .

Jung differentiates between the personal unconscious, which contains "the forgotten, the repressed, the subliminally perceived, thought and felt,"[6] and a deeper layer of the psyche, which he regards as the creative primal ground of man's mental life. In the collective unconscious, there are dynamic contents at work which Jung called *dominants, primal images,* and, later, *archetypes.* The word *archetype* is derived from the Greek *archetypon,* that which was made first: the primal image, the original form, the model. The *ideae principales* of Augustinus originally inspired Jung to choose the name of archetype, which has more or less the same meaning. According to Augustinus, the *ideae principales* are eternal, changeless, contained in the divine wisdom. The archetype is one of the most difficult and more frequently misunderstood concepts in Jung's psychology. During his lifetime Jung himself changed and differentiated his archetype concept as his researches progressed. In this connection, I would like to mention his essay "On the Nature of the Psyche" in volume 8 of his *Collected Works.* His clearest and most inclusive ideas on the archetype are formulated there.

It is important to keep in mind a differentiation in the concept of the archetype: Jung makes a distinction between the "archetype as such" and archetypal images and ideas. The archetype as such is the unconscious disposition, the abstract pattern of images and ideas. It is not perceivable, but remains "a hypothetical and irrepresentable model."[7] Since its existence cannot be proved directly but only through its manifestations, the archetype must remain a hypothesis for the scientist. It effects the patterns of images and ideas in myths, fairy tales, visions, dreams, and fantasies. These patterns, which *are* perceptible to our consciousness, are the archetypal images and ideas. They are produced by the "archetype as such." At the same time they point to its hidden activity.

■   ■   ■   ■

In examining the relation between literature and psychology the following is important: the "archetypal images" that Jung mentions in his work are equivalent to what we commonly refer to as symbols. The word *symbol* comes from the Greek *symballein*, which literally means "to throw together." A symbolon in ancient Greece was a fragment of a cube or some other object that could be fitted back together with the other half of the object. Friends would each take one such half to seal a friendship that often extended to every member of their respective families. The pieces were used as means of identification and were handed down through the generations in each family. If two halves fitted together to make a whole, the bearer of the fragment was legitimately identified and made welcome.

From this original concrete meaning, the symbolon came to stand for a contract or agreement in the legal field. In the aesthetic sphere, it came to mean what in German is aptly called *Sinnbild* (i.e., a "sense image" or "image of meaning"). An image becomes a symbol when he who looks at it sees in it a meaning beyond that which it depicts. This meaning swings within the image, shines through it. An image that strikes us as a living symbol points beyond itself and appears rich in meaning. For Jung, a symbol is the "best possible description, or formula of a relatively unknown fact . . . which cannot conceivably, therefore, be more clear or characteristically represented."[8]

■   ■   ■   ■

. . . It is especially in respect to the symbol-concept that we can see how enormously Jung's work has extended and deepened psychological knowledge. Freud, too, speaks of symbols. But in his view they invariably serve to mask the sexual realm and its activity. In short, Freud always reduces the "unfathomable" to something known, namely, sexuality and its organs. But if the symbols that occur in works of literature are always interpreted and reduced in this manner, they always lead to the author's personal sexual wishes and their sublimation. Such results may be accurate in many cases, but in the last analysis they remain of marginal interest both for the psychology of creativity and for the study of literature. This is why Jung says, "Whether something is a symbol or not depends first of all on the way in which our consciousness approaches it."[9] In other words, it is quite possible for our consciousness to remain closed to the wealth of meaning contained in a symbol and to reduce its meaning to some well-worn, generally known facts. When this happens, the symbol loses its depth, it no longer points to the "unfathomable," to that which transcends consciousness; it becomes a mere sign. In Jung's view a symbol is alive only "when it is the best and highest possible expression of something divined but not yet known even to the observer."[10]

Jung's particular endeavor is to make consciousness receptive to symbols in order to strike a possible chord of meaningful experience. He sees neurosis largely as "the suffering of a soul which has not discovered its meaning."[11] The ultimate purpose of translating symbolic images into the language of psychology, the "interpretation" of dreams and fantasies, which can at best be only partially successful, is to open the subject's consciousness to the events in his own unconscious mind.

Jung ascribes great importance to these "Relations between the Ego and the Unconscious,"[12] and for the following reasons: his psychotherapeutic experience made him regard the entire psyche, which includes both the conscious and unconscious part of the mind, as a self-regulating system striving for wholeness. This means that the unconscious activity manifested in dreams and fantasies contributes to the psyche's equilibrium in a compensatory manner. Modern experimental dream researchers have impressively corroborated this thesis of Jung's.[13] Our consciousness can be compared to the eye whose field of vision includes only a tiny part of the universe. Consciousness differentiates and decides according to space and time, causality, value, and so on. Out of all possibilities it chooses those which appear important for its particular life-experience and for the necessary life-adaptation. It sets its own direction, gives its own directives. Thus, contents and possibilities that do not lie in the chosen direction never enter the field of our consciousness. Therefore, consciousness is always more or less one-sided. There is a danger that this one-sidedness may become absolute, possibly leading to an unhealthy narrowing of the conscious mind, to a sense of emptiness and meaninglessness. The splitting-off of consciousness from its sources is, according to Jung, the cause of many neuroses; and man's "self-estrangement," so often mentioned in these days, is also based on the same thing. Jung says: "The more one-sided his conscious attitude is, and the further it deviates from the optimum, the greater becomes the possibility that vivid dreams with a strongly contrasting but purposive content will appear as an expression of the self-regulation of the psyche."[14] This is why he regarded the notation and understanding of dreams and fantasies as therapy of the first order.

The theory of compensation and the hypothesis of the collective unconscious led to new lines of inquiry about the handling and understanding of dream symbols. Jung inquired into the possibilities of new experience, new insights and attitudes, as revealed and divined through symbols in dream and fantasy, which help us overcome stagnation of consciousness and achieve self-realization. The natural drive toward wholeness in the household of the soul is really, when seen in temporal sequence, nothing else but the vital urge toward self-realization, the psychic necessity of what Jung called the process of individuation.

In order to gain a better understanding of archetypal images in dreams and fantasies, Jung worked out a method that he called the method of amplification. "In Jung's method of amplification, the various dream motifs are enriched through analogous, meaning-related material that consists of images, symbols, sagas, myths, etc. The dream motifs are thus shown in every nuance of their possible meanings, and in all their various aspects, until their meaning becomes utterly clear. Then, each element of meaning that has been granted by this method is linked to the next element and so on until the entire chain of dream motifs has been laid bare and can be verified as a united whole."[15] This method, which can be used for the better understanding of all collective symbols, does not reduce—it expands. The parallels taken from myths, fairy tales, religious history are a kind of philogenetic association; they stem from a collective memory on which, in the final analysis, our entire culture is based. They direct the mind toward man's essential being as it has been created, shaped, and reshaped in the course of the millennia, and as it continues to echo in our soul. "Creation, change—the eternal pastime of the eternal mind"—Goethe's words may well describe the way our psyche works.

We have seen that Jung set a very high value on human imagination. The unconscious is creative, and this makes its irrational picture-language extremely valuable. All his life Jung defended its importance against the one-sided overvaluation of rational thinking. The unconscious regulators, the archetypes, make the human imagination possible. They are the seeds from which the conscious mind unfolds. The work of our imagination, no matter how free it may seem, is unconsciously guided by general-human principles and patterns. If this were not so, no reader would ever be able to reexperience the contents and structure of a work of art. Imagination does not originate in conscious volition or whim, it occurs—which is why, in the realm of poetry, it is called inspiration. Jung's research into the working of the human imagination thus also implies the question of the origins of poetic creativity. Here is where the sciences of literature and psychology meet.

II

Throughout Jung's work, we find numerous interpretations of literary themes. But there are three essays which deal directly with literature.[16] The following is an attempt to summarize his most important ideas.

Jung endeavored to find a clear-cut dividing line between the psychological and the aesthetic consideration of literature.

> Only that aspect of art which consists in the process of artistic creation can be a subject for psychological study, but not that which constitutes its essential nature. The question of what art is in itself can never be answered by the psychologist but must be approached from the side of aesthetics. A similar distinction must be made in the realm of religion. A psychological approach is permissible only in regard to the emotions and symbols which constitute the phenomenology of religion, but which do not touch upon its essential nature. If the essence of religion and art could be explained, then both of them would become mere subdivisions of psychology. (*CW,* 15:65)

This was Jung's first formulation in his essay, published in 1922, "On the Relations between Analytical Psychology and Literature." In "Psychology and Literature," published in 1930, the psychological part was expanded. "The investigation of the psyche should therefore be able on the one hand to explain the psychological structure of a work of art, and on the other to reveal the factors that made a person artistically creative" (*CW,* 15:86). Here, Jung assumes that the work of art itself has psychological structures which do not necessarily derive from the psychological conditions of its creator. This is a new view, as against Freudian psychoanalysis, which always explains the work of art through the personal complexities of its author. Jung's view is based on the hypothesis of the creative collective unconscious. He regards not only the individual psyche but also the collective psyche as a self-regulating system. Experience shows that contents and value systems which constitute the "spirit" of a period and philosophy are of necessity incomplete and one-sided. There is no philosophical system so all-embracing, so generally valid, that it cannot be attacked and contested; there is no article of faith so firm that human doubt did not have to reject or, at least, reinterpret it in the course of time. Currents of thought succeed each other; what was valuable for one period often becomes valueless for the next. Seen in psychological terms, this would mean that changing archetypal ideas attain validity and develop into the cultural canon of an era. Out of all the possible modes of human existence those which best lend themselves to coping with existing conditions are unconsciously selected. Views which help us come to terms with the greatest variety of encountered conditions and which, at the same time, produce meaningful relations, constitute the valid prototypes of the collective consciousness.

To repeat: one of the most important results of Jung's researches is the insight that the human soul strives toward totality; that is, toward the realization of all its innate possibilities. This is a goal we can never quite reach. This may well be the reason why conscious collective ideas and their unconscious prototypes, with their necessary one-sidedness, are continually being undermined from within. The result is "Civilization and Its Discontents," a condition that calls for relief. New ideas emerge which try to compensate, to complete, or to replace the old philosophy. These ideas usually occur to individual, creatively gifted people, such as the poet who can receive them, give them shape, and so make them accessible to the general public. While Freud believes that the poet refashions his own unconscious wish into a work of art, Jung sees him as the instrument of a collective creative power. "Whenever the creative force predominates, life is ruled and shaped by the unconscious rather than by the conscious will, and the ego is swept along on an underground current, becoming nothing more than a helpless observer of events (*CW*, 15:103). Friedrich Hölderlin, the German poet, saw himself as "an arrow of the god Apollo. The god shall make use of the poet to let his divine rhythm leap forth from the bow."[17] The poet becomes an instrument destined to give expression and form to those yet unformed ideas that lie dormant in our souls. They take possession of him, transcending his personal life-sphere with their wealth of memories; otherwise they could not become generally meaningful. Artistic sensibility and talent are usually characterized by the vividness of fantasies rising from the unconscious and striving to take on form; and also by the ability to *give* them form. According to Jung's psychology, the unconscious mind stands in a compensatory relation to its own conscious contents and drives, so that works of art illuminate and compensate for the one-sidedness of the spirit of the time. Jung

says: "Thus, just as the one-sidedness of the individual's conscious attitude is corrected by reactions from the unconscious, so art represents a
process of self-regulation in the life of nations and epochs" (*CW*, 15:83).
We find a similar trend of thought in Goethe:

> All supreme productivity, every important observation, every inven-
> tion, every great idea that bears fruit and has lasting effect, stands
> not in anyone's power and is above all earthly force. Man must re-
> gard these things as gifts from on high, as pure children of God, and
> he must receive and venerate them with joyful gratitude. It is re-
> lated to the daemonic which can overpower him and do with him as
> it pleases and to which he gives himself up unconsciously, while be-
> lieving himself to be active under his own power. In such cases man
> can often be regarded as the tool of a higher world government, as a
> vessel that has been found worthy to receive a divine influence. I say
> this while I think how often a single idea has given new form to an
> entire century, and how certain individuals have put their stamp on
> whole epochs and have remained a recognizable and salutory influ-
> ence for generations.[18]

The fact that totalitarian dictatorships expend so much effort on controlling and censoring art reveals an instinctive knowledge of the compensatory aspects of works of art. Wherever the live mental processes are to be
hamstrung in favor of a rigid collective system, creative-artistic freedom
must first be curtailed. The artist must be allowed only to glorify existing
conditions; his work is to have an educational effect in accordance with
the ruling ideas, the ideology.

Given this knowledge, Jung finds it wrong to try to explain the creative act and the literary work through the personal history and problems
of the writer alone—although depth psychology at first tended to do so. It
is true that the biographies of writers often are treasure troves of psychopathological phenomena. Neuroses, psychoses, addictions, sexual per-
versions quickly reveal themselves to the psychiatrist's trained eye. But
all attempts at interpretation which try to dissect works of literature on
the basis of their author's personal difficulties reduce the work to a demonstration of symptoms. "The personal psychology of the artist may explain many aspects of his work, but not the work itself. And if ever it did
explain his work successfully, the artist's creativity would be revealed as
a mere symptom. This would be detrimental both to the work of art and
to its repute." Jung offers the following example: "A knowledge of Goe-

the's particular relation to his mother throws some light on Faust's excla-
mation: 'The mothers, the mothers, how eerily it sounds!' But it does not
enable us to see how the attachment to his mother could produce the
Faust drama itself, however deeply we sense the importance of this relationship for Goethe the man from the many telltale traces it has left behind in his work" (*CW,* 15:86).

Jung tries to explain the writer's personal problematic through the
fact that the writer has to subordinate his humanity to his need to create.
His conflict consists in the fact that "two forces are at war within him: on
the one hand the justified longing of the ordinary man for happiness,
satisfaction and security, and on the other a ruthless passion for creation
which may go so far as to override every personal desire" (*CW,* 15:102).
Rilke alludes to this basic conflict in his requiem for Paula Becker-
Moderssohn: "For, there is somewhere an ancient hostility between life
and the great work."[19] A deeply moving document testifying to the extent and power of this "hostility" is to be found in the correspondence
between Kafka and Felice Bauer.[20]"How can we doubt," says Jung, "that
it is his art that explains the artist, and not the insufficiencies and conflicts
of his personal life? These are nothing but the regrettable results of his
being an artist, a man upon whom a heavier burden is laid than upon
ordinary mortals." He usually must "pay dearly for the divine gifts of
creative fire" (*CW,* 15:102–3). Thus, if we are to regard the author's
human-personal problems from the viewpoint of the creative work, his
suffering becomes psychologically meaningful; it stems from the fact that
he is, as a rule, not allowed to travel "the broad highway of normal man"
(*CW,* 15:83) or to identify completely with the conscious trends of his
epoch. He feels lonely and "thrown back upon himself," as Heidegger
says. This condition again has meaning in regard to the work, but "the
artist's relative lack of adaptation turns out to his advantage; it enables
him to follow his own yearnings far from the beaten path, and to discover
what it is that would meet the unconscious needs of his age" (ibid.). Jung
is quite generally of the opinion that the artist's suffering—for himself,
his world, and the general spirit of his age—is the very thing that opens
his consciousness to those compensatory images and ideas that arise from
the unconscious. Jung arrived at this knowledge through countless experiences with mental patients undergoing psychotherapy. This is why he
sees neurosis not merely as a negative, senseless pattern, but in some
cases even as a signal or a call to deeper self-awareness, self-knowledge,
and self-realization. No doubt this is why he never delved into the personal diagnoses or neuroses of literary personalities for a key to the un-

THE ANALYTICAL PSYCHOLOGY OF C. G. JUNG

derstanding of their work; to him, "every great work of art is objective and impersonal, and yet profoundly moving. And that is also why the personal life of the artist is at most a help or a hindrance, but is never essential to his creative work. He may go the way of the Philistine, a good citizen, a fool, or a criminal. His personal career may be interesting and inevitable, but it does not explain his art" (*CW*, 15:105). I consider this formulation of Jung's a little exaggerated; but it is as legitimate a position as are the psychoanalytical interpretations of the Freudian school that merely dissect the author's instinctual conflicts. How far the artist's personal sphere has influenced his work—the relationship between private biography and the contents of literary creations—is a matter that must be examined in each individual case and that will, of course, show very different results with different artist personalities.

Thus Jung's main interest is the work itself and its archetypal background. In considering the work of art from the psychologist's viewpoint, Jung first of all makes a basic distinction between categories of artistic creation which can be clearly recognized. The first category contains "works, prose as well as poetry, that spring wholly from the author's intention to produce a particular result. . . . He exercises the keenest judgement and chooses his words with complete freedom." In this type of work the conscious artistic knowledge seems to have been responsible for everything, including the idea. Certainly, it has arranged the idea, related it to the whole, and determined its form. The poet "is wholly at one with the creative process, no matter whether he has deliberately made himself its spearhead, as it were, or whether it has made him its instrument so completely that he has lost all consciousness of this fact" (*CW*, 15:72). At any rate, the material from which he fashions his works seems not to be foreign to his conscious mind; it consists of

> materials drawn from man's conscious life—with crucial experiences, powerful emotions, suffering, passion, the stuff of human fate in general. All this is assimilated by the psyche of the poet, raised from the commonplace to the level of poetic experience, and expressed with a power of conviction that gives us a greater depth of human insight by making us aware of those everyday happenings which we tend to evade or to overlook because we perceive them only dully or with a feeling of discomfort. The raw material of this kind of creation is derived from the contents of man's consciousness, from his eternally repeated joys and sorrows, but clarified and transfigured by the poet. (*CW*, 15:89)

For the sake of clarity, Jung calls these works *psychological*, because "the poet has done the psychologist's work in them . . . no obscurity surrounds them, for they fully explain themselves in their own terms" (ibid.). The psychologist, in turn, can at best annotate or criticize such works; they remain throughout within the boundaries of what is psychologically comprehensible. "Countless literary products belong to this class: all the novels dealing with love, the family milieu, crime and society, together with didactic poetry, the greater number of lyrics, and drama both tragic and comic" (ibid.). They "have been known from the beginning of time—passion and its fated outcome, human destiny and its sufferings, eternal nature with its beauty and horror" (*CW*, 15:90).

But there is a different class of literary works, which comes,

> as it were, fully arrayed into the world, as Pallas Athene sprang from the head of Zeus. These works positively force themselves upon the author; his hand is seized, his pen writes things that his mind contemplates with amazement. The work brings with it its own form; anything he wants to add is rejected, and what he himself would like to reject is thrust back at him. While his conscious mind stands amazed and empty before this phenomenon, he is overwhelmed by a flood of thoughts and images which he never intended to create and which his own will could never have brought into being. Yet in spite of himself he is forced to admit that it is his own self speaking, his own inner nature revealing itself and uttering things which he would never have entrusted to his tongue. He can only obey the apparently alien impulse within him and follow where it leads, sensing that his work is greater than himself, and wields a power which is not his and which he cannot command. Here the artist is not identical with the process of creation. He is aware that he is subordinate to his work or stands outside it as though he were a second person; or as though a person other than himself had fallen within the magic circle of an alien will. (*CW*, 15:73)

Jung calls this type a *visionary* work of art. It often comes over the poet as a kind of primal vision and it can "rend from top to bottom the curtain upon which is painted the picture of an ordered world, and allow a glimpse into the unfathomable abyss of the unborn and of things yet to be. Is it a vision of other worlds, or of the darkness of the spirit, or of the primal beginnings of the human psyche? We cannot say that it is any or none of these" (*CW*, 15:90–91). Such works in which we encounter the primal vision are, according to Jung: Dante's *Divina Commedia,* Goethe's *Faust,* part 2, William Blake's drawings and poems, the grand and sometimes scurrilous images in E. T. A. Hoffmann's novel *The Golden Pot*; James Joyce's *Ulysses,* which "is a work of the greatest significance in spite of or perhaps because of its nihilistic tendencies" (*CW,* 15:91, n. 7).

"In more restricted and succinct form" (*CW,* 15:91), according to Jung, such works as *She* by H. Rider Haggard, *L'Atlantide* by Benoit, *The Other Side* by Kubin, or *The Green Face* by Gustav Meyrink are also based on a primal vision. Contrary to the "psychological" works in which well-known and familiar things are described and expressed, in visionary literature "we are reminded of nothing in everyday life, but rather of dreams, night-time fears, and the dark, uncanny recesses of the human mind" (ibid.). This is why such works are not accessible to the spontaneous understanding of the general reader; they call for interpretations and commentary.

We can see why Jung, the explorer of the unconscious ground of the soul, was powerfully attracted to works of visionary literature. They gave him profound insights into the secret workings of man's collective-psychological life. These same forces, conjured up by the artist, can also, in a negative sense, erupt in individual psychoses or in religious and pseudoreligious mass hysteria, flooding the conscious mind. What matters most is whether such experiences can be accepted, sufficiently understood, and integrated into the conscious mind and thus enrich it profoundly, or whether they completely overwhelm it and carry away its powers of discrimination whence they are anchored in everyday life—into unknown and no longer controllable regions. This is why we almost always find, in cases of insanity, that archetypal images have taken over the sufferer's consciousness and have produced a state of "possession." But the primal images can also release those helpful forces "that ever and anon have enabled humanity to find a refuge from every peril and to outlive the longest night" (*CW,* 15:82). This is why Jung, the physician and psychotherapist, was mainly interested in the relations between the ego, its radius of consciousness, and the basic archetypal data, the contents of the collective unconscious. When the ego is made aware of its own boundaries and allows them to open out toward the unconscious life in an understanding, orderly, and even value-judging manner, the result may well be a relation to the ground of one's own soul, the end of self-estrangement, and a maturing of the entire personality. Jung's extensive research into symbols also serves to facilitate a proper understanding of the unconscious contents of our mind and the way they function, so that they cannot produce dangerous obsessions by taking our consciousness unawares. Instead, these unconscious contents should

enlarge and deepen our consciousness and enrich the entire personality.
For this reason, Jung rated the visionary type of literature, with its deep-
probing symbolism, so highly, for "he who speaks in primal images, speaks
as a man with a thousand voices; he grasps and overpowers us and at the
same time he raises that which he describes from the particular and transitory sphere into the eternal; he elevates individual destiny to the destiny of
man" (*CW*, 15:82).

    This brings us back to the actual problem of literary evaluation.
Jung's valuation, which was psychological in viewpoint, cannot possibly
be identical with aesthetic-artistic values. It would be utterly absurd to
ascribe greater artistic value to a book like Haggard's *She* than to, say,
Goethe's *Wahlverwandschaften* (Elective Affinities) or to *Faust*, part 1,
which Jung cites as examples of "psychological" literature. Jung was fully
aware of this discrepancy. He wrote: "There is a fundamental difference
of attitude between the psychologist's approach to a literary work and
that of a literary critic. What is of decisive importance and value for the
latter may be quite irrelevant for the former. Indeed, literary products of
highly dubious merit are often of the greatest interest to the psychologist" (*CW*, 15:87–88). Literary critics have reproached the depth psychologists for their interest in literary works of extremely doubtful
value.[21] But Jung explains quite clearly that his interest in literature
stems from quite another side. For him as a scientist, literary products are
primarily documents of a mental activity he wishes to illuminate in
depth. He asks: "what is the human psyche like?; what laws can be in-
ferred from its functioning?; and how is human consciousness to cope
with unconscious problems of the psyche for its own good? The words of
the visionary poets, being "products of the unconscious," provided him
with the most valuable insights for these researches. I would here like to
call attention to the work of Jung's student, Aniela Jaffé, about *The
Golden Pot* by E. T. A. Hoffmann, a beautiful example of psychological
interpretation and illumination of archetypal contexts in a literary work.

III

■　■　■　■

    A psychologist cannot evaluate works of literature in the aesthetic-
artistic sense or create criteria for them in that sense. But evaluation and
the search for general value standards is an activity of the psyche that can
be studied from the psychological point of view. And here it becomes
apparent that the literary value categories cited above correspond with
general value ideas that have been discovered in the human soul. We

have said that the archetype of the highest good, with its unconscious call to action, motivates us to strive for value and to recognize value; in other words: to become aware of our own unconscious values. The further we progress in increasing awareness and recognizing the relative importance of certain values we had unquestioningly accepted from our families or peer groups, the more we shall discover the contents of a "fabric of relations" that is both inexhaustible and timeless. We thus gain a far larger sense of values and may experience an encounter with the "ultimate values" of our existence.

We find such images, symbols of the supratemporal, everywhere in the great literature of all times. They are fraught with meaning and are experienced as values by us. The criteria of literary evaluation cited earlier are based on this same spontaneous, archetypally determined value experience. As value categories, they appeal to our emotions and assume a living relationship between the work and the value-conscious reader. The question is, whether the "inexhaustibly reflective fabric of relations"[22] of which Emrich speaks is intrinsic to the work, or whether the work merely acts as a catalyst, stimulating within the reader his own fabric of relations which, in turn, is projected back onto the work and so conveys a sense of value through it. There is no unequivocal answer to this question, since the experience of value becomes possible only in fruitful mutual relation; the poet touches something in me which seems to me of high value and, reciprocally, makes me receptive to the work's larger message. The value categories described above seem to be the result of such mutual relations between the work of art and the discriminating, emotional reaction of the reader or critic. In their emphasis on the supratemporal, in their infinite reflexibility, in their relation to the primal image, they point to an infinitely meaningful highest value which we can only vaguely sense as the deepest meaning of our life, and which our conscious mind can grasp only in a fragmentary way. Thus they leave enough room for appreciation of the irrepeatable uniqueness of the work on the one hand, and for its translucency for eternally human questions of existence on the other.

We now must ask ourselves how far we can do justice to contemporary literature with such criteria. Do they not create the impression that everything great has already been written, once and for all, by authors we consider classical in the widest sense? The psychologist's answer to this basically literary question might be that, as Jung has pointed out, the primal images have—at all times—the effect of extremely potent life forces. We cannot say that they have been revealed once and for all in the Bible, in the Upanishads, in Dante, Shakespeare, or, if you wish, in Goethe's *Faust*; that

they have been given their final validity only in those works. The classics
are historic documents we must, first of all, understand in the contexts of
their periods. But, in addition to this, their "infinite reflexibility" as Emrich
calls it, provokes a search for new approaches in *every* period. There are
libraries full of interpretations of all the works named above. But the primal
images or archetypes are not historic entities. As Muschg says,[23] the relation to archaic contents is not to be understood as a historical activity but
rather as something that takes place within the psyche. The archetype itself
is abstract, but it can take on the guise of thousands of possible symbols in
which it manifests itself to the human consciousness. And so, ever new
symbols arise, conveying a connection between the modern consciousness
and the eternally human in a vaguely sensed way and, at the same time,
opening up new possibilities of consciousness.

In literature, too, new types of word construction and word combinations can continually arise behind which there sounds the "primal
word" as Gerhard Hauptmann has said. Whether anything of the kind is
happening in our period, how far certain authors working in the style of
surrealism, or the *nouveau roman,* or the theater of the absurd, are opening up such new dimensions and creating space for the inexhaustible
"fabric of relations," is a question which, as we well know, contemporary
criticism cannot really answer, because lack of distance means lack of
perspective. But there is room, and need, for detailed discussion and
evaluation.

All in all, the psychologist can state that the literary value criteria
mentioned above correspond to general human archetypal value ideas:
that they bring those ideas to mind and are therefore of sufficient depth
and breadth to allow us to approach true literature without being hampered by prejudgments or narrow, preconceived notions.

The criterion of "infinite reflexibility" of a "poetic fabric of relations" corresponds, in the realm of psychology, to the archetype that is
inexhaustible for the conscious mind. A conscious valuation, no matter
how broad, can never grasp more than the fragments of the creative unconscious which manifests itself in a work of literature. This is why literary evaluation as such becomes a problem; this is why a work of art must
be studied and considered anew in every period. As W. B. Yeats wrote:

> Man can embody truth
> But he cannot know it.

(1969)

6   THE FASHIONING OF LIVING MYTHS

Joseph Campbell

$\mathbf{J}$*oseph Campbell is widely known today for his extensive writing and lectur-ing, especially via television, on the importance of myth, but he was also a perceptive and influential critic of the relationship of literature and psychology. In 1944 he coauthored* A Skeleton Key to "Finnegans Wake." *His* The Hero with a Thousand Faces *(1949) analyzed the ubiquitous story of the hero, found in both legend and literature, as a "monomyth" having a universal, psychological meaning. Although his editor, William McGuire, notes that Campbell had a Freudian orientation when he wrote* Hero, *he moved toward Jung thereafter; his popular video and book,* The Power of Myth *(1988), makes frequent reference to Jung and his psychology.*

This selection discusses in Jungian terms a much-remarked literary phe-nomenon: the explosion of interest by authors such as Joyce, Mann, and Eliot in the archetypes of mythology during the socially chaotic period surrounding World War I. Employing Jung's principle that visionary art compensates for the imbalances of its age, Campbell psychologizes this historical interest in myth, relating it to a felt need for order in an unstable time. He analyzes the theme of individuation in the lifework of these three writers, carefully balancing the art-ist's inner necessity against society's conditioning from without. He thus presents a psychological explanation of two central questions of myth study, and of liter-ary myth criticism: what was the origin of myths in the past, and what are the possibilities for creating new and powerful myths?

In Joyce's *A Portrait of the Artist as a Young Man* there is represented, stage by stage, the process of an escape from a traditional and the fashioning of a personal myth, adequate to the shaping of an individuated life. From the first page, attention is focused on the feelings and associated thoughts of a growing boy in response to the sights, sensations, teachings, personages, and ideals of his Irish-Catholic environment, his home, his schools, and his city. The key to the progress of the novel lies in its stress on what is inward. The outward occasions of the inward feeling-judgments are thereby emptied of intrinsic force, while their echoes in the boy's—then the youth's—interior become enriched and recombined in a growing context of conscientiously observed subjective associations. Steadily, a system of sentiments, separate and increasingly distant from that of his fellows, takes form, which he has the courage to respect and ultimately to follow. And since these guiding value judgments are conceived in relation, not only to the accidental details of life in late-nineteenth-century Dublin, but also both to the "grave and constant" in human sufferings and to the dogmas and iconography of the Roman Catholic Church—together with the school classics of the Western world, from Homer to his own day—the inward life and journey is by no means an isolating, merely idiosyncratic adventure, but in the best sense a mystery-flight from the little bounds of a personal life to the great domain of universals. The novel is introduced, on the title page, by a line from Ovid's *Metamorphoses* (Book VIII, line 188): *Et ignotas animum dimittit in artes,* "And he turns his mind to unknown arts." The reference in Ovid is to the Greek master craftsman Daedalus, who, when he had built the labyrinth to house the monster Minotaur, was in danger of being retained in Crete by King Minos; but turning his mind to unknown arts, he fashioned wings for himself and for Icarus, his son; then warned the boy:

> "Remember
> To fly midway, for if you dip too low
> The waves will weight your wings with thick saltwater,
> And if you fly too high the flames of heaven
> Will burn them from your sides. Then take your flight
> Between the two."[1]

Icarus, however, disobeyed; he flew too high and fell into the sea. But Daedalus reached the mainland. And so Joyce would fly on wings of art from provincial Ireland to the cosmopolitan Mainland; from Catholicism to the universal mythic heritage of which Christianity is but an inflection;

and through mythology, on wings of art, to his own induplicable immortality.

Thomas Mann, likewise, in his early novelette, *Tonio Kröger*, tells of a youth who, guided by the inward compass of his own magnetic pole, dissociates his destiny, first, from his family—in this case, German Protestant—but then, also, from "those haughty, frigid ones," as he calls them, the literary monsters of his day, "who," as he discovers, "adventure along the path of great, demonic beauty and despise 'mankind.' " He consequently stands "between two worlds, at home in neither," where it is darkest, so to say, and there is no way or path; or, like Daedalus, in flight between sea and sky.

In his masterwork, *The Magic Mountain*, which appeared shortly after World War I, Mann turned this mythological theme of the inwardly guided passage between opposites to the representation of the psychological metamorphosis, not of an artist this time, but of an ingenuous though attractive young marine engineer, Hans Castorp, who had come for a brief visit to a Land of No Return—the timeless playground of Aphrodite and King Death (an Alpine tuberculosis sanatorium)—where he remained to undergo a sort of alchemical transmutation, for a span of exactly seven years. Mann extended the import of this adventure to suggest the ordeal of contemporary Germany between worlds: between the rational, positivistic West and the semiconscious, metaphysical East; between *eros* and *thanatos*, liberal individualism and socialistic despotism; between music and politics, science and the Middle Ages, progress and extinction. The noble engraving by Dürer of "A Knight Between Death and the Devil," might stand as the emblem of Mann's thesis in this work. He expands the image further to signify Man, "life's delicate child," walking the beveled edge between spirit and matter, married in his thinking to both, yet in his Being and Becoming, something else—not to be captured in a definition. Then, in the biblical tetralogy of *Joseph and His Brothers*, Mann passes altogether into the sphere of mythological archetypes, sounding once more, but now fortissimo, his life-song of the Man of God, *Homo Dei*, in adventurous passage between the poles of birth and death, from nowhere to nowhere, as it were. And, as in the novels of James Joyce—from the autobiographical *Portrait*, through *Ulysses*, to the cycling mythologic nightmare ("whirled without end") of *Finnegans Wake*—so in those of Thomas Mann, from the life-adventure of his Tonio, through that of his unassuming yet gifted Hans, to the unashamedly self-serving, cheating yet imposing and beloved heroes of his tales of Jacob and Joseph, we may follow, stage by stage, the flight of a highly conscious, learned, and superbly competent artist, out of the "Crete" (so to say) of the naturalistic imagery of his accidental birthplace, to the "Mainland" of the grave and constant mythological archetypes of his own inward being as Man.

As in the novels of Joyce, so in those of Mann, the key to the progression lies in the stress on what is inward. The outward occasions represent, however, substantial external contexts of their own, of historical, sociopolitical, and economic relationships—to which, in fact, the intellects of the minor characters of these novels are generally addressed. And that such relationships have force, and even make claims on the loyalties of the protagonists, not only is recognized, but is fundamental to the arguments of the adventures. In the words of Joyce's hero: "When the soul of a man is born in this country there are nets flung at it to hold it back from flight. You talk to me of nationality, language, religion. I shall try to fly by those nets." Obviously, an outward-directed intellect, recognizing only such historical ends and claims, would be very much in danger of losing touch with its natural base, becoming involved wholly in the realization of "meanings" parochial to its local time and place. But on the other hand, anyone hearkening only inward, to the dispositions of feeling, would be in equal danger of losing touch with the only world in which he would ever have the possibility of living as a human being. It is an important characteristic of both James Joyce and Thomas Mann, that, in developing their epic works, they remained attentive equally to the facts and contexts of the outward, and the feeling systems of the inward, hemispheres of the volume of experiences they were documenting. They were both immensely learned, furthermore, in the scholarship and sciences of their day. And they were able, consequently, to extend and enrich in balanced correlation the outward and the inward ranges of their characters' spheres of experience, progressing in such a way from the purely personal to the larger, collective orders of outward experience and inward sense of import that in their culminating masterworks they achieved actually the status, the majesty, and validity, of contemporary myth.

Carl Jung, in his analysis of the structure of the psyche, has distinguished four psychological functions that link us to the outer world. These are sensation, thinking, feeling, and intuition. Sensation, he states, is the function that tells us that something *exists*; thinking, the function that tells us *what* it is; feeling, the function that evaluates its *worth* to us; and intuition, the function that enables us to estimate the *possibilities* inherent in the object or its situation.[2] Feeling, thus, is the inward guide to value; but its judgments are related normally to outward, empirical circumstance. However, it is to be noted that Jung distinguishes, also, four psychological functions that unlock, progressively, the depth chambers of our nature. These are (1) memory, (2) the subjective components of our conscious functions, (3) affects and emotions, and (4) invasions or possessions, where components of the unconscious break into the conscious field and take over.[3] "The area of the unconscious," he writes, "is enormous and always continuous, while the area of consciousness is a restricted field of momentary vision."[4] This restricted field, however, is the field of historical life and not to be lost.

Jung distinguishes two orders or depths of the unconscious, the personal and the collective. The Personal Unconscious, according to his view, is composed largely of personal acquisitions, potentials, and dispositions, forgotten or repressed contents derived from one's own experience, etc. The Collective Unconscious, on the other hand, is a function rather of biology than of biography: its contents are of the instincts, not the accidents of personal experience, but the processes of nature as invested in the anatomy of *Homo sapiens* and consequently common to the human race. Moreover, where the consciousness may go astray and in the interest of an ideal or an idea do violence to the order of nature, the instincts, disordered, will irresistibly protest; for, like a body in disease, so the diseased psyche undertakes to resist and expel infection: and the force of its protest will be expressed in madness or, in lesser cases, morbid anxieties, troubled sleep, and terrible dreams. When the imagery of the warning visions rises from the Personal Unconscious, its sense can be interpreted through personal associations, recollections, and reflections; when, however, it stems from the Collective, the signals cannot be decoded in this way. They will be of the order, rather, of myth; in many cases even identical with the imagery of myths of which the visionary or dreamer will never have heard. (The evidence for this in the literature of psychiatry seems to me now to be beyond question.) They will thus be actually presentations of *the archetypes of mythology* in a relation of significance to some context of contemporary life, and consequently will be decipherable only by comparison with the patterns, motifs, and semantology of mythology in general.[5]

Now it is of the greatest interest to remark, that, during the period immediately following World War I, there appeared a spectacular series of historical, anthropological, literary, and psychological works, in which the archetypes of myth were recognized, not as merely irrational vestiges of archaic thought, but as fundamental to the structuring of human life and, in that sense, prophetic of the future as well as remedial of the present and eloquent of the past. T. S. Eliot's poem, *The Waste Land,* Carl Jung's *Psychological Types,* and Leo Frobenius's *Paideuma* appeared in 1921; James Joyce's *Ulysses* in 1922; Oswald Spengler's *Decline of the West* in 1923; and Thomas Mann's *The Magic Mountain* in 1924. It was very much as though, at a crucial juncture in the course of the growth of our civilization, a company of sages, masters of the wisdom that arises from the depths of being, had spoken from their hermitages to give warning and redirection. However, what men of deeds have ever listened to sages? For these, to think is to act, and one thought is enough. Furthermore, the more readily communicable to the masses their driving thought may be, the better—and the more effective. Thus the nations learn in sweat, blood, and tears what might have been taught them in peace, and as Joyce's hero in *A Portrait* states, what those so-called thoughts and their protagonists represent are not the ways and guides to freedom, but the very nets, and the wielders of those nets, by which the seeker of freedom is snared, entrapped, and hauled back into the labyrinth. For their appeal is precisely to those sentiments of desire and fear by which the gate to the paradise of the spirit is barred. Didacticism and pornography are the qualities of the arts that they inspire (their hacks I would term, very simply, a bunch of didactic pornographers!), and their heroes are rather the monsters to be overcome than the boon-bringers to be praised.

And so, I come to my last point.

There are (and, apparently, there have always been) two orders of mythology, that of the Village and that of the Forest of Adventure. The imposing guardians of the village rites are those cherubim of the garden gate, their Lordships Fear and Desire, with, however, another to support them, the Lord Duty, and a fourth, her holiness, Faith: and the aims of their fashionable cults are mainly health, abundance of progeny, long life, wealth, victories in war, and the grace of a painless death. The ways of the Forest Adventurous, on the other hand, are not entered until these guardians have been passed; and the way to pass them is to recognize their apparent power as a figment merely of the restricted field of one's own ego-centered consciousness: not confronting them as "realities" without (for when slain "out there," their power only passes to another vehicle), but shifting the center of one's own horizon of concern. As Joyce's hero, tapping his brow, muses in *Ulysses:* "In here it is I must kill the priest and the king."[6]

Meanwhile, those under the ban of those powers are, as it were, under enchantment: that is the meaning of the Waste Land theme in T. S. Eliot's celebrated poem, as it was also in the source from which he derived it, the Grail legend of the twelfth- and thirteenth-century Middle Ages. That was a period when all had been compelled to profess beliefs that many did not share, and that were enforced, furthermore, by a clergy whose morals were the scandal of the age. As witnessed by the pope himself, Innocent III (himself no saint): "Nothing is more common than for even monks and regular canons to cast aside their attire, take to gambling and hunting, consort with concubines, and turn jugglers or medical quacks."[7] The Grail King of the legend was one who had not earned through his life and character his role as guardian of the supreme symbol of the spirit, but had inherited and had simply been anointed in the part; and when riding forth, one day, on a youthful adventure of *amor* (which was appropriate enough for a youthful knight, but not for a king of the Grail), he became engaged in combat with a pagan knight, whom he slew but whose lance simultaneously unmanned him; and, magically, his whole kingdom thereupon fell under an enchantment of sterility, from which it would be released only by a noble youth with the courage to be governed not by the social and clerical dogmas of his day but by the dictates of a loyal, compassionate heart. Significantly, in the leading version of the tale, by the poet Wolfram von Eschenbach, every time the hero Parzival behaved as he had been taught to behave, the case of the world became worse, and it was only when he had learned, at last, to follow the lead of his own noble nature that he was found eligible to supplant and even to heal the anointed king, lifting thereby from Christendom the enchantment of a mythology and order of life derived not from experience and virtue, but authority and tradition.

In T. S. Eliot's modern poem a similar point is made, referring, however, to a modern Waste Land of secular, not religious, patterns of inauthentic living:

> Unreal City,
> Under the brown fog of a winter dawn,
> A crowd flowed over London Bridge, so many,
> I had not thought death had undone so many.[8]

And again, the answer to the spell of death is understood to be psychological, a radical shift in the conscious center of concern. Eliot turns for a sign to India, to the same *Bṛihadāraṇyaka Upanishad,* by the way, from which my figure came of the primal being who said "I" and brought forth the universe. That same Prajāpati, "Father of Creatures," speaks here with a voice of thunder, DA—which sound is variously heard by his three classes of children: the gods, mankind, and the demons. The gods hear *damyata*, "control yourselves"; mankind hears *datta*, "give"; and the demons hear *dayadhvam*, "be compassionate."[9] In the *Upanishad* this lesson is declared to epitomize the sum of that sacred teaching by which the binding and deluding spell of egoity is undone, and in the modern poem equally, it is again pronounced as a thunder voice, releasing a rain of enlivening grace from beyond the hells and heavens of egoity. Joyce, also, in *Ulysses*, invokes a thunderclap (which then resounds through every chapter of his next work, *Finnegans Wake*) to break the self-defensive mask of his young hero, Stephen Dedalus, whose heart thereafter is open through compassion to an experience of "consubstantiality" with another suffering creature, Leopold Bloom. And finally—to close this sample series of timely modern works renewing timeless mythological themes—Thomas Mann's hero Hans, on the Magic Mountain, his spirit set in motion by the same two powers by which the Buddha had been tempted—namely, Death and Desire—follows courageously, unimpressed by all warnings of danger, the interests of his heart, and so learns to act out of a center of life within, or, to use Nietzsche's phrase, as "a wheel rolling from its own center" (*ein aus sich rollendes Rad*). Whereupon, once again, there is heard a "thunderclap," the *Donnerschlag*, as Mann calls it, of the cannon-roar of World War I, and the same young man who formerly had found an office job too much for him finds the heart to enter voluntarily the battlefields of his century and thus to return to life.

For what to the young soul are nets, "flung at it to hold it back from flight," can become for the one who has found his own center the garment, freely chosen, of his further adventure.

(1970)

7 ROBERT BLY'S *SLEEPERS JOINING HANDS:* SHADOW AND SELF

Michael Atkinson

This selection elucidates a contemporary example of what Joseph Campbell called "timely modern works renewing timeless mythological themes"; it is a quest-book of poetry and prose by Robert Bly, surely today's best-known Jungian poet and storyteller (Iron John: A Book for Men). Michael Atkinson, a professor of literature whose experience of Jung's psychology includes some years of analysis, discusses not only the long autobiographical poem Bly structured on Jung's individuation process, "Sleepers Joining Hands," but the entire book of that name, including the 1969 poem "The Teeth Mother Naked at Last" (arguably the finest poem to come from America's Vietnam War period) and Bly's essay on the American psyche's need for values associated with the Great Mother.

   Atkinson outlines Bly's pervasive debt to Jung, presented most clearly in the Great Mother essay, and then displays his own education in Jung by following the poet through his imaging of the psyche in its various archetypal manifestations. Atkinson explains the shadow poems of the book's first part, showing how Bly follows Jung in implicating the personal in the political by tracing the roots of the Vietnam War back to the psyche and the shadow denied; Atkinson then follows Bly through "The Teeth Mother" and its symbol of the anima turning to devour the psyche that it normally nourishes. At this nadir enters the title poem of the book, "Sleepers Joining Hands," which follows the path of the individuation process, ultimately culminating in a redemption of the Self imaged in

psychospiritual terms. Atkinson is clear about the difficulties Bly's use of Jung-
ian psychology and its terms pose for a general readership, but he demonstrates
convincingly that this important book does constitute a coherent, powerful
whole.

   In *Sleepers Joining Hands,* Robert Bly offers his readers a various
weave of the personal and the public, the psychological and the political
modes of experience. Each mode illuminates the other, though, as I hope
to show, the collection is most fundamentally and formally psychological.
The layout of the book is pleasantly indirect: two dozen pages of poems,
ranging from haiku-like meditation moments to longer poems of protest.
Then there is the essay, a short course in the Great Mother, an analysis of
the disturbing but finally nourishing configuration of feminine archetypes in the collective unconscious. And finally we have the oneiric title
sequence: four poems and a coda, written at different times and published in different places, but here offered as a single structure, a whole.
   The poems on either side of the essay seem to point back and forth
to each other. And so naturally we ask: what is the relation of the earlier
poems to the later sequence? what is the final shape of the book?
   The essay points the way. Like most poets who pause to explain
themselves, Bly works obliquely. His essay focuses on the work of Bacho-
fen and Neumann; yet the pattern of the book rests firmly on the thought
of a successor to the first and the teacher of the second—Carl Jung. The
essay coordinates the variety of anima archetypes that inhabit our sub-
consciousness: the Good Mother who gives us life; the Death Mother
who takes it away; the Ecstatic Mother, muse of joy; and the Stone or
Teeth Mother who reduces us to the stupor of psychic annihilation. But
the title sequence, which is the key to the book's integrity, focuses on
two other Jungian dream archetypes—the shadow and the Self.
   The symbols of the earlier poems gain resonance in the schematic
context of the later sequence: imagist poems move toward plotted action,
oracles toward ritual, archetypes toward myth. Here, I would like to present the scheme of the sequence and show its relation to the shorter
poems, delineating the system of archetypes that coherently applies
throughout the book, linking biblical allusions to contemporary consciousness and connecting dream images with myth.
   After sketching in the profiles of the Great Mother, Bly warns that
we should not examine his "poems for evidence of them, for most of
[the] poems were written without benefit of them." And further to guide
us, he lifts the penultimate paragraph of his essay from Jung: it virtually

diagrams the concern and shape of the "Sleepers" sequence, shifting our attention from "the woman within" to the shadow and the Self.

> It would be far better simply to admit our spiritual poverty. . . . The spirit has come down from its fiery high places . . . but when the spirit becomes heavy, it turns to water. . . . Therefore the way of the soul in search of its lost father . . . leads to the water, to the dark mirror that lies at the bottom. Whoever has decided to move toward the state of spiritual poverty . . . goes the way of the soul that leads to the water. [Bly's ellipses]

In Jung's overall schema, the personality striving for full individuation or integration has four aspects, which are personified in our dreams: (1) the ego (or persona), that person (or role) we consider ourselves to be in normal waking consciousness; (2) the shadow, that figure of the same sex as the ego who embodies negative or positive traits which might have been conscious but which have now been repressed; (3) the anima, the woman within the man, that feminine consciousness with which he has to come to terms—or the animus, the man within the woman, representing the male consciousness with which the woman must reconcile herself; and finally, (4) the Self, that perfect wholeness which the individual can become, when he has reconciled himself with his shadow and anima (or she with her shadow and animus) and become his own potentiality for being.

The first poem of the "Sleepers" sequence hearkens back to the time when the ego became split from its shadow by repression, and is appropriately entitled "The Shadow Goes Away." It records the fragmentation of the questor, chronicles his separation from that lost aspect which he must again come to recognize in himself. Until he incorporates his shadow, he is powerless to act effectively. We feel his powerlessness as we gaze with him upon "The woman chained to the shore," Andromeda-like, and hear him express his fear of going into the ocean to fight for her, to liberate her. (In mythic compression, the woman *is* the ocean—*la mer, la mère*—the womb from which he must be reborn whole). He fears the sea. Juxtaposed to his feeling of impotence is its cause: his loss of the shadow.

Often—perhaps most frequently in dream and art—the shadow is a figure that embodies the negative aspects of the personality; the negativity provides the reason they are repressed. Thus we have Jekyll's hidden Hyde, Dimmesdale's Chillingworth, Gatsby's Wolfsheim, and the like. But, as Jung notes, we may just as easily deny parts of ourselves that—grown wiser—we would consider good. Because something about them threatens the fragile, narrowly defined persona or ego, they too may be repressed. But ultimately they must be admitted to our consciousness and assimilated, or the results will be disastrous. Ishmael's savage Queequeg, Willy Lowman's Charley, Macbeth's Banquo: each contains "values that are needed by consciousness, but that exist in a form that makes it difficult to integrate them into one's life."

The protagonist in Bly's poems has a shadow that is protean but consistent. The dreamer first imagines himself a brother (probably Judah) to Joseph of the many-colored coat; he recalls selling his brother-shadow into slavery. Joseph possesses the qualities the dreamer so desperately needs to complete his life. In Genesis (chapters 37–50) Joseph is sent into the moral wilderness of Egypt, banished, repressed from the consciousness of the family (except the mind of the father, the wise old man, the Self, who yearns for Joseph's return). Despite (or because of) the banishment, Joseph gains mastery over the alien realm, understands its laws by understanding dreams both positive and negative, and eventually provides his brothers with what they need to sustain their lives, when they at last seek him out.

Bly's shape-shifting protagonist repeatedly dreams of selling his brother, notably to be carried away into the desert or out to sea (archetypal equivalents for the unconscious, which may be a realm of danger and potential death for the fragmented and brittle ego). Joseph is transformed into an American Indian: he is "taken in by travelling Sioux," and he learns to "glide about naked, drinking water from his hands, / to tether horses, follow the faint trail through bent grasses." The questor's shadow—and, the poem suggests, ours—is the natural man, the primitive, at home in the world of nature and the unconscious. The pillagers of the tribal village and the Marines who appear late in the poem are intended to remind us how we have duplicated our oppression of the Indian in the bombing of Vietnam. Equations that seem both familiar and strained in political rhetoric are here given greater coherence and vitality in a psychological connection. In each case we have attempted to destroy (or repress) the people who best exemplified the very qualities we most need to acknowledge and cultivate in ourselves—positive shadows.

"The Shadow Goes Away" gives a larger context for a number of the other poems—poems, already integers themselves, now resonate within the larger pattern. "The Condition of the Working Classes: 1970" is blamed not on those above them, but on those they have trod under—

blamed not on the oppression that workers might suffer, but on the repression of their shadows, inwardly and outwardly. Thus, we eat "a bread made of the sound of sunken buffalo bones" and drink "a water turned dark by the shadows of Negroes"; the "Sioux dead sleep all night in the rain troughs on the Treasury Building," and because of this our sons are "lost in the immense forest" of the unintegrated unconscious.

As the repression intensifies, so does the terror of living with it. Denying the shadow drives us into the maw of "The Teeth Mother Naked at Last." Here the horror hits its highest pitch, and an unfamiliar list toward stereotype and stridence appears. Maybe it is unavoidable—so many have spoken out against the war for so long that even the most telling analysis has deteriorated into formula and finally come to rest in cliché. Bly's poem cannot shake itself free of stereotypy, even though it has considerable power. The power comes not just from its imagery—

> If one of those children came near that we have set on fire, . . .
> If one of those children came toward me with both hands
> in the air, fire rising along both elbows
> I would suddenly go back to my animal brain
> I would drop on all fours, screaming,
> my vocal cords would turn blue, so would yours.
> it would be two days before I could play with my own children
>   again

—but from the analysis of cause and effect that is given in the hard terms of imagery which will not allow the luxuries and niceties of rationalization. These cause-effect concatenations generate both the strengths and weaknesses of the poem. I suspect each reader will find different equations effective. But when they work, they work; when they don't, they grate.

The poem begins with a deft and horrific picture of planes lifting off on bombing missions. The first stated cause for the missions—Hamilton's plan for a centralized bank. This is entirely too easy. And, though he does return to such, fortunately Bly gets beyond the familiar accusations of economic materialism to a perspective that still has the capacity to arrest us. He tells us to save the tears we shed for exploding children.

> Don't cry at that—
> Do you cry at the wind pouring out of Canada?
> Do you cry at the reeds shaken at the edge of the sloughs?

He asks us to hold our tears and, Yeatsian but joyless, to see the terrible destruction as a natural law working itself out. The natural wind that shakes the reeds and brings the snow is not just meteorological—it is the inner wind of the spirit that blows where it lists.

> This happens when the seasons change,
> This happens when the leaves begin to drop from the trees
>   too early
> *"Kill them: I don't want to see anything moving."*
> This happens when the ice begins to show its teeth in the
>   ponds
> This happens when the heavy layers of lake water press
>   down on the fish's head, and send him deeper, where his
>   tail swirls slowly, and his brain passes him pictures
>   of heavy reeds, of vegetation fallen on vegetation . . .
> Hamilton saw all this in detail:
> *"Every banana tree slashed, every cooking utensil smashed,*
>   *every mattress cut."*

The key here is the aquatic imagery, which so pervades the poem (and the book). Allegorically read, the passage limns in a picture of repression—a freezing of the sensitive living waters, the ice pressing down on the fish, denizen of the unconscious, our evolutionary precursor. And the dying, descending fish sees the pictures of previous repressions, impressions from the coal age, compressed, petrified, transformed, ancient, yet still leaving, layer upon layer, the imprint of their repression deep in the lake floor, beneath the now frozen surface.

Although it is pretty clear that Hamilton did *not* see all this in detail, we can see that these are natural psychic laws we are following. This is why we lie to others and to ourselves (section II)—to cover with further layers the skin we have already put on things, and so to mask the mask. And, from this, a further equation is posited. "These lies mean the country wants to die"—self-denial is self-denial is self-denial. Killing our shadows betokens hunger for our own death.

The poem's other analyses—economic primarily—look best when seen in light of this larger pattern of repression.

> It is because the aluminum window shade business is doing
>   so well in the United States that we roll fire over
>   whole villages

fortunately cedes to

> It is because we have so few women sobbing in back rooms,
> because we have so few children's heads torn apart by high
>   velocity bullets,
> because we have so few tears falling on our own hands
> that the Super Sabre turns and screams down toward the
>   earth.

And it is from this analysis that the poem's final prayer comes:

> Let us drive cars
> up
> the light beams
> to the stars . . .
>
> And return to earth crouched inside the drop of sweat
> that falls
> from the chin of the Protestant tied in the fire.

If we have become cruel it is because we cannot remember our own suffering: in our righteousness we have forgotten our pain. Our only hope lies in remembering.

   "The Marines think that unless they die the rivers will not move." At a conscious level, we believe we are fulfilling a chosen, comprehensible destiny; but at the unconscious level we are following the path to a destiny not nearly so manifest, though much more powerfully certain. We are rushing to the edge of the sea as "pigs rush toward the cliff," driven by our own demons, and there below us we see our history and our destiny, balanced:

> the waters underneath part: in one ocean luminous globes
>   float up (in them hairy ecstatic men—)
> in the other, the teeth mother, naked at last.

She is naked and terrible. But at least we can see her now, as our forebears perhaps could not. In the terror of Vietnam she has become clear to us, our own creation. As Bly explains in his essay, the Teeth Mother "stands for numbness, paralysis, catatonia, being totally spaced out, the psyche torn to bits, arms and legs thrown all over." For the alternative path—the path that leads down into the ocean where "luminous globes float up (in them hairy ecstatic men)"—we must wait until "Sleepers Joining Hands" outlines a map to recovery. Though the outrage of the poem is certainly justified, it looks better in the context of the book as a whole than it does standing alone. "The Teeth Mother Naked at Last" offers a diagram of despair, a brittle anatomy of agony with only a gesture to indicate the possibility of healing, of wholeness.

Here, then, is a picture of the U.S.A. at our most culturally destructive, annihilating our own shadows—Indians, Blacks, Vietnamese—with whom we must be reunited if we are to have psychic fullness and dimensionality; if we are to be solid enough to cast shadows. Concern for oppression of our shadows pervades the book, essay and poems. But it is neither a continuing accusation nor an extended *mea culpa* that Bly chants, as "Calling to the Badger" shows. This poem, like all of Bly's work on the shadow, is pervaded by a "sadness that rises from the death of the Indians," and that is a sadness for our own loss. "We are driven to Florida like Geronimo" because our imaginations cannot function fully with such a large psychic space blocked out, repressed. Or, in the imagery of "Pilgrim Fish Heads," the Indian we have displaced "vanishes into water. . . . / The Mattapoiset is in league with rotting wood." Thus the denied shadow softens and rots whatever structures we might consciously build.

This backward look over the shadow poems that begin the book can help define the conditions that apply as the title sequence opens. As in most myths (whether the king be impotent, the land waste, or the virgin guarded by a dragon—all of which conditions more or less obtain as we return to the opening of the "Sleepers" sequence), the call to the quest begins with a perception of a lack, an imbalance. Whereas the earlier, shorter poems mainly expressed despair at the loss, "The Shadow Goes Away" proceeds from recognition to restorative action. Our fugitive imaginations are personified in the protagonist who, too, calls to the badger and otter, animals still in touch with the renewing waters of psychic life, the stream that emerges from beneath the ground.

Bly's seeker goes in search of his shadow, which hides in all dark peoples: Negro, Eskimo, Indian, Asian. He enters the inner and outer desert and sees the Sioux "struggling up the mountain in disordered lines" or opens a drawer, a compartment of the unconscious, and sees "small white horses gallop away toward the back" in retreat. He links the destruction of his shadow with his inability to recognize and unite with his anima, the woman within, his own gentleness and intuition:

> I have been divorced five hundred times,
> six hundred times yesterday alone.

Yet even now he has begun to incorporate the shadow's consciousness
and values. He will no longer participate in the repression, for he sees
where it leads: "The Marines turn to me. They offer me money. / I turn
and leave." With the consciousness of the shadow resuscitated, he sees
the disfiguration of his land. "The suppressed race returns: [it sees]
snakes and transistors filling the beaches." Even the planets are de-
spoiled: "The Sea of Tranquility scattered with dead rocks / and black
dust resembling diesel oil." Beneath this polluted moon "pilots in ar-
mored cockpits [are] finding their way home through moonlit clouds."
The equation between past and present betrayals, between Indian and
Asian wars, is now complete, clear to the protagonist as well as the
reader. Refusing to continue along the old path of inner denial and outward oppression, he turns from the zeal of battle to view the littered land
with primitive consciousness and compassion. He has begun to assimilate
the consciousness of the shadow, and can now continue his journey of
integration.

The second poem of the sequence finds the dreamer momentarily
awake, noting but not yet comprehending the femininity of the earth on
which he finds himself: "fragments of the mother lie open in all low
places." But his task here is "Meeting the Man Who Warns Me," and the
substance of the warning is that he may not understand, may not proceed
further without realizing from a transcendental viewpoint where he has
already been.

Dreaming again, the sleeper experiences everywhere the death of
the father:

> I dream that the fathers are dying.
> Jehovah is dying, Jesus' father is dying.
> the hired man is asleep inside the oat straw.
> Samson is lying on the ground with his hollow hair.

Even the father's emissary, the Christlike visitor whose circumcising
touch puts the protagonist back into a dream, is seen as inhumanly remote, extraterrestrial. The dreamer experiences absolute separation
from the presence of the father because he has seen the father only as
external; he has not yet recognized the father-energy as a part of himself,
waiting to be actualized.

But now that vision can change, for in the paradoxical logic of myth, once the shadow figure has become visible, the light may be seen.

> My shadow is underneath me,
> floating in the dark, in his small boat bobbing among the
>   reeds.
> A fireball floats in the corner of the Eskimo's house—
> It is a light that comes nearer when called!
> A light the spirits turn their heads for,
> suddenly shining over land and sea!
> I taste the heaviness of the dream,
> the northern lights curve up toward the roof of my mouth.
> The energy is inside us. . . .

This energy, this light, is the light of the Self, that truly integrated individual, that near divinity which each human being has the potential to become.

Jung notes that the Self can be symbolized by many sorts of things: a geometric figure, a radiation of light, a tree, stone, well, or any number of "world navel" configurations. But the most prevalent literary and mythical representations of the Self are the babe and the wise old man. It is appropriate that the Self could be represented by youth and age, since it is that nuclear source of energy within us at birth (or reborn in self-discovery), which, if we integrate our lives, comes to the fullness of its wisdom in our maturity. Quite strikingly, as the protagonist of the poem "sees the light" and realizes that "The energy is inside us," he immediately encounters a personification of the Self:

> I start toward [the light], and I meet an old man.
> ....
> And the old man cries out: "I am here.
> Either talk to me about your life, or turn back."

When the protagonist pauses for breath and begins to account for his experience, the rendering is most startling; for it comes from a greater completeness, and a greater mythic awareness than either reader or dreamer knew he had. He begins by announcing his own shadow-including nature and proceeds to recount a mythical journey that neither we nor he knew he had taken.

"I am the dark spirit that lives in the dark.
Each of my children is under a leaf he chose from all
    the leaves in the universe.
When I was alone, for three years, alone,
I passed under the earth through the night-water
I was for three days inside a warm-blooded fish.
'Purity of heart is to will one thing.'
I saw the road."

And when the Self urges him—"Go on! Go on!"—he continues:

A whale bore me back home, we flew through the air . . .
Then I was a boy who had never seen the sea!
It was like a King coming to his own shores.
I feel the naked touch of the knife,
I feel the wound,
this joy I love is like wounds at sea . . . "

Suddenly he has discovered in his own experience, not only the realization of the shadow (which we had shared with him), but also the shape of
a quest—complete with a three-day immersion in the belly of a whale,
the traditional typological symbol for a descent into the most terrifying
aspects of the unconscious (viz. Jonah, Christian iconography, Pinocchio,
et al.). Until now, he had, like a child born again, forgotten his links with
the sea; he was like a king, stranger to his own shore, suddenly realizing
the extent of his right and rule. His realization is as sudden as it is complete, as astounding for the dreamer as for the reader. Having thought all
the fathers were dead (i.e., having felt the lack of his own origin), he now
discovers the light of illumination within himself, and encounters a fa-
therly wise old man who corresponds to that light in the outer world, only
to realize that he, the dreamer himself, is both father and child, "dark
spirit" and "boy." Wounded—that is, born and circumcised into the
adult male world—the protagonist stops to reflect.

    We, too, might take a moment to stop and reflect—to consider the
poem's method of proceeding. In the last few paragraphs I have been
concerned to establish and outline the continuity of the poem—a continuity that is so far from obvious as to be truly problematic. The obscurity
arises, primarily, from the high degree of compression with which the
poem was written. (The sequence, I was told casually, was originally five
times its present length.) The epiphanic mode, not so unusual in itself, is

further complicated by a reversal of the usual relation between outer event and psychic response; here the changing phenomena are dictated by shifts in psychic states (as in dream) rather than the other way around. In order to manage this material, Bly replaces the conventional narrative structure with an implicit and continuous parallelism to Jung's schema of dream imagery in the individuation process.

Though Jung's way of reading the language of dreams is enormously insightful, it is legitimate to ask whether it is so essential a part of our culture that it may be alluded to as a structural principle, as Joyce, say, uses the *Odyssey*. Following archetypal patterns, of course, produces neither merit nor defect in poems, novels, or situation comedies. But requiring external knowledge of patterns is problematic, especially when what is required is not just a general sense of the quest, but Jung's interpretation of it. For without the Jungian frame, and a fair amount of time to apply it, most readers will find some real problems of coherence; and no matter how telling the individual images or how striking the poem's particular emotional effects, difficulties with coherence will diminish the final effect of the poem. Clearly, various readers will count the cost in differing ways— based largely, I suspect, on the ways they have already decided to handle matters such as Eliot's classical eclecticism, Yeats's esotericism, Roethke's Emersonianism, Kinnell's magic, and the like. But a problem that some feel worth overcoming is a problem nevertheless.

The synoptic recollection of the journey of the protagonist, which appears in the last lines of "Meeting the Man Who Warns Me," is expanded in "Night Journey in the Cooking Pot," which is a flashback composed of reflections on the experience and meaning of his immersion, of the dark, still uncomprehended part of his quest. Here, again, a problem of continuity confronts us; but the apparently confused and confusing emotional swings of "Night Journey" can be understood once we see that the poem divides itself into two movements, describing two phases of the mythic journey: the departure into the realm of mystery and also the return to the ordinary world. As the seeker begins to reexperience and rearticulate his journey retrospectively, we hear a familiar pattern: "I was born during the night sea journey." That he "love[s] the whale with his warm organ pipes" is less expected, but perfectly consonant: for Bly, this going-out is an *ecstasis*, a standing-outside-of the ego, an ecstasy; it is the return to the world of ordinary men and affairs that proves the difficult leg of the journey.

The departure into the water is a journey into ego-dissolving solitude, a necessary prelude to finding a path of effective action in the ordinary world: "I float on solitude as on water . . . there is a road" (Bly's ellipsis). The poem's first movement explores his privacy, which for Bly is sister word to privilege, not privation. Here we see the rejuvenating exhilaration of going a little crazy in private, deprived of human contact in the "womanless loneliness." The enthusiasm for isolation expressed in "Night Journey" is reinforced and clarified by several of the book's earlier poems. Because it rejuvenates, solitude itself becomes a welcome state, well-captured "In a Mountain Cabin in Norway" where "No one comes to visit us for a week." The short poems that begin the volume deal frequently with solitude in both its aspects, as a going-out and as a coming-in to center. Ecstasy as *ecstasis* animates "Six Winter Privacy Poems":

> There is a solitude like black mud!
> Sitting in this darkness singing,
> I can't tell if this joy
> is from the body, or the soul, or a third place."

Conversely—as a gloss on "Night Journey" 's oracular exhortation "inward, inward, inward"—the "Shack Poem" muses, "How marvelous to be a thought entirely surrounded by brains!"

Finally, of course, this privacy is the solitude of the womb, for the voyage he recalls in "The Night Journey in the Cooking Pot," is the night sea journey in the womb of *la mer, notre mère*. The cooking pot of the title, like the oven and hearth, as Bly explains in his essay, is the province of the woman and symbol of the womb. In the opening movement of "Night Journey" images of rebirth abound: "I feel . . . / the baby whirling in the womb," and "Nuns with faces smoothed by prayer peer out from holes in the earth." When he sees and realizes the possibilities brought by the visitants from the realm of snow and death ("sleeping in anguish like grain, whole, blind in the old grave"), when he intuits the chants of the shamans "with large shoulders covered with furs, / Holy ones with eyes closed," then he comes to rejoice in all signs pointing toward the death that precedes rebirth:

> Leaves slip down, falling through their own branches.
> The tree becomes naked and joyful.
> Leaves fall in the tomby wood.

And it is out of the experience of the retreat, the death, the hibernation
that he sings his song of joy.

> Suddenly I love the dancers, leaping
> in the dark . . .
> I start to sing.

But this song is not an easy one, and he knows it. In the second movement of "Night Journey" he faces the difficulty of returning to the world
of ordinary experience. Like Buddha, whose ultimate temptation was
simply to stay in the oceanic trance of nirvana, like the silent Lazarus and
other such questors, this seeker sees how difficult it will be to communicate the joy of going beyond the ego, the personality, the boundaries of
our daily round. But, like Whitman in "Crossing Brooklyn Ferry," he
urges us to realize that we are not separated from him, but united by a
common experience we sometimes forget.

> I am not going farther from you
> I am coming nearer,
> green rain carries me nearer you,
> I weave drunkenly about the page,
> I love you,
> I never knew that I loved you
> Until I was swallowed by the invisible.

Here, in his protagonist's plea for understanding, it would seem that we
have Bly's apologia for his own method. By writing in the language of
dream and vision, he does not hope to remove himself from our experience, for we are all dreamers, and can eventually intuit the scheme of our
dreams. If we do not immediately see our waking and sleeping lives as
whole and one, it is because the waters of sleep's deep well give the
illusion of discontinuity.

> For we are like the branch bent in the water . . .
> Taken out it is whole, it was always whole. . . .
>   [Bly's ellipses]

Though he acknowledges that the poem's oracular words may seem skew
and difficult, he assures us that when he emerges from the water (night,
mother, chaos, unconscious, dream) his speech will be straight as the

branch—a promise, as we have seen, difficult to fulfill. What he hopes for
(as he said in an earlier poem) is a day in which "if only the fragments in
the unconscious would grow as big as the beams in hunting lodges, . . . /
we would find holy books in our beds, / Then the Tao Te Ching would
come running across the field!" If only.

But such a conclusion is far too optimistic, or else many would have
returned and spoken, and redemption would be daily for all men. Bly
realizes that—and in the second movement of "Night Journey," the
questor suffers the inexorable difficulty of returning to the realm of ordinary experience while preserving his vision. Used to mental traveling, he
finds himself constricted by the physical limitations of waking reality: "I
think I am the body / the body rushes in and ties me up." Aware of his
new clumsiness, he is "ashamed looking at the fish in the water," for he is
a fish out. The new being born inside him—the "child in the old moonlit
villages of the brain"—is threatened with execution by that Herod, the
waking ego and the social system of which, as ego or persona, he finds
himself a part. He discovers himself in a role that his deeper, nascent Self
had not intended. Hearkening back to the imagery of the early West that
characterized "The Shadow Goes Away," he realizes

> Suddenly I am those who run large railroads at dusk,
> who stand around the fallen beast howling,
> who cannot get free, . . .
> This is not the perfect freedom of the saints.

Having become one of the very people he would fight against, he realizes
the difficulty of action after vision, the dichotomy between what he
knows in the absolute realm and the position he occupies in the relative
realm. With a fuller understanding, he has arrived at the point at which
he began the journey we have shared with him in "The Shadow Goes
Away."

The personality is divided against itself: with fuller vision now, he
sees how he has become his brother's vendor, betrayer of the shadow:

> I fall into my own hands,
>   fences break down under horses,
> cities starve, whole towns of singing women carrying to the
>   burial fields
>   the look I saw on my father's face,
> I sit down again, I hit my own body,

I shout at myself, I see what I have betrayed.
What I have written is not good enough.
Who does it help?
I am ashamed sitting on the edge of my bed.

He is ashamed looking into the limpid pool of his dreams. The poem has
moved fully from the ecstasy of the journey to the restrictions of the return. And those restrictions include the difficulty of making the poem
"good enough."

In the fourth poem, Bly spells out the nature of the journey as explicitly as possible:

Here is some prose
Once there was a man who went to a far country
to get his inheritance and then returned.

This, of course, is (in the phrase of James Joyce and the system of Joseph
Campbell) the "monomyth" in its briefest form: the story of the hero
who is called from the ordinary world of experience into the realm of the
mysterious, where he battles various foes, conquers or converts them,
and gains a boon, his "inheritance," a life-restoring elixir with which he
recrosses the threshold and with which, after some readjustment, he
transforms the world or his vision of it.

Bly uses his water imagery to suggest an intriguing relation between the realm of mystery and the boon snatched from it. The pool, the
lake into which he has gazed, the night sea through which he has traveled
in dream vision, all now become "Water Drawn Up Into the Head." The
questor now encompasses what once encompassed him. In the same way
that, in the Judaic tradition, the redeemed feast on the now delicious
flesh of the devouring monsters Behemoth, Leviathan, and Ziz, so the
very ocean of the night sea journey becomes the elixir which nourishes
the poet, granting him the serenity of the final poem and the joy of the
"Extra Chorus" that follows it.

This liquid optimism has already found voice in "Water Under the
Earth": "everything we need is buried . . . , it's under the water guarded
by women." (And in "The Turtle," "huge turtle eggs / lie inland on the
floor of the old sea.") The promise of the water is that consciousness can
be bathed in, nourished by, and brought to rebirth via the fluid world of
the unconscious. If tapped, the subterranean sea can yield the healing
balm that unites the diverse aspects of fragmented man within his Self

and joins him with all other men. Progression begins with regression,
conscious realization with a descent into the unconscious.

> There is a consciousness hovering under the mind's feet,
> advanced civilizations under the footsole,
> climbing at times upon a shoelace!
> It is a willow that knows of the water under the earth,
> I am a father who dips as he passes over underground rivers,
> who can feel his children through all distance and time!

The mind, like a funerary willow, draws the water from beneath the earth
and manifests it in leaves and swaying branches: water drawn up into the
head produces that fluid and protean vision of the poems Bly has created,
nourishes his vision of himself and all men.

"When alone," when in privacy with the wellspring of the unconscious, "we see that great tomb [the material world] is not God," and
"We know of Christ, who raised the dead, and started time. / He is not
God, and is not called God." Trying to find God outside ourselves, Bly
suggests, is to deny the inner springs, the water drawn up into the head.
"Best is to let them lose themselves in a river": best to immerse yourself
in the energy of the unconscious, energy of the Self, and learn from your
dreams, visions, and intuitions that you yourself are the transcendental;
and then to drink from that knowledge continuously.

> So rather than saying Christ is God or he is not,
> it is better to forget all that
> and lose yourself in the curved energy.
> I entered that energy one day . . .

The God he discovers himself to be a part of has no name, because he is
beyond the pairs of opposites, good and evil, kine and predator:

> We have no name for you, so we say:
> he makes grass grow upon the mountains,
> and gives food to the dark cattle of the sea,
> he feeds the young ravens that call on him.

There is a nascent realization, a new Self, "another being living inside"
the poet: "He is looking out of my eyes. / I hear him / in the wind through
the bare trees." It is the wind in the barren trees that alerts him to his

own birth, it is the death of the old self that so confidently presages the new. And "that is why I am so glad in fall." The poet beside the bare and naked tree trunk waits for true nakedness to come to him as well. And as Jung observes, the tree is often a symbol for the developing self, bringing forth energy from the invisible underground reservoir of the unconscious to be manifested in the world of light and form.

As Ginsberg ended *Howl* with a joyous footnote—not as a palinode, but to affirm the divinity of the horror he chronicled—so to this strange and often painful oneiric journey, Bly appends "An Extra Joyful Chorus for Those Who Have Read This Far." In several ways the chorus alludes heavily to Whitman. Its closing lines (and, indeed, the very title of the entire "Sleepers Joining Hands" sequence) bear strong resemblance to the opening of the last section of Whitman's poem "The Sleepers":

> The sleepers are very beautiful as they lie unclothed,
> They flow hand in hand over the whole earth from east
>   to west as they lie unclothed.

And, chiasmatically, lines that Whitman uses to close his poem on a cyclical note—

> I will stop only a time with the night . . . and rise
>   betimes.
> I will duly pass the day O my mother and duly return
>   to you

—Bly transforms into a paradoxical opening for his "Joyful Chorus":

> I love the Mother.
> I am an enemy of the Mother.

The allusions are clear. Yet, though both poems record psychological night sea journeys, and though both close with affirmations, the similarities between the poems are not continuous. Bly borrows from Whitman for his own ends, as we shall see.

And so with technique. The "Joyful Chorus," Bly's chant of polymorphous identity, which echoes and goes beyond his handling of the protean shadow in "The Shadow Goes Away," also recalls Whitman's chants of universal identity. Here again, there are some important differences to balance the similarities. Whitman's sympathetic identifications are usually directed toward the commonplace and the possible, encouraging the reader to follow along:

> I am the actor and the actress . . . the voter and
>   the politician . . .
> ....
> A shroud I see—and I am the shroud . . . I wrap a
>   body and lie in the coffin. . . .

Most typically, in the words of "Song of Myself," "I am the man . . . I suffered . . . I was there." Bly, on the other hand, opts to include the fantastical and folkloristic along with the ordinary and credible, which encourages the reader to relate these elements to other symbolic quests or to translate them into his own terms, but not to engage directly in the protagonist's own identification:

> I am the ball of fire the woodman cuts out of the
>   wolf's stomach,
> I am the sun that floats over the Witch's house,
> I am the horse sitting in the chestnut tree singing.

While both poets work within the tradition of the psychic quest, Bly is also *referring* to it, and asking the reader to refer to it, schematically.

Like Whitman, Bly makes use of the transcendent power of the aggregate. The catalogue of beautiful and ordinary and terrible beginnings which dominates the first sixty lines of section 15 of "Song of Myself" yields the aggregate exhilaration of Beginning; in "The Sleepers" the catalogue of actor, nominee, stammerer, and criminal in an averaged aggregate of sleeping humanity allows Whitman to say

> The soul is always beautiful
> The universe is duly in order . . . every thing
>   is in its place. . . .
> ....
> The diverse shall be no less diverse, but they shall
>   flow and unite . . . they unite now.

For Bly's protagonist the transcendent aggregate is the experience of the completed quest: its component parts, no matter how painful, finally be-

come redeemed because of their place in the whole. Even "fleeing along
the ground like a frightened beast" or being "the last inheritor crying out
in deserted houses" become fit matter for a "Joyful Chorus" when the
protagonist realizes that he is at every moment "an eternal happiness
fighting in the long reeds." Each act contains the imprint of all others,
and of the completed sequence. Bly's questor images his life everywhere
at once and at all stages simultaneously. Perhaps most summatively, he is
"the man locked inside the oakwomb, / waiting for lightning, only let out
on stormy nights." He is that core of life in the tree of the Self, drawn
from subterranean waters and waiting, now that the old foliage has died,
to manifest himself in the new spring. He is everyone and "no one at all"
simultaneously, for he is prior to personality. Thus, in the womb, aching
to deliver himself, he can paradoxically say:

> I love the Mother.
> I am an enemy of the Mother, give me my sword.
> I leap into her mouth full of seaweed.

For he honors the womb of the unconscious and arational which he has
reentered as embryo, and he honors the rational and masculine desire to
translate that primeval wholeness into the articulate world of forms—
water to leaves, sea to sword.

Further, he sees and feels the archetypal nature and universal possibility of his experience—new incarnations and new Bethlehems for all
men who attend to their dreams:

> Our faces shine with the darkness reflected from the
>   Tigris. . . .
> The panther rejoices in the gathering dark.
> Hands rush toward each other through miles of space.
> All the sleepers in the world join hands.

(1976)

8 EMILY DICKINSON AND THE DEERSLAYER: THE DILEMMA OF THE WOMAN POET IN AMERICA

Albert Gelpi

Albert Gelpi, a professor of American literature, has written a number of Jung-oriented literary studies, including The Tenth Muse: The Psyche of the American Poet (1975), as well as an essay in this book on H. D. and Adrienne Rich. Here Gelpi skillfully profiles a social/feminist level of significance in both the poetry and the figure of Emily Dickinson by backlighting it with an archetypal reading of the nineteenth-century zeitgeist. To put Dickinson's "man," a frequent but mysterious animus-muse figure in her poetry, in his proper context, Gelpi invokes James Fenimore Cooper's Deerslayer and provides a psycho/socio/sexual interpretation of the frontiersman-pioneer myth that still dominated the national psyche in Dickinson's time. Gelpi analyzes this cherished symbol of a patriarchal society as it was confronted and reinvented in Dickinson's art. Gelpi successfully uses archetypal psychology to align these different categories in order to generate a new understanding of Dickinson as a feminist poet-psyche engaging her own time and its myths about her gender. In doing so, he demonstrates the especial suitability of Jung's psychology for literary gender criticism, a subject he addresses again in his archetypal-feminist essay in this book's section "Jung and Gender Criticism."*

In nineteenth-century America there were many women poets—or, I should better say, lady poets—who achieved popular success and quite lucrative publishing careers by filling newspaper columns, gift

books, and volumes of verse with the conventional pieties concerning
mortality and immortality; most especially, they enshrined the domestic
role of wife and mother in tending her mortal charges and conveying
them to immortality. Mrs. Lydia Sigourney, known as "the Sweet Singer
of Hartford," is the type, and Mark Twain's Emmeline Grangeford is the
parodic, but barely parodic, recreation. Emily Dickinson was not a lady
poet, but she was the only major American woman poet of the nineteenth
century—in fact, a poet of such great consequence that any account of
women's experience in America must see her as a boldly pioneering and
prophetic figure.

In the Dickinson canon the poem that has caused commentators
the most consternation over the years is "My Life had stood—a Loaded
Gun—." It figures prominently and frequently in *After Great Pain,* John
Cody's Freudian biography of Dickinson, and more recently Robert
Weisbuch prefaces his explication in *Emily Dickinson's Poetry* with the remark that it is "the single most difficult poem Dickinson wrote," "a riddle to be solved." The poem requires our close attention and, if possible,
our unriddling, because it is a powerful symbolic enactment of the psychological dilemma facing the intelligent and aware woman, and particularly the woman artist, in patriarchal America. Here is the full text of the
poem, number 754 in the Johnson variorum edition,[1] without, for the
moment, the variants in the manuscript:

> My Life had stood—a Loaded Gun—
> In Corners—till a Day
> The Owner passed—identified—
> And carried Me away—
>
> And now We roam in Sovreign Woods—
> And now We hunt the Doe—
> And every time I speak for Him—
> The Mountains straight reply—
>
> And do I smile, such cordial light
> Upon the Valley glow—
> It is as a Vesuvian face
> Had let it's pleasure through—
>
> And when at Night—Our good Day done—
> I guard My Master's Head—

'Tis better than the Eider-Duck's
Deep Pillow—to have shared—

To foe of His—I'm deadly foe—
None stir the second time—
On whom I lay a Yellow Eye—
Or an emphatic Thumb—

Though I than He—may longer live
He longer must—than I—
For I have but the power to kill,
Without—the power to die—

Despite the narrative manner, it is no more peopled than the rest of Dickinson's poems, which almost never have more than two figures: the speaker and another, often an anonymous male figure suggestive of a lover or of God or of both. So here: I and "My Master," the "Owner" of my life. Biographers have tried to sift the evidence to identify the "man" in the central drama of the poetry. Three draft-"letters" from the late 1850s and early 1860s, confessing in overwrought language her passionate love for the "Master" and her pain at his rejection, might seem to corroborate the factual basis for the relationship examined in this poem, probably written in 1863. However, as I have argued elsewhere,[2] the fact that biographers have been led to different candidates, with the fragmentary evidence pointing in several directions inconclusively, has deepened my conviction that "he" is not a real human being whom Dickinson knew and loved and lost or renounced, but a psychological presence or factor in her inner life. Nor does the identification of "him" with Jesus or with God satisfactorily explain many of the poems, including the poem under discussion here. I have come, therefore, to see "him" as an image symbolic of certain aspects of her own personality, qualities and needs and potentialities which have been identified culturally and psychologically with the masculine, and which she consequently perceived and experienced as masculine.

Carl Jung called this "masculine" aspect of the woman's psyche her "animus," corresponding to the postulation of an "anima" as the "feminine" aspect of the man's psyche. The anima or animus, first felt as the disturbing presence of the "other" in one's self, thus holds the key to fulfillment and can enable the man or the woman to suffer through the initial crisis of alienation and conflict to assimilate the "other" into an integrated identity. In the struggle toward wholeness the animus and the anima come to mediate the whole range of experience for the woman and the man: her and his connection with nature and sexuality on the one hand and with spirit on the other. No wonder that the animus and the anima appear in dreams, myths, fantasies, and works of art as figures at once human and divine, as lover and god. Such a presence is Emily Dickinson's Master and Owner in the poem.

However, for women in a society like ours, which enforces the subjection of women in certain assigned roles, the process of growth and integration becomes especially fraught with painful risks and traps and ambivalences. Nevertheless, here, as in many poems, Dickinson sees the chance for fulfillment in her relationship to the animus figure, indeed, in her identification with him. Till he came, her life had known only inertia, standing neglected in tight places, caught at the right angles of walls: not just *a* corner, the first lines of the poem tell us, but corners, as though wherever she stood was thereby a constricted place. But all the time she knew that she was something other and more. Paradoxically, she attained her prerogatives through submission to the internalized masculine principle. In the words of the poem, the release of her power depended on her being "carried away"—rapt, "raped"—by her Owner and Master. Moreover, by further turns of the paradox, a surrender of womanhood transformed her into a phallic weapon, and in return his recognition and adoption "identified" her.

Now we can begin to see why the serious fantasy of this poem makes her animus a hunter and woodsman. With instinctive rightness, Dickinson's imagination grasps her situation in terms of the major myth of the American experience. The pioneer on the frontier is the version of the universal hero myth indigenous to our specific historical circumstances, and it remains today, even in our industrial society, the mythic mainstay of American individualism. The pioneer claims his manhood by measuring himself against the unfathomed, unfathomable immensity of his elemental world, whose "otherness" he experiences at times as the inhuman, at times as the feminine, at times as the divine—most often as all three at once. His link with landscape, therefore, is a passage into the unknown in his own psyche, the mystery of his unconscious. For the man, the anima is the essential point of connection with woman and with deity.

But all too easily, sometimes all too unwittingly, connection—which should move to union—can gradually fall into competition, then contention and conflict. The man who reaches out to Nature to engage his basic physical and spiritual needs finds himself reaching out with the hands of the predator to possess and subdue, to make Nature serve his own ends. From the point of view of Nature, then, or of woman or of the values of the feminine principle, the pioneer myth can assume a devastating and tragic significance, as our history has repeatedly demonstrated. Forsaking the institutional structures of patriarchal culture, the woodsman goes out alone, or almost alone, to test whether his mind and will are capable of outwitting the lures and wiles of Nature, her dark children and wild creatures. If he can vanquish her—Mother Nature, Virgin Land— then he can assume or resume his place in society and, as boon, exact his share of the spoils of Nature and the service of those, including women and the dark-skinned peoples, beneath him in the established order.

In psychosexual terms, therefore, the pioneer's struggle against the wilderness can be seen, from this viewpoint, to enact the subjugation of the feminine principle, whose dark mysteries are essential to the realization of personal and social identity but, for that reason, threaten masculine prerogatives in a patriarchal ordering of individual and social life. The hero fights to establish his ego-identity and assure the linear transmission of the culture that sustains his ego-identity, and he does so by maintaining himself against the encroachment of the Great Mother. Her rhythm is the round of Nature, and her sovereignty is destructive to the independent individual because the continuity of the round requires that she devour her children and absorb their lives and consciousness back into her teeming womb, season after season, generation after generation. So the pioneer who may first have ventured into the woods to discover the otherness which is the clue to identity may in the end find himself maneuvering against the feminine powers, weapon in hand, with mind and will as his ultimate weapons for self-preservation. No longer seeker or lover, he advances as the aggressor, murderer, rapist.

As we have seen, in this poem Emily Dickinson accedes to the "rape," because she longs for the inversion of sexual roles which, from the male point of view, allows a hunter or a soldier to call his phallic weapon by a girl's name and speak of it, even to it, as a woman. Already by the second stanza "I" and "he" have become "We": "And now We roam in Sovereign Woods— / And now We hunt the Doe—," the rhythm and repetition underscoring the momentous change of identity. However, since roaming "in Sovereign Woods—," or, as the variant has it, roaming "the—Sovereign Woods—" is a contest of survival, it issues in bloodshed. "To foe of His—I'm deadly foe," she boasts later, and here their first venture involves hunting the doe. It is important that the female of the deer is specified, for Dickinson's identification of herself with the archetype of the hero in the figure of the woodsman seems to her to necessitate a sacrifice of her womanhood, explicitly the range of personality and experience as sexual and maternal woman. In just a few lines she has converted her "rape" by the man into a hunting-down of Mother Nature's creatures by manly comrades—Natty Bumppo and Chingachgook in *The Last of the Mohicans*, Natty Bumppo and Hurry Harry in *The Deerslayer*.

Nor are we imposing a psychosexual interpretation on the naive innocence of an earlier Romantic idyll; the implications of the myth are all there in Cooper. Here is the first appearance of Natty and Hurry Harry in chapter 1 of *The Deerslayer*. They hack their way out of "the tangled labyrinth" of the Great Mother's maw or belly. The description acknowledges the awesome solemnity of the "eternal round" of the Great Mother's economy but acknowledges as well the threat to the individual snared in her dark and faceless recesses and unable to cut his way free. Initially there is no sign of human life; then from her timeless and undifferentiated "depths" emerge, first, two separate voices "calling to each other" and, at last, two men, "liberated" and "escaped" into lighted space where they can breathe. The passage reads:

> Whatever may be the changes produced by man, the eternal round of the seasons is unbroken. Summer and winter, seed-time and harvest, return in their stated order, with a sublime precision, affording to man one of the noblest of all the occasions he enjoys of proving the high powers of his far-reaching mind, in compassing the laws that control their exact uniformity, and in calculating their never-ending revolutions. Centuries of summer suns had warmed the tops of the same noble oaks and pines, sending their heats even to the tenacious roots, when voices were heard calling to each other in the depths of a forest, of which the leafy surface lay bathed in the brilliant light of a cloudless day in June, while the trunks of the trees rose in gloomy grandeur in the shades beneath. The calls were in different tones, evidently proceeding from two men who had lost their way, and were searching in different directions for their path. At length a shout proclaimed success, and presently a man of gigantic mould broke out of the tangled labyrinth of a small swamp, emerging into an opening that appeared to have been formed partly by the ravages of the wind, and partly by those of fire. This little area, which afforded a good view of the sky, although it was pretty well filled with dead trees, lay on the side of one of the high hills, or

few mountains, into which nearly the whole of the adjacent country
was broken.

"Here is room to breathe in!" exclaimed the liberated forester, as
soon as he found himself under a clear sky, shaking his huge frame
like a mastiff that had just escaped from a snow-bank. "Hurray,
Deerslayer, here is daylight at last, and yonder is the lake."

Man "proves" "the high powers of his far-reaching mind" by "compas-
sing" and "calculating" (that is, by comprehending and thus holding
within bounds in the mind) the cycle of generation. From an elevated
perspective above the woods, "the brilliant light of a cloudless day in
June" may grace "the leafy surface," but "in the shades beneath," where
the men "had lost their way," was the oppressive gloom of the tree-
trunks and "the tenacious roots." The two "gigantic" men emerge into
an area cleared by wind and fire, the lighter and more spiritual elements,
from the "small swamp," compounded of mud and water, the heavier
elements conventionally associated with the feminine matrix.

True to the archetypal meaning of the situation, the first conversation between Hurry Harry and Natty turns on the question of proving
one's manhood. The immediate victim is the doe, slain by Natty's rifle,
Killdeer, but soon the real contention becomes clear. As the moral and
sensitive woodsman, Natty finds himself defending his brother Delawares, arguing with the coarse Hurry Harry that they are not "women,"
as Hurry charges, but "heroes," despite the fact that they are dark children of the Great Mother. The conversation begins as follows:

> "Come, Deerslayer, fall to, and prove that you have a Delaware
> stomach, as you say you have had a Delaware edication," cried
> Hurry, setting the example by opening his mouth to receive a slice
> of cold venison steak that would have made an entire meal for a
> European peasant; "fall to, lad, and prove your manhood on this
> poor devil of a doe, with your teeth, as you've already done with your
> rifle."
>
> "Nay, nay, Hurry, there's little manhood in killing a doe, and that
> too out of season; though there might be some in bringing down a
> painter or a catamount," returned the other, disposing himself to
> comply. "The Delawares have given me my name, not so much on
> account of a bold heart, as on account of a quick eye and an actyve
> foot. There may not be any cowardyce in overcoming a deer, but,
> sartin it is, there's no great valor."

"The Delawares themselves are no heroes," muttered Hurry
through his teeth, the mouth being too full to permit it to be fairly
opened, "or they never would have allowed them loping vagabonds,
the Mingoes, to make them women."

"That matter is not rightly understood—has never been rightly
explained," said Deerslayer, earnestly, for he was as zealous a friend
as his companion was dangerous as an enemy; "the Mengwe fill the
woods with their lies, and misconstruct words and treaties. I have
now lived ten years with the Delawares, and know them to be as
manful as any other nation, when the proper time to strike comes."

"Harkee, Master Deerslayer, since we are on the subject, we may
as well open our minds to each other in a man-to-man way; answer
me one question: you have had so much luck among the game as to
have gotten a title, it would seem; but did you ever hit anything
human or intelligible? Did you ever pull trigger on an inimy that was
capable of pulling one upon you?"

Not yet; but the subtitle of the book is *The First War-Path,* and in the
course of the action Natty spills human blood for the first time, all of it
Indian. Natty may be a doeslayer with a difference, but even his unique
combination of the best qualities of civilization and nature does not ex-
empt him from the conflicts and contradictions of the pioneer myth.
Though a man of the woods, roaming the realm of the Great Mother, he
must remain unspotted from complicity with her dark and terrible aspect, just as his manhood has to be kept inviolate from the advances of
Judith Hutter, the dark and sullied beauty in *The Deerslayer,* and from his
own attraction to Mabel Dunham in *The Pathfinder.*

In the psychological context of this archetypal struggle, Emily
Dickinson joins in the killing of the doe without a murmur of pity or
regret; she wants the independence of will and the power of mind that
her allegiance with the woodsman makes possible. Specifically, engagement with the animus unlocks her artistic creativity; through his inspiration and mastery she becomes a poet. The variant for "power" in the last
line is "art," and the irresistible force of the rifle's muzzle-flash and of
the bullet are rendered metaphorically in terms of the artist's physiognomy: his blazing countenance ("Vesuvian face"), his vision ("Yellow
Eye"), his shaping hand ("emphatic Thumb"), his responsive heart
("cordial light"). So it is that when the hunter fires the rifle, "I speak for
Him—." Without his initiating pressure on the trigger, there would be
no incandescence; but without her as seer and craftsman there would be

no art. From their conjunction issues the poem's voice, reverberant enough to make silent nature echo with her words.

In Hebrew the word "prophet" means to "speak for." The prophet translates the wordless meanings of the god into human language. Whitman defined the prophetic function of the poet in precisely these terms: "it means one whose mind bubbles up and and pours forth as a fountain from inner, divine spontaneities revealing God. . . . The great matter is to reveal and outpour the God-like suggestions pressing for birth in the soul."[3] Just as in the male poetic tradition such divine inspiration is characteristically experienced as mediated through the anima and imaged as the poet's muse, so in this poem the animus figure functions as Dickinson's masculine muse. Where Whitman experiences inspiration as the gushing flux of the Great Mother, Dickinson experiences it as the Olympian fire: the gun-blast and Vesuvius. In several poems Dickinson depicts herself as a smoldering volcano, the god's fire flaring in the bosom of the female landscape. In her first conversation with the critic Thomas Wentworth Higginson, Dickinson remarked: "If I feel physically as if the top of my head were taken off, I know *that* is poetry. . . . Is there any other way?"[4]

But why is the creative faculty also destructive, Eros inseparable from Thanatos? To begin with, for a woman like Dickinson, choosing to be an artist could seem to require denying essential aspects of herself and relinquishing experience as lover, wife, and mother. From other poems we know Dickinson's painfully, sometimes excruciatingly, divided attitude toward her womanhood, but here, under the spell of the animus muse, she does not waver in the sacrifice. Having spilled the doe's blood during the day's hunt, she stations herself for the night ("Our good Day done—") as stiff, soldierly guard at "My Master's Head," scorning to enter the Master's bed and sink softly into "the Eider-Duck's / Deep Pillow." Her rejection of the conventional sexual and domestic role expected of women is further underscored by the fact that the variant for "Deep" is "low" ("the Eider-Duck's / Low Pillow") and by the fact that the eider-duck is known not merely for the quality of her down but for lining her nest by plucking the feathers from her own breast. No such "female masochism" for this doeslayer; she is "foe" to "foe of His," the rhyme with "doe" effecting the grim inversion.

Moreover, compounding the woman's alternatives, which exact part of herself no matter how she chooses, stands the essential paradox of art: that the artist kills experience into art, for temporal experience can only escape death by dying into the "immortality" of artistic form. The fixity of "life" in art and the fluidity of "life" in nature are incompatible. So no matter what the sex of the deer, it must be remade in the artist's medium; the words of the poem preserve the doe and the buck in an image of their mortality. These ironies have always fascinated and chilled artists. Is the vital passion of the youthful lovers on Keats's "Grecian Urn" death or immortality? In Eudora Welty's "A Still Moment" Audubon shoots the exquisite white bird so that he can paint it. In John Crowe Ransom's "Painted Head" the artist betrays the young man he has painted by shrinking him into an image. It seems a death's-head now, yet this painted head of a now-dead man radiates unaltered health and happiness. No wonder Audubon is willing to shoot the bird. No wonder a poet like Emily Dickinson will surrender to painful self-sacrifice. The loss of a certain range of experience might allow her to preserve what remained; that sacrifice might well be her apotheosis, the only salvation she might know.

Both the poet's relation to her muse and the living death of the artwork lead into the runic riddle of the last quatrain. It is actually a double riddle, each two lines long connected by the conjunction "for" and by the rhyme:

> Though I than He—may longer live
> He longer must—than I—
> For I have but the power to kill,
> Without—the power to die—.

In the first rune, why is it that she *may* live longer than he but he *must* live longer than she? The poet lives on past the moment in which she is a vessel or instrument in the hands of the creative animus for two reasons—first, because her temporal life resumes when she is returned to one of life's corners, a waiting but loaded gun again, but also because, on another level, she surpasses momentary possession by the animus in the poem she has created under his inspiration. At the same time, he *must* transcend her temporal life and even its artifacts because, as the archetypal source of inspiration, the animus is, relative to the individual, transpersonal, and so in a sense "immortal."

The second rune extends the paradox of the poet's mortality and survival. The lines begin to unravel and reveal themselves if we read the phrase "Without—the power to die—" not as "lacking the power to die" but rather as "except for the power to die," "unless I had the power to die." The lines would then read: unless she were mortal, if she did not have the power to die, she would have only the power to kill. And when we straighten out the grammatical construction of a condition-contrary-to-fact to conform with fact, we come closer to the meaning: with mortality, if she does have the power to die—as indeed she does—she would not have only the power to kill. What else or what more would she then have? There are two clues. First, the variant of "art" for "power" in the last line links "the power to die," mortality, all the more closely with "the power to kill," the artistic process. In addition, the causal conjunction "for" relates the capacity for death in the second rune back to the capacity for life in the first rune. Thus, for her the power to die is resolved in the artist's power to kill, whereby she dies into the hypostasized work of art. The animus muse enables her to fix the dying moment, but it is only her human capabilities, working in time with language, which are able to translate that fixed moment into the words on the page. The artistic act is, therefore, not just destructive but in the end self-creative. In a mysterious way the craftsmanship of the doomed artist rescues her exalted moments from oblivion and extends destiny beyond "dying" and "killing."

Now we can grasp the two runes together. The poet's living and dying permit her to be an artist; impelled by the animus, she is empowered to kill experience and slay herself into art. Having suffered mortality, she "dies into life," as Keats's phrase in *Hyperion* has it; virgin as the Grecian urn and the passionate figures on it, her poetic self outlasts temporal process and those climactic instants of animus possession, even though in the process of experience she knows him as a free spirit independent of her and transcendent of her poems. In different ways, therefore, each survives the other: she, mortal in her person but timeless in her poems; he, transpersonal as an archetype but dependent on her transitory experience of him to manifest himself. The interdependence through which she "speaks for" him as his human voice makes both for her dependence and limitations and also for her triumph over dependence and limitations.

Nevertheless, "My life had stood—a Loaded Gun—" leaves no doubt that a woman in a patriarchal society achieves that triumph through a blood sacrifice. The poem presents the alternatives unsparingly: be the hunter or the doe. She can refuse to be a victim by casting her lot with the hunter, but thereby she claims herself as victim. By the rules of the hunter's game, there seems to be no escape for the woman in the woods. Emily Dickinson's sense of conflict within herself and about herself could lead her to such a desperate and ghastly fantasy as the following lines from poem 1737:

> Rearrange a "Wife's" affection!
> When they dislocate my Brain!
> Amputate my freckled Bosom!
> Make me bearded like a man!

The violent, exclamatory self-mutilation indicates how far we have come from the pieties of Mrs. Sigourney and her sisters.

Fortunately for Dickinson, the alternatives did not always seem so categorical. Some of her most energetic and ecstatic poems—those supreme moments that redeemed the travail and anguish—celebrate her experience of her womanhood. The vigor of these dense lyrics matches in depth and conviction Whitman's sprawling, public celebration of his manhood. At such times she saw her identity not as a denial of her feminine nature in the name of the animus but as an assimilation of the animus into an integrated self. In that way "he" is not a threat but a force— and a source. As part of herself, "he" initiates her into the mysteries of experience that would otherwise remain "other"; "his" mind and will summon her to consciousness—not the fullness of manhood but the completion of her womanhood. There, in the privacy of her psyche, withdrawn from the world of men and even of family, she would live out all the extremes of feeling and response, all the states of mind that fall under the usual rubrics of love, death, and immortality.

Poem 508, probably composed a year or so before "My life had stood—a Loaded Gun—," describes her psychological metamorphosis in terms of two baptisms that conferred name and identity: the first the sacramental baptism in the patriarchal church when she was an unknowing and helpless baby; the second a self-baptism into areas of personality conventionally associated with the masculine, an act of choice and will undertaken in full consciousness, or, perhaps more accurately, into full consciousness. Since Emily Dickinson was not a member of the church and had never been baptized as child or adult, the baptism is a metaphor for marking stages and transitions in self-awareness and identity. The poem is not a love poem or a religious poem, as its first editors thought in 1890, but a poem of sexual or psychological politics enacted in the convolutions of the psyche:

I'm ceded—I've stopped being Their's—
The name They dropped upon my face
With water, in the country church
Is finished using, now,
And They can put it with my Dolls,
My childhood, and the string of spools,
I've finished threading—too—

Baptized, before, without the choice,
But this time, consciously, of Grace—
Unto supremest name—
Called to my Full—The Crescent dropped—
Existence's whole Arc, filled up,
With one small Diadem.

My second Rank—too small the first—
Crowned—Crowing—on my Father's breast—
A half unconscious Queen—
But this time—Adequate—Erect,
With Will to choose, or to reject,
And I choose, just a Crown—

Some of the manuscript variants emphasize the difference between the two states of being. The variants for "Crowing" in "Crowned—Crowing—on my Father's breast—" are "whimpering" and "dangling," as contrasted with "Adequate" and "Erect" later. The variants in the phrase "A half unconscious Queen—" are "too unconscious" and "insufficient." As the poet comes to consciousness in the second and third stanzas, she assumes, as in the previous poem, something of the phallicism and privileges of the masculine. "Power" is the variant for "Will" in the second-to-last line, but now the power of will is the Queen's. She has displaced the Father, the crown he conferred replaced by her round diadem; she calls herself by her "supremest name."

Dickinson wrote several "Wife" poems on the same theme. Poem 199, written a little earlier than the one above, probably in 1860, sums up the situation:

I'm "wife"—I've finished that—
That other state—

I'm Czar—I'm "Woman" now—
It's safer so—

How odd the Girl's life looks
Behind this soft Eclipse—
I think that Earth feels so
To folks in Heaven—now—

This being comfort—then
That other kind—was pain—
But why compare?
I'm "Wife"! Stop there!

The passage from virgin girlhood to "wife" and "Woman" is again accomplished through the powerful agency of the animus, in this poem the
"Czar." The "wife" and "Czar" couple into the androgynous completion
of her woman's Self. However, for Dickinson it is a womanhood reached
at heavy cost, a wifehood consummated on peculiarly private terms, withdrawn from the risks and dangers of contact with actual men in a man-
dominated culture. Only alone and in secret could this royal pair wed and
be joined in the hierogamy, or mystic marriage, of identity. As the poem
warns us, "It's safer so—."

Until recently, women poets since Emily Dickinson have found
themselves caught in the same quandary, and, in exchange for more
public recognition, have chosen to repress the "feminine" or the "masculine" aspects of themselves. Some, such as Marianne Moore and Elizabeth Bishop, tended to obscure or deflect passion and sexuality in favor of
fine discriminations of perceptions and ideas. Others, such as Edna St.
Vincent Millay and Elinor Wylie, took as their woman's strain precisely
the thrill of emotion and tremor of sensibility which rendered them susceptible to the threats of the masculine "other." In the isolation of her
upstairs bedroom, Emily Dickinson refused finally to make that choice;
but in the first half of the century perhaps only H.D., especially in the
great poems and sequences of her old age, commited head and heart,
sexuality and spirit, to the exploration of her womanhood: a venture perhaps made possible only through an expatriation from American society
more complete than Gertrude Stein's or Eliot's or Pound's. During the
last decade or two, however, in the work of poets as diverse as Sylvia
Plath and Denise Levertov, Muriel Rukeyser and Robin Morgan and
Jean Valentine, and, most importantly, I think, in the work of Adrienne

Rich, women have begun to explore that mystery, their own mystery, with a new sense of calling and community. Sometimes ecstatically, sometimes angrily, sometimes in great agony of body and spirit, but always, now, with the sustaining knowledge that they are not living and working alone, that more and more women and a growing number of men are hearing what they say, listening to them and with them. Such a realization makes a transforming and clarifying difference in the contemporary scene. And it is an important aspect of Emily Dickinson's enormous achievement that she pursued the process of exploration so far and so long on her own.
(1977)

9 THE RHIZOME AND THE FLOWER: THE PERENNIAL PHILOSOPHY—YEATS AND JUNG

James Olney

*L*ike Henderson, Hinz and Teunissen, Pratt, and others, James Olney, a professor of literature and editor of The Southern Review, addresses the question of the relationship of a Jungian literary criticism, and of Jung's psychology, to history. In an earlier book, Metaphors of Self: The Meaning of Autobiography *(1972), Olney had shown how Jung's psychology could inform a critical understanding of the literature of self-history. In this selection he quests beyond the conventional comparative study, even beyond the usual boundaries of intellectual history, to explore "the psychology of ideas." Olney presents Yeats and Jung as two blossoms from a common root, but one that is twofold, with "both an historical rhizome and a psychical rhizome . . . in ancient Greece and in the collective depths of the unconscious." Both writers developed metaphors within their respective disciplines for an idea historically developed within the perennial philosophy that Olney declares to be also a universal, archetypal act of the human mind: its dividing and unifying of experience.*

Thus Olney's book is an experiment in interdisciplinary analysis. "Prolegomena" describes the problem and alternative solutions. Olney's strategy is to develop a "third language" capable of discussing both Yeats's poetics and Jung's psychology. Further, he acknowledges that his analysis implicates and transforms the critic himself. Indeed, he declares that by being a ré-performance of that process, a "creative reenactment" of the mind's "virtually instinctive urge," his book pays double homage to the archetypal act it describes in Yeats and Jung.

NOTE TO THE READER

This book is not a study of the poetry or the poetics of W. B. Yeats; it is not a study of the psychology of C. G. Jung; it is not a study of the pre-Socratic philosophers; and it is not a study of Platonism. Neither is it a study of the similarities between Yeats and Jung. I say this at the outset merely to discourage certain conventional (but perhaps natural) expectations. The book is a study of what I have chosen to call "The Rhizome and the Flower," or, in other words, a study of "the Perennial Philosophy" and of "Yeats-and-Jung." *The Rhizome and the Flower* is, of course, concerned in part with the poetics of Yeats, in part with the psychology of Jung, in part with the manifold similarities between Yeatsian poetics and Jungian psychology, and in part with that perennial philosophy that in ancient Greece spoke the language of the pre-Socratics, Plato, and Platonism; but in the end the various subjects merge and interpenetrate to the degree that they cannot be set off and apart from one another. Hence the unconventional shape of the book and hence this request: that readers approach this book on its own terms, not on any others (those terms being described fully in the "Prolegomena"), and that they not expect the conventional in a book that in plan, in purpose, and in structure is designedly and necessarily unconventional.

PROLEGOMENA

■ ■ ■ ■

While one spoke the language of poetry and the other the language of psychology, Yeats and Jung are nevertheless in astonishing agreement on all the following concepts, doctrines, and beliefs:

> The relation between the collective unconscious (Jung) and *Anima Mundi* (Yeats) on the one hand and the personal unconscious and *anima hominis* on the other hand.
>
> Jung's concept of the archetype and Yeats's theories of the archetypal symbol in life, in magic, and in poetry.
>
> Their ideas on Unity of Being (Yeats's term), on individuation (Jung's term), and on the nature of the self (a shared term).
>
> Jung's theories of "synchronicity" and Yeats's of minds flowing into one another, their shared feeling that both time and space may be relative when psychic phenomena are in question, and their joint belief in prevision, precognition, and extrasensory perception.

The division and unification of human types and of humanity
in *Psychological Types* and in *A Vision.*

Their schematic representations (drawings of antinomies, circles, and quaternities in Jung's "Red Book" and in Yeats's *Vision*) of
psychological and cultural processes.

Their notion that all energy and all creativity arise from a conflict of opposites and that human history itself moves in perpetual
cycles that oppose, reverse, and complement one another.

Jung's theory of shadow figures and of anima and animus and
Yeats's theory of masks and images.

Their shared idea that tradition—familial, cultural, national,
and intellectual—finds its culmination in present creativity.

Their beliefs about the relation of the living to the dead and
about the relation of emotions and instincts.

A belief in what both of them called "the *daimon.*"

Their concepts of symbolism as a creative transformation of
psychic and spiritualistic energy.

The symbolic significance (psychological and poetic) of their
towers in Bollingen and Gort.

While this list by no means exhausts the number of points at which Yeats
and Jung touch and merge, it does at least demonstrate that it is not at all
out of poverty that one would decline to accept simple—or complex—
comparison as a sufficient subject. Who cares simply that Yeats and Jung
were in some ways alike—of course they were—if there is not more to it
than that? If the only conclusion to which we can come is that they had
similar thoughts, then this is more than unfortunate, because it is not a
conclusion at all: it is instead the accepted *premise*, the *donnée* from which
the study would properly start.

The wrong way to begin, I am thoroughly convinced, would be by
reading Yeats through Jungian spectacles or Jung through Yeatsian spectacles. Yeats had no great love for psychology; Jung had even less for what
he called "modern art," and modern poetry he found especially offensive. To adopt either literary criticism or psychology as a discipline and an
exclusive mode for approaching the subject would be to murder the one
man in order to dissect the other. Not that literary criticism and psychology should be abandoned altogether: Yeats demands to be approached as
a poet, and in ways appropriate to poetry; Jung demands to be approached as a psychologist. What is necessary is to discover—while not
altogether abandoning literary criticism or psychology—a *tertium quid,* as

Jung might call it, or a *tertium comparationis:* a third language that displays a syntax and grammar similar to the syntax and grammar of Yeats's poetics and at the same time similar to the syntax and grammar of Jung's psychology. Refusing the language of psychology or the language of literary criticism as our sole speech, what we must attempt is to find a *tertium* between the two conflicting opposites that would integrate them at a higher level and provide the grounds for a valid comparison between them if and because they both share, through the uniting third, a similar underlying structural configuration. Moreover, this *tertium* must be a twofold "higher third," comprehending both historical and psychical origins of an idea, an image, or an expression.

If we must give up literary criticism as an exclusive discipline, if we must abandon psychology as an exclusive analytical tool, and if there are no direct, lateral ties to be discovered between Yeats and Jung, then where do we stand? There still remain, it seems to me, various ways in which to account for the many similarities in thought, image, expression, and intention discoverable in the works of the two men. It could be, for example, that (1) the personal and cultural circumstances in which the bodies of work were produced caused them to be alike—that the works were, in a manner of speaking, precipitated out by the times; or (2) it could be argued that Jung's notion of "synchronicity" was a valid one and in this case potently operative; again, (3) it might be that the systems implicit in Yeats and Jung answer to some basic configuration and archetypal need of the human mind and at the same time, perhaps, to an ontological and metaphysical reality outside the mind; and finally, (4) it is possible that the two men participated in and were to a large extent shaped by the same philosophical tradition—behind the systems, in other words, was what might be called "The System," a historically evolved, humanly articulated structure of thought and feeling. Moreover, if (3) and (4) were joined, it might be that the systems/System would bear legitimate reference, not only within, to the structure of the mind that shaped it, but outside itself as well, to the structure of the cosmos. I think it best not to reject out of hand either of the first two possible explanations, but there can be no doubt that the latter two explanations, especially if seen as corollaries that serve to extend one another, provide a far richer subject for our consideration. There is no lateral or temporal line that connects Yeats with Jung, but there are parallel lines which one could demonstrate and retrace, stretching back from both so far into the past of human history that, as they reach the limits of our vision and our historical perspective, they cease to be parallel and come together on the horizon of human thought in such primal figures as, first, Plato, and then, beyond Plato (in the order in which we meet them as we trace our lines back into the past), Empedocles, Parmenides, Heraclitus, and Pythagoras. Seen in this light, the works of Yeats and Jung are present moments of a long past, a creative surfacing in geographically discrete places of a continuous and unbroken, though sometimes chthonic and subterranean, body of slowly developed and developing human thought and performance. Thus a great tradition is discoverable behind these two very individual talents, and here is the first face of our *tertium quid*: the Platonic system, shaped by Plato himself out of his four great predecessors and issuing in that immense tradition called Platonism.

"I ceased to read modern books that were not books of imagination," Yeats tells us in a volume of his *Autobiographies,* "and if some philosophic idea interested me, I tried to trace it back to its earliest use, believing that there must be a tradition of belief older than any European Church, and founded upon the experience of the world before the modern bias" (p. 265). Thus also the intention and the mode of the present book: to trace back to their earliest use, many centuries before Yeats and Jung, those ideas, images, figures, and expressions that the poet and psychologist shared so lavishly, but unknowingly, with one another. Having observed the two contemporaneous flowers, so strikingly alike in form and structure but growing in different gardens and alien soils, I should like to examine the rhizome from which they have grown and blossomed and to which they return. . . .

■   ■   ■   ■

To go behind the similarities of thought, image, and expression in Yeats and Jung and so to discover the tradition that issued in their works (and in many another man's work also, of course) is only one step of the way, however; for that merely leaves us with the perception of multiplied similarities: Yeats is like Jung is like Blake is like Swedenborg is like Boehme is like Paracelsus is like Nicholas of Cusa is like Saint Augustine is like Plotinus is like Plato is like Pythagoras . . . almost to that infinity which we cannot reach only because our vision cannot extend indefinitely into the past. This tradition has been developing for so long and in so many places that it seems never to have begun, to have almost no limits, and to be the natural and necessary creation of a corporate human consciousness: the intellectual/emotional complement of human life as such. The other necessary step of the way, then, beyond the first step of delineating a tradition, is to abandon historical and chronological order and to go not only behind the surface similarities between Yeats and Jung but also behind the tradition. What is it, not in history but in the human mind—what creative forces, what inner impulses or structures or necessities—what is it that impels these individual creations, all established, as it would appear, on the one essential ground plan?

Writing of his and Lady Gregory's experience in collecting stories from peasants in the West of Ireland—stories in which he discovered precisely that the same ancient "tradition of belief" mentioned in the *Autobiographies*—Yeats says, "Again and again, she and I felt that we had got down, as it were, into some fibrous darkness, into some matrix out of which everything has come. . ." (*Essays and Introductions* [London: Macmillan, 1961], p. 429). Let it be noted that though Yeats felt that in the stories he had discovered the same ancient tradition of belief as he could find by tracing a philosophic idea back to its earliest use, he specifically describes himself as going *down* rather than *back* into a "fibrous darkness," and his choice of adverb clearly indicates that the journey in this case was psychic rather than historic. What is that "matrix out of which everything has come"? Jung gave it a name—a name not lovelier but perhaps more scientific than "fibrous darkness"—for Yeats's matrix is the unconscious (or subconscious, as Yeats called it: "down" beneath consciousness), which is a dark, teeming, creative matrix that is also, in one of its aspects, collective. "The unconscious is the matrix of all metaphysical statements, of all mythology, of all philosophy," according to Jung (*CW*, 11, par. 899). Elsewhere in the same volume of the *Collected Works*, Jung writes: "Because the unconscious is the matrix mind, the quality of creativeness attaches to it. It is the birthplace of thought-forms such as our text considers the Universal Mind to be. . . . In so far as the forms or patterns of the unconscious belong to no time in particular, being seemingly eternal, they convey a peculiar feeling of timelessness when consciously realized" (par. 782). If this is true (and Yeats certainly would have found himself in passionate agreement with what Jung says), then the ideas that we give Pythagoras credit for are products of the human psyche—of the unconscious and especially the collective unconscious—and in that "fibrous darkness," the "matrix out of which everything has come," we can expect to find still in our time, as in any time, a shadowy Pythagoras, Heraclitus, Parmenides, and Empedocles, all of them known to us and yet unknown, all of them unconscious but forever rising into consciousness. This necessitates, as I earlier remarked, that our *tertium* be twofold. The Yeatsian and Jungian blossoms that we now observe are of the present and of consciousness, but there is both a historical rhizome and a psychical rhizome from which they draw their life, for those two momentary flowers have their roots, alike and together, in ancient Greece and in the collective depths of the unconscious. This is the other, the second face of our *tertium comparationis,* to be made out not on the surface level, not even on the first subsurface level, not so much in history or in written texts, but further down in that "fibrous darkness" that is the emotional and mental makeup of humanity itself. This may seem very like saying that Yeats and Jung will serve as little more than pretexts for unfolding a drama of the human mind and of human creativity, a drama that is not, at least not in any limiting sense, Jungian or Yeatsian. Against such a charge—that I have "used" Yeats and Jung for my own purposes—I have no defense to offer, nor any apology—unless it be apology to remark that both Yeats and Jung did the same thing in their works and in their days and so gave the example for our work and our day.

■ ■ ■ ■

In "Leda and the Swan"—which began as a political poem, "but as I wrote, bird and lady took such possession of the scene that all politics went out of it"—Yeats tells us that he imagined "the annunciation that founded Greece as made to Leda. . . . But all things are from antithesis," he continues, "and when in my ignorance I try to imagine what older civilisation that annunciation rejected I can but see bird and woman blotting out some corner of the Babylonian mathematical starlight" (*Vision,* p. 268). Much the same thing happens to the explorer who goes far back in Western thought and deep down in the human psyche toward beginnings. Like Yeats, he discovers the same basic configurations realized again and again until finally the contours of specific civilizations, like politics, disappear, as do also the distinguishing features of individualized men, leaving those primordial images (bird and woman) and those generalized patterns (mathematical starlight) according to which human behavior shapes itself and has always shaped itself. There, approaching as near to the ground and beginning as he can, the investigator finds images with a high degree of internal organization but with, as yet, little or no realized, individualized content: beyond Zeus and Leda there is bird and woman; beyond bird and woman there is masculine and feminine, divine and human; beyond these, once more, there are, in Yeats's terms, images of sphere (divine) and gyre (human), and there are, in Jung's terms, the numbers three and four—the ultimate abstractions from the concrete realities of history. For four, according to the discoveries of Jung's science, is not only the number of wholeness but also the feminine number, and three is not only an incomplete quaternity but also the masculine number.

We can, if we like, call this ultimate abstraction of the image and the numerical pattern from the confusion of experience "number mysticism" and thus go a certain distance toward dismissing it; but it would be as well to observe at the same time that men, apparently everywhere and at all times, have felt numbers to possess arcane properties prior to and quite outside human imaginings. Numbers, that is, or so men have always believed, were there in the structure of reality before the human mind existed to observe the fact; indeed, the human mind, according to such a belief, is itself a part of that structure of reality that is determined by number and number relations, and numbers therefore have not been shaped and invented by the human mind but, on the contrary, have shaped and invented it. To Philip Wylie, who had offered an objection to something in Jung's numerology, Jung wrote (in 1957), "Don't worry about my mathematics. I never dreamt of adding anything to mathematics, being myself utterly 'amathematikós.' My affiliation to it consists only in the equation $3 + 1 = 4$, which is a psychological fact indicating the fundamental relation between psychology and mathematics" (*Letters,* 2:404). This, which is Jung's equation for wholeness, is simple enough in mathematical terms; simple though it be, however, in Jung's view it also represents the most profound mystery—it is, he says, "the mystery of the psychologist" (ibid.)—for just such a simple equation as this is the bond that joins mind and nature, *psychē* and *physis,* and makes them a single, indissoluble unity beyond our capacity to see or to conceptualize. It was on this ground that Jung could say (quoting the mathematician Leopold Kronecker), "Man created mathematics, but God created whole numbers: ὁ θεὸς ἀριθμητίζει ['God arithmetizes']" (*Letters,* 2:23). This god that arithmetizes, as Plato argued in the *Timaeus,* to the entire satisfaction and agreement of Yeats and Jung, does so throughout his creation both physical and psychic. How exquisitely the mind is fitted to nature, with number as the preexistent, analogical, and informing bond, was Platonic doctrine (and before Plato it was Pythagorean), which Wordsworth turned into Romantic psychology and poetry and which Yeats and Jung embraced heart and soul; nor could they do otherwise, since heart and soul are themselves numerically, rhythmically organized.[1]

Pythagoreans (and neo-Pythagoreans of all times and places) consider numbers to be archaic in the most literal sense: for such *mathematici,*

numbers are the *archai,* the primordial principles, the generative source
of all created beings, and as such they provide a formal replacement for
the physical *archai* of the Ionian philosophers. That is to say, according to
Pythagoreans, the cosmos had its beginning in numbers and in the formal
relations of numbers rather than in some such substance as water, air, etc.
Given the fact that he wanted to be taken for an empirical scientist, it was
rather daring of Jung—but as Pythagorean as daring—to write that
"Whole numbers may well be the discovery of God's 'primal thoughts' "
(*Letters,* 2:302). It is not the higher mathematics, as Jung saw it—and so
also the ancients—but simple number that rules throughout the cosmos,
both micro- and macro-. "Thus Number," the Pythagorizing Plotinus
tells us, "the primal and true, is Principle and source of actuality to the
Beings." In Jung's terminology, numbers would be said to be archetypal,
and it is certainly true that schematic representations of Jungian archetypal figures (e.g., mandalas) display a very great instress of numerical
organization. Bringing the question back to a psychological focus, one
might take numbers to be the structural dominants of the psyche and,
going a step further, take the procession and recession of numbers (that
is, the multiplying of numbers out of oneness and the return of multiplicity to original unity) to be the twofold analogue to the intricate, double
movement of the mind in its typical mode of operation: analyzing and
synthesizing, dividing and unifying. This would be to suggest the possibility that there is a configurational correlation between typical thought
patterns and basic mental structure determined on a simple mathematical ground.

　　While other numbers may have equal potency in certain regards,
the human mind has repeatedly viewed reality, in the schematizing light
of the first four integers, as being monadic, dyadic, triadic, or quaternal—
or sometimes, and this is perhaps more interesting as well as more complex, as alternating between the monadic and one or more of the other
three. Greek philosophic history, conveniently enough, provides the
prototypes for each of these readings of the way things really are. Parmenides' poem stands as the great statement in antiquity of an uncom-
promising philosophical monism; Heraclitus is the primal antinomist;
Pythagoras apparently reverenced various numbers (one, four, and ten,
for example), but it could well be argued that three had a special force for
him (Aristotle: "As the Pythagoreans say, the whole world and all things
in it are summed up in the number three; for end, middle and beginning
give the number of the whole, and their number is the triad. Hence we
have taken this number from nature, as it were one of her laws, and make

use of it even for the worship of the gods" [*De caelo* 268a10]); and Empedocles was the stoutest exponent of quaternal arrangements (albeit with occasional glances toward monism and dualism) until Jung came along twenty-three or twenty-four centuries later as champion of the number four. So these four pre-Socratics, individually and in sum, offer us a story occurring in time that is nicely parallel in its character, its plot, and its structure—and ultimately parallel also in its significance—to the nontemporal story of the human psyche in its efforts, conscious and unconscious, to analyze and synthesize all the experience that it encounters.

■　■　■　■

To describe the way in which the mind has countless times over set about dividing and unifying experience—for the division and unification of experience is what the thought of mankind has always been about: the systole and diastole of human creativity—is in effect to perform that division and unification once again. The most compelling description of human performance will always be found in reperformance, and this is one way of stating what the present book proposes: a creative reenactment that would hope to be more meaningful and persuasive than any mere stitching or pasting can ever be. What I intend, after the manner of the Aristotelian imitation of an action, is an imitation of the subject—which is the action of the mind in ancient Greece and the action of the mind in the contemporary West. Not that the great predecessors, Yeats and Jung, Heraclitus and Empedocles, have failed, leaving their job yet to be done. On the contrary, precisely because they have done their job, we are obliged to do ours. What Yeats does in *A Vision* and Jung in *Psychological Types* is different of course from what Empedocles does in his two poems or Heraclitus in his dark and riddling aphorisms; but it is different only as to the superficial content on which their minds operated, not as to the way the mind operates and the patterns it seems to discover simultaneously within itself and in the universe without. This is the same difference and the same similarity that Yeats discovered to exist between Greek and Christian annunciations: on the one hand, Leda and the Swan are unquestionably different from Mary and the Holy Ghost, just as the two civilizations they heralded were opposites; on the other hand, however, in both cases, and at deeper levels of image, pattern, and meaning, we have woman and bird, human and divine, sphere and gyre, female and male, four and three. And just so, too, with Yeats and Jung, Heraclitus and Empedocles, who differ one from another on the surface but not at all

on deeper levels of the psyche where archaic ideas, primal patterns, and
the passion to divide and unify experience have their origins. At that
deep level, we discover archetypal "images that yet / Fresh images beget," and, as they are archetypal, they can scarce be distinguished and
differentiated individually. One might well suppose, as I have implied,
that this virtually instinctive urge to division and unification—a double
movement compounded of halves opposed and complementary—is
somehow a reflection, an analogy, and a consequence of a deep, inner
life-rhythm: something in the structure of the brain and the central ner-
vous system, something also in unconscious imitation of the flow out and
back of blood from the heart, or of breath, *pneuma,* taken in and out of the
lungs, and in imitation of a cosmic system as well, for *pneuma* is not only
breath but also the wind that "bloweth where it listeth" and that moves
all things in rhythm and pattern throughout the cosmos.
(1980)

10 HEALING FICTION

James Hillman

James Hillman is a Jungian analyst, former editor of Spring: An Annual of Archetypal Psychology and Jungian Thought, and the central figure in a recent Jungian movement known as imaginal or archetypal psychology, the topic of Part 2, sec. B. Hillman's many books include Re-Visioning Psychology (1975) and Archetypal Psychology: A Brief Account (1983). He was the first director of studies at the C. G. Jung Institute in Zurich and now resides in his native America.

Hillman re-visions Jung's psychological method as essentially a literary method. Hillman's Jung, in the first selection, "The Pandaemonium of Images: Jung's Contribution to 'Know Thyself,'" explores the text of his dreams and fantasies, envisioning psychic reality as "poetic, dramatic, literary in nature," and treating the archetypal "daimones" of his inner life as personified images. As an analyst, Hillman suggests that imaginative art plays a central role in therapy. The exercise of active imagination—giving concrete form to dream-images—succeeds, says Hillman, primarily because it lifts the patient out of "the disease of literalism" and restores him to living "fictionally."

"The Fiction of Case History: Genre and Archetype" shows how Hillman's vision of the primary act of analysis parallels in some important ways the deconstructionists' vision of literature: both emphasize the significant effect of the linguistic structure and its various formal relationships upon the reality-content it purports to express. Thus Hillman's archetypal psychology attempts to *shift the focus of analytical psychology toward "the poetic basis of therapy, of biography, of our very lives."*

THE PANDAEMONIUM OF IMAGES: JUNG'S CONTRIBUTION TO "KNOW THYSELF"[1]

It is not possible to speak rightly about the Gods without the Gods.
—Iamblichus

JUNG'S DAIMONES

When we inquire into Jung's contribution to our culture, one virtue appears to me to stand out. Jung gave a distinct response to our culture's most persistent psychological need—from Oedipus to Socrates through Hamlet and Faust—Know Thyself. Not only did Jung take this maxim as the leitmotif of his own life, but he gave us a method by which we may each respond to this fundamental question of self-knowledge. It is in respect to this *how*, the art or method of proceeding with oneself, which is as well the grounding impetus within all psychology, that we can especially learn from Jung. So, the angle I wish to develop here is Jung's psychological method seen as his most valuable gift to us.

You may remember how this began: it is told by Aniela Jaffé in Jung's autobiography. Jung was deluged by "an incessant stream of fantasies," a "multitude of psychic contents and images." In order to cope with the storms of emotion, he wrote down his fantasies and let the storms transpose themselves into images.

You remember also when this took place: it happened shortly after the break with Freud—so much so that Stanley Leavy[2] has suggested that the Salome in the vision which I shall soon come to is none other than a disguised Lou Andreas-Salomé, and the Elijah none other than Freud. At this moment in his life Jung was spiritually alone. But in this isolation he turned neither to a new group, nor to organized religion, nor to refuge in psychosis, nor to security in conventional activities, work, or family: he turned to his images. When there was nothing else to hold onto, Jung turned to the personified images of interior vision. He entered into an interior drama, took himself into an imaginative fiction, and then, perhaps, began his healing—even if it has been called his breakdown. There, he found a place to go that was no longer Vienna, figures to communicate with who were no longer the psychoanalytic circle of colleagues, and a counselor who was no longer Freud. This encounter with these personal figures became the first personifications of his mature *fate*—which is also how Jung speaks of the personifications we meet when we interiorize to Know Thyself.[3] It was in this time, during which the dove-maiden spoke to him in a crucial dream, that Jung found his vocation, his psychological faith, and a sense of personality.[4] It is from this point onward that Jung becomes that extraordinary pioneering advocate of the reality of the psyche.

■   ■   ■   ■

Know Thyself in Jung's manner means to become familiar with, to open oneself to and listen to, that is, to know and discern, daimons. Entering one's interior story takes a courage similar to starting a novel. We have to engage with persons whose autonomy may radically alter, even dominate, our thoughts and feelings, neither ordering these persons about nor yielding to them full sway. Fictional and factual, they and we are drawn together like threads into a *mythos,* a plot, until death do us part. It is a rare courage that submits to this middle region of psychic reality where the supposed surety of fact and the illusion of fiction exchange their clothes.

■   ■   ■   ■

[Jung's] move between the two orthodoxies of theological religion and clinical scientism reestablished in experience the middle realm that he was to call "psychic reality." This psychic reality discovered by Jung consists in fictive figures. It is poetic, dramatic, literary in nature. The Platonic *metaxy* speaks in mythical fictions. Freud's fictioning appeared disguised in his case histories and his cosmogonic theories; Jung's appeared overtly in the history of his own case. Freud entered the literary imagination by writing about other people; Jung, by envisioning himself as "other people." What we learn from Freud is that this literary imagination goes on in the midst of historical fact. What we learn from Jung is that this literary imagination goes on in the midst of ourselves. Poetic, dramatic fictions are what actually people our psychic life. Our life in soul is a life in imagination.

We have already been given the clue in the instructor's manual as to how this third realm traditionally called "soul" can be reestablished—and by anyone. Jung says he treated the figures whom he met "as though they were real people." The key is that *as though,* the metaphorical, as-if reality, neither literally real (hallucinations or people in the street) nor irreal/unreal ("mere" fictions, projections which "I" make up as parts of "me," auto-suggestive illusions). In an "as-if" consciousness they are

powers with voice, body, motion, and mind, fully felt but wholly imaginary. This is psychic reality, and it comes in the shape of daimons. By
means of these daimonic realities, Jung confirmed the autonomy of the
soul. His own experience connected again the realm of daimons with that
of soul. And ever since his move, soul and daimons imply, even require,
each other.

■ ■ ■ ■

DEMONS AND DAIMONES

The plurality of worlds, *psychologically,* refers to the plurality of perspectives that determine our subjectivity, the many eyes that see through
ours. For it is not that there are many distinctly different worlds, each
ruled by one God, rather, as Kerényi often insisted, there is one and the
same world which we partake in but always and only through the cosmos
of one or another leading imaginal figure in a particular constellation or
mytheme. These are the divine backgrounds to what existential humanism from Nietzsche onward calls "perspectives." These figures shape our
so-called real worlds in the images of this hero, that angel, anima, daimon, or God.

Demonology in its widest sense thus becomes the logos of the
imaginal persons who stand within all our ideas and deeds.

Demonology in its widest sense is also *anthropology,* for, as Stevens
also writes: " . . . the study of his images / Is the study of man. . . . "⁵
Moreover, demonology in its widest sense that includes all persons, even
the angels of imagination, becomes a basis not only of our *psychopathology*
but of our *epistemology,* of all knowledge whatsoever. Modes of knowing
are never altogether purified of the "subjective factor," and this factor is
one or another imaginal person who casts our consciousness into specific
epistemological premises.

Thus the first task of knowledge is knowledge of these premises, or
Know Thyself. The pluralities of the imagination precede even our perception of them, not to speak of our understanding of them. ("We are
lived by Powers we pretend to understand," said W. H. Auden.) As well,
these persons who appear to us as our daimons make possible the modes
of our perception and our styles of participation in the reality of things.
As first task—and as first enjoyment too—Know Thyself is the self-
reflexive moment, a psychological a priori within all moments, that laugh
of self-recognition glimpsed in the images of one's selves in all things.

ACTIVE IMAGINATION: THE HEALING ART

We break off here to conclude this chapter with an observation about the intention of active imagination,[6] which Jung links, at the conclusion of his final major work, *Mysterium Coniunctionis,* with Know Thyself.[7] Also, I believe, it is by means of active imagination that Jung joins together again the Hellenistic, Neoplatonic tradition of image-work and the analytical mode of self-knowledge of Sigmund Freud. This connection is more important, I believe, than is the usual separation of Platonism and Freud: for one of the great potentials in Jung's approach lies precisely in making possible a rereading of Freud.

When we study Jung carefully as to *why* one undertakes active imagination, we find these basic reminders. They can be presented as a *via negativa* of cautions, similar to the sober restraint that imbues Freud's analytical mode with a religious piety:

■   ■   ■   ■

(2) Active imagination is not an artistic endeavor, not a creative production of paintings and poems. One may aesthetically give form to the images—indeed, one should try as best one can aesthetically—though this is for the sake of the figures, in dedication to them and to realize their beauty, and not for the sake of art. The aesthetic work of active imagination is therefore not to be confused with art for exhibition or publication.

■   ■   ■   ■

So, Jung's method of interior imagining is for none of these reasons—spiritual discipline, artistic creativity, transcendence of the worldly, mystical vision or union, personal betterment, or magical effect. Then what for? What is the aim?

Primarily, it aims at healing the psyche by reestablishing it in the metaxy from which it had fallen into the disease of literalism. Finding the way back to the metaxy calls up a mythical mode of imagining such as the Platonic Socrates employed as a healer of souls. This return to the middle realm of fiction, of myth, carries one into conversational familiarity with the cosmos one *inhabits.* Healing thus means Return, and psychic consciousness means Conversation, and a "healed consciousness" lives fictionally, just as healing figures like Jung and Freud become under our very eyes fictional personages, their factual biographies dissolving and coagulating into myths, becoming fictions so they can go on healing.

Therefore, active imagination, so close to art in procedure, is distinct from it in aim. This is not only because active imagination foregoes an end result in a physical product, but more because its intention is Know Thyself, self-understanding, which is as well its limit—the paradoxical limit of endlessness that corresponds with the Heraclitean endlessness of psyche itself. Self-understanding is necessarily uroboric, an interminable turning in a gyre amid its scenes, its visions and voices.[8]

From the viewpoint of narrative, the visions and voices are an unfolding story without end. Active imagination is interminable because the story goes into death and death is endless—who knows where it has its stop? From the viewpoint of narrative, self-understanding is that healing fiction which individuates a life into death. From the imagistic viewpoint, however, self-understanding is interminable, because it is not in time to begin with. Know Thyself is revelatory, nonlinear, discontinuous, it is like a painting, a lyric poem, biography thoroughly gone into the imaginative act. We may fictionalize connections between the revelatory moments, but these connections are hidden like the spaces between the sparks or the dark seas around the luminous fishes' eyes, images Jung employs to account for images. Each image is its own beginning, its own end, healed by and in itself. So, Know Thyself terminates whenever it leaves linear time and becomes an act of imagination. A partial insight, this song now, this one image; to see partly is the whole of it. Self-understanding healed by active imagination.

Know Thyself is its own end and has no end. It is Mercurial.[9] It is a paradoxical hermetic art that is both goal-directed and without end, much as the aged Freud, in a last paper before exile from Vienna, said of analysis, both of its end as goal and its end in time: "Not only the patient's analysis but that of the analyst himself has ceased to be terminable and become an interminable task." There is no other end than the act of soul-making itself, and soul is without end.

THE FICTION OF CASE HISTORY: GENRE AND ARCHETYPE

A Jungian friend, Wolfgang Giegerich, while exposing the archetypal pattern within the writings of Erich Neumann, makes the remark:

> Something (some "factor") obviously keeps us from the truly psychological orientation and makes our thinking unpsychological by making us wish for, or even need, empirical verification, scientific truth, and systematizations. This "factor" is our containment in the

Great Mother/Hero myth, whose nature is to create the (mythic!)
fantasy of the possibility of heroically breaking out of myth, into
"fact," "truth," "science."[10]

He then develops the theme, showing that a narrative account in evolu-
tional terms is a genre which belongs to the perspective of the Hero/
Great Mother. This implies that when we conceive our life story as a
Battle for Deliverance from the Great Mother—as Jung called it—we are
engaged in heroics; these heroics reflect in such concepts as ego development, ego strength, and personal identity. The theory emerging from this
archetypal perspective is that of Neumann's *Origins and History of Consciousness*. That book is not a statement of *faith* in progress or a work of
science in evolution. Nor is it, as Giegerich shows, a *history* in any other
sense of that word but "story." It is, rather, an archetypal fantasy held
together by a captivating plot: the development of Ego, an Everyman,
with whom each of us can identify. Its persuasiveness rests upon this
same archetypal foundation—the rhetoric of the archetype—which in
this example casts each of us readers into an ontogenetic recapitulation of
the heroic battle of deliverance from maternal uroboric claustrophobia.

Giegerich links a genre of psychoanalytical writing with an archetype.
In a short paper of my own I also tried to show that a certain style of presenting psychology, Jung's in particular, by means of diagrams, numbers,
and crystals, by references to introversion and slow patience, and by images
of the Old Wise Man, uses of ancient wisdom and magic, belongs to the
senex consciousness of Saturn.[11] Again, the rhetoric of an archetype. Again,
a genre which determines our plots and our styles in writing case history.

The relationship between archetype and genre has been worked
out most famously by Northrop Frye in his *Anatomy of Criticism*, where
the four classical genres of literature are each given a season in the year,
so that literature follows a cycle of the corn god. Actually Frye's system,
though fourfold, still remains within the single myth of the Great
Mother, the God-Hero her son, and the cycle of nature.

More fundamental than any of these attempts at the problem of
genre and archetype is an approach that can be extrapolated from a paper
by Patricia Berry. She considers that narrative as such cannot help but
reflect the ego's concerns, because narrative is essentially the genre of
the hero archetype. She writes:

Narration is also reinforced by therapy. As we tell our dreams, so we
narrate our life stories. Not only the content of our dreams is influ-

enced by analysis but the very style of our remembering. . . . Since
the narrative style of description is inextricably bound with a sense
of continuity—what in psychotherapy we call the ego—misuse of
continuity because of the ego is also close at hand. . . . The most
important difficulty with narrative: it tends to become the ego's trip.
The hero has a way of finding himself in the midst of any story. He
can turn anything into a parable of a way to make it and stay on top.
The continuity in a story becomes *his* ongoing heroic movement.
Hence when we read a dream as narrative there is nothing more ego-
natural than to take the sequence of movement as a progression culminating in the dreamer's just reward or defeat. The way story en-
capsulates one into it as protagonist corrupts the dream into a mirror
in which the ego sees only its concerns.[12]

A similar thought has been put succinctly in Roger Fowler's dictionary:
"The narrative without a hero remains a critical fiction."[13] Even the anti-
hero is what we in psychology would refer to as a negative inflation of the
ego. Whether invoked or not, ego is always present. If we are going to tell
tales in narrative form we are going to come out with ego theory. Berry
implies that the genre of narrative itself determines the plot by which we
form our case history and understand it.

The question now arises: is our style of case-history writing, even of
interpreting individual dreams and situations, the result of ego psychology, *or* is it possible that ego psychology—as presented first by Freud,
then by one division of his school, and now by the therapeutic establishment—results from our style of case-history writing? Have we produced
ego psychology through our way of writing cases? And are our case histories not so much empirical demonstrations of the way the psyche works
but empirical demonstrations of the way that *poiesis* works in organizing
our vision?

This means we would begin to read case histories with an archetypal eye toward their form. We would be interested in the genre in
which the case is fantasied, even the rhythm, the language, the sentence
structures, the metaphors; for we find archetypes not only in the content
of a case history: form, too, is archetypal. There is an archetypal psychology of form. Thus we would open ourselves to the idea that, were the
story written in another way, by another hand, from another perspective,
it would sound different and therefore *be a different story*. I am suggesting
the poetic basis of therapy, of biography, of our very lives.

Perhaps the examples of the heroic ego and the picaresque are not enough to show what I mean. Let us return to the abstractions of senex consciousness where we move away from narrative altogether, both epic and episodic.

We find in this senex style of case writing, both Freudian and Jungian, an emphasis upon reductions, either downward to castration anxiety, omnipotence fantasy, primal scene, etc., or upward to wholeness, self, fourfoldedness. The work of analysis is presented less in terms of what happened next than in terms of descriptive states of being, basic abstractions of powers at work in the soul. The abstractions and reductions can be theoretical in terms of libido and its quantifications, or historical, numerical (quaternio), or configurative (mandala). The images of a dream, instead of being primary and irreducible, as Jung's own theory itself states, become representations of something more abstract. The lady in the shop window repairing carpets is not that precise image and its metaphorical implications, but is a representation of a nonrepresentational and abstract mother image to which it can be reduced. The scenes of childhood are not taken either as images, or linked into developmental narrative, but become exemplars of theoretical universals, anal or oedipal. Events do not tell a story but expose a structure. This structure is then applied to other events across time and to images regardless of context—attempts to be best in school, obsession with changing underwear, fear of the dark forest in camp—uniting them as manifestations of the one root principle.

No longer is it a question of what happened next and how one moved through this situation into the next one. Rather, it is a question of instances exemplifying principles, images as allegories, scenes as enactments in time of eternal verities. In this genre of examining a case—and I say examining deliberately—the function of consciousness, represented by the writer-analyst, is that of seeing abstractions, a keen-sighted perspicacity into structures and laws.

Here the connecting function of consciousness is defined, not hermetically in terms of significances, or martially in terms of activation, or erotically or Dionysianally, but systematically, through a paranoid ability to see defenses and resistances as mechanisms (not as obstacles in the heroic course of progression). Finally, the denouement in this genre is less in terms of a goal for the patient (improvement, say), which belongs to the narrative style and to ego development, than it is an instruction in the science of analysis, a contribution to theory, adding another stone to its monument. Saturn, the senex.[14]

You will have noticed that I threw in a few alternatives that we have not yet discussed: hermetic writing where connections do not close up but open and reveal; Aphroditic where the eye is on sensate value, personal relatings, perhaps, or sex; Dionysian where flow matters most. I also have left only as a hint the point of view of the anima which, as I see it, would stay with images and fantasies themselves, never translating them or organizing them into narrative or through plot, but responding to them in a metaphorical style where consciousness is one of innuendo, reflection, echo, tone, and elusive movements.

The idea that there is a god in our tellings and that this god shapes the words into the very syntax of a genre is not new in literary studies, even if it might come as a shock to my colleagues who really believe they are only writing clinical accounts of facts. Annabel Patterson,[15] for instance, has taken up again "The Seven Capital Stars" or description of the seven ideas of style employed in Renaissance compositions. There we see how different gods can be linked with genres—i.e., gravity with Saturn, speed with Mercury, beauty with Venus, vehemence with Mars, and the like. Of course, these one-to-one parallels should not be forced: polytheistic psychology can't speak straight on, one-to-one. Rather, they are to be imagined as suggestive perspectives toward writing and reading clinical accounts and toward listening to the language of the patient.

My point in this section has already been made in that same article by Berry: "The way we tell our story is the way we form our therapy." The way we imagine our lives is the way we are going to go on living our lives. For the manner in which we tell ourselves about what is going on is the genre through which events become experiences. There are no bare events, plain facts, simple data—or rather, this too is an archetypal fantasy: the simplistics of brute (or dead) nature.

Rhetoric means the art of persuasion. And the rhetoric of the archetype is the way in which each god persuades us to believe in the myth that is the plot in our case history. But the myth and the god are not something set apart, to be revealed in numinous moments of revelation, by oracle, or through epiphanies of images. They are in the rhetoric itself, in the way we use words to persuade ourselves about ourselves, how we tell what happened next and answer the question *why*. To find the gods in psychology we ought to look first at the genres of our case-history writing.

Our reflection needs to turn to psychoanalytic literature *as literature*. I am suggesting that literary reflection is a primary mode of grasping where one is ignorant, unconscious, blind in regard to the case because one has not differentiated the subjective factor, the gods in one's work. (1983)

11 WAR, LOVE, AND INDUSTRIALISM: THE ARES/APHRODITE/HEPHAESTUS COMPLEX IN *LADY CHATTERLEY'S LOVER*

Evelyn J. Hinz and John J. Teunissen

Hinz and Teunissen are professors of literature in Canada (Hinz is editor of Mosaic as well); the two have coauthored many essays on such writers as Lessing, Atwood, and Lawrence. This selection represents a much more overtly psychological approach when compared to the critics' argument for their brand of archetypal criticism of eleven years before (see Chapter 16).

In part 1 the critics differentiate between "mythic literature," where the author "gives voice to the myth that truly informs his culture," and the more common but inferior "literature about myth." After reviewing the Homeric myth and its historical "signatures," in part 2 they present a detailed reading of how Lawrence's mythic novel displays and reworks this archetypal complex with an appropriately modern signature, which they sum up in parts 3 and 4.

Especially interesting is their use of the archetypal approach in part 4 to pursue a psychocritical analysis of the author's relationship with his text during its composition. Hinz and Teunissen persuasively argue that the archetypal complex that inheres in Lawrence's novel is in fact to be found also in his own psyche, a position that has much in common with the analyst Hillman's discussion in Healing Fiction (Chapter 10). They recount a "complete history of Lady Chatterley's Lover," interweaving elements of its social, personal, and textual past, wherein they discover the drama of Lawrence's "reluctant surrender to the myth" after "overcoming resistance" (all psychological resonances surely intended).

*What would you say again to the tale . . . of how Hephaestus, because of similar goings-on, cast
a chain around Ares and Aphrodite?*

—Plato, *The Republic*

I

An underlying assumption of much criticism of *Lady Chatterley's Lover* is
that its mythic dimension is to be found in its Frazerian motifs and, accordingly, that the work's "redemptive" value has to do with Lawrence's
attempts to revitalize ancient fertility rituals. Though he himself is partly
responsible for the situation—in terms of some of his comments in "A
Propos of *Lady Chatterley's Lover*"—Lawrence has elsewhere also made
clear that the qualities of a truly mythic modern work are of a very different kind.

Specifically, in his review of Frederick Carter's *Dragon of the Apocalypse,* Lawrence defines myth as a *story* about a fundamental truth of the
human condition: "Myth is an attempt to narrate a whole human experience . . . a profound experience of the human body and soul, an experience which is never exhausted and never will be exhausted, for it is being
felt and suffered now, and it will be felt and suffered while man remains
man." The modern scientific world, however, has tried to "explain the
myths away," ignoring their phenomenality and splitting their original
integration of the cosmic and the psychic into two abstract and theoretical
parts: either myths are regarded as psychological paradigms or they are
treated as allegories about the operations of the universe. The consequence of this loss of ancient humanistic history is that modern man
thinks his experiences are unique, and it is in countering this egocentric-
ity by illustrating that history repeats itself that the real "redemptive"
value of modern mythic work resides. For to be ignorant of the myth one
is in "only means [that] you go on suffering blindly, stupidly, 'in the
unconscious,' instead of healthily and with the imaginative comprehension playing upon the suffering" (*Phoenix,* 295–96).

This is not to suggest, however, that the artist sets out to write a
mythic work; indeed, if this is the case then the end result will not be
"mythic literature" but "literature about myth"—literature characterized by nostalgia or by the deliberate manipulation of parallels between
the past and the present.[1] Mythic literature, in contrast, originates in the
artist's *discovery* that the modern story he is telling is an old one, just as it
is because the story is an archetypal one that the symbolism of the myth
invariably manifests itself in the realistic details. Thus, if we begin this
study with a consideration of the extent to which *Lady Chatterley's Lover*

has precedents, our purpose is not to imply that these are the sources that Lawrence consulted and refashioned; rather, we draw attention to these artifacts merely as a strategy for bringing to consciousness the modern reader's intuitive recognition that there is something eternal about Lawrence's lovers and their situation. Furthermore, having provided this context, we shall then examine the genesis of *Lady Chatterley's Lover* with a view toward demonstrating that in the initial phases of its composition, far from wanting to realize the mythic dimensions of this material, Lawrence struggled against the recognition.

. . . Stripped to its essentials, *Lady Chatterley's Lover* is the story of the love between the wife of a crippled industrialist and an erstwhile soldier and of the humiliation they experience and the entanglements that ensue when their relationship is exposed. As such, this story of love, war, and industrialism is also the same in kind as that told by Homer over three thousand years ago, when the blind bard Demodocus sang of the love of Ares and Aphrodite and of the revenge of Hephaestus.

As redacted in the Greek epic, Ares (the god of war) was the clandestine paramour of Aphrodite (the goddess of love), their meetings taking place within the wronged husband's domain. Aphrodite's husband was the lame smith-god Hephaestus, who was finally informed of his cuckolding by the all-seeing Sun. Instead of taking immediate or direct action, Hephaestus fashioned a gossamer-sheer bronze net and suspended it over the bed where the lovers were wont to have their trysts. Upon their next encounter, the adulterous pair were thus ensnared, and Hephaestus called the other gods to witness his dishonor and to adjudicate his rights—complaining, however, not about the blow to his masculinity but about the violation of the marriage contract. Focusing upon the enchained condition of Ares, one of the gods moralized that here was a case of the triumph of the mental and the mechanical over the physical; focusing upon the beauty of Aphrodite, Hermes concluded that her love was worth any price one might have to pay.

Nor, paradoxically, does the sense of déjà vu diminish when one notes that Mellors is as much a "god of the woods" as a "god of war," or that Clifford is as much associated with the "upper" as with the "nether" regions. On the contrary, these seeming disparities serve to emphasize the fact that mythic expression always takes the form of *eadem, sed aliter* and that, to discover both what is constant and the forms which this constant can take, one must examine a variety of "signatures." Thus it is that in the Roman counterparts of the Greek trio—Mars, Venus, and Vul-

can—one finds the elements "missing" in the Homeric version: Mars
was an agricultural deity as well as a military god, Vulcan's abode was the
"volcano," and as a patron of crafts he was regarded as an agent of civilization.

In turn, much that seems missing from the Roman "signature" is
to be found in the articulations provided by various Renaissance
painters. . . .

II

The symbolism of the myth pervades the texture and diction of *Lady
Chatterley's Lover*. What, for example, could be more evocative of the
sounds and smells of Hephaestus at his forge than Lawrence's description of "the rattle-rattle of the screens at the pit, the puff of the wind-
ing-engine, the clink-clink of shunting trucks, and the hoarse little
whistle of the colliery locomotives. . . . The air always smelt of something under-earth: sulphur, iron, coal, or acid" (47). Similarly, the visual atmosphere of the god who served as craftsman for the other Greek
deities (as well as his "volcanic" dimension in Roman mythology)
emerges unmistakably from Lawrence's long-range view of the area:
"The vast plumes of smoke and vapour rose from . . . the great
'works', which are the modern Olympia with temples to all the gods.
. . . And Uthwaite, on a damp day, was sending up a whole array of
smoke plumes and steam, to whatever gods there be" (207). As for the
crippled smith-god himself, his essential lineaments are well embodied
in Clifford Chatterley, whose "shoulders were very broad and strong,
his hands were very strong"; "he was very strong and agile with his
arms" (38, 87). Mentally, as well, Clifford perfectly embodies the
qualities of Hephaestus, amazing Connie with "his shrewd insight into
things, his power, his uncanny material power over what is called practical men" (157). Like Hephaestus, too, Clifford is a proponent of
technology, thrilling to "the ingenuity and the almost uncanny cleverness of the modern technical mind, [it was] as if really the devil himself had lent fiend's wits to the technical scientists of industry"
(153–54). In particular, furthermore, Hephaestus invented two objects—a mechanical chair and a self-powered table on wheels—which
are conflated in Clifford's major prop: his motorized wheelchair. And
just as Clifford is presented as an emotional cripple before he becomes
a physical one, so there are two stories concerning the origin of Hephaestus's lameness: in the *Odyssey* he complains that he was born that

WAR, LOVE, AND INDUSTRIALISM 143

way, whereas in the *Iliad* he explains that he was crippled when he was hurled from Olympus by Zeus for taking his mother's side in a domestic dispute.

In his characterization of Mellors, Lawrence seems to incline more toward Roman than Greek mythology, emphasizing the "agricultural deity" side of the Ares figure. At the same time, however, his "god of war" dimension is never lost sight of. . . .

Whereas Clifford and Mellors thus incarnate their prototypes from the very beginning, as it were, Connie must be awakened to her identity as Aphrodite, and accordingly Lawrence's first evocation of the goddess of love takes the inverted form of a quotation from Swinburne in which the poet evokes "the Cytherean" in the course of lamenting her demise (128). For the same reason, when Connie does experience her apotheosis as a woman born to love, she at first sees Mellors/Ares as an agent of destruction. . . . If Clifford has a distinctively "Greek" cast and Mellors a distinctively "Roman" one, Connie is most allied with "Renaissance" signatures. . . .

Perhaps what brings the Ares/Aphrodite/Hephaestus complex into clearest focus, however, is the recurrent net and chain symbolism. Pervasive in Lawrence's description of the industrial world—where the "steel threads of the railways" link town to town (208)—the symbolism comes especially to identify the plight of lovers trapped in this world and in their legally binding marriages. In fact, the plot of the novel begins when Clifford explains to Connie that he wants a son, because "one is only a link in a chain," and that he does not care if it should be fathered by another man, since he and Connie are "interwoven in a marriage." Not being very "keen on chains," Connie thinks to herself: "Was it actually her destiny to go on weaving herself into his life. . . . She was to be content to weave a steady life with him. . . . How could one say Yes? for years and years? . . . Why should one be pinned down by that butterfly word?" (81–84).

■   ■   ■   ■

But, of course, the episode that is most explicitly directive in its use of "net" symbolism is the one wherein Duncan Forbes agrees to "pose" as the father of Connie's child on the condition that she "pose" as a model for him. For when Forbes states his condition, Mellors's response is: "Better have me as a model at the same time. . . . Better do us in a group, Vulcan and Venus under the net of art" (357).

"*Vulcan* and Venus"? Thus no sooner does the myth come into sharp focus than everything begins to seem confused. For although Mellors has the right iconographic configuration, it is Mars not Vulcan who was ensnared with Venus, and accordingly it is with the former that he should identify. Nor can the "mistake" be dismissed as a slip on Lawrence's part, since he has Mellors go on to explain, "I used to be a blacksmith." But what, then, is Lawrence's point?

One possible answer would seem to lie again in Lawrence's distinction between myth and allegory—specifically in his observation that mythic figures always have a "Janus" aspect and that mythic works always have a dialectical nature: not *a* "meaning" or even "meaning *within* meaning: but rather, meaning against meaning" (*Phoenix,* 295). For the fact that Mellors was a blacksmith is not the only point of affinity between him and Vulcan. . . .

But Mellors's identification of himself with Vulcan cannot be justified and so must be regarded as a mistake that Lawrence deliberately has Mellors make.

As for the significance of the mistake, here the explanation is to be found in the extent to which Mellors's recourse to an explicit and "literary" allusion is totally "out of character" and contrary to the entire direction of the novel thus far. . . . Mellors's *invocation* of "Vulcan and Venus under the net of art" is therefore in itself indicative that something is wrong, that he does not have a sure sense of his mythological identity.

Supporting such an interpretation, furthermore, is the fact that leading up to the faulty recognition scene there is a conversation between Mellors and Connie concerning his true nature, a conversation in which he admits to being confused at the same time that Lawrence himself subtly evokes his Ares/Mars qualities: "I can feel something inside me, all mixed up with a lot of rage. But what it really amounts to, I don't know" (345–46). Connie knows, however, and by explaining that he has "the courage of [his] own tenderness" she unobtrusively identifies the combination of strength and softness which is symbolized by the union of Ares and Aphrodite.

If Ares and Aphrodite symbolize this ideal fusion, however, Vulcan and Venus are husband and wife, and herein lies a related way of accounting for Mellors's mistake: namely, as a kind of wish fulfillment, as a recasting of himself in a role that will make for a happy outcome for him and Connie. For, according to mythology, upon being released from the net, Aphrodite blithely left Ares to return, first to her native abode, but ultimately to Hephaestus, who "had no real intention of divorcing her."[2] If Mellors can see himself as Hephaestus, in short,

then he can rest assured that in due time Connie—who has also returned to her native land, Scotland—will come back to him. And this
dream of reunion, of course, is the motivating force behind Mellors's
concluding "hopeful" letter to Connie, and accounts for his further attempts to identify with Vulcan. . . .

What makes his attempt so desperate, furthermore, is the teller-
versus-tale nature of his letter—the extent to which everything about his
situation unmistakably identifies him as an Ares/Mars figure who is
caught in a Hephaestus system. . . .

III

If *Lady Chatterley's Lover* has a moral, therefore, it is that mythic configurations inexorably shape our lives, and that a failure to realize where one fits
in the cosmic scheme is the real cause of modern man's anxiety. For it is not
the fact that he is away from Connie that bothers Mellors as much as a
general sense of alienation; his total investment in their love, indeed, is the
result of a feeling that he has no other connections. Although in theory he
knows that a man must "trust in something beyond himself" and that "a
higher mystery" controls events, in practice his frame of reference is limited to "the little flame between us. For me now, it's the only thing in the
world. I've got no friends, not inward friends. Only you" (373). As such,
Mellors is a perfect example of the alienated type that Lawrence describes
in *Apocalypse:* "When I hear modern people complain of being lonely then I
know what has happened. They have lost the cosmos.—It is nothing human and personal that we are short of."[3] What this loss of the cosmos also
entails, as Lawrence explains in his review of Carter's *Dragon,* is a shift from
an immediate enjoyment of life to a view of fulfillment in the future:
"While life itself is fascinating, fortune is completely uninteresting, and the
idea of fate does not enter. When men become poor in life then they become anxious about their fortune and frightened about their fate. By the
time of Jesus, men had become so anxious about their fortunes and so
frightened about their fates, that they put up the grand declaration that life
was one long misery and you couldn't expect your fortune till you got to
heaven; that is, till after you were dead" (*Phoenix,* 299). Mellors, of course,
does not go quite so far. He repeatedly tells Connie not to worry, but his
assertions are undermined by the equal repetition of "Patience, always patience" and "Wait." Even more ironic is his long polemic on the subject of
"living" versus "spending" and his advocacy of "old group dances" as a
solution to the "industrial problem"; for what lies behind his conviction

that "the mass of people oughtn't even to try to think" but should be "alive and frisky, and acknowledge the great god Pan" is his own problem in this very respect: "I'm sure you're sick of all this," he tells Connie. "But I don't want to harp on myself, and I've nothing happening to me. I don't like to think too much about you, in my head, that only makes a mess of us both. But of course, what I live for now is for you and me to live together" (371–73).

To the very extent that Mellors is "hopeful" about the future, therefore, so much is he Christian rather than pagan in his orientation. . . . we begin to see why Clifford is presented as a "Christ" figure in his "rebirth" as an industrialist, and why he identifies with Plato, that precursor of Christian attitudes. In turn, we also see the tragic significance of the change in Mellors from a man of passion to a man of peace, from a pagan who speaks the language of the body to a Christian who sends a wordy epistle about chastity to his "brothers in love"—in short, from a man who *incarnated* the qualities of Ares/Mars to a man who *likens* himself to Hephaestus/Vulcan: all of these changes are forms of the triumph of mind over body that is described in the myth.

IV

If *Lady Chatterley's Lover* seems to qualify as a genuinely "mythic work" by reason of the way in which the Ares/Aphrodite/Hephaestus complex *inheres* within its plot and texture, the genesis of the novel presents a very different situation, points indeed to an antimythic attitude. For the crippling of Clifford—the thing that distinguishes this myth from others concerned with adultery—was something Lawrence personally disliked: "It made it so much more vulgar of [Connie] to leave him." As for why he nevertheless went against his personal feelings, Lawrence's explanation was that "the story came as it did, by itself, so I left it alone," and that "in the sense of its happening" the crippling of Clifford was "inevitable" (*Phoenix*, 2:514).

A better description of the driven artist—of the artist who does not set out to write a mythic work—would be hard to find, and when one realizes that the story that "came" to Lawrence was that of Ares/Aphrodite/Hephaestus, then his argument that Clifford had to be paralyzed because the story demanded it does not sound at all like question begging. It can also be demonstrated that Lawrence was not speaking loosely when he attributed the plot and symbolism of *Lady Chatterley's Lover* to a surrender to "inevitability." For the genesis of the novel has a long history, and Lawrence's willingness to "let the story alone" really represents the climax of an almost lifelong resistance to the myth—a resistance, significantly, that roughly coincided with the war and initially took the form of a critique of inorganic mythic literature.

In a November 1916 letter to Lady Cynthia Asquith, Lawrence begins by criticizing her husband's poetry for not being true to "his own realities" and by arguing that "it needs the death of an old world in him, and the inception of a new. Not Ares, not Aphrodite—these two are old hat, and not *real* in us." But he then contradicts himself when he observes that "the war is and continues because of the lust for hate and war"—in short, because of the "worship of Ares and Aphrodite—('But a bitter goddess was born of blood and the salt sea foam')—both gods of destruction and burning down." Nevertheless, he stubbornly concludes that "Ares and Aphrodite have ceased to be gods. We want something else: it is fulfilled in us, this Ares-Aphrodite business" (*CL*, 486–87).

A similar latent admission and conscious rejection characterizes Lawrence's handling of the Ares/Aphrodite motif in the novel he was writing at the time, *Women in Love*. On the one hand, there is a positive evocation of the birth of the goddess of love in the description of the bride—"a sudden foaming rush . . . like a sudden surf-rush, floating all white"—but, on the other hand, there is Birkin's denunciation of her as "the flowering mystery of the death-process. . . . Aphrodite is born in the first spasm of universal dissolution." To the same effect, but conversely, when Birkin attempts to enunciate the "star equilibrium" theory, Ursula retorts: "There you are—a star in its orbit! A satellite—a satellite of Mars—that's what she is to be! . . . You want a satellite, Mars and his satellite."[4]

This same recourse to mockery as a mode of resistance also characterizes a novel that Lawrence began in 1920 but never completed, a novel that in many ways anticipates the central situation of *Lady Chatterley's Lover*. Entitled *Mr. Noon*, the novel is concerned with "the tripod footing" of the universe, as Lawrence mockingly describes the "eternal triangle" (*Phoenix*, 2:190). Actually, there are two triangles, with the titular hero as the link between them, and with the first—which involves his sexual entanglement with an engaged girl—serving to prevent one from taking the second as seriously as its dramatization seems to warrant. This second plot focuses upon the relationship between the hero and a frustrated married woman, a relationship that is sparked by his account of Mars: "Mars, its canals, and its inhabitants . . . ah, how wonderful it was! And how wonderful was Mr. Noon, with his rough bass voice, roughly

and laconically and yet with such magic and power landing her on another planet" (*Phoenix*, 2:115). The effect of their relationship is her
emergence as "a new Aphrodite from the stiff dark sea of middle-aged
matronliness . . . ivory-white and soft, woman still, leaving the sea of all
her past . . . Aphrodite, mistress, mother of all the worlds of unknown
knowledge" (*Phoenix*, 2:141–44).[5]

Putting *Mr. Noon* aside, Lawrence turned his attention to explicating his theory of the dynamics of the unconscious, and in the process once
again found himself tangling with the Aphrodite material. In attempting
to define the relationship between man's daytime self and the night-self,
for example, he explained in *Fantasia* that "you must start every single
day fresh from the source. You must rise every day afresh out of the dark
sea of the blood. . . . The self which rises naked every morning out of the
dark sleep of the passionate, hoarsely-calling blood: this is the unit for the
next society. . . . This is under the spell of the moon, of sea-born Aphrodite, mother and bitter goddess."[6] Later, when he goes on to suggest how
Christianity blocks this renewal, Hephaestus is also brought into the picture: "We bruise the serpent's head. . . . But his revenge of bruising our
heel is a good one. . . . The serpent has bruised our heel till we limp.
The lame gods, the enslaved gods, the toiling limpers moaning for the
woman" (*FU*, 216). At the conclusion of *Fantasia*, furthermore, the third
member of the triangle is also introduced in terms of Lawrence's critique
of a recent scientific thesis, which argued that "It is almost as certain that
there's life on the moon as it is certain there is life on Mars" (*FU*, 224).
But if he ridicules this scientist for reducing the symbolic significance of
these planets by attempting to make them familiar—"All I can say is:
'Pray come in, Mr. Moony. And how is your cousin Signor Martian?' "
(*FU*, 225)—he himself ridicules Aphrodite by presenting the Statue of
Liberty as her avatar, emerging from the waters of New York harbor still
clutching in her raised hand the severed phallos of Uranus.

Lawrence's next strategy involved an attempt simply to ignore
Aphrodite—in the political novels of the so-called leadership period.
But, in the last of these, *The Plumed Serpent*, he also deliberately tried to
announce her demise by having Kate, in her sexual relationship with Ci-
priano, realize "the death in her of the Aphrodite of the foam: the seeth-
ing, frictional, ecstatic Aphrodite. . . . [H]e, in his dark, hot silence,
would bring her back to the new, soft, heavy, hot flow, when she was like
a fountain gushing noiseless and with urgent softness from the volcanic
deeps."[7] But in rejecting one aspect of the Aphrodite complex, Lawrence
is betrayed into drawing attention to another; for the volcanic imagery is

as central to the myth as the foam, evoking as it does Aphrodite's "Roman" husband, Vulcan. Similarly, the more Lawrence succeeds in substituting the religion of Quetzalcoatl for Christian beliefs, the more he evokes the cult of Aphrodite; for though the "Morning Star" is the symbol of Quetzalcoatl, astrologically the morning star is Venus.

Where one finds evidence of his final capitulation, in turn, is, significantly, in two of his "philosophical" works which are most concerned with defining the true nature of myth and mythic consciousness. In *Apocalypse*, for example, he observes that "our idea of time as a continuity in an eternal straight line has crippled our consciousness cruelly," and he traces our loss of an organic relationship to the mythic past to the early explicators' tendency to "fix" the meaning of symbolism (*A*, 87, 97). And even more pointedly, in *Etruscan Places*—which he wrote, one should recall, in the interval between the second and the final versions of *Lady Chatterley's Lover*—Lawrence argues that the old religious sense of man's essential harmony with nature "changed with the Greeks and Romans into a desire to resist nature, to produce a mental cunning and a mechanical force that would outwit Nature and chain her down completely, completely, till at last there should be nothing free in nature at all, all should be controlled, domesticated, put to man's meaner uses."[8]

If the complete history of *Lady Chatterley's Lover* thus takes the form of a reluctant surrender to the myth, so too is its immediate genesis characterized by overcoming resistance. Though the first and the last drafts of the novel structurally have the same plot, the first version is less a story of exposed lovers than it is an exposé of what goes on behind the scenes in upper-class society. Similarly, instead of leaving the story alone in the second version, Lawrence made it the vehicle for social criticism, and attempted to deflect its mythic direction by introducing a series of literary analogues: *Romeo and Juliet, Wuthering Heights, Jane Eyre,* and *Ulysses.*[9] The overcoming of resistance, in turn, can be charted in the changes that serve to bring the myth to the foreground and into clearer focus. Thus, one of the essential differences between the gamekeeper in the first and the final versions is Lawrence's characterization of Mellors as a military man, a change that makes Connie's attraction to him more that of Aphrodite for Ares and less that of a sexually deprived woman willing to sacrifice decorum for a virile male.[10] A second major change was to make Clifford not merely an industrialist but also a writer,[11] a change that again is required if he is to reflect not merely the smithy side of Hephaestus but also his mental cunning and his basically spiteful nature; and once more Lawrence draws attention to the significance of the change by describing Clifford's stories as "curious, very personal. . . . Clever, rather spiteful" and by emphasizing their similarity to Hephaestus's contrivance: "A display! a display! a display!" (50, 90).

A third change, seemingly minor but important if one is to appreciate the contemporary relevance of Hephaestus's attitude toward adultery, involved the renaming of a key site. In *John Thomas and Lady Jane,* there is mentioned in passing a spring, called "Robin Hood's Well," in the vicinity of the gamekeeper's hut. In *Lady Chatterley's Lover,* the site is called "John's Well": it is there that Connie rests before her first encounter alone with Mellors; it is there that he gives her the key to his hut; it is there that they drink in anticipation of their first night together. From being initially dry, furthermore, the spring becomes active, as the love between Connie and Mellors develops. Easily overlooked by those unfamiliar with the biblical story of Jesus' encounter with the adulterous Samaritan woman at Jacob's Well, as told by "John" (4:6–26), the name change draws attention to the fact that the mortality of Hephaestus finds its counterpart in the Christian view that only the man to whom one is legally married can be called one's "husband."

This is not to suggest, however, that even in the final version of *Lady Chatterley's Lover* all traces of resistance have vanished; on the contrary, the last draft is best described as a recapitulation of Lawrence's earlier struggles and as his only gradual capitulation to the myth. The opening of the novel, for example, is about as unmythic as could be, consisting not only of glib generalizations but also of a parody of the Isis/Osiris myth—Clifford is shipped home to Connie "more or less in bits," with Connie searching for the missing piece, as "the bits seemed to grow together again" (37). In Connie's affair with the bounderish Michaelis, one has a direct parody of the adulterous Ares/Aphrodite relationship, just as the discussion of proper sexual relations on the part of Clifford's cronies—a discussion that begins with the key refrain, "Blest be the tie that binds"—may be seen as an ironic portrayal of the gods' discussion when Hephaestus summoned them to witness the adulterous lovers and to uphold his legal rights.

Nor, finally, are the concluding chapters of the novel without their component of mockery of the myth, although indicative of Lawrence's own changed attitude is the fact that his ridicule is now presented through Clifford and as an aspect of the Hephaestus mentality. Thus, in his letter to Connie detailing the return of Bertha Coutts to Mellors's hut, Clifford writes: "Unable to evict the somewhat manhandled Venus from his couch, he beat a retreat and retired, it is said, to his mother's house in Tevershall. Meanwhile the Venus of Stacks Gate is established in the cottage, which she claims is her home, and Apollo, apparently, is domiciled in Tevershall" (328). Clifford's contempt for mythology, in short, is matched only by his ignorance of the myth he is in, and to criticize him even further on this account Lawrence has Mrs. Bolton express her scorn of Clifford in terms that clearly recall Hephaestus's recourse to a trick rather than direct confrontation when he learns of his wife's infidelity: "If he would have admitted it, and prepared himself for it; or if he would have admitted it, and actively struggled with his wife against it: that would have been acting like a man"; and she concludes by evoking an image of Hephaestus caught in his own net: "he's like a mummy tangled in its own bandages" (360).

Similarly, Lawrence presents Mrs. Bolton's attempts to "comfort" Clifford as an ironic version of the "Aphrodite calming the tempestuous Ares" motif: "And she drew him to her, and held her arms round his great shoulders, while he laid his face on her bosom and sobbed, shaking and hulking his huge shoulders, whilst she softly stroked his dusky-blond hair." Though there is an "oedipal" aspect to this relationship, Lawrence makes clear that this is not the myth in question when he describes this "perverted child-man" as otherwise being "impervious as a bit of steel," with "an almost uncanny shrewdness, hardness," and when he has Mrs. Bolton express her reaction in terms suggestive of the degrading objective of the Hephaestean net: "It was so ridiculous! It was so awful! such a come-down! so shameful!" (361–63).

Where the importance of an oedipal echo in *Lady Chatterley's Lover* does lie is in drawing our attention to Lawrence's first attempt to give mythic articulation to the crippling nature of modern trends, for in so doing it emphasizes the fact that the mythic artist is compelled to keep going over the same material until he truly gives voice to the myth that truly informs his culture. *Sons and Lovers* was inadequate on both accounts: first, Lawrence was too close to his subject matter to "leave the story alone" or to realize its wider implications; second, the Oedipus myth does not concern itself with two of the primary features of modern culture—its technological orientation and its puritanical and legalistic morality. As a result, the real value of Lawrence's articulation of the Oedipus myth in *Sons and Lovers* was that it enabled him to come to terms with his own psychological problem—a necessary first stage, since until the artist has contended with his personal unconscious he is incapable of becoming the spokesman of the collective unconscious.

This is not, of course, to suggest that an artist should be remote from the myth of his times. On the contrary, it could be argued that Lawrence's initial resistance to the Ares/Aphrodite/Hephaestus complex derived from a lack of personal identification, and conversely that his ultimate capitulation had to do with the adulterous triangle—he, Frieda, and Ravagli—in which he found himself at the time of writing *Lady Chatterley's Lover*. The relevance of this experience to *Lady Chatterley's Lover* has been discussed elsewhere,[12] however, and for the present, what is important is simply to point out that such biographical considerations are not alien to a mythic reading of Lawrence's novel. For, by way of conclusion, we want to address two related misconceptions about myth criticism and the nature of myth in *Lady Chatterley's Lover*.

One is the complaint that mythic interpretations accommodate only a part of Lawrence's novels and as a result end up distorting their full meaning;[13] the other is that the "symbolic" and the "naturalistic" dimensions of *Lady Chatterley's Lover* are not well integrated.[14] From our discussion, however, it should be clear that a mythic approach can accommodate the complete range of *Lady Chatterley's Lover*, and that to see the mythic as existing in contrast to the realistic is to have misidentified the novel's informing myth. For the Ares/Aphrodite/Hephaestus complex has within it both an "idyllic" and a "social consciousness" side: it is as much concerned with industrialism as with love; with marriage and divorce as with the rightness of passion; with a puritanical as with a pagan morality. To provide a discussion of how this myth informs the novel, therefore, does not involve ignoring the world outside the "sacred wood" or rejecting the latter part of the novel as anticlimatic.

Nor, finally, does such a reading interpose between the text and the reader's emotional response. Rather, its effect is a kind of "unconsciousness raising," an awakening not to new insights but to forgotten knowledge. Of course there will always be those who resist, but in doing so they will be providing a related kind of evidence of the reality of eternal recurrence: they will simply be registering the same modernist reaction to myth that itself characterized the genesis of *Lady Chatterley's Lover*.

(1989)

12 SPINNING AMONG FIELDS: JUNG, FRYE, LÉVI-STRAUSS, AND FEMINIST ARCHETYPAL THEORY

Annis V. Pratt

Annis V. Pratt has been referred to authoritatively as "the leading feminist archetypal literary theorist." This selection, taken from a much longer essay, traces her own search for ideas suitable to weave into a personal yet feminist theory of archetypes that could be useful for literary criticism. She analyzes Jung's work on archetypes and then explores some of the difficulties that she and others have found with Jung. She then goes on to discuss the competing positions held by feminist archetypal critics such as Goldenberg, Ulanov, and Singer.

Pratt concludes her investigation of Jung by sketching out the kind of literary criticism that comes from her approach. She treats the archetypal rebirth quest or journey, discussing why it is not the same for women as for men. The selection ends with a coda, a defense of her position in terms of the feminist movement, both in society and in the university community. Pratt's essay in this book's section "Jung and Gender Criticism" is a demonstration of her archetypal feminist theory put into practice.

Literature is a particularly apt field for the joining of the ideal and empirical approaches because it brings together both the ideal and the real in a relationship of tension and conflict. This tension was present in many British and American novels written by women between 1700 and 1978. In searching more than three hundred such works for recurrent patterns of plot symbolism, characterization, and theme, I was struck by the conservatism of even purportedly feminist writers, whose women characters showed a kind of mindless, tacit accommodation to gender norms. Patriarchal values proved to be far heavier a burden for these women authors than I had expected. At the same time, though, they wove into their texts strands of a more fully human potential self that contradicted gender norms. These two conflicting tendencies produced an ambivalence of tone, irony in characterization, and strange disjunction in plotting, which indeed mirror women's social experience.

   In spite of the rigid patriarchal ideology that has prevailed in much of women's literature over the past three centuries, portrayals of more ideal possibilities for women characters—images of total feminine self-hood in which sexuality, intellect, and creativity have developed in the same person—have occurred quite frequently. When women heroes explored their unconscious, they came up against ancient archetypes, often encoded, frequently hieroglyphic, but nevertheless present as possibilities to be assimilated and emulated. There seems to be some kind of forgotten code or buried script underlying the normative plots that women authors in a patriarchal culture internalize. If, in the early years of the new feminist movement, consciousness-raising, or becoming aware of gender roles, was the primary task, in recent years "unconsciousness-raising" has assumed equal importance. Whether or not they derive from some golden age of women in our actual past, the archetypes we find in our literature represent vital psychological possibilities. The feminist archetypal critic seeks to elucidate these feminine counterstructures, to show how gender norms affect tone, attitude, imagery, characterization, and plotting, to trace the counterstructures through the total work of an author and then throughout the field of women's literature as a whole.

■ ■ ■ ■

I have always enjoyed the story of Jung's attempt to break away from Freud in order to develop his own theory because it offers a valuable lesson. Coming up against all sorts of emotional resistances and mental impediments, Jung took to playing with stones, building cottages and castles and whole villages down by the lakeshore. New theories do not necessarily spring like Athene from Zeus's frontal lobes. They depend as much on intuitions that arise while fooling about with ideas, building up and knocking over hypotheses, as on sophisticated thought processes. Lewis Thomas has argued that new ideas are discovered by making mistakes, erring by being errant, wandering from idea to idea, "being flung off into blind alleys, up trees, down dead ends, out into blue sky, along wrong turnings, around bends," leaping "across mountains of information to land lightly on the wrong side."[1]

Jung developed a definition of the unconscious, which he differentiated from Freud's subconscious as being less subordinate to than in balance with consciousness, and less inferior to reason than valuable to the personality as a whole. Although both Freud and Jung saw the purpose of psychoanalysis as a balance between the ego and the subterranean realms of the self, Jung emphasized the destructive capacity of too much ego, on the one hand, and, on the other, insisted on the positive, beneficial qualities of the unconscious.

One would think that, in valuing the unconscious, Jung would have transcended the dualistic sexism that pervades Freudian theory. But Jung's association of emotion and illogic with women and logical rationality with men led him to a similar dichotomy. "Although man and woman unite," wrote Jung, "they nevertheless represent irreconcilable opposites which, when activated, degenerate into deadly hostility. This primordial pair of opposites symbolizes every conceivable pair of opposites that may occur: hot and cold, light and dark, north and south, dry and damp, good and bad, conscious and unconscious."[2] Although his theory valued the feminine and the unconscious, Jung placed these ideas on one side of a dualistic value system along with things "cold," "dark," "south," "damp," and "bad," and this categorizing undermined his integrative goals.

Jung admitted that he and his colleagues had little perspective on the feminine personality: "The elementary fact that a man always presupposes another's psychology as being identical with his own aggravates the difficulty and hinders the correct understanding of the feminine psyche."[3] Jung himself fell into difficulties when he tried to analyze women's dreams as if they were identical in configuration to men's. He once had a woman patient whose dreams and fantasies featured very powerful feminine archetypes, including sphinxes, Egyptian queens, and an Aztec god-lover.[4] Ironically, Jung derived his theory of the heroic quest from this single female patient, who was diagnosed as schizophrenic. Later in his career, however, Jung recognized that there were specifically feminine archetypes, like the Demeter-Kore narrative, that were probably only accessible to and definitive of women.

Jungian psychoanalysis tends to assume that archetypal patterns derived from male experience are applicable to women's as well. As a consequence, female archetypes are interpreted according to male patterns, and the male patterns may be allowed to eclipse women's experience altogether. The feminine may be reduced to an attribute of the masculine personality rather than seen as an archetype deriving from women's experience that is a source of power for the self.

I once tried to explain to a Jungian therapist what I faced as a woman employed in a largely male academic world. "I wish that *you* could be a women for just one day!" I finally burst out. "I don't have to do that," he replied smugly. "I come to terms with my anima every day." Even though femininity in the form of the anima, an assimilated attribute, must be experienced quite differently from being a woman oneself, the therapist felt that experiencing his anima was equivalent to understanding the experience of a real woman in the real world. He also regarded it as a secret internal source of power. Once one has decided that the internal experience of a quality is more valuable than the external phenomena from which the quality devices, one is open to an extremely dangerous kind of conceptual narcissism. The idea that men and women are inherently androgynous, each containing masculine and feminine qualities, is transformed into an assumption that if one has come to terms with these qualities internally, the problems associated with being a man or a woman in the social world will handle themselves.

The focus on internal integration of masculinity and feminity assumes that what goes on inside the human mind is of more importance than what goes on in the world of other humans and the world of nature. Although Jung thought that society would benefit as individuals became more attuned to their psyches, he demonstrated an idealistic valuation of mind over matter. From the dualistic assumption that mind is ontologically other than and superior to matter, it is a short step to the notion that matter is derived from mind. Since men have been associated with mind and women with nature, or matter, there has been a tendency, given this idealistic bias, to see women as extensions or even creations of male imagination. If women are taken as attributes of the male psyche, or if women as representations of nature, the body, and the chthonic are understood only as others in relation to male questers, then women cannot be analyzed as creators and questers in their own right.

So easily does Jungian theory fall into this posture toward women that some feminist scholars have been wary of adapting Jung's ideas on the unconscious for feminist purposes.[5] But just as I am not willing to deny the richness and depth of women's dreams (which individual women, and not Jung or Jungians, create from within themselves), so I am not willing to discard useful archetypes because Jung happened to formulate them. When I use the word "archetype" to describe images,

symbols, and narrative patterns recurrent in women's literature, however, I am not defining myself as a Jungian. Some feminist scholars, assuming that the use of the term "archetype" constitutes a pledge of
allegiance to Jung's system, prefer the term "archetypal" or even "prototypical" because it suggests a more fluid description of unconscious configurations. Naomi Goldenberg, in *Changing of the Gods,* prefers the word
"archetypal" because "archetype" seems infected with the Jungian assumption that archetypes contain absolute and transcendent power:
"While we must recover lost history and buried images of women, we
ought not to set up these images as archetypes. If we do, we run the risk
of setting bounds to experience by defining what the proper experience
of women is. This could become a new version of the ideology of the
Eternal Feminine and it could result in structures just as limiting as those
prescribed by the old Eternal Feminine."[6] The new "Eternal Feminine"
would consist of feminist scholars' descriptions of recurrent archetypes of
feminine power, but it is not inevitable that the concepts we arrive at
become as rigid as Jungian formulations. Archetypes, to take the dread
example of the swastika, are value-free in themselves, though they can
have a considerably destructive impact when used as cultural weapons.

   Two further tendencies among women Jungians may account for
Goldenberg's hesitation about promulgating the feminine as an eternal
archetype. First is the tendency, best exemplified in Ann Bedford Ulanov's work, to posit a polarized model of the human psyche, with the
feminine as one pole complementary to the masculine pole. Second is
the insistence, as in June Singer's work, that archetypes remain absolutes, separated from experience in a psychic realm of their own.

   Ulanov, in *The Feminine in Jungian Psychology and in Christian Theology,* affirms the polar Jungian concept of the feminine as a "matrix,"
"container," "anima," a "central resource of the human spirit."[7] Ulanov's books, however, do contain other descriptions of women's experience that are recognizable and worth exploring for typical or recurrent
patterns, such as the development of intuitive cognition, a nonlinear
sense of time, and an adaptation to natural cycles. The works of women
such as Mary Esther Harding, Toni Wolff, Emma Jung, and Marie Louise
von Franz, all of whom Jung encouraged to undertake research on
women's archetypes, similarly fascinate us with their descriptions of tri-
ply powerful moon goddesses, magic cauldrons, golden bowls filled with
generative power, and magical feminine landscapes. But at the same
time they repel us with statements that these archetypes make up half of
a transcendent dualistic system in which men belong to the realm of light

and logic while women, to quote Harding, derive from "the primordial slime."[8] We need to spin among these writings as among masculine fields, taking those ideas that can best elucidate our lives, dreams, art, and literature.

When feminist archetypal critics adapt Jung's system to their own purposes, they come up against Jungians who insist that they are in error. Thus June Singer, an American Jungian who has explicitly abjured Jung's gender bias, contends that we should not confuse the word "archetype," in the literary sense of a recurrent image, symbol, or narrative pattern, with Jung's definition of an acultural, wordless, and transcendent essence. In her view, the patterns I describe in my study of women's literature are not archetypes but archetypal images derived from inchoate and indescribable forms. "When we speak of images as if they were the archetypes," she writes, "they lose the quality of numinosity and the sense of power that characterize them."[9] It is this belief in the absolute transcendence of archetypes that both Goldenberg and I find disquieting.

Goldenberg prefers to abandon the idea of fixed sets of archetypes along with the separation of the archetype from its expression in images that Singer posits. For Goldenberg, it is "the separation of the absolute from experience which lies at the base of all patriarchal experience."[10] I, likewise, am not willing to separate the archetype from its expression in images, to divorce concepts from life. In concentrating on women's experience as expressed in literature, I have taken care that my descriptions fit rather than distort the text. Freed of the conceptual absolutism that grips both Jungians and the "theoretically sophisticated," feminist scholars can redefine Jung's concepts in accord with women's experiences. With the knowledge that not only men but also women undertake quests, encounter shadows, and deal with figures of the same and the opposite sex, we can adapt Jung's formulations to our own purposes.

The literary critic rarely encounters feminine archetypes in their purely feminist form in women's texts. Because gender norms are often unconsciously internalized by women authors, their writings are adulterated to a great degree with patriarchal cultural material. Symbols and narratives of feminine power are secrets kept hidden not only from men but from women as well. For thousands of years women have been forced to disguise and deny the heady mixture of intellectual, sexual, inventive, political, and procreative powers embodied in the ancient goddesses. When archetypal figures appear in works by women, one author may dread and another admire the same figure.[11] Moreover, a single author may take different attitudes toward such a figure within a single text, creating an ambivalence in tone and an ambiguity in attitude that literary critics need to scrutinize. As we reconsider existing criticism that deals only with male heroes as questers and excludes consideration of texts dealing with women's quests for selfhood, we must be careful not to dismiss women heroes who are less than absolutely authentic in transcending gender norms. Feminine aspirations, existing in dialectical relationship to societal prescriptions against women's development, create textual mixtures of rebellion and repression that can be discerned by careful textual critics.

■   ■   ■   ■

We can see how men's and women's archetypal experiences diverge by examining a typical narrative pattern, described by Jung, which often structures women's fiction: the rebirth quest or journey. (This pattern was most thoroughly described by Jung in *Symbols of Transformation*.) Many feminist critics would agree with Jung that patterns found in myths and stories, in fables and in more formal literary productions, reflect the psychological development of the individual. In Jung's archetypal rebirth journey, the male hero crosses the threshold from the conscious to the unconscious world in an attempt to come to terms with his internal nature, seen not only as his own individual inner state but as part of a collective unconscious whose archetypes correspond to known cultural patterns. The male hero journeys from the day-to-day world of society into a different realm that is nevertheless translatable in cultural terms. One of the figures he encounters is his "shadow," which represents a collection of antisocial tendencies, his opposite or wicked self, himself as a self-hater and social rebel. The attributes that gather around the shadow at the first stage of the journey are social in the inverted sense, deriving from feelings repressed by the hero's good-citizen persona. As the male hero moves from the realm of the personal unconscious down into the collective unconscious, the shadow changes sex, merging alarmingly with his buried feminine self. The shadow and anima together form a powerful "autonomous complex" which Jung calls the "dual mother" or "terrible mother." The crux of the adventure is the hero's struggle with this powerful feminine component of himself; his goal is to absorb her import, master her autonomous control over his impulses, and then return, a reborn psyche, to everyday life.

Jung does not suggest that the hero is easily reintegrated into society. In fact, the hero can expect suspicion and ostracism for having assimilated the anima figure, that is, for becoming androgynous. His rebirth journey is nonetheless socially beneficial. Even if he remains less than fully acceptable, his story becomes, as in the cases of Jesus and of Virgil in Dante's *Divine Comedy,* the stuff of legend and religion. Both figures are prototypical, and worthy of ritual emulation. When women heroes emerge from such quests, the least suggestion of androgyny makes them fearfully odd creatures, and they become social outcasts. Demeter, to use a classical example, effected the rescue of her daughter Persephone without ever being admitted to Olympus; and in American local-color fiction, strong autonomous country women are often under suspicion of being witches. Thus, when feminist archetypal critics interpret women's literature with this pattern in mind, warps and distortions arise.

When I began my research on women's novels, my initial hypothesis was that women's literature would reveal patterns parallel to the male rebirth quest with only incidental variations. I expected, for example, a dual god, or powerful male figure, where Jung found the dual mother. Maud Bodkin had suggested that Heathcliff is to Catherine, in *Wuthering Heights,* as Beatrice is to Dante,[12] and Heathcliff, like the Aztec god of Jung's female patient, at first seems to exemplify a blend of shadow and animus at the core of feminine consciousness. In accepting Bodkin's suggestion, I overlooked the fact that Beatrice, acting as inspiration and guide, leads Dante straight up to heaven, whereas Heathcliff, acting as demon lover, drives Catherine to a socially correct marriage and later to her death. The sublimated love of Dante for Beatrice gave him a vision of paradise and allowed him to pen a masterpiece understandable to his reading public; the Eros that Heathcliff called up in Catherine ruined her for life in society and allowed Emily Brontë to produce a "freakish" book whose unfavorable reception may have contributed to her death. The difference is not merely between medieval spiritual love and romantic libido. Whenever women encounter erotic, godlike figures in literature, the encounters are often natural, antisocial, and above all antimarital; the women end up socially outcast, mad, or dead. An integrated feminine self, particularly when it includes full-fledged Eros, is frightening to society. Thus women's rebirth literature casts its heroes *out of* the social community rather than, as in men's rebirth literature, elevating them to the status of hero.

Very few women heroes are so fortunate as to encounter a Heathcliff, or "green world lover" who represents a natural Eros. This combination of the shadow and animus figure corresponds to Pan, Dionysus, and the horned god of the Celts, and is always antimarital and antisocial. More often, in women's literature, the male figure has only social content;

he represents not the animus but the shadow, which plays quite a different role in female than in male experience. Jung's male shadow, or antiself, is antisocial, for man's dark impulses spring from rebellion against cultural norms and mores. Women's shadows are socially conformist, incorporating women's self-loathing for their deviations from social norms, specifically the norms of femininity. Women heroes in the novels of Edna O'Brien, Mary McCarthy, Olivia Manning, and Joyce Carol Oates, as in nineteenth-century fiction such as George Eliot's, punish themselves for violating gender norms. Their shadows are swollen with self-administered opprobrium for rebelling against what society wants them to be. For example, they punish themselves for any erotic feelings that spring from authentic, self-ish, desire. Should the female hero fail to reproach herself, the author accomplishes the task for her in a disproportionately punitive denouement. We do not find men punishing themselves for their libido (or other normal human desires); quite the contrary, they celebrate their sexuality. Women's shadows, rigidly social in content, fill them with self-hate for the very forces that should carry them toward greater development.

Whereas Jung's male hero encounters the dread figure of the dual mother, giving birth to himself in relationship to a loathed and revered femininity, the woman hero often encounters a "horrible husband" who stops her dead in her tracks. In women's experience, the gynophobic shadow and the animus are often fused in a masculine character who loathes the woman character every bit as much as she loathes herself, reinforcing her self-blame and dragging her into masochistic compliance with social standards. Examples of such male characters are Harald in Mary McCarthy's *The Group*, Sam Pollit in Christina Stead's *The Man Who Loved Children*, Jonathan in Sue Kaufman's *Diary of a Mad Housewife*, and husbands and lovers in novels by Fay Weldon, Doris Lessing, Katherine Anne Porter, Edna O'Brien, and Joan Didion. Confronting the horrible husband, the female character falls into madness, determines to commit suicide, or lapses into a zombielike state that precludes further development.

These novels describe partial, truncated, or failed rebirth journeys. The women heroes are unable to go beyond the personal realm of the unconscious because of the destructive messages communicated to women in everyday social experience. Male characters more easily get past the internalized social messages because social norms do not restrict men to the extent they do women. Because men are considered to be primary beings in our culture, and their physical and sexual development is regarded as a valuable part of their identity, men more easily overcome self-hate. Women, by contrast, tend to devalue their own bodies. A significant number of women's novels (Olive Schreiner's *The Story of an African Farm,* Sylvia Plath's *The Bell Jar*) feature characters blocked in growth by a hatred of their bodies as well as an emotional self-hate projected onto dismal lovers and horrible husbands. Such portrayals suggest that the journey through personal to unconscious experience is far more perilous for women than men. Women heroes are seldom able to assimilate these animus-shadow constellations, which embody proscriptions against women's maturation. The green world lover, who embodies a powerful and amarital feminine eroticism, and the anima, often represented in the strong mother or goddess archetype, remain inaccessible. Thus novels in which women go mad or die at the hands of "perfectly nice" husbands outnumber by far novels in which women achieve rebirth and transformation.[13]

In some novels by women authors, the characters do overcome the animus-shadow block and reach a deeper and more holistic sense of the feminine. Examples are Lily Briscoe in Virginia Woolf's *To the Lighthouse,* the narrator in Margaret Atwood's *Surfacing,* and Martha in Doris Lessing's *The Four-Gated City.* Characters who do get past sadistic lovers, horrible husbands, and their own self-hate often do so in a journey of rebirth structured along the line of the archetypal narrative of Demeter and her daughter Kore. In broad outline, Demeter's daughter Persephone is seized by Pluto, god of the underworld, while gathering flowers; he takes her away to his underground kingdom where she is forced to marry him. Grieving deeply, Demeter wanders the earth in search of her daughter until she meets Hecate, who has heard Persephone's cry. In fury, Demeter goes to Olympus to complain to Zeus, who refuses to help her. She then refuses to allow vegetation to grow upon the earth until her daughter shall be restored to her. After various adventures Demeter is finally able to effect the raising of Persephone from the land of the dead, although, as a compromise, she may only spend the spring and summer months with her mother and must return to Pluto for a third of the year. Jung found this narrative so specifically feminine that he felt it held no import for the masculine personality.[14] That Jung was able to recognize an archetypal pattern of primary concern to women shows that he realized that the feminine psyche has characteristics different from those of the masculine pscyhe.

Whereas Jung's male heroes often confront the terrible mother at the nadir of their journey, women characters at the core of their quest often encounter a powerful integrative mother figure who offers regeneration. Like Martha at the end of Lessing's *The Four-Gated City*, the hero herself sometimes becomes such a mother or generative being. And often, as in Esther Broner's *Her Mothers* and Margaret Laurence's *The Diviners*, the daughter questing for a mother achieves transcendence in reconciling herself to her own daughter. The hero of Laurence's novel, Morag, is typical, in that her journey does not lead her back into society but leaves her on its perimeter, writing in an isolated country house about her life's experiences. Woman's incursion into the unconscious is much more tinged with the personal and the social. For Jung's male quester the socially rebellious shadow leads the way to adventure; for the woman hero the shadow in the unconscious *is* society, the marital norms and sexual prohibitions that impede her full development. In the male version the ultimate encounter is with an "other" and takes the form of a struggle with and taking over of the feminine within the male psyche. The woman's encounter with a feminine figure at the depths of her psyche, when it occurs, is more a fusion than an agon; the woman encounters a being similar to herself, which empowers even as it exiles her from the social community. Although women's journey to a core of being where a holistic goddess provides beneficence and strength do not reconcile them to a society dominated by men, the journey itself continues to provide the structure of novels, poems, and dramas.

■   ■   ■   ■

Ever since women writers began to circulate their productions on a wide scale after the European renaissance, they have used mythological archetypes in poems and stories. A task for feminist archetypal critics is to analyze these texts for the interplay of images. Puzzlingly, what we often find is a combination of attitudes toward goddesses in a single text similar to the ambivalence that I noted in women's novels. Again, the patriarchal overlayer of gender prescription seems to come into conflict with an underlayer of women's desire for authenticity as human beings. For example, a sampling of poems about Medusa by male and female poets reveals attitudes ranging from horror (Robert Lowell's "Near the Ocean," Sylvia Plath's "Medusa") to affirmation (May Sarton's "The Muse as Medusa"), with the majority of poems falling between the two poles. From a preliminary study of these poems, however, I have found that although both men and women poets express ambivalence about her—combinations of awe, reverence, and loathing—the poems by women move to an identification with Medusa, while the men, however hypnotized into complicity, remain separate from her, at a distance. We need to explore the psychoanalytic theories about male and female development in relation to the mother in order to comprehend these distinctly different quests; our knowledge of the divergence between the romance quest of Frye's male hero and the development of the woman hero in women's novels should provide us with initial hypotheses.

Although there are thus noticeable distinctions between male and female poets writing on the same archetypal figure, the relationship between reverence for goddesses and fear and loathing of their powers cannot be reduced to simple dualism, with masculine literature viewed as gynophobic and feminine literature as affirmative. The archetypal perspectives are not as gender-rigid as one might believe. Feminine archetypes are depicted according to the respect for authentic feminine being by a particular writer at a particular time in history, and it thus becomes necessary to pay close attention to how both personal and historical elements influence an individual poet's writing.

My research in Canadian literature and in the folklore of native peoples suggests that archetypal descriptions of feminine images, symbols, and narratives can be found not only in women's literature but in western male literature as well as in native American and Canadian works. I am thus moving beyond a study of women's literature in isolation to an exploration of male as well as female writing. Since such an undertaking is unmanageably vast, I have developed a method of focusing on one symbol or archetype at a time. Thus my analysis of poems and other artifacts concerning Medusa, and an exploration of a variety of texts that focus on the archetype of the bear. Since the symbol of the bear appears in a large sample of masculine, feminine, and native texts, I have found it useful and feasible to examine it as a single recurring element. The crucial question left hanging in the air by my analysis of specific texts, on the one hand, and my exploration of prehistoric religious practices, on the other, is the link between (in this instance) Old European bear worship and recent poetry about bears. Am I positing a specific historical link between prehistory and the present? This question cannot be answered without much further study into the transmission of symbols; however, it is an interesting question, which might lead us at least to posit the hypothesis that some link exists, whether in the unconscious or through recurrent instances of the same image producing similar responses, between prehistoric archetypes and modern writers' fascination with them. Since only a limited number of animals—crows, owls, frogs, toads, turtles, snakes, bears, and deer, for example—were associated with Old European religions, these animals could serve as the focus of continued archetypal study.

"Good Lord!" I can hear some skeptical feminist scholars exclaiming. "How can one take the study of recurrent images of snakes and toads seriously in a world where the ERA is in jeopardy, the lust for war rises afresh, and men are devising ever more subtle ways to defeat women at the polls and abhorrent ways to rape us on our streets?" The academic study of archetypes, I propose, empowers women both personally and politically, since the ancient worship of goddesses suggests truths vital for the survival of the human race today. In discussing the contributions that psychoanalytic thought can make to feminism, Jean Elshtain calls for "the articulation of a philosophy of mind that repudiates the old dualism with which we are still saddled in favor of an account that unites mind and body, reason and passion, into a compelling account of human subjectivity and identity, and the creation of a feminist account of human subjectivity and indentity, and the creation of a feminist theory of action that, complicatedly, invokes both inner and outer realities."[15] Elshtain's philosophy of mind is already available to feminist scholars, not only in the figurines and paintings unearthed by our archaeologists and in the habits and customs described by our anthropologists, but in rich archetypal images and themes embedded in our literature.

Archetypes are value-free. Like deeply buried stores of uranium, they can be exploited by whoever gets to them first and has the power to employ them most broadly. In 1982 a television presentation by an articulate and clearly powerful woman advertising researcher illustrated the potential for the amoral and unethical use of archetypes.[16] The researcher made a persuasive case that advertisers should employ feminine archetypes in order to sell products. Her research had proven that a compelling feminine archetype or archetypal story produces a galvanic response on the surface of the target's skin, a change in temperature signifying the impact of the archetype upon the body. She suggested using the archetypes of the willful woman, the hetaira, the mother, and even the rebirth narrative implicit in the family reunion, since her research had proven conclusively that these figures and themes elicit strong galvanic reactions. Her research went beyond her readings in Jung to analyses of data derived from a broad sample of American women. She was spinning among fields for her own profit and that of commercial advertisers. As damaging as the use of such mass-media images can be, the same sorts of archetypes could be employed by propagandists to produce even more harmful social effects inimical to women and to humanity as a whole. In light of such uses, feminist scholars can hardly afford *not* to study archetypes.

Archetypal criticism is neither a solitary nor a short-term task, and spinning among fields turns out to be a not so lightfooted activity. There are unconscious blocks against trespassing. Self-doubt holds one back like the bogs that immobolize one's legs in nightmares; and once one has seized the sought-after fleece, there is always somebody following along after trying to reclaim it or deny its importance. More than these obstacles, however, the problem of time looms largest for feminist scholars. Women themselves and women's experience have been excluded from academe for so many years that we are impatient for results that cannot be garnered as quickly as we want. As Carol Christ writes:

> The discovery and recovery of women's experience will not be accomplished overnight. The alienation of ourselves from our own experience is deep; the resources that can aid our journey of self-discovery are slim. To ask for definitive conclusions prematurely is to misjudge the depth of the problem. We are in a time for ripening. . . . We must discover a mode of thinking about the ultimate which can be modulated by a sense of timing, a mode which will not require the definitive word in a time when soundings are more appropriate.[17]

In universities where young women are overlooked and then pushed out of revolving doors without time to publish, where tenured women are alone on so many committees that they either succumb to or are driven crazy by masculine standards and behaviors, where all of us swing between a false masculine self and authentic feminine being, we keep right on setting deadlines for ourselves that are impossible to meet. Significant scholarly research requires thirty or forty years to complete; we need time to test and discard various hypotheses, and time to sit back and muse. These activities, in turn, require freedom from attack, fewer committee duties, lighter teaching loads, and the opportunity to sit quietly alone in our studies doing the intellectual work so vital to our future. That we have constructed, in the midst of hostile or apathetic academies, viable women's studies programs engaged in a multiplicity of interdisciplinary projects is a tribute to our individual endurance and collective strength.

(1985)

13 C. G. JUNG: A DEBT ACKNOWLEDGED

Kathleen Raine

Kathleen Raine is well known for both her poetry and her scholarship, and recently, as editor of the British journal Temenos. Her numerous works include Blake and Tradition and Blake and the New Age. In an essay written for Harvest, the journal of the London Analytical Psychology Club, Raine speaks with the authority of one whose life spans nearly the entire period of Jung's "transforming presence" upon "the context, the climate, the mental universe in which we live." She cites the manifestations of that presence in her own work and that of the distinguished artists and thinkers she has known. Jung was most important for rediscovering that aspect of the perennial philosophy which she calls "the learning of the imagination," not only as a neglected tradition for scholars to study anew but also as a way of life for all people seeking to better experience and explore life itself. In presenting her case for Jung's reinvigoration of this tradition, Raine gives an account which, both in its restlessly questing energy and its reasoning, is a classic expression of the appeal of Jung to a non-Jungian (Raine declares herself so). Raine exemplifies a type of Jungian literary criticism that is broadly philosophical, like that of James Olney (who dedicated his Yeats and Jung book to her).

It is inevitable that a follower of Blake must be, if not a follower of Jung, at all events a fellow traveler, for both Blake and Jung draw upon, and themselves represent, the mainstream and fulfillment of the Protes-

167

tant tradition of the "Kingdom within." I feel that in my writings I have been ungrateful to Jung and intend to write something in belated acknowledgment of my indebtedness; which is indeed the indebtedness of all poets and artists of the imagination in this century. It was Jung who restored to us in the West the key to the long-closed door of the inner worlds and their symbolic language—the door to our own inner universe, trapped as we were in the prison of prevailing materialist ideologies and a religious iconography located, in Jung's words, "all outside." I have never undergone a Jungian analysis. I would not call myself a "Jungian"—Blake is my Master—but I have read most of Jung's works as these appeared, published by the Bollingen Foundation; and my heart has assented to Jung's thought as to no other great mind of this century. (Here I am not speaking of poetry, of Rilke or of Yeats, and indeed other poets, painters, and musicians, whose worlds have opened great realms of beauty.) Jung was no poet, but he too was a master of the language of symbol, and the image is the language of psyche. Jung taught us to read our dreams as if these were poems; as we should read poetry of the imagination as the discourse of our inner worlds. Jung taught us to listen to the oracle in the heart, that speaks to each his own truth, in symbols we ourselves can read, since we are their creators. Perhaps it is as well that Jung seems to have had little aesthetic appreciation of the arts, and that his relationship therefore to the soul's language of symbols and the exploration of the worlds of imagination is in no way confused with "art" and its value-judgments. His work on the language of image and symbol is radical and unadulterated; he discovered the ground of the "numinous"—the sacred source—in what Yeats calls "the foul rag-and-bone-shop of the heart."

Jung's personality, for all his imaginative greatness, does not particularly attract me—his robust Germanic temperament. Yeats's mental presence, by contrast, is to me almost as myself—his birthday, on June 15th, is the day after my own, in the sign of Gemini, and with Yeats I feel a temperamental sympathy, an affinity. I follow his thought as if it were my own— even his faults and weaknesses are congenial. (I do not of course compare myself in any way with his stature.) But I have been too ambiguous, too cursory in my acknowledgment of my debt to Jung. Perhaps when a whole age is under that same debt we take for granted what, as a personal indebtedness not shared with half the Western world, we might have acknowledged. Jung's very greatness makes us ungrateful, for the enlightenment he has brought into our Western world is indeed for Everyman, not an intellectual elite. Jung, neither poet nor prophet, speaks to our common humanity in the soul's universal forgotten language.

I first heard the name of Jung mentioned in Cambridge days by Humphrey Jennings, who had a way of not following fashion; and while the rest of us were obediently reading Freud as the new gospel, Humphrey spoke of a wonderful book entitled *The Secret of the Golden Flower*. I read Jung's *Psychological Types*, which did not too much challenge Freudian orthodoxy, and which appealed to the young in the same way as does astrology, in our desire to discover who and what we are. Then came *Modern Man in Search of a Soul*. It had not occurred to me that Modern Man *was* in search of a soul, having myself most thankfully put religion behind me at that time, for the freedom from constraints that Freud seemed to offer my generation. But I—and how many more—did secretly rejoice that Jung had perhaps made possible again the inner adventure, yet freed from the trammels of religion: the quest for the Holy Grail, the journeys to that lost holy land which all seek. Thereafter I read all of Jung's works as these appeared, with assent and unfailing delight, as region beyond region of unknown inner worlds opened in each successive volume. I have them all to this day. They were the food I needed, and have remained so even though in my studies I have pursued other themes. My work on Blake, too, was undertaken from a thirst for knowledge of the inner worlds of the imagination which Blake and Jung have in common, and the end of Blake's Golden String I was to follow through many volumes in the North Library was that whole excluded tradition of knowledge of the *mundus imaginalis* known to Jung and Blake alike. It has never been my way to apply to works of another age some theory of the present unknown to their author; and in studying the sources of Blake's knowledge I infinitely extended my own. I sought to understand Blake through those writings he himself knew, and quickly abandoned all thought of giving a "Jungian" interpretation of Blake, as I had at first intended. But in Jung I was to find constant confirmation of the picture of inner reality gradually built up in the course of my Blake studies. Indeed, Blake's reading and Jung's covered much the same ground. Thus I have remained always a fellow traveler with the Jungian school without at any time being committed to it.

No doubt my work on Blake originated in my interest in the similarity of his cosmology to Jung's, but as I followed Blake's sources in the excluded "learning of the Imagination" on which Jung had also drawn—the Western esoteric tradition, Neoplatonism, alchemy, the Gnostic and Hermetic writings, and the rest—I became more concerned with these sources and origins than with modern affinities. In pursuing my Blake and Yeats studies I had no occasion to invoke Jung; as I would have done no doubt had I remained ignorant of these sources and continued to suppose Blake's mythological world to be a pure product of "the unconscious." Yet Jung's thought all along formed a structure that continually supported my work on Blake; as indeed it has inspired and illumined other Blake scholars. Jung has changed the course of thought in my own lifetime in a manner that affects, not intellectuals alone, but the mental universe and climate of the present and the future. He has helped to make Blake himself intelligible.

In retrospect I realize that the shortcoming of my own work on Blake—the tracing of his many sources within that excluded tradition which I have called "the learning of the Imagination"—was that which is inherent in all modern scholarship: I did not experience and explore that world imaginatively, as Blake did, and as did Jung, but in terms of academic "history of ideas" and "sources" and "influences"; in exploring the writings of Jakob Boehme, the Neoplatonists, alchemists, and the rest, I didn't myself enter those regions of the imagination as these were inhabited and explored by the cabbalists, mystics, and visionaries themselves. True, I wrote of these with the assumption that their view of reality was the truth itself, not an old cosmology superseded by modern science. These were regions of knowledge likely to be rediscovered with the change of premises now taking place in the West, belatedly and uneasily awakening from three centuries of domination by materialist ideologies. I was even impassioned in my advocacy of that universe of thought opening before me with every volume I studied in those happy days in the North Library, but I made little effort to live my thought. Certainly I made interesting and useful discoveries of some of Blake's sources—mainly Neoplatonic—and insofar as I did so, uncovered affinities with regions of experience—I will not say "schools of thought," for the affinities are of a deeper and a different kind from what is comprised under the term "history of ideas"—neglected by academic orthodoxy. These regions, in terms of scholarship, need never be experienced or entered into any more than anatomists enter into the lives and modes of consciousness of dead animals on a dissecting-table. But Porphyry, that "thaumaturgist," whose *de antro nympharum* is the theme of Blake's Arlington Court tempera-painting, and indeed Plotinus himself, were describing realities of the soul's realm, Blake's "eternal worlds" of the inner universe, long neglected and uninhabited, not to say denied, in the modern West, where "reality" has for so long been equated with external measurable phenomena of "nature," conceived—misconceived—as an autonomous mechanism. These things had long, at best, been studied as "history"

and "history of ideas." But there again, much as I then strove to understand this long-neglected domain of thought, and afterward—concur-
rently rather—to make known its regions in my writings, my labors have
already been overtaken by the "new age." Locke and Descartes and the
Newtonian universe are themselves now old lumber in the storehouse of
"the history of ideas." In my studies I, no less—or only a little less—than
others, was hampered by the habit of mind that equates book-learning
with knowledge. Blake made no such mistake, but inhabited his own
inner regions; and so did Yeats in his magical and other esoteric studies.
In such inner explorations I was only intermittently and superficially engaged. But Jung understood "knowledge"—as did Boehme and Blake
and all mystics, cabbalists, Gnostics, holy men, and indeed true poets and
musicians, and all who enter into the realms of the imagination—as the
thing itself and not book-learning about those living regions. Jung placed
in our hands the key that leads into Blake's "bosom of God, the Human
Imagination." But many still continue to read books and to write them
about these realities rather than confronting them and themselves ven-
turing into those inner regions that Jung, like Blake, invites us to explore.
My own work on "sources" and affinities, whatever its value to students,
was no more than a signpost to those seeking that reality itself.

■　■　■　■

. . . Jung has been the prophetic voice of our time, illuminating a
way forward into the discovery within ourselves of those regions to
which all religions and their iconographies are but guides on the way.
He had a redemptive message to communicate to his world. His influence is irreversible; the ideas he has liberated into the Western world
are living ideas. If "God" is a word Jung hesitated to use with the facil-
ity of professional theologians, it is because his concern was with unnameable realities of life itself, and his reticence has been offensive
only to those who are (in A. N. Whitehead's words) given to paying
God "metaphysical compliments." Jung, who believed in "thinking his
thoughts to the end" was, with Blake, with Jacob Boehme, aware of the
dark side of "God." But in his now famous television interview with the
journalist John Freeman, when asked, "Dr. Jung, do you now believe
in God?" he replied that he found the question difficult to answer and
added, "I *know*. I don't need to believe. I know." These words seem to
me as central to the consciousness of our age as were Descartes's *cogito
ergo sum* to his rational century. "Beliefs" are more or less consciously
adopted postulates to which we assent; modern man in search of a soul

is not in search of "beliefs" but of spiritual realities, insights, epiphanies. It is the destiny of our New Age to reenter and repossess the inner worlds. Blake also announced a "new age" (following Swedenborg) and his task likewise was

> To open the Eternal Worlds, to open the immortal Eyes
> Of Man inwards into the Worlds of Thought, into Eternity
> Ever expanding in the Bosom of God, the Human Imagination.

Jung's traditionalist critics have failed to recognize the magnitude of his contribution to the reversal of the age of secular materialism, not by a return to some "revealed" tradition, however venerable, but by a return to the source of all revelations and prophecies.

∎ ∎ ∎ ∎

. . . "It is strange that God should speak to man formerly and not now, because it is not true," Blake, in true Protestant spirit, commented on the opinion of a bishop who held that view, and on no better authority than his own experience; and yet what my orthodox Christian and Muslim friends constantly insist is that "revelation" belongs only to the founders of great religious traditions, as Christians insist that only Jesus Christ was the Son of God. There too Blake had his answer; asked what was his opinion concerning Jesus Christ, he replied, "He was the Son of God." But then he added, "and so am I, and so are you." Jung would have agreed. Indeed, he saw the spiritual task of this time as "individuation"—the transition from religious collectivities to the discovery by each individual of that inner universe to which each is heir. The unit of humanity is the individual, each "sole heir" (as Traherne long ago understood) of the world, indivisibly; we do not enjoy a portion of sun, moon, and stars, of daisies and apples and trees and birds—to each of us all is given. So with our inner worlds. Those churches full of statues and icons cannot speak to us with that immediacy of dream or vision, or indeed of sun or moon or tree or bird. Does not religious conformity mask a deep inner insecurity—not to say fear—the need to cling to external props, anything rather than confront the Presence itself, which is with all, everywhere and always, inescapably?

Not, indeed, that Jung is dismissive of religions—on the contrary. In the light of Jung's guidance, the symbols of religion themselves take on meaning as realities of our inner worlds, long lost by a Church that has insisted on the Christian mysteries as natural and historical fact; which in the domain of meaning, of the sacred, of the soul's country, is neither here nor there.

Not only has Jung enabled us to discover the symbolic values and meanings of our own dreams; no less has he restored meanings to all that we encounter in the natural world, to sun and moon, the elements, the creatures. These are the long-forgotten language of nature itself, a language older than words, innate, universal, understood by all. A material science has denied all meaning to the natural world save of quantity. Yet the language of correspondences of whatever is in nature to qualities and values of the soul's universe is age-old, as old as the universe itself, which speaks to us in that language it has itself taught us, as children of the cosmos. To a civilization dominated by abstract thought, Jung restored the language of image, symbol, correspondences, and signatures. Not through books and the accumulated transmitted knowledge of mankind but in our dreams and visions, and from the world ever before our eyes, come revelations, continually. A living universe has replaced, for those with eyes to see, that mechanism under whose compulsion Western mankind has suffered too long. A few mystics and saints may have escaped or eluded that tyranny, but the intellect of the West long has been its victim; and a view of the universe as a mindless mechanism has created the climate, the light in which our civilization as a whole has received its everyday experience. Jung has been the liberator from countless implicit assumptions and has restored life and meaning to the phenomena of the natural world.

The regions of psyche, with its images, symbols, living metaphors, are of course the same world whence the arts of all times and places have originated. Blake understood that the arts are not the adornments of religious truths but are themselves visions of those truths, immediate and from the source. "The Religions of all Nations are derived from each Nation's different reception of the Poetic Genius which is everywhere call'd the Spirit of Prophecy." In the same way we might say that Jung's reading of dreams is in no way different from an imaginative poet's disposal of poetic images. One may read a poem—*Kubla Khan* or *The Rime of the Ancient Mariner,* and not these alone—as if it were a dream, a dream as if it were a poem—imaginative poetry, that is. Of course there are other categories, and even these, as Blake himself allowed, "seldom without some vision," for imaginative vision is the essence of poetry—vision, that is, of the realities of the imagination, whether received from within the mind or from the world of apparently external nature. To the materialist, forms belong only to the external world, from which the internal world derives all its terms. To those for whom spirit and soul are realities, the opposite is true.

It was Jung's genius that discerned in the psyche an ordered realm in which archetypal forms inhere—the Tree of Life, Eden and the Four Rivers of Paradise, the serpent and the androgyne, Temple and Holy City, and all the gods and celestial hierarchies are of that inner world. Blake, too, had written of the error of supposing that "before the creation all was Solitude and Chaos." "Eternity Exists and All things in Eternity," which is, for Blake as for Jung, the inner universe of the human psyche. "There Exist, in that Eternal World, the Permanent Realities of Every Thing which we see reflected in this Vegetable Glass of Nature. All Things are comprehended in their Eternal Forms in the divine body of the Saviour, the True Vine of Eternity, the Human Imagination." The reality of that world will pass a "last Judgment" on all temporal things, seemingly so solid yet in reality impermanent and insubstantial. Whatever order we discover in the outer world in reality belongs to the inner, Soul (as Plotinus had long ago understood) beholding itself in the "vegetable glass of nature." What lies beyond psyche's world is in its nature unknowable otherwise than as it is reflected in that interworld.

What Jung has changed is the context, the climate, the mental universe in which we live. We have entered another domain, long lost to the West, confined as it has been within the dimensions of a materialist science. This being so, one might find it surprising that hitherto Jung's reopening of the inner worlds—Blake's for that matter—has not resulted in a great flowering of the arts. Edwin Muir is the most notable poet to have explored his dreams and fantasies and to have used them as the basis of many of his poems. Taking a small seminar of students of analytical psychology last year, I found the symbolic images of Muir's poems immediately and directly comprehensible in terms of Jung's thought. Not the images alone, but that ambience, atmosphere of feeling, which pervades Muir's poems is, like that of dreams, inexplicable in terms of our experience of the outer world but familiar to all dreamers of those intensities of the "savage and beautiful country," whose images are inseparable from their content of meaning. In childhood indeed it was so also with the world of nature—birds and beasts and flowers and rivers, mountains and seas, all these once conveyed their powerful meanings to us, we read the language of nature as Jung has taught us to read the language of dreams. "Nature-poetry" then was not what some meticulous observer of detailed appearances writes about fish or fowl, but what these living presences communicated to us. Gaston Bachelard's books on the four Elements have in great measure recaptured this experience— his thought also surely moving within the new context created by Jung.

Jung's friend Laurens van der Post has written of the world of the African Bushmen, the immediacy of their experience of stars and insects, flowers and animals, in all their living qualities of life itself, not observation of experiences but living empathy with their "natures" in quite another sense. Far from creating confusion by returning to these nameless forms, so remote from the prescribed symbols of Christian (or any other) orthodox iconography, these images emerge with all the freshness of the newly created reality itself. . . .

. . . At present it seems that the followers of Jung—and indeed the New Age in its whole rediscovery of the soul's country—are concerned not so much with "art" as an end in itself as with art or poetry as a means and aid to the exploration of the inner worlds. Is there not a reaction from a civilization that places too high a value on the object—the "work of art"—to a rediscovery of life itself as the supreme art, and works of art as, at best, aids on the way of the soul's quest? I find more meaning in the dreams and visions recounted to me by my friends—many of whom are neither poets nor painters—than in most current so-called poetry and painting. Will some great storyteller or maker of myths, some poet or painter, arise from this change in our inner ground? Anything is possible, and the new is never foreseen. But in truth I doubt it, for what, after all, are poems and paintings but the records of that world, traveler's tales, and when we ourselves are the travelers, the explorers, we have less need of them; and it is to this exploration that Jung has summoned. May not the future prove to be a time in which young people will no longer work on canvases or paper but, as in our own middle ages, on their own lives? May not "being" rather than "doing" once more engage a society weary of technology's worthless satisfactions, so unable to meet the soul's desire for invisible, intangible values and joys and visions and meanings? May faces once more become beautiful and illuminated from dreams? It may well be so and would be no cause for despair if "the arts" have no immediate future of any remarkable achievement. In that context, drawing or writing could become rather a means to an end, and the materialist idolatry of "works of art," exaggerated and falsified by commercial interests, lose its hold.

■　■　■　■

. . . None knows what a dream "means" better than the dreamer, that meaning being the experience itself. Jung it was who sent us in search of sacred meaning in such experiences. He has changed the context, the climate, the light in which we are now able to receive and to use such epiphanies of the "eternal worlds." Or to receive them at all, and not, as my parents' generation would have done, either dismiss them altogether or (like my mother, who was a great dreamer) been unable to make use of them in the better understanding of the living of a life. I see in Jung the term—the flower—of the Protestant tradition of the Inner Light, the opening of what my old friend the mystic Gay Taylor was shown as "a church in the hearts of men." (Her visionary dreams, unlike mine but like some Rosamund Lehmann has described in her *Swan in the Evening*, often took Christian form.) I find it most wonderful, and infinitely liberating to those of us irked by the prescribed iconography of church and creed, to have been shown by Jung that the forms assumed by the Holy Spirit are for each of us that which is for us, individually, most appropriate; whether in some familiar traditional guise or mysteriously as a figure nameless yet recognizable always.

What I have written about Jung is solely in terms of my own experience of his great presence in my world—this is in no sense a critical evaluation of even a small aspect of his work, which I am not qualified to make. But there must be few indeed whose concern is with the thought and the arts of this time who are not aware of his presence as a transforming influence; and this is so above all—contrary to all that the Guénonists level against him—in the sphere of religion itself, and the restoration of meanings and values of symbols that had lost their power to speak to the imagination. Edwin Muir, who had undergone Jungian analysis, never abandoned Christian symbolism and tells in his *Autobiography* how at a certain moment he "found that he was a Christian," doubtless in part thanks to Jung's transformation of the way in which we now are able to perceive the nature of the symbolic world, not excluding the "mysteries" of Christianity. I have to thank Jung for enabling me to make the opposite discovery—that I am not a Christian at heart or by nature—although like Blake I would make a distinction between "the religion of Jesus"— the universal and eternal "everlasting gospel"—and the teaching of Church and churches. The transforming influence on Western civilization of Christendom has been wonderful indeed, and the flowering of the arts that accompanied the Christian vision testifies to the reality of the vision itself. But being myself now in my eightieth year, neither "art" nor "religion" any longer concerns me as ends in themselves but, like the images of dreams, I see them as traces of the passage of the sacred reality itself—of "Thought's eternal flight."
(1988)

JUNG AND CRITICAL THEORY

Part II

A. "MYTH" AND "ARCHETYPE": CRITICS AND ANALYSTS

These selections present descriptions and definitions of a few crucial interrelated terms that remain central to the interdisciplinary field of Jungian critical theory (see also Drew, Baird, and Jacoby, in Part 1). There are essays by both literary critics and analytical psychologists. When viewed together as attempts to formulate a consensual understanding of the terms for each discipline, these selections suggest the range of possible meanings of "archetype" and "myth" in the interdisciplinary discourse. Obviously, the very different tasks of analysts and literary critics govern their sense of the terms' meanings, their realization of the necessity and value of fixed meanings, and finally, the strength of their desire to avoid imprecision in their use of the terms. Since the passing of the New Criticism, literary critics have become more comfortable using "working definitions"; analysts, at least Jungians, have always been more interested in the heuristic value of the concept of archetypes for their daily psychotherapeutic work with patients. Today there clearly is increasing interdisciplinary commerce between critical theory and analytical psychology. The new imaginal archetypal psychology (Section B of Part II) is only the most recent example.

14 ARCHETYPE AND ARCHETYPAL IMAGE

Renaldo J. Maduro and Joseph B. Wheelwright

These two Jungian analysts, affiliated with both the University of California (Berkeley) Medical School and the C. G. Jung Institute of San Francisco, composed this authoritative statement to be presented in a standard psychology text. It offers the psychologists' definition of the archetype, along with descriptions of three archetypal symbols frequently encountered in personal analysis as well as in myth and literature: symbolic death and renewal, the child, and anima-animus.

ARCHETYPES FUNCTION AS ORGANS OF THE COLLECTIVE UNCONSCIOUS PSYCHE

Jung initially used a variety of words, such as *primordial image,* to describe an early and relatively undifferentiated formulation of the archetypal dimension of the psyche, but the word *archetype* appeared in 1919 for the first time. For the remainder of his life, the major focus of his theoretical work and clinical practice was devoted to the serious exploration and elucidation of the role of the collective unconscious, or what he later came to call the *objective psyche* in human development.

From the very beginning Jung widened and deepened Freud's position, which he did not so much dispute, reject, or supplant as go beyond. Jung felt his colleague's views were correct but not comprehensive enough to describe adequately the complicated workings of the mind. He could not accept Freud's exclusive emphasis on sexuality and personal psychobiological determinism.

In the light of Jung's balanced approach to the psyche, a relevant remark made by the anthropologist Clyde Kluckhohn is paraphrased here: *Every man is in certain respects like all other men, like some other men, like no other man.* This statement is particularly helpful in putting Jungian psychology and the concept of the archetype into proper perspective. Although Jung never denied the importance of culture and strictly personal life history variables in the development of an individual, he contributed most richly to psychoanalysis by addressing himself to the psyche's phylogenetic heritage and to the psychic unity of mankind. It was Jung's holistic contention that the psyche and the unconscious cannot be understood without a consideration of the interpenetration of sociocultural, personal, and archetypal (transpersonal) forces. With Jung's approach in mind, Kettner refers to Kluckhohn and puts it well: "That, in a nutshell, is how an archetype works—a basic theme, recognizable patterns of variation, and the unique individual twist taken in a specific case."[1]

Having touched briefly on how, when, and why Jung discovered the importance of the transpersonal psyche, we shall now turn more specifically to questions related to what an archetype is, and when it functions as it does.

Jungian theory holds that the mind is not a tabula rasa at birth but that there is an archetypal ground plan built into the structure of the human brain. It would take us too far afield here to discuss modern biology in relation to the theory of archetypes. Such a focus would have to include research on the limbic system and on right-left hemispheres of the brain, modern behavioral genetics, and how natural selection and the mutation of germ plasm are viewed by modern scientists.[2] These studies would clearly indicate, moreover, that there need be nothing "mystical" about archetypes, which are inherited predispositions to apperceive typical or nearly universal *situations and figures.* The archetype can further be described as a "system of readiness" that responds to environmental cues, a dynamic nucleus of concentrated psychic energy ready to be actualized, as an affect-image and as an *autonomous,* numinous structural element outside the comprehension of the ego. Fordham sheds further light on the problem of defining archetypes.

> Though most studied in their complex symbolic forms, i.e., in dreams, fantasies, mythology, folklore and religion, the essential core that emerges from Jung's work is that an archetype is a psycho-

somatic entity having two aspects: the one is linked closely with physical organs, the other with unconscious and potential psychic structures. The physical component is the source of libidinal and aggressive "drives"; the psychic one, the origin of those fantasy forms through which the archetype reaches incomplete representation in consciousness.[3]

Although at first Jung considered mainly archetypal images, he later considered patterns of emotions and predispositions to species-specific behavior as well. Jung's concept of the archetype, as developed and refined,[4] provides for two essential distinctions: (1) *the archetype as such,* and (2) *the archetypal image.* It is important to keep these two distinctions in mind, since Jung's contributions have been greatly misunderstood and misrepresented by confusing these theoretical issues. Misinformed opinion would have it, for example, that actual ideational content is inherited. Although Jung never ruled out such a possibility, he could never accept Freud's strictly Lamarckian concept of a "racial memory."

The Archetype as Such. Archetypes are not inherited ideas or images but are a priori possibilities.

For Jung the "primordial image" or "archetype as such" belonging to the deepest unconscious is an a priori, phylogenetically transmitted predisposition or "readiness" to apperceive a universal, emotional core human experience, myth, or thought-image-fantasy. This "archetype as such" can never be exactly pinpointed or apprehended because it exists in such a primitive formal state. Jung summarizes his views:

> The archetypal representations (images and ideas) mediated to us by the unconscious should not be confused with the archetype as such. They are very varied structures which all point back to one essentially "irrepresentable" basic form. The latter is characterized by certain formal elements and by certain fundamental meanings, although these can be grasped only approximately. The archetype as such is a psychoid factor that belongs, as it were, to the invisible, ultra-violet end of the psychic spectrum. . . . It seems to me probable that the real nature of the archetype is not capable of being made conscious, that it is transcendent, on which account I call it psychoid (quasi-psychic). (*CW,* 8:213)

The Archetypal Image. There is a dynamic relationship between environmental situations and archetypal response. Unlike the archetype as such, the image is a representation already perceived by at least a portion of ego-consciousness: "A primordial image is determined as to its contents only when it becomes conscious and is therefore filled out with the material of conscious experience" (*CW,* vol. 9, pt. 1, p. 79).

Jung's theory stresses the role of culture in activating and symbolically structuring ("clothing") archetypal activity arising from the deep conscious. It follows that the same environmental experience may evoke different archetypal responses and that various environmental factors may evoke the same or similar archetypal responses. To turn again to Jung: "There are as many archetypes as there are typical situations in life. Endless repetition has engraved these experiences into our psychic constitution, not in the forms of images filled with content, but at first only as *forms without content,* representing merely the possibility of a certain type of perception and action" (*CW,* vol. 9, pt. 1, p. 48).

The passage above indicates that Jung considers the archetypes to be innumerable. Yet certain archetypal images, situations, and experiences are more commonly encountered than others during a personal analysis, in the course of individual human development, or in everyday life. They are found in dreams, literature, religious mythologies, art forms, symptoms, and so on. Several examples are presented below.

Symbolic Death and Renewal. A common archetypal situation experienced cross-culturally relates to Jung's emphasis on potentiality in the human psyche for symbolic transformation involving reconstitutive experiences of death and rebirth, and on his extremely positive evaluation of therapeutic regression. For Jung it is clearly the birth of the ego, or part of the ego, which renews the sense of self (feeling centered and whole). Ego-consciousness is reborn, experiences growth, is expanded; it emerges dynamically from a state of projective identification or fusion with a primordial state of unconsciousness (non-ego). This healthy process in later life repeats the earliest separation of the ego from identification and containment in the primary self. The ego feels threatened by death and experiences (perceives) rebirth.[5]

The concept of symbolic death and rebirth, as an archetypal/transpersonal motif, came to characterize Jung's overall theoretical approach to man's unconscious psychological growth during analysis,[6] as well as patterns of initiation or rites de passage.[7] While there are no specific *contents* common to the death-rebirth motif in all cultures, the mythological *form* may be seen as an important archetypal given.

The Child. The symbol of an infant or child is an example of a common archetypal *figure.* It can foreshadow or accompany forward movement and progression through creative regression leading to symbolic death and renewal in the psyche.[8]

The meaning of the child symbol is highly overdetermined. In addition to all the personal (e.g., a sibling) and biological (e.g., child-penis-breast) associations, the archetypal dimension can at times assume great importance. The appearance of a child in dreams may signify a turning point in one's life or analysis; it may also indicate a good prognosis. The image of the "divine child" is found in many cultures and can stand for new life and direction, the free playful child in oneself, new awakenings, new beginnings, new symbolic identities, futurity, creativity, potential, and growth (the good internalized breast or fecundating phallus). The child image may stand for the self, the process of individuation or self-actualization, and symbolic rebirth. The child may also be infernal, monstrous, and sadistic.

Children in fantasy life may stand for potentiality and creativity, because they are always on their way to developing into something else. Babies stand for wholly new ideas born out of the unconscious and therefore not yet known, as against the mere juggling of old ideas into forming what appear to be new ones. But original ideas are growths, not constructions. They gestate and, when ready, are born, and this is the difference between creativity and imitation.

It is easy to see that this particular archetypal figure, when analyzed, takes on an added future-oriented significance. Narrow causal-reductive (personal) explanations alone cannot account for its full symbolic meaning. Jungian theory posits the appearance of this particular symbol (the child) at different phases of human development and asserts that it is more a question of symbolic transformation requiring teleological explanation than one of simple causalities. The true symbol, according to Jung, looks not only backward in time but also forward. It may accompany positive or negative transformations.

Anima-Animus. Two part-personalities frequently encountered in dreams, visions, literature, male-female interaction, analytical treatment, and myth are the contrasexual archetypes of the anima and animus: the inherited potential carried by a man to experience the image of woman (his anima) and, in a woman, the experience of man (her animus).

The unconscious of a man contains a complementary feminine component which takes the image of a woman: "An inherited collective image of woman exists in a man's unconscious, with the help of which he apprehends the nature of woman" (*CW*, 7:190). When a man has repressed his feminine nature, undervalued feminine qualities with contempt and neglect, or conversely has identified with his anima image, he is cut off from his own creativity and wholeness. The anima performs a mediating role to the creative unconscious and can stand for the whole unconscious in general (*CW*, vol. 9, pt. 1, pp. 54–74).

The anima is expressed in projection upon women and in creative process involving fantasies. With regard to the anima and the mother who first carries this projection for a man, Frieda Fordham writes:

> The image only becomes conscious and tangible through the actual contacts with woman that a man makes during the course of his life. The first and most important experience of a woman comes to him through his mother, and is most powerful in shaping and influencing him: there are men who never succeed in freeing themselves from her fascinating power. But the child's experience has a marked subjective character and it is not only how the mother behaves, but how he *feels* she behaves that is significant. The image of his mother that occurs in each child is not an accurate picture of her, but is formed and colored by the innate capacity to produce an image of woman—the anima.[9]

Likewise, the personal father first embodies the animus image for a girl.

Thus, in addition to parental figures who first activate and symbolically structure the contrasexual images in culturally patterned ways, anima and animus are derived from the inherited collective images of man and woman, as well as the latent masculine and feminine principles found in all individuals who are, according to psychoanalytic theories, assumed to be fundamentally bisexual.

(1977)

15 ARCHETYPE, MYTH, NUMINOSUM

Andrew Samuels, Bani Shorter,
and Fred Plaut

The 1986 Critical Dictionary of Jungian Analysis *composed by these analysts from London is a valuable resource for the Jungian literary critic. Here are the book's description/definitions of three related terms, one of them including a brief account of the concept of the archetype during the historical development Jungian psychology.*

archetype The inherited part of the psyche; structuring patterns of psychological performance linked to instinct; a hypothetical entity irrepresentable in itself and evident only through its manifestations.

Jung's theory of the archetypes developed in three stages. In 1912 he wrote of primordial images, which he recognized in the unconscious life of his patients as well as by way of his own self-analysis. These images were similar to motifs repeated everywhere and throughout history, but their main features were their numinosity, unconsciousness, and autonomy (see NUMINOSUM). As conceived by Jung, the collective unconscious promotes such images. By 1917, he was writing of nonpersonal dominants or nodal points in the psyche that attract energy and influence a person's functioning. It was in 1919 that he first made use of the term *archetype,* and he did so to avoid any suggestion that it was the content and not the unconscious and irrepresentable outline or pattern that was fundamental. References are made to the archetype per se to be clearly distinguished from an archetypal image realizable (or realized) by man.

The archetype is a psychosomatic concept, linking body and psyche, instinct and image. This was important for Jung, since he did not regard psychology and imagery as correlates or reflections of biological drives. His assertion that images evoke the aim of the instincts implies that they deserve equal place.

Archetypes are recognizable in outer behaviors, especially those that cluster around the basic and universal experiences of life such as birth, marriage, motherhood, death, and separation. They also adhere to the structure of the human psyche itself and are observable in relation to inner or psychic life, revealing themselves by way of such inner figures as anima, shadow, persona, and so forth. Theoretically, there could be any number of archetypes.

Archetypal patterns wait to be realized in the personality, are capable of infinite variation, are dependent upon individual expression, and exercise a fascination reinforced by traditional or cultural expectation; and, so, carry a strong, potentially overpowering charge of energy which it is difficult to resist (someone's ability to do so being dependent upon his stage of development and state of consciousness). Archetypes arouse affect, blind one to realities, and take possession of will. To live archetypally is to live without limitations (inflation). To give archetypal expression to something, however, may be to interact consciously with the collective, historic image in such a way as to allow opportunities for the play of intrinsic polarities: past and present, personal and collective, typical and unique.

All psychic imagery partakes of the archetypal to some extent. That is why dreams and many other psychic phenomena have numinosity. Archetypal behaviors are most evident at times of crisis, when the ego is most vulnerable. Archetypal qualities are found in symbols, and this accounts in part for their fascination, utility, and recurrence. Gods are metaphors of archetypal behaviors, and myths are archetypal enactments. The archetypes can neither be fully integrated nor lived out in human form. Analysis involves a growing awareness of the archetypal dimensions of a person's life.

Jung's concept of the archetype is in the tradition of Platonic Ideas that are present in the minds of the gods and serve as the models of all entities in the human realm. Kant's a priori categories of perception and Schopenhauer's prototypes are also antecedents.

In 1934 Jung wrote:

The ground principles, the *archetypoi*, of the unconscious are indescribable because of their wealth of reference, although in themselves recognisable. The discriminating intellect naturally keeps on trying to establish their singleness of meaning and thus misses the essential point; for what we can above all establish as the one thing consistent with their nature is their *manifold meaning*, their almost limitless wealth of reference, which makes any unilateral formulation impossible. (*CW*, vol. 9, pt. 1, para. 80)

Ellenberger identified the archetype as one of the three main conceptual differences between Jung and Freud in defining the content and behavior of the unconscious. Following Jung, Neumann saw the archetypes recurring in each generation but also acquiring a history of forms based upon a widening of human consciousness. Hillman, founder of the school of archetypal psychology, cites the concept of archetype as the most fundamental in Jung's work, referring to these deepest premises of psychic functioning as delineating how we perceive and relate to the world. Williams argued that, since the archetypal structure remains skeletal without personal experience to flesh it out, the distinction between personal and collective dimensions of experience or categories of the unconscious might be somewhat academic.[1]

Notions of innate psychological structure exist in present-day psychoanalysis, notably in the Kleinian school: Isaacs (unconscious fantasy), Bion (preconception), and Money-Kyrle. Jung's theory of the archetypes may also be compared to structuralist thought (Samuels, 1985a).[2]

With increasing use of the term, we meet frequent references to such phenomena as "a necessary shift in the paternal archetype" or "the shifting archetype of femininity." The word was included in the Fontana *Dictionary of Modern Thought* in 1977. The biologist Sheldrake finds relevance between Jung's formulation and his theory of "morphogenetic fields."[3]

myth Jung's investigations of the contents of dreams as well as the hallucinations of his psychotic patients led him to the conclusion that there were innumerable psychic interconnections for which, he said, he could find parallels only in mythology. Ruling out previous associations on the part of his patients or any kind of "forgotten knowledge" of such connections, he felt that he was presented with elements separate from any conscious influences. Consequently, he reached the conclusion that the preconditions for myth-formation must be present within the structure of

the psyche itself. He hypothesized the existence of a collective unconscious or reservoir of archetypal structures, experiences, and themes.

Myths are stories of archetypal encounters. As the fairy tale is analogous to the workings of the personal complex, so the myth is a metaphor
for workings of the archetype per se. Like his ancestors, Jung concluded,
modern man is a mythmaker; he reenacts age-old dramas based upon
archetypal themes and, through his capacity for consciousness, can release himself from their compulsive hold.

In a sequence of myths, the earliest of the gods and goddesses are
representative of a basic design that unfolds or is differentiated in the
stories of their descendants. Mythic tales illustrate what happens when
an archetype has free rein and there is no conscious intervention on the
part of man. By contrast, individuality consists of confrontation and dialogue with such fateful powers in recognition of their primal force but
without submission to it.

Modern psychology, Jung concluded, must treat the products of
unconscious fantasy, including mythological motifs, as statements of
the psyche about itself. We do not invent myths; we experience them.
"Myths are original revelations of the pre-conscious psyche, involuntary statements about psychic happenings" (*CW*, vol. 9, pt. 1, para.
261). For example, Jung wrote that they did not *represent*, but rather
were the psychic life of primitives. When such motifs crop up during an
analysis, they convey a vital meaning. The analyst should not assume
that they simply correspond to certain collective elements but be aware
that, for better or worse, these elements are reactivated in the soul of a
present-day person.

Not only does the behavior of the unconscious resemble the workings of myth, but we ourselves participate in "living and lived myth."
Pathology is mirrored in myth, while consciousness has the opportunity
to extend or enhance mythic themes. Hence, Jung's view of mythology is
in direct contrast to that held by Freud and has a bearing upon regression. Regression, which always involves archetypal behavior, can be seen
not only as an attempt to avoid reality, but also as a search for new mythologems with which to reconstruct reality. Again, Jung felt that analysts
misuse mythological motifs if they attach them only as labels for certain
patterns of psychic behavior rather than seeing them as symbols dynamically activating and enabling the discovery of new possibilities.

There is also danger in taking myth literally. Myth is analogous to
certain aspects of personal experience, but it cannot be seen as a substitute without consequent inflation. It provides a metaphorical perspective

but is not an explication or a portent to be fulfilled. It is a nonpersonal image that provides psychic space for individual expression.

numinosum In 1937 Jung wrote of the *numinosum* as "a dynamic agency or effect not caused by an arbitrary act of will. On the contrary, it seizes and controls the human subject, who is always rather its victim than its creator. The *numinosum*—whatever its cause may be—is an experience of the subject independent of his will. . . . The *numinosum* is either a quality belonging to a visible object or the influence of an invisible presence that causes a peculiar alteration of consciousness" (*CW*, 11, para. 6). It defies explanation but seems to convey an individual message which, though mysterious and enigmatic, is also deeply impressive.

Jung felt that belief, conscious or unconscious—that is, a prior readiness to trust a transcendent power—was a prerequisite for experiencing the *numinosum*. The numinous cannot be conquered; one can only open oneself to it. But an experience of the *numinosum* is more than an experience of a tremendous and compelling force; it is a confrontation with a force that implies a not yet disclosed, attractive, and fateful meaning.

This definition was consistent with that given by Otto in *The Idea of the Holy*[4] and Jung saw an encounter with the *numinosum* as an attribute of all religious experience. Numinosity is an aspect of a supraordinate god-image, whether personal or collective. Investigations of religious experiences convinced him that, at such times, previously unconscious contents break through the constraints of the ego and overwhelm the conscious personality in the same way as do invasions of the unconscious in pathological situations. However, an experience of the *numinosum* is not habitually psychopathological. Presented with reports of individual encounters with the "god-like," Jung maintained that he did not necessarily find proof of the existence of God; yet, in all instance, the experiences were of such profundity that mere descriptions could not convey their effects.

Contemporary humanistic psychology speaks of such impressive happenings as "peak experiences."
(1986)

16 CULTURE AND THE HUMANITIES: THE ARCHETYPAL APPROACH

Evelyn J. Hinz and John J. Teunissen

In this essay the literary critics Hinz and Teunissen distinguish their view of the archetype, especially in its relationship to myth and history, from the rather different definitions of archetype posited by the structuralist or comparativist critic. Further, they discuss how an archetype both is and is not connected to history. They know well that in defining myth and the archetype they are also suggesting its usefulness for literary criticism, and so they carefully situate their definition within a tradition of critical rather than psychological practice. However, the belief that archetypes originate in the psyche's collective unconscious— not the artist's imagination or the work of art itself—is of the essence in their definition of archetypal criticism. And their commitment to the psychological basis of the archetype is further evidenced in their argument for a creative response to archetypal art by the archetypal critic. Interestingly, Hinz won the PMLA award for best article in 1976 for her essay "Hierogamy versus Wedlock: Types of Marriage Plots," a subject addressed also in the following selection. Further understanding of these critics' archetypal approach is provided by their essay on D. H. Lawrence in Part 1, written eleven years after this piece.

In the appendix to *Till We Have Faces*, after deliberately acquainting his reader with the story of Cupid and Psyche as it appears in *The Golden Ass*, and also after drawing his reader's attention to the fact that *The Golden Ass* contains the first known telling of the story, C. S. Lewis then goes on to make what at first glance might seem to be an utterly outrageous or facetious claim: namely, that his version of the story of Cupid and Psyche in *Till We Have Faces* is truer and consequently closer to the spirit of the myth than that provided by Apuleius. Far from being an irresponsible denial of his indebtedness to his source, however, and even less an attempt to precipitate a search for the ur-mythos, Lewis's claim is a serious enunciation of what is the controlling premise of archetypal criticism, a premise from which, accordingly, stem all the radical differences between such criticism and those of the more traditional kinds but also between archetypal criticism as the authors have come to understand it and much other criticism that currently goes by the title.

The basis for Lewis's claim that his version of the Cupid and Psyche myth is truer than that of Apuleius is to be found, first of all, in an interdisciplinary understanding of the nature of archetypes, just as it is in this matter of definition itself and what it implies that certain of the major differences initially begin to manifest themselves. In contrast to critics like Eliot and Frye, for whom the archetype is relatively synonymous with the literary prototype or recurring pattern, and equally in contrast to those who take their definition wholly and singly from the work of such nonliterary theorists as Mircea Eliade, Jung, or Erich Neumann, our own definition derives from a syntheses of what these and a great many others—Plato, G. E. Lessing, the later Walter Otto, Rudolf Otto, Schopenhauer, Wagner, Nietzsche, Maritain, the later Otto Rank, the later N. O. Brown, the later Joseph Campbell, and Jean Seznec (to name a few at random and in no particular order)—have written, and it takes into consideration what has already been said on the subject by interdisciplinary critics such as James Baird (*Ishmael*) and Leslie Fiedler ("Archetype and Signature"), and such artist/critics as D. H. Lawrence, James Branch Cabell, Charles Williams, and C. S. Lewis himself. And this is why, after having brought through practice our own theory to relative maturity, we feel that we now have not only the right but the duty to be both critical of what others have done and assertive of our own position; if we seem to speak with the authority of only two, we nonetheless draw upon the wisdom of many.

Even from that vantage point, however, we have to resort to metaphor in an attempt to define the individual archetype, and for our present purposes the metaphor of vulcanism will suffice. The archetype is an irruption of energy from below which manifests itself above in complexes of symbols—both creative and destructive—in art and society (history). Archetypes are always irrupting into the consciousness from the level of the unconscious or the numinous, but different archetypes and complexes of archetypes emerge at different times. Thus Promethean irruptions seemed inevitable in the nineteenth century; the Great Mother makes herself everywhere visible in the twentieth. Whether one particular temporal society is more amenable than another in another time and place, or whether the archetype, becoming obsessive, creates that society in all its historic trappings, is a question which space and the very nature of archetypal manifestations will not allow us to answer here. But the archetype is synchronous; as the common denominator that lies outside time, it links all humans to the collective unconscious on the numinal level, and on the phenomenal level it unites them through art and its symbols. Given such a definition, it would seem to follow that a twentieth-century artist is as susceptible to the influence of a particular archetypal complex (C. S. Lewis) as the first-century artist (Apuleius) who "preceded" him in time and is the product of a "different" culture; and in turn to find in a modern work the same archetype which informs an earlier one is not grounds, ipso facto, for assuming that the modern artist was working under the influence of a particular human predecessor. The great artist neither steals nor borrows, although he may be inspired by a familiar muse.

In theory, what the recurrence of archetypes proves, rather, is the hegemony of the collective unconscious—in which two artists or two societies respond to the same "source"—and the disdain which that collective reveals when confronted with notions of evolution or historical progress. To use the example with which we began this discussion, that one finds in Lewis's story much of the same archetypal content as in Apuleius's is not evidence for treating *The Golden Ass* as Lewis's source or, worse still, is not an excuse for concluding a discussion of the two works once one has reduced them to their common archetypal denominator. In practice, nonetheless, plagiarism we shall always have with us.

In many respects, furthermore, the extent of the archetypal critic's interest in drawing attention to the similarities between a later work of art and an earlier one should be in demonstrating that an archetype is in operation and that much of the power of a given work derives from its appeal to a constant in our psyches that we share with humans of all times and places. As such, the notation of archetypes is essentially a tactical measure, designed to correct equally the romantic idea that the appeal of the classics consists in their remoteness from contemporary experience and the modernist prejudice that the appeal of the best contemporary works is to be found in their newness or originality, their "novelty," perhaps. In contrast to the structuralist or the comparatist, the archetypalist is not motivated—as unfortunately were Otto Rank in *The Myth of the Birth of the Hero* and Joseph Campbell in *The Hero with a Thousand Faces*—by a desire to find a basic plot or monomyth and reduce all art to its level. Nor, indeed, is it his concern to demonstrate that history repeats itself. The archetypalist's concern with historical repetition has mainly to do with the fact that it is through recurrence that an essence beyond history makes its presence felt, its reality known. It is with the interaction between this extrahistorical force and the temporal that he is concerned, not with the relationship between things in time. What distinguishes the archetypal critic is not so much that he uses a different set of critical tools but that he proceeds from an entirely different philosophical orientation and that, consequently, what is an end in itself all too often for the traditional critic is for the archetypal critic a means to a cultural end.

Moreover, what functions as the starting point for critics like Eliot and Frye—literature—is what we must regard as the second, or product, stage in the archetypal process, and it is precisely the omission of the primary stage, together with the conventional linearity of his philosophy of history, that makes Frye's archetypology so narrowly literary, so static, so theological, and yet so secularly scientific.

As we have observed, though it may manifest itself most creatively in a work of art, the archetype does not originate there, nor does it originate in the consciousness or imagination of the artist; and it never dissolves itself completely into its temporal manifestation, always retaining its autonomy and independence in the collective unconscious. Conversely, what identifies a work of art as being informed by an archetype is that it commands an emotional response which is often seen to be disproportionate to the vehicle and that it reflects the numinous and mysterious nature of its source in the nonrational and "holy" character of the feelings that it arouses. Thus it is not the fact that the plot of a given work follows a typical pattern, nor that the plot can be correlated with a myth, which makes the work archetypal; what makes a work archetypal is that it generates in the artist and in his audience a sense of the otherworldly, of the divine (as Walter Otto puts it, "die goetter sin da"), and does so inexplicably or by reason of the thing which cannot be rationally explained.

Accordingly, while all works of art may be said to contain archetypes, being the products of artists whose personal unconscious involves them willy-nilly in the collective, not all works of art—or political movements or madnesses—are archetypal in the sense in which we have defined the term. And the justification for restricting the definition as we have done is that to broaden it would have the effect of defeating the purpose for which such criticism, in one respect, is designed: namely, as a way of approaching those works of art to which full justice cannot be done through the application of traditional aesthetic or belletristic theory. There is, for example, really little if anything about "The Rape of the Lock" or *Pride and Prejudice* that cannot be discovered or discussed through the use of conventional critical tools and vocabulary, but there is a great deal about works like *Till We Have Faces* or *All Hallows' Eve* which cannot be accommodated, and such works are misunderstood or ignored within the confines of the established critical tradition.

If our definition of archetypal criticism is justifiable, it is only in such a critical approach, eclectic and paying due regard to the nonrational or precognitive content of the artistic work, that there is to be found a rationale for treating works of art simultaneously, i.e., without regard to chronological placing. Similarly, such criticism provides the only rationale whereby—without recourse to progressivist theory—the autonomy of the modern work is preserved in the light of the knowledge that it evidences basic similarities with works that preceded it.

To explain: because the archetype does not originate in history and is therefore not a construct or motif that can be traced "back" to any one literary source or individual expression, for the purposes of archetypal analysis it does not matter which artistic redaction came first. Archetypes, deriving from a context outside history and unaffected by history, are not governed by temporal priorities or changes which would guarantee that one is purer, more direct, or simpler than another. The earlier manifestation is not by definition closer to the source, since the source is made up of constants and is constantly available. Thus there is no *reason* why Lewis's version of the myth of Cupid and Psyche should or should not be closer to the spirit of the original than Apuleius's; but if one associates the primitive mentality with an unquestioning acceptance of fate, then the harrowing directness with which Lewis dramatizes the psychological implications of the story does indeed seem more "primitive"—and therefore prior?—than the picaresque framework and happy ending that characterizes Apuleius's rendition.

As much as the archetypal critic seems, then, to be in a position to ignore chronology and the historical differences between cultures, so much, however, is he concerned as well with the historical context of given works when it comes to actual practice. For, just as he does not regard the work of art as the primary stage in the archetypal process, so neither does he regard the purely literary explication of the text as the end of archetypal criticism as a process. The long-range objective of archetypal criticism is to understand how archetypes operate *culturally*, and to this effect a central concern of the archetypal critic is with the way in which certain periods of history or cultural climates are conductive—or seem to be—to the manifestation of recurring archetypal patterns and symbols: he asks himself, what, for example, do the cultural milieus of Lewis and Apuleius have in common that might explain their obsessions with the myth of Cupid and Psyche. Similarly, the archetypal critic is concerned with the relationship between a given archetype and the style of the works in which it manifests itself: are there, for example, perceptible differences in style between *Till We Have Faces* and Lewis's other fiction? are there perceptible differences, that is, between *Till We Have Faces* and fictions that derive their creative energy from other sources? Finally, it is one of the axioms of archetypal criticism that just as the archetype cannot be contained in its individual manifestation—its temporary location—so neither can it be extracted from or observed independently of the frame in which it manifests itself.

Consequently, the archetypal critic is concerned with what Leslie Fiedler, in his 1956 essay, "Archetype and Signature," calls signature. For Fiedler, what distinguishes the archetypal critic from the more historically oriented variety is not that he is exclusively concerned with identification of the archetype but rather that he is "delivered from the bondage of time, speaking of 'confluences' rather than 'influences,' and finding the explication of a given work in things written later as well as earlier than the original piece."

Where the explicatory value of the modern/later work resides for the archetypal critic, however, it is not in direct commentary, i.e., critical observations on a predecessor's work, or in such self-conscious manipulation of mythic motifs as has become the happy hunting ground of the pseudoarchetypalists who expound upon the works of Eliot, Joyce, or Mann (who produced literature *about* archetypes, as Fiedler puts it). No, the later work aids our understanding of the earlier because it is itself a manifestation of the archetype, and by alerting us through its symbolic language, a language we learn to understand—or perhaps remember?— it warns us that we are once more in the presence of those gods once thought dead. What *Moby-Dick* gives us is not a modern version of the Book of Job or *Prometheus Bound* but an immediate revelation of how we are, and have always been, Job and Prometheus. What Doris Lessing's *Briefing for a Descent into Hell* gives us is not new things said in an old way

or an updated version of the *Odyssey* but a direct insight into the nature of
the eternal Odyssean plight. These later works do not provide us so much
with a new way of looking at the earlier ones as they do with an understanding, nowadays nowhere else available, it seems, of *how it has always
been*. They let us see what we have missed along the way, or have mis-
taken for something else, or have come to forget. What they assert is that
only books were burned at Alexandria.

It is, then, not by responding critically to the manifestation but
rather in responding creatively to the archetype manifested in the earlier
work that the later writer helps to explicate that work—and herein is to
be found the reason why Lewis at once acknowledges his familiarity with
The Golden Ass and at the same time denies that Apuleius was his source.
In another area of his endeavor, Lewis also provides a paramount example of the way in which the creative response provides a better explication of an earlier work than does the more conventionally critical
discussion: there is no question in our minds that Lewis's *Perelandra* constitutes a better critical introduction to *Paradise Lost* than does his *Preface
to Paradise Lost*. In the same way, Milton's *Paradise Lost* provides far
more profound insights into Genesis than his own *De Doctrina Christiana*.
This same rationale may explain why the archetypal critic is characteristically more passionate—sometimes risking the charge of subjectivity—in
his treatment of literary texts than might seem decorous to a critic of
more conventional persuasion. (One frequently wonders, though,
whether the emphasis upon objectivity and dispassionate analysis and the
concomitant suspicion of enthusiasm by certain critics and teachers does
not really reflect a less defensible subjective reaction.)

What might most disturb the conventional critic, and particularly
the specialist in the classics, is the conclusion that could very well be
drawn from the argument that later works of art and literature provide
essential insights into the nature of earlier ones: namely, that all the effort and scholarship expended upon the earlier work is, at one blow, one
explication of the modern work, rendered useless if not invalid and, if
neither of these, of interest only to the antiquarian. Who, to use our continuing example, would want to labor through critical interpretations of
The Golden Ass when one can better understand the complexities of that
work through a pleasant reading of *Till We Have Faces*? Paradoxical as it
may sound, unobserved though it may be, the answer is simple and positive: the student of C. S. Lewis, of the modern work. By virtue of the fact
that both works are informed by the same archetype, those questions
which classical scholars have raised about *The Golden Ass* can be used as

points of departure for discussions of *Till We Have Faces*. Far from bringing about the death of scholarship surrounding an earlier work, therefore, archetypal criticism can serve as a means of bringing it to renewed life.

The cultural relevance of archetypal criticism should by now be obvious. Let one example, however, provide a conclusion to our discussion. Earlier we noted that the Great Mother seems to have become the archetype of our time. It should be noted that this is not so because the Jungians suddenly discovered the pervasiveness of the Magna Mater in her many forms in our culture. The reverse is certainly true. Jung discovered her, Neumann and others discussed her, because she was already there. She had irrupted irresistibly into our present. But a true archetypalist will not stop with a discussion of the statuary of Henry Moore, for example. He will want to ask himself whether the same archetypal irruption is responsible for the rise of feminism in our time; he will want to ask himself, and in the asking to inform his contemporaries, whether such a phenomenon reveals the Mother in her creative or destructive phase.

(1978)

17 FEELING, IMAGINATION, AND THE SELF

William Willeford

These two sections from Willeford's 1987 book display to full advantage their author's long dual career as both practicing Jungian analyst and professor of literature. Unlike his earlier The Fool and His Sceptre *(see Part 3, Chapter 23), this recent book is oriented more toward psychological theory and practice—specifically, the transformations of the crucial archetypal Mother-Baby relationship. However, throughout, Willeford interweaves literary and psychological criticism to explain the complex interrelationships that link the three elements of psyche named in its title.*

"Mythic Forms and Images," the first selection, surveys theories of myth and discusses the relationship of myth and the individual's psychic life. The second selection, "Myth as Formal and Final Cause," draws upon Shakespeare to illustrate how the psychologist-literary critic Willeford would envision not only mythic symbols (weddings) but also mythic forms (plot development) in terms of how they structure the individual's psychic life, of how, as Jung said, a person lives a myth onward. Both selections are clearly responsive to the issues addressed by Hinz and Teunissen in the previous chapter.

MYTHIC FORMS AND IMAGES

Having spoken of mythic forms and images as archetypal, structuring our experience in ways that endow it with certain kinds of meaning, I wish now to offer a brief defense of this way of speaking, as well as a further note of caution.

Kerényi raises the issue of whether similar myths in different cultures are related through transmission or as diverse expressions of an archetypal foundation. Regarding the distinction as misstated, he remarks, "The question is, rather: spontaneous acquisition on an archetypal foundation or transmission on the same foundation. The term 'archetypal' seems to contain implications which compel one to accept it but which, for that very reason, make it a commonplace that arouses no particular interest. We must take care not to attach too much importance to the *word*."[1] He nonetheless continues to employ the term in his later works, presumably because the mythical materials with which he is concerned in important respects accord with "types," and they have been imagined as—or imagined in relation to—beginnings or first principles, *archai*. But he also offers another reason when he speaks "of *archetypal facts of human existence*."[2]

An example that occurs to me of an "archetypal fact of human existence" is birth. Over the earth as a whole, human births take place at the rate of a large number per minute; women have been giving birth as long as the human race has existed; and births are recorded as statistics of various kinds. In this sense the archetypal fact of birth is a commonplace. But a particular birth may be fraught with the profoundest personal meaning, may indeed seem a miracle, and birth as a fact of human existence has been elevated to the status of a mythic form or image in countless rituals and birth-stories of gods or heroes. Similarly, falling in love is a commonplace of much kitschy song and fiction but may also be experienced as a fateful gift from another world and has been so elevated in myths and great works of literature.

When I speak of mythic forms and images, I have in mind certain ways in which what Kerényi called archetypal facts of human experience have been apprehended and expressed. Indeed, I assume that in calling such facts archetypal, Kerényi means, in part, that they are significant in such ways as to lend themselves to embodiment in mythic forms and images.

In speaking of mythic forms and images, I have in mind such statements of Jung as these: "The collective unconscious . . . appears to consist of mythological motifs or primordial images, for which reason the myths of all nations are its real exponents. In fact, the whole of mythology could be taken as a sort of projection of the collective unconscious."[3] And " 'myth-forming' structural elements must be present in the unconscious psyche," producing not "myths with a definite form, but rather mythological components which, because of their typical nature, we can call 'motifs,' 'primordial images,' types or—as I have named them—*archetypes*."[4] Thus, "mythic forms and images" basically translates *archetypes* in light of such definitions.

By "mythic" I mean pertaining to the kinds of elements to be found in myths. From a psychological point of view, there are various reasons for using the term "mythic," and for using it in an open and partly figurative way. First, the foremost students of myths do not agree on a several-point definition of myth that cannot be contested on the basis of counterexamples, whereas a minimal definition such as "traditional tales" ignores essential characteristics of a great many myths—such as their sacredness, their concern with divine beings, and their association with cult.[5] Second, myths in the sense of traditional tales are not the only imaginative products containing mythic or mythlike elements. Thus, in *Symbols of Transformation* Jung justifiably brought together mythical religious texts, passages from such poets as Goethe, dreams, and psychotic delusions. Third, it sometimes makes sense to allow *mythic* also to refer to cultic and ritual elements associated with myths but also distinguishable from them. (For example, one might have reason to call the eucharist "mythic.") And fourth, though myths have their context in a community, one may also have reason to speak of a life-shaping "personal myth," which may or may not be drawn from living religious tradition.

The "forms" of myths include such aspects of mythic "logic" as the binary oppositions studied by the structural anthropologist Claude Lévi-Strauss."[6] To speak of mythic "images" is implicitly—and rightly—to link them with imagination. Another advantage of the term *mythic image* is, as Kerényi points out, that it suggests the question of what the mythic image is an image *of*, as such a term as *figure* does not.[7] This question may not be in any simple way answerable, as mythic images are often symbols in the sense of referring ultimately to something unknown, of which the symbol is the best possible but only an approximate expression. (If it could be said simply what the Christian eucharist refers to, millions of words would not have been uttered in trying to explain it.) To have such a mercurial question in mind is to remain aware that mythic experience is transcendent as a reaching toward a certain psychic content—a reaching toward that is also, through imagination, a way of already gaining and having contact with it.

This transcendent quality of a myth is what gives it its capacity to transform psychic energy and to structure consciousness in accordance with the myth. (This may be seen, for example, in the myth of the mother-daughter pair Demeter and Persephone as celebrated in the Eleusinian mysteries, one aim of which was clearly to bring about a certain state of mind in the participants.) This quality is experienced as revelation, the content of which functions on the order of a formal and final cause. In saying this I am assuming that mythic forms and images are important in the reality of the psyche, and that they have a bearing on unconscious and conscious processes in their interrelations, which have both personal and collective aspects. That these interrelations are hard to trace and talk about does not make them unreal or unimportant.

One danger constantly attendant upon attempts to express these interrelations must, however, be admitted. It is to forget that conscious and unconscious systems are ultimately complementary, are a polarity within an overall whole, so that there is continuous feedback between the two. To forget this is to invite the reifying of archetypes in such a way that they are aligned with the unconscious and made causative, to the neglect of conscious action and knowledge. The result is a covert idealism (or even solipsism), to be seen, for example, in the implications of an oversimplifying diagram by the analytical psychologist Erich Neumann. It shows nuclei-like "archetypes" situated in the collective unconscious, whence they are constellated as contents of collective consciousness, a role that gradually depotentiates them: leaving husks behind, they then sink back into the collective unconscious.[8] It is surely this sort of danger that leads Kerényi to qualify his reference to archetypal facts of human existence by saying that they "cannot be mere realities of the psyche."[9] Of course, for Jung—as my discussion of participating consciousness should have demonstrated—the reality of the psyche is anything but "mere." Yet once it is recognized, attention subtle enough to befit the enterprise is needed to explore the openness of psyche to the world. This issue I have already raised in my reflections on the polarities of God and man, and of man and nature.

My account of mythic forms and images needs to be further qualified by the admonition that the many things that have been called "myth" make up a sprawling variety difficult to classify. Thus G. S. Kirk maintains "that there are *myths*, which are traditional tales of many different kinds and functions, but no such thing as 'myth.' "[10] It is surely true that some earlier students of Greek and other myths generalized too broadly, for example, in describing the relations of "myth" to "cult," as though these relations were fixed rather than variable or sometimes even nonexistent. And there are, as Kirk avers, problems about making a cate-

gory of "mythical thinking."[11] But when Kirk also sees "no reason to
suppose that most myths are especially symbolic," we may surmise that
his clean-up operation on earlier thinking about myth has been at a high
price, that he has clarified some issues by ignoring the intuitive grasp—
shared, with differences, by Jung, Kerényi, Walter F. Otto, and others—
of certain important things. These concern the nature of imaginative
symbols as apprehended especially in the mode of feeling.

Otto might seem to fall into the kind of one-sidedness I noted in
Neumann when he speaks of "der ursprüngliche Mythos"—original,
primitive, initial myth—in contrast to secondary (and partly debased)
versions of it.[12] this is related to the distinction that Jensen has drawn
between a creative phase of culture and its secondary "application." And
the justification I adduced for Jensen, that he is saying something true
about the bearing of religion (as distinct from magic) on feeling and
imagination, I would also adduce for Otto. That is, I propose granting
that a human urge to find and create meaning is not derivative but primary, and that feeling and imagination are necessary to some of the deepest kinds of meaning which find their fullest expression in some myths—
in mythic forms and images. If, then, we make an ideal type of such
myths, as Otto does, we are regarding them as realizations of a formal and
final cause inherent in man's capacity and propensity for mythmaking.
This view seems to me in principle compatible with also granting that
myths draw upon the most diverse psychic functions and embody the
most diverse concerns.

If it troubles us that such an ideal type cannot be neatly demar-
cated—not as neatly, at least, as Otto seems to assume—we should recall
that where feeling and imagination are alive, boundaries are typically
fluid. ("These things seem small and undistinguishable, / Like far-off
mountains turnèd into clouds"; "Methinks I see these things with parted
eye, / When everything seems double" [A Midsummer Night's Dream,
IV.i.188–91].) This fluidity—the reader may recall references earlier to
deintegration—is a necessary concomitant of the quality of revelation
Otto finds characteristic of the myths with which he is chiefly concerned.
Whatever historical issues he oversimplifies, his view is in keeping with
what I have maintained about the role of mythic forms and images in the
transformation of psychic energy and the creation of consciousness.

The full title of Otto's essay is "Primitive Myth in Light of the
Sympathy of Man and World"; this implies the polarities of man and God
and of man and nature. I take this sympathy to be real. "Lebt' nicht in
uns des Gottes eigne Kraft, / Wie könnt' uns Göttliches entzücken?"

Goethe asks: "If the god's own power did not live in us, / How could the divine enrapture us?" Goethe also observes that only because the eye is sunlike can it see the light of the sun.[13] And I take this sympathy to be as fundamental in the reality of the psyche as are the workings of our instrumental intelligence.

That synthetic imagination is continuous with more prosaic forms of fantasy I have already maintained, as I have that utilitarian and more contemplative concerns are often densely interwoven. Though giving mythic forms and images an important kind of primacy, I would also propose that imagination and feeling live in the real world of nature and other people and their God or gods. As the phenomenological philosopher Max Scheler (1874–1928) usefully reminds us, "We live with the *entire fullness of our spirit* chiefly among *things*; we live in the *world*."[14] To call mythic forms and images "archetypal" is to emphasize the causative power they may sometimes have in the reality of the psyche. But, as we saw in the preceding section, this power is a function of interest—in nature, other people, and their God or gods.

The mother-infant relationship bears on these matters, since to be born is to enter a world of community, an animated world, perceived by a creature disposed to be interested in its animation. To see links between mythic animation more generally and the infant's interest in animate objects and, early in its second year, in fantasy stories is not to reduce gods to infantile projections. It is simply to affirm that imaginative apprehension of the gods draws on psychic capacities at work very early in the life of the individual. Further, Otto cites the philosopher Schelling as saying (in *The Ages of the World*) that each thing is more than its appearance, more than the eyes see and the hands can grasp, something that is true of every event and every condition of existence. As Otto remarks, this "more" is not something additional, that could also be lacking; rather, without this aura-like "more" the thing would have no existence. Otto is thus talking about what Goethe called *Urphänomene*, primordial phenomena, behind which, in Goethe's view, stands divinity.[15]

In talking about this "more," I have related it to nonconsummatory mutuality and the infant's sense of more than enough. Surely the mythic "more" rests and draws upon the infant's knowledge of plenty.

Myth as Formal and Final Cause

If abstract concepts (such as "atoms" and "particles") are fictions of one kind, mythical forms and images are fictions of another. The two kinds

may be interrelated, but each has its own distinct and apparently necessary kinds of truth. Thus, the "soul" of the systematic theologian and the
"soul" of the shaman might both be treated in the same encyclopedia
article, but in different sections of it.

"Soul" belongs to the order of cause. (It is an ancient idea, for
example, that the body lives *because* the soul inhabits it.) In its less abstract and theological manifestations "soul" belongs among the mythic
forms and images that fictionally represent causation.

We may try to understand "cause" by translating it with such terms
as "meaning construct."[16] In so doing we usefully remind ourselves that
we are talking not about the Real but about models of our experience. As
models of our experience, mythic forms and images especially accord
with formal and final causes—among Aristotle's four kinds of causation
(material, efficient, formal, and final). This is to say, mythic forms and
images are expressive of the broad patterning and goal-directedness of
psychic life. We use them, as we use abstract concepts, to live our lives
meaningfully. Yet to say that we "use" mythic forms and images is to
make them products of our instrumental intelligence, and is thus to oversimplify.

The view that our fictions are instrumental assumes that something
is using them to some purpose. Partly this something is the knowing,
acting subject that we call "I." But this something may also, on a deeper
level, be the unknowable *x* that Schopenhauer has called Will and Berg-
son the Life Force (or *élan vital*). Whether our fictions are not only instrumental but also true we cannot in the larger view know, since—as
Nietzsche has argued—there is no way to be certain that whatever agent
and organizing principle is at work in the ongoing of life cherishes truth
more than deception, no way to be certain that deception serves its purposes less effectively than truth. (A man and woman fall in love and
marry; their union produces children. Is their falling in love deception or
truth?) We may prefer truth, make of it an ultimate term, and persuade
ourselves that it will prevail. To assume such an affirmation is to exceed
rational and empirical knowledge, though we normally remain unaware
of this. More cautiously, and at the price of greater ambiguity, we may
say with Jung that even in our scientific constructions we are living the
myth, some myth, onward. I will return in a moment to what it means to
live a myth—and to live it onward.

If, then, I say that "I" live my life, I must be fully aware that this
"I" is by no means identical with the conscious ego, and that the *x* that
lives in and through my life also lives in and through the kinds of nonego

psychic components that we have explored in various personal vignettes. Moreover, this x also lives in and through my life in my encounters with the world as the world corresponds to my inner dispositions. I mean by this, among other things, that I meet images of my problems, my aversions, my inclinations, in outer objects, people, and events. (Thus, for example, exactly Hamlet, with his capacity for "thinking too precisely on the event," is given a chance to kill Claudius exactly when Claudius is trying to pray.)

We may assume or conclude that there is some form of correspondence or even identity between the x I am describing now and the still larger x that causes there to be something and not nothing, and causes that something to have whatever character it has, with and despite my limited participation in it. But one cannot be rationally and empirically certain that one knows what one thus assumes or concludes. Nor can one call the larger x "God"—a concept—and then say that one knows this concept in experience. One can do neither of these things because the qualification "as if" must always be part of the ultimate rounding out of our conception—since we can at best "stammer about Being," to quote von Weizsäcker—and because in important respects conceptual and nonconceptual experience so radically transcend one another. (If I talk about the nature of pain, I am not talking about *my* pain *now*.)

Mythic forms and images may take us to the limit of the known, and even of the knowable. We may recognize in them the structures of the x that lives in and through our lives. This is the purport of the statements about myth by Jung and Otto—and about primordial phenomena (*Urphänomene*) by Goethe—cited in the previous section. And yet mythic forms and images are and must be logical if they are to function within a symbol system, even if they do so in a way that provides glimpses of a reality that transcends it. That a god is capable of assuming human form is in part a sign of his extraordinary power. That mythic forms and images accord with logic contributes to our sense of their deep necessity, a point to which I will return in a moment.

In archaic societies myths performed two interrelated functions bearing on the issues I am now raising—the functions of effecting a detachment from the flux of particular experience, and of relating the individual to a total world. (These functions may also be performed by cultural artifacts other than myths—such as works of art and contemplative practices. Myths may also perform a host of other functions. And some myths may not perform these functions at all. But even if these functions do not offer the basis of an exclusive definition of myth, this

admission need not hinder us from singling them out as especially important to an understanding of what myths are and do.)

One can see the function of detachment most clearly in myths of
creation, which reveal a deeper and more embracing reality that our personal interests and projects in the world cause us to neglect. Such myths
free us, in the words of Mircea Eliade, from a "false identification of
Reality with what each of us *appears to be or to possess*" and thus enables us
"to approach a Reality that is inaccessible at the level of profane, individual existence."[17] As Polanyi comments on this view of creation myths:
"Our personal involvement in the world is *with some parts of the world*,
while the conception of creation encompasses the *whole* world—the
world that lies beyond or under or through all its parts. The one is concerned with things as parts, while the other ignores these matters and has
the totality of all conceivable experiences as its object. . . . In this sense,
therefore, myths of creation are untranslatable into terms that apply to
things within the world."[18] In reciting or listening to such a myth, according to Eliade, one transcends "the 'historical situation.' In other words,
one goes beyond the temporal condition and the dull self-sufficiency
which is the lot of every human being simply because every human being
is 'ignorant'—in the sense that he is identifying himself, and Reality,
with his own particular situation."[19] And so the detachment effected by
myths in archaic societies is also an opening to a total world having, for
the person entering it by means of the myth, a more objective character.
It is this line of reasoning, and this positive valuation of mythic forms and
images, that led Jung to consider them expressions of the "objective
psyche."

The reader will, however, recall my insistence that an objective
view of the world is impossible. This, coupled with my insistence (just
now) on the subjectivity of our living among fictions, and on their fiction-
ality, should raise doubts as to how nearly the term "the objective psyche" resolves issues raised in the preceding section. Further, even if
myths in archaic societies may be said to create a total world, we may still
wonder how unified or multifarious such a total world is—questions to be
explored in the following section. I would emphasize, too, the way in
which consciousness not only makes the unconscious conscious, but beyond this helps to form it by being manifest in conscious attitudes to
which the unconscious creatively responds. Moreover, the segregation of
sacred life that I have just been describing is always incomplete, a failed
attempt to realize a desideratum. There is laughter in church, Judas

among the disciples, the altar built for venal ends. We live in divided and distinguished worlds that we nonetheless cannot in our minds and hearts securely divide and distinguish when it seems most important for us to do so.

Still, the butterflylike life of the psyche is real—indeed, in important respects primary and irreducible. And there are important respects in which unconscious processes are primary within that life. Though we experience mythic forms and images as phenomena of consciousness, and though they may in part be consciously created in accord with conscious aims and values, there are also important respects in which they bring unconscious processes to conscious expression. In so doing, mythic forms and images mediate between consciousness and its unconscious background and matrix. Conscious products, they have a resonance of unconscious implications that enables them to point beyond the known. This resonance, apprehended in glimpses, is essential to their efficacy as transformative symbols.

I want now to discuss two characteristics of Shakespearean comedy that are "mythic" in the sense in which I am using the word. They belong to the class of what I have been calling mythic forms and images—appearing here in a nonmythic context, though they also figure in what we would call myths in a more limited sense. Further, they function as formal and final cause—they are structuring elements—in the interactions between consciousness and the unconscious, as such interactions are implied in the drama. The first of these characteristics is the contrivance of events to serve the exigencies of the plot; the second is the wedding concluding the main action.

By "contrivance" and "exigencies" I mean to suggest the radically nonnaturalistic, dancelike movement of the comic form, which unfolds in accordance with what could be called a mythic logic, a logic of higher powers, superior to individual volition. (One may grant at least some manifestations of *mythos* as having a special authority with respect to *logos*—as being in some sense truer. Writers I have cited do this, persuasively. Still, myth has its own form of logic, partly according with the logic followed in mundane affairs.)

For example, in the story of the three caskets in *The Merchant of Venice*, the choice of the correct one can only come last, since with that choice the story of the rival suitors will be wound up. Moreover, since the first casket is of gold, the second must be of silver, and the third of lead, since this series is a single, clear, and logical progression. Moreover,

when Bassanio declares his love for Portia it is logical, since the Venetian
friends share a common fate, that Gratiano should declare his love for
Nerissa, offering no more explanation than this:

> My eyes, my lord, can look as swift as yours:
> You saw the mistress, I beheld the maid.
> You loved, I loved. . . .
>
> [III.ii.197–99]

Further, once Antonio's bond with Shylock is signed, it is inevitable
that Antonio's ships should miscarry and the bond be forfeit, since this
development accords with the logical principle of fairy tales (described
by Vladimir Popp), whereby every explicit injunction in the story is to be
violated.

To see the relations between such contrivance and the weddings at
the close, we must ask ourselves *what* weddings are an image *of*—to return to Kerényi's question about myths considered in the preceding section. And to begin to answer this question we might consider the feelings
and emotions aroused by weddings in real life.

One striking fact about weddings is that they make some people
cry. Why? Partly, one may guess, because the bride and groom are making an immense commitment for obscure reasons that one would have to
sum up in the unenlightening word *love*, and are doing so while completely unaware of what will result from that commitment. One gains a
measure of their ignorance if one imagines a married couple with grown
or half-grown children and then thinks back to the wedding of the couple,
when those children, in all their particularity and complexity, were, in
effect, a cipher, a nothing. Further, though matrimony is a haven, it is
better to be well hanged than ill wed, and the tears at a wedding may also
be in response to the immense risk with which the scarcely definable
promise of marriage is suffused. Moreover, though this was earlier clearer
than it is now, there is still an important sense in which marrying is not
something two people do, like actions performed by their conscious egos,
but is, rather, something done to them by personal and historical circumstances, by society, and—to use a word I have already applied to the
Venetian friends—by fate. But what does *fate* mean in such a connection?
It means a formal and final pattern of that which lives in and through our
lives, as that pattern is manifest at the limits of the known. Such a pattern
is of emotional import.

In what someone takes to be a fateful event, a special value is revealed in a way that seems to be both fortuitous and the expression of a transpersonal order. There is, it is supposed, a level of reality on which one's future is already known—written, for example, in the Book of Fate. What knows one's future, it is assumed, makes it happen. And what knows it and makes it happen is thought to foretell it by making order out of chance, or by revealing apparent chance as secretly ordered. Refined and elaborated, such "magical" views become metaphysical concepts of the preestablished harmony of the universe. Whatever we may think of such concepts, experiences of fortuitous—magical—order are available to all but the most hardened rationalists among us.

Shakespeare records such experiences, on the one hand, because as a dramatist he is concerned with action, which is formed, which moves to some goal, but which may be dissipated in random events. He records such experiences, on the other, because he is concerned with the soul, which in some of its most important expressions views the world magically. Thus, he sometimes presents twilight subjective states in which the distinction between subject and object does not obtain.

But in Shakespeare's plays events in the outer world, and coming to the subject from others, also sometimes assume the character of magically induced *actions*, or of actions suggestive of magic. In *King Lear*, for example, the storm on the heath *is* Lear's passionate madness. Or rather, between storm and madness there is a causal relation, not so much material and efficient—though also that—as formal and final.

Let us return to our question concerning the relation between the "contrived" logic of Shakespeare's comic design and the weddings rounding out the main action. In a sense, the plot of such a play as *The Merchant of Venice* is partly, in effect, the product of a process of reasoning backward from its weddings. The characters are "fated" to be married; the exigencies of the plot force them to that intended end. Marriage is the mythic form of their relation to the unknown, is for them the experienced structure of spirit, from which the formal and final meaning of their lives has been emerging since the outset of the action. To be fated to marriage in this way is to be subject to such higher powers as those that find expression in the nuptials of Zeus and Hera bringing fertility to the fields,[20] or of the Bridegroom Christ and the Church or the soul.

To elaborate upon these remarks about the x that lives in and through our lives, I want to comment briefly on two utterances made by Jung that bear upon myth as formal and final cause.

The first is the motto he had carved over the entrance to his house in Küsnacht: "Called or not called, God is present." If *God* is understood as, on the one hand, the result of the metaphorical extension we have been considering, and, on the other, as the lived experience of spirit, and if the irreducible discrepancy between these two senses of *God* is kept in mind, the thought expressed in this saying is, I believe, not only true but psychologically invaluable.

The practical wisdom implied by this saying (thus understood) is elaborated in the second of these utterances, in Jung's essay "On the Nature of the Psyche," in which he compares instinct with the infrared part of the color spectrum and "archetype" with the ultraviolet part. One would expect blue to be a more apt equivalent of the spirit than violet, he observes, implying that the ultraviolet of his metaphor stands for the spiritual form of instinct. Spirit would thus be continuous with instinct, and partly of the same nature as it, but without being reducible to it. Since we do not know what thing or multitude of diverse things instinct may be—some 14,000 "instincts" have been proposed—this attempt to ground "archetype" in instinct does not say anything very specific. It nonetheless says something important, which Jung summarizes thus: "The realization and assimilation of instinct never take place at the red end, i.e., by absorption into the instinctual sphere, but only through integration of the image which signifies and at the same time evokes the instinct, although in a form quite different from the one we meet on the biological level."[21]

We could imagine the body-ego or body-subject as the infrared part of the color spectrum and spirit as the ultraviolet part. Thus qualified, Jung's remarks about the integration of the image are profoundly true: psychological problems serve the purpose of impelling the person suffering them to make contact with the relevant spiritual factors. These are the mythic forms and images, the souls, spirits—and demons—of lived experience. Such contact must precede integration of spiritual contents, which is in any case possible only to a limited extent, since spirit remains finally "other."

And yet, as the metaphor of the spectrum suggests, "other" need not be assimilated to the "Wholly Other" that the theologian Rudolf Otto regarded as the primary object of religious experience.[22] (Such assimilation would make "other" not violet but blue.) Rather, the otherness that makes persons and things into "It" is first known in the shared life of mother and infant, in which "Thou" appears even earlier, and the spirit that can be known as "Wholly Other" can also be known in the intimacy of "nearer to me than I am to myself." (This intimacy is implicit in a central tenet of Meister Eckhart, that "God is in us and we are in

God.")[23] In relation to the body-ego or body-subject, the image—at the ultraviolet end of the spectrum—is always significantly "other"; yet it remains mine, however much it may sometimes seem not-mine in lived experience.

(1987)

18 OUTLINE OF A JUNGIAN AESTHETICS

Morris Philipson

*P*hilipson, trained as a philosopher, published this study while a university professor; currently he is a novelist and director of the University of Chicago Press.
Here, he opens up Jung's writings in the direction of formal philosophy as well as
philosophically oriented literary criticism; his book is a systematic presentation and
analysis of an aesthetics that is both explicit and implicit in Jung's psychology.

"Symbolism and Epistemology" examines why Jung's interpretation of
symbolism and its crucial role in furthering the wholeness and well-being of the
human psyche—whether in day-to-day living or in the special, psychodynamic
transaction between artist, artwork and audience—has been immensely important in attracting artists and the audience for art to his psychology.

"Jungian Psychology and Aesthetics" delineates Jung's psychological justification of literary criticism. Philipson underscores Jung's position that psychology
can complement, without supplanting, the many culture-based approaches to literary criticism. For Jung, artists and their art have important, collective knowledge
to communicate to an audience, not merely individualized, infantile wishes. Thus
the critic fulfills an important role too. The skillful critic is like the effective analyst in helping the audience to interpret symbolic materials.

I. SYMBOLISM AND EPISTEMOLOGY

Ira Progoff has pointed out that there was a strong influence of Kantian
thought on the formulation of Jung's primary principles. "He accepted

214

Kant's fundamental restriction that we cannot know things in them-selves, and he concluded that the only reality we can study with confi-dence is *Esse in Anima*, Being in the Soul." Subsequently developing his interpretation of what is "psychologically real," Jung maintains that "the phenomena of the psyche constitute an area of reality which may be stud-ied in their own terms." "In interpreting Jung's point of view, we must always remember the fact that all his doctrines about the world as cosmos are based, not on the world itself, but on the analysis of psychic content."[1]

What is loosely called "the world itself," then, may be generally thought of as "physical reality" in contradistinction to "psychic reality." The problems of knowledge concerning "physical reality" may be con-ceived as essentially theoretical, and studied by methods appropriate to it. But the problems of knowledge concerning "psychic reality" must be recognized to be essentially practical and, therefore, "studied in their own terms." The "terms" of "psychic reality" are conditioned by the manifestations of psychic life in unconscious as well as in conscious activ-ity. This is the radical originality of Freud's interpretation of psychology.

Jung believes he has made an important improvement over the Freudian system by introducing an equally radical distinction within the area of unconscious manifestations. Such phenomena *are* what they *do* for us. What they do is governed by laws inherent in the psyche, some of which can be known and expressed in the language of instincts and their transformations. Manifestations of these will be *signs*. What they do for us is offer "hints" as to why we are as we are; and by a causal-reductive analysis, with the help of such "clues," the analyst can discover the etiol-ogy of the condition they represent.

But the practical concern for psychotherapy is that of curing the patient and, even when all such etiological analysis has been made, the most important question remains: how should the patient *develop* health-ily? Unless this is imposed from some public system of behavior indepen-dent of the individual patient, the source of such "knowledge" must be, somehow, within him. In other words, even after the reductive analysis of the *signs* has revealed the causes and, it is hoped, removed the power of such causes, so that the patient is "free" where he had previously been "possessed," the problem remains of what he *should* "freely" make of himself.

Jung's conception is that there are such psychic manifestations as must be designated *symbols* which, arising from the unconscious, offer "hints" or "clues" of what one ought to become. These are necessarily individual, and must *not* be retrospectively analyzed, but interpreted appropriately to the individual's prospective development. Such phenomena as these, likewise, are governed by laws inherent in the psyche, but they are not clearly known. They are not to be described in terms of instincts and their transformations. They appear as "images" and, being recognized in a variety of universal manifestations, are characterized as archetypes of a collective unconscious. The "terms," then, of their description will be metaphoric and their vocabulary mythological.

By interpretation of them what is gained is "knowledge" of the individual, for the individual. This is *personal knowledge* of the psychic reality of the individual, oriented toward the future and conceived as contributing to that individual's psychic health (expressed metaphorically as "wholeness"). Either such an intuition is proved "right" because the development undertaken on the basis of the interpretation does conduce to "wholeness" or it is proved "wrong" when that does not happen. The interpretation is always problematic, but it is supported by the fact that Jung finds much evidence of there being successfully interpreted intuitions.

It is necessary to recognize that Jung considers the symbol to be a spontaneous formation, the content of which is from the collective unconscious. It is able to function in consciousness only when it has been "channelized" by interpretation. "If the symbol is joined with the ego so that it becomes the center of consciousness, and if it is experienced inwardly with an intimate sense of personal identification, it becomes the focus for the major energies of the individual."[2] Without the operation of critical consciousness, it is unlikely that the symbol can have this effect; in its place, then, the public symbols of the individual's culture serve as "impersonal" substitutes. The result is that the individual never achieves *personal knowledge* and never achieves the "wholeness" that is authentic to himself.

Among the "impersonal" substitutes are the symbols of religion and art. The most striking difference between the two, of course, is that "art" never functions in an official or systematic way.

Theoretical knowledge may be intellectually possessed without making any appreciable difference whatsoever to the individual's inner life. But "knowledge" of one's own psychic reality is meaningless except as practical knowledge—such interpretations as contribute to changing how one lives. Analogously, the kind of "knowledge" derived from interpretations of works of art is practical knowledge; it reorganizes the psychic reality as a whole. The essential elements of this reality are consciousness, the personal and the collective unconscious. Works of art in the Psychological Mode, it would seem, act as mediators between consciousness and the personal unconscious. Works of art in the Visionary Mode act as mediators between consciousness and the collective unconscious. Since these symbols are public or "impersonal" (suprapersonal), they are not, comparatively, as powerfully effective as individual symbols. But their "psychic significance" is that they demand interpretation from the person who is "seized" by them; and, insofar as an individual takes from his interpretation of them some insight of a prospective nature for himself, the symbolic work of art is of comparable value. In this sense, art is the public dream of society. Relative to the degree of integration of a society, its art will be expressive of the archetypes of the collective unconscious working out compensatory "indicators" of how it should tend to develop. That is, it presents an intuition of what is "missing."

There is a lack in Jung's presentation of his ideas concerning the creative process in art, despite the fact that he sees it as analogous with the process of symbol formation in individual psychology. This is because a "vision," as experienced by a patient in analysis, exists apart from its expression, whereas no "work" of art can. As to the "spontaneous formation," Jung explains it as a result of an autonomous complex in the artist, as in the patient. But he never makes an adequate statement of what constitutes the *creative* autonomous complex. This is clearly related to the fact that he does not pay any close attention to the so-called formative process. As a result, he does not specify the differentia by which the creative autonomous complex in the arts can be distinguished from the autonomous complex operating in other spheres of creativity—"the seer, prophet, leader, and enlightener."

This also reminds the reader of a certain imprecision and consequent ambiguity in Jung's expressions concerning "form" and "matter" in a work of art. Sometimes the content of a symbol is spoken of as the "matter" that the collective unconscious produces spontaneously (of an archetypal nature). When this is true of a work of art, the artist is said to "form" (shape) the matter. On the other hand, some of the time Jung speaks of the archetype as a "form" (in the sense of a blueprint) which the artist then "shapes" his "material" (his medium?) in order to objectify. The ambiguity, perhaps, arises not so much from the metaphoric language Jung employs as from the comparisons of statements made at different times and in different contexts, while within any one such context of thought Jung uses the words consistently. This is why I have preferred to speak of "subject matter" and "method" when dealing with these questions.

Despite this lack and this ambiguity, it must be recognized that from the very beginning of this inquiry it has been obvious that Jung is interested in symbolism as a heuristic device. "The effective symbol" is a guide to discovery. The genuine symbol, both private and public, is conceived as enabling the individual and the society to fulfill an educative requirement. It is true that it is not the theoretical knowledge of the physical sciences which he has in mind, but the "practical knowledge" of "psychic reality." He is not interested in what is fruitless for psychic life, but in what is "pregnant with meaning." Only the "event" that may be interpreted successfully attracts him; not the would-be-symbol, a "manufactured" item that is impotent. And success is discoverable through effectiveness in what actually develops in the future.

This aspect of futurity, the concern with what is tending to become, the intuitive perception with prospective value leading to further discovery in enacted life, valued more highly because of its consequent contribution to "wholeness"—all of these aspects of the symbol bespeak its function as a heuristic device in the service of practical personal knowledge. The most distinguishing feature of all of this is the concern with "the possible" as contrasted with "the actual." Reductive analysis of *signs* operates in the service of discovering the conditioning causes of "the actual." Synthetic interpretation of *symbols* operates in the service of discovering what the indications from the collective unconscious are for the future. It is in this respect that they are seen to be concerned with what is the most appropriate "possible" for an individual. From Jung's point of view, it is patently arbitrary to speak of any other source of information as to what any particular person ought to become.

Such indications—adumbrations, intimations, intuitions—of "the possible" can be formulated as *personal knowledge* only through the activity of interpretation, and validated only through the pragmatic test. This is the structure of an epistemological analysis of Jung's conception of symbolism. His greatest concern is with the usefulness of such means for the ongoing understanding of "psychic reality." But, by extrapolation, he indicates that such an epistemological analysis might also be made of the rational sciences of "physical reality." Between the world of private "psychic reality" and the public world of scientific "physical reality," stand the public symbolic systems of religion and art. Halfway between—in virtue of the fact that, while they take their "subject matter" from the realm of what is psychologically real, they use such "methods" as are appropriate to an interpersonal rather than an individual application.

When writing on a general theory of individual psychology, Jung distinguishes such psychic manifestations as *signs*, in the service of Life, from *symbols*, in the service of Spirit. When he speaks of public symbolic systems, Life is equated with "Nature," Spirit with "Culture"; and Culture is no substitute for the gratifications of Nature. The difference between his system of thought and Freud's is that Jung requires more than one kind of principle for explanation.

It is curious that Freud considers his psychology "dualistic" and that of Jung "monistic." Freud writes:

> Our views have from the very first been *dualistic*, and to-day they are even more definitely dualistic than before—now that we describe the opposition as being, not between ego instincts and sexual instincts but between life instincts and death instincts. Jung's libido theory is on the contrary *monistic*; the fact that he calls his one instinctual force "libido" is bound to cause confusion, but need not affect us otherwise.[3]

The confusion arises, obviously, over the fact that for Freud two kinds of instincts (life and death), neither of which is reducible to the other, constitutes a dualism of principles for explanation. Whereas, from Jung's point of view, since both life and death instincts are *instincts*, Freud's system is "monistic." It is Jung's theory that is genuinely a dualism. Psychic energy in the service of "life" cannot be reduced to psychic energy in service of "spirit," or vice versa. But only the libido of "life" energy is *instinctual*. The psychic energy of all manifestations of the unconscious in the service of "spirit" is *symbolical*. Exactly what it has its source *in* is not known. Jung never defines the "objective reality" of the archetypes of the collective unconscious; he makes no statements whatsoever concerning their "ontological nature." It is only a misinterpreter like Edward Glover who believes that Jung has so defined them—perhaps in the sense of an "Objective Spirit" such as one finds in nineteenth-century German Idealism—who, therefore, accuses Jung of "animism."[4]

Jung speaks of the archetypes only as a "subjective reality"—they are psychologically real. But since they are of a radically different nature than *instincts,* which have their sources in biological reality, it is his system, in contrast with Freud's, that is "dualistic." Instincts and archetypes are truly two different, opposed principles for the interpretation of individual psychology; whereas "life instincts" and "death instincts" are both of the same causal nature.

In a sense, Freud had conceived the opposition in psychology to be ultimately rooted in the conflict between what is biological and what is inorganic. For Jung, this would be explained by the fact that Freud had not taken seriously all of the special characteristics of what is "psychologically real." The cause of this would be Freud's desire to approximate the methods of scientifically analyzing the "physically real" in constructing his conceptual analysis of "psychic reality." Since the archetypes cannot be reduced to biological instincts, therefore, Freud's own reflections on phylogenetic traces in psychic heredity remained unintegrated with his general system. What is at stake, on the one hand, is (*a*) the nature of "knowledge" in psychology; on the other hand, it is (*b*) an adequate conception of "psychic reality."

(*a*) If it is stipulated that only what satisfies the logical empiricists' criteria of "scientific language" can qualify as "knowledge," then Freud's system is, at least, *closer* to being knowledge than Jung's is. But this is because Freud himself was trying to maintain the kind of standards that the (subsequent) development of positivistic thought has sharpened and codified. On the other hand, Jung appeals to the Kantian rather than the Comtian tradition in respect to epistemology. And, in so doing, his theory of symbolism, itself, offers a challenge to the philosophy of science. Such a philosopher as Cassirer may be called upon to give support to his efforts. Polanyi's recent book on *Personal Knowledge* must be considered an example of the work possible in the direction of a more accurate epistemology, taking into account the conception of personal, practical, knowledge implicit in Jung's position.

> Man lives in a symbolic universe. Language, myth, art and religion are parts of this universe. They are the varied threads which weave the symbolic net, the tangled web of human experience. . . . No longer can man confront reality immediately; he cannot see it, as it were, face to face. Physical reality seems to recede in proportion as man's symbolic activity advances. Instead of dealing with the things themselves man is in a sense constantly *conversing with himself.* He has so enveloped himself in linguistic forms, in artistic images, in mythical symbols or religious rites that he cannot see or know anything except by the interposition of this artificial medium. His situa-

tion is the same in the theoretical as in the practical sphere. Even here man does not live in a world of hard facts, or according to his immediate needs and desires. He lives rather in the midst of imaginary emotions, in hopes and fears, in illusions and disillusions, in his fantasies and dreams.[5]

Cassirer's metaphoric phrase of man "conversing with himself" is an analogue for what Jung has been trying to describe all along as the "conversation" between the conscious mind and the collective unconscious, in which "himself" becomes the facet of psychic reality which is suprapersonal. As a practising psychotherapist, for Jung the most obvious importance of this "conversation" is that it results in the discovery of "lines" for future development. His position is perfectly clear: any psychology that does not reckon with his source of *personal knowledge* cannot offer a basis for coping with any other manifestation of "Spirit" or "Culture." And, by the same token, no epistemology that ignores the function of intuition can be adequate for all kinds of knowledge.

(*b*) Glover interprets Jung's conception of the function of a collective unconscious as a "devaluation of individual factors"[6]—the empirical conditioning of the individual. And, as a result, Jung carries this "devaluation" "to its logical conclusion by denying the individual man whatever credit or comfort he might derive from his artistic achievements."[7]

What the Freudian assumes is that we understand with certainty what constitutes *the individual man*. But this is precisely what differences among psychological theories point out that we do not understand with certainty. The Freudian Glover appears to be defending the individual's "credit" relative only to this victory at the conscious level in the struggle between consciousness and the (Jungian) personal unconsciousness. Were the Jungian hypothesis of a collective unconscious confirmed, Glover feels that the individual's "credit" would be lost, because consciousness was not the source of the subject matter or method out of which artistic achievements are accomplished.

It is only if we are blinded by the idea of the archetypes, so that we no longer recognize all that has been said about the role of consciousness in interpreting as well as in objectifying symbols, that we can imagine Jung means that all the "credit" for such "achievements" goes to the collective unconscious.

But the problem is analogous in Freudian psychology itself. What is the relationship, in terms of "credit" (responsibility, praise, and blame), between the impersonal factors (the id) and the personal ones (ego con-

sciousness)? Jung's distinctions would make the impersonal factors not
simply opposed to the personal-conscious ones but participating with
them in order to achieve a progressive development. In both cases there
is a social relativity between what is characterized as personal and impersonal. The element of struggle is described in one system as the conflict
between life and death instincts; in the other, as the conflict between
Life and Spirit. Jung's concern with the element of futurity as a positive
"interest" of the unconscious is the crucial difference to set in contrast
with the exclusive concern of Freudian retrospective reductive analysis.
The better psychology is the one that gives us more practical knowledge
of "psychic reality."

II. JUNGIAN PSYCHOLOGY AND AESTHETICS

The question should be raised whether Jung offers nothing more to aesthetics than literary critics or cultural historians can contribute in virtue
of their descriptive classifications. This would bring us to the heart of the
matter.

For Jung, literary and pictorial typologies such as "Classical" and
"Romantic" are primarily concerned with distinctions laid down in respect to *style*. Both Freud and Jung speak of the possible contribution of
psychology to aesthetics in respect to *subject matter*, having in mind such
"material" as exists outside of the work of art and to which it "refers."
They leave questions of style to what they both imply is the sphere of
"formal aesthetics." But the difference between them seems to me perfectly clear.

The effect of the Freudian approach is that the interpretation of art
would consist of (1) formal aesthetics, and (2) psychoanalytic interpretations of artworks, producing retrospective "meaning," and these together would exhaust the field of art criticism. What implications formal
aesthetics might draw for the nature and meaning of art-in-general would
be discounted by the Freudians as unacceptable unless it were grounded
in Freudian psychology. What judgments critics of any of the arts might
make would be discounted for the same reason, were they sociologically,
historically, philosophically, and/or economically oriented. They would
not be able to interpret and explain the "meaning" of artworks.

By contrast, the effect of Jung's approach is precisely to "underwrite" just such criticism. He offers a psychological justification for all
efforts at "taking art seriously." That is to say, while "formal aesthetics"
seems to remain something independent—unexamined by psychoanaly-

sis—all the various facets of art *criticism* are supported insofar as they are attempts to formulate that "previously unknown" into which the work of art gives us an intuition. Either such efforts achieve the goal of interpreting the artwork effectively, so that it functions as a reconciling (transcending) symbol, or they go beyond that to exhaust the implicit or potential reference, in which case the image that has been completely explained ceases to possess the power of a symbol and becomes a sign. But the possibilities for valuable criticism by other than psychoanalysts remain limitless.

If I read Jung correctly, then, the implication of his position is that *critical interpretations of works of art are to a culture what the analyst's interpretations of private symbolic contents are to the individual patient in therapy.*

There is no intention whatsoever inherent in Jung's writing on the subject that would support the idea that the analyst should supplant the critic and treat works of art as if they were patients undergoing analysis. On the contrary, his writing clearly indicates the analogy between what the patient and analyst do in trying to "read the symbol rightly" for the individual and what the audience and the critics do in trying to appreciate a work of art: the problem is to grasp as consciously as possible the prospective significance of something that is ostensibly unintelligible but "driven deeply" into consciousness, and which "stimulates."

The Freudian position seems to be that critics deal only with the "surface" of a work of art and cannot (because they do not have the necessary principles and method for interpretation) understand its psychological essence—its "meaning." This is like saying, if the artwork is compared with a dream, that critics are restricted to trying to draw significance from the "manifest content" without being aware of the more important "latent content."

But Jung's position is that, even if one were to compare the work of art with a dream, only some dreams are signs to be understood retrospectively, by a reductive method; but there are also dreams that are symbols, and these are to be taken as giving "lines" for future development, interpreted by the "synthetic" method appropriate to *them.* The consequence of such a point of view is that, from certain works of art we can derive further understanding, new knowledge, intellectually conceivable formulations of what had been intimated. The role of the critic is to make explicit, as well as he can, what is implicit in the artwork. And Jung considers this an entirely legitimate, valuable, intellectual function—independent of psychology.

In effect, Jung's writings on art present a defense of criticism. Analytic psychology is not the only means of interpreting artworks. It is no substitute for criticism, for formal aesthetics, or for philosophies of art. Its sole function is *to give a psychological justification for efforts to interpret works of art* as an enterprise worthy of respect in its own right. If the theory of psychology that Jung has elaborated—including ideas of the archetypes of the collective unconscious—is directly of use to art critics, so much the better. But his general theory is no substitute for actual criticism, any more than it is a substitute for a patient's psychoanalysis. Nor does he claim for it the importance that followers of Freud have made for reductive art criticism. In his two relatively short essays on the arts, Jung himself has produced practically none of the possible consequences that might be derived from a careful and detailed application of his principles and method to particular works of art. (Actually, a number of critics have begun trying to do this, with varying degrees of success. There are such examples as Theodora Ward's study of Emily Dickinson, Sir Herbert Read's criticism of painting in *Education through Art*, James Baird's study of *Moby-Dick*, Wingfield Digby's *Symbol and Image in William Blake*, Erich Neumann's analysis of the "Cupid and Psyche" of Apuleius, Walter Abell's *The Collective Dream in Art*, and Maud Bodkin's *Studies of Type-Images*.) On the other hand, in his numerous and extensive books, Jung has attempted to make a substantial contribution to the theory of symbolism that would assure the validity of the critical enterprise in general, within which the above cited examples can be included; they would not constitute the exclusive body of what "qualifies" as criticism.

■   ■   ■   ■

When a literary critic such as William York Tindall, writing specifically about symbolic literature, speaks of the artwork as suggesting "more thoughts and feelings than we could state," so that "if we stated as many as we could . . . some would be left over and some would remain unstable,"[8] he is both implicitly supporting Jung's thesis and explicitly affirming the function of criticism, namely to abstract and conceptualize, as well as possible, the thought and feeling content of the artwork. This does not explain "away" the artwork by uncovering causal connections or the creative process; rather, it draws the implications of "meaning" (psychic significance) by establishing warrantable relations between what is present in the work and something else, whether the latter comes from sociological, historical, mythological, or political thought, etc. Such specific criticisms are bound to overlap. But this is an advantage, not a draw-

back. It has the advantage of increasing and extending conscious
understanding (new knowledge) that could be met with opposition only
by such an "aesthetics" as sees just one form of criticism as exclusively
exhaustive of "meaning."

Whether Lionel Trilling writes criticism of Jane Austen (whose
novels seem to exemplify the Psychological Mode, both in subject matter
and method), whether Wallace Fowlie writes criticism of Arthur
Rimbaud (whose poetry seems to exemplify the Visionary Mode, both in
subject matter and method), or whether Erich Auerbach writes of Virginia Woolf (whose novels seem a complex of method and subject matter
in both modes)—the nature of criticism is approximately the same: to
abstract and conceptualize the thought and feeling content implicit in
the work, and to elicit its meaning in relation with other relevant values.
It is precisely this function which Jung's reflections on art serve as a
means of defense; it "protects" it by offering, in a conceptual framework,
a psychological justification for its validity.

To be sure, in making his defense, Jung appears to have been interested in symbolic art to the exclusion of art in the Psychological Mode.
But I think this is only a consequence of his having "bent over back-
wards" to support as useful for society just that kind of art which Freudian analysis implies is most idiosyncratic and therefore of "meaning" only
in the psychology of the individual artist. Consequently, given Jung's distinction between signs and symbols, it may be seen that *works in the Psychological Mode function as signs; works in the Visionary Mode function as
symbols.* Obviously, the acid test is whether the "signal" artwork does
reaffirm one's previously established knowledge and values, and whether
the "symbolic" artwork does *stimulate* one to new knowledge and new
values.

New knowledge of what? It is clear that works of art are not prop-
ositions of a scientific nature. Their "statements" are not to be taken as
referring to "matters of fact" or "a state of affairs" in any physical scientific sense. Such "statements" may be included as constituents within a
verbal or iconographic unit, but the work-as-a-whole is not reducible to
them. They are, as Lionel Trilling has put it, among the "elements"—
rational, moral, or emotional—that are organized and controlled by the
form. Therefore, the effect of the whole (controlled by an "idea-form") is
the subject matter of the critic's interpretation. Now, this will be true of
both cases. In Psychological ("signal") Mode artworks as well as in Visionary ("symbolic") Mode works, it is the idea-form of the whole from
which the critic is making his abstractions and to which he is bringing his

relevant comparative data. In both cases, the effect of the whole artwork is on the whole psychic reality of the audience. What else can be meant by the work of art making possible communication from "the spirit and heart of the *poet as man* to the spirit and heart of mankind," as Jung puts it?

The organization that this "whole" determines is conventionally divided, by critics, between "thought and feeling." The new knowledge, critically derivable from the artwork, therefore, is usually spoken of as a reorganization of thought or of feeling. But Jung points out that there is more to consciousness than that, and there is more to psychic life than just consciousness. Among conscious functions must be included, besides thinking and feeling, also sensing and intuiting. The former two are more amenable to criticism because they are both "rational" functions—i.e., they give conceptual meaning and understanding by means of causal relations (thinking) and make value judgments (feeling). The latter two are less amenable to criticism because they are both "irrational" functions—i.e., the content of perception (sensing) and insights into future possibilities (intuition). Beyond consciousness must be included both the personal and collective unconscious.

The result of this psychological differentiation is that Jung must say: the organization that the idea-form gives to the "whole" of the work of art has its effect on the whole psychic life of the audience. The effect, then, is a reorganization of psychic life in general, not just an appeal to thought or feeling. In any case, it is always true that the work of art must appeal first to sensing, and this in itself is not adequately understood. But, besides that, it would seem to follow that criticism has limited itself unfairly by concentrating on thought and feeling.

Granted that these are the two conscious functions to which works of art in the Psychological Mode do appeal, it is a Procrustean bed on which to mutilate symbolic values if critics limit themselves to interpreting artworks in the Visionary Mode by the same standards. In effect, Jung is offering the critics a justification for a truer, fuller, more accurate and adequate interpretation of symbolic works by establishing a psychological theory in which *intuition* has an understandable role to play, or purpose to fulfill.

It is comparable to the role that individual symbols play in a patient's therapy, that is, a compensatory function between archetypes of the collective unconscious and a present state of consciousness, and a prospective significance, intuitive of a line for future development. For culture, just as for therapy, symbols are not intuitions by themselves;

they are only the brute facts that must be interpreted. Herein lies the inestimable importance of the critical enterprise. Without the "right" conscious interpretation, the symbol remains only an uncomprehended "event." With the right interpretation it can become a "living experience"—contributing to the betterment of the patient, in one case, and of the society, in the other.

Whether or not an interpretation is right is decided pragmatically, i.e., by whether it does *work* to bring about an advance. The "betterment" in both cases rests on the reconciling power of the symbol, a potentiality that can become effective in practice only by way of conscious appreciation. In the case of culture, it is critical intelligence, the activity of criticism, that performs this function.

At the very least, then, such "new knowledge" as is derived from a symbol by the critical appreciation is of value to the progressive reorganization of psychic life as a whole. It cannot qualify as knowledge in the sense that logical empiricism limits "knowledge" to the mathematical and physical sciences. It would appear to be closer to such knowledge as we call wisdom. Wisdom literature is conventionally thought of as concerned with making connections between knowledge and life. And, in this respect, it would be easy to see that the popularity and importance of literary criticism, in particular, exemplifies the common public desire for contemporary wisdom literature. By drawing out relationships between certain artworks and other relevant values, such criticism offers interpretations of artworks that "stimulate" but are not self-evident. The new knowledge (the "wisdom") of such criticism lies in its appreciation of the intuitive or prospective values of the artworks; and its effectiveness lies in its ability to make connections between the symbol and a reorganization of psychic life. If the interpretation is right, it does bring about an improvement in the service of wholeness. If it is not right, and the advance is not derived from it, then the symbol remains only an uncomprehended event. The valuable critic, like the effective analyst, is the one who helps the audience (like the cooperating patient) to interpret those manifestations that are symbolic in purport. By so doing, he exemplifies the expression of wisdom, relating what is known to proposals for how to live better.

This is not the only function of criticism, just as the interpretation of genuine symbols is not the only function of therapy. But by concentrating his defense of artworks on this special interest, Jung has offered a *psychological* justification for the critical enterprise in general.
(1963)

B. IMAGINAL ARCHETYPAL CRITICISM

This subsection of Part 2, Jung and Critical Theory, presents three selections related by their attention to the implications for Jung-and-literature of the radical reorientation of Jung's psychology that James Hillman *(Re-Visioning Psychology,* 1975; *Archetypal Psychology: A Brief Account,* 1983) has urged since the early 1970s. The selections and their accompanying headnotes outline the position of this movement, certainly one of the most important and most debated recent developments for Jungian critical theory. The reader is referred also to the selection from Hillman's *Healing Fiction* in Part 1, to Samuel's definition of *archetype* in subsection A of Part 2, and to the selections by Pratt ("Spinning Among Fields") and Elias-Button ("Journey into an Archetype") for discussion of the importance of Hillman's work in the context of feminism. The reader should note that Hillman and his followers use the term "archetypal psychology" to distinguish their movement from the older "Jungian psychology."

19 DECONSTRUCTIVE PHILOSOPHY AND IMAGINAL PSYCHOLOGY: COMPARATIVE PERSPECTIVES ON JACQUES DERRIDA AND JAMES HILLMAN

Michael Vannoy Adams

Michael Adams is a professor of literature. In this essay he reveals the linkage between the ideas of a younger generation of Jungian critics, influenced by James Hillman's re-visioning of Jung's psychology into their renamed "archetypal psychology," and Continental thinkers such as Derrida, whose writings form the basis for much of America's contemporary literary criticism.

Adams begins with an extended exposition of Derrida's deconstructive philosophy. He presents it in terms that not only display its many ramifications for literary criticism but also, eventually, enable Adams to compare it to, and thereby to elucidate, Hillman's less-well-known imaginal psychology, which is the purpose of the essay. Especially important for Adams in this comparison is Derrida's attack on the structuralists' signifier/signified (i.e., image/concept) opposition, which Derrida believes has served as "justification for all the other oppositions" characteristic of Western thought. Derrida's rebellion against this unjustified habit of thought is similar in both content and style to Hillman's questioning of Jung's position concerning the archetypal image/archetype opposition, and to Hillman's call for analogizing, rather than allegorizing, the image.

In a real sense, the deconstructive philosophy of Jacques Derrida is a reaction to (or against) the structural anthropology of Claude Lévi-Strauss. At the very least, deconstruction is a departure from structuralism—or, perhaps more precisely, from the oppositional logic of structuralism. Lévi-Strauss asserts that the mind, whether "savage" or "civilized," categorizes phenomena in oppositions. (Savage/civilized would be one such opposition, as would such classic oppositions as mind/body, subject/object, space/time, form/content, and nature/culture.) The *phenomena* that the savage mind selects as relevant to categorize in oppositional terms may be different from those that the civilized mind regards as pertinent, but, according to Lévi-Strauss, this in no way implies that the *structure* of the civilized mind is qualitatively (that is, evolutionarily) either different from or superior to that of the savage mind. In contrast to Lucien Levy-Bruhl, who maintained that the savage mind was "prelogical" (although he did eventually repudiate the notion), Lévi-Strauss insists that the savage mind is just as logical as the civilized mind. In fact, he contends that the logic in both cases is identical—and it is a logic of oppositions (perhaps the most famous of which, at least in structural anthropology, is the "raw" and the "cooked").

The structuralist studies myths (and other texts). What interests him is not the contents (the mythemes, or gross constituent units of a myth) as they happen to be narrated diachronically, but rather the form (the oppositional logic of the myth) as it may be schematized synchronically. In short, the structuralist is by definition a formalist. Thus he systematically extracts or abstracts the oppositions that inform or structure a myth, in order to represent diagrammatically the logic that governs the relations between and the transformations of these oppositions (for example, the transformation of the raw into the cooked or the savage into the civilized)—or at least that is what the structuralist supposes he does. The structuralist argues that these oppositions are implicitly present— objectively inherent, if tacitly so—in the text and, in addition, that they existed in the savage mind that more or less unconsciously composed the myth. In *Structuralist Poetics* Jonathan Culler suggests that such oppositions may not be in the text—much less in the mind of any savage or, as the case may be, in the mind of any poet—but may merely be in the mind of the structuralist, who arbitrarily imputes these oppositions to the text—that is, imposes certain assumptions on the text: conventions, or heuristic devices, that enable him to study the text in one rather than another, perhaps equally valid, way. If so, such "structures" would simply be constructs, and the only justification for them would be pragmatic expedience.

As practiced by Derrida in such inimitable style, deconstructive philosophy subjects to scrutiny certain metaphysical assumptions and value judgments that he asserts the West has accepted and applied uncritically in order to categorize phenomena. The very word *deconstruction* epitomizes the effort to subvert and transcend the logic of oppositions (for example, the opposition construction/destruction). In short, deconstruction is not a contradiction in terms but a pun with the logic of a paradox. According to Derrida, the West has categorized phenomena differentially or oppositionally, but it has not been content simply to differentiate one phenomenon from another and then to oppose one to the other. The West has also *privileged* one phenomenon *over* another. It has judged one to be more valuable than the other. It has considered one to be superior (primary and originative) and the other to be inferior (secondary and derivative)—or, as Derrida says, merely supplementary. Thus the logic of oppositions is the logic of the supplement.

In *The Conquest of America: The Question of the Other*, Tzvetan Todorov demonstrates in practical terms what the deconstructive "method," for lack of a better word, can accomplish. According to him, the encounter between Europeans and native Americans (in this instance, the Spaniards and the Indians) in the period immediately after the discovery of America in 1492 is a case with paradigmatic implications for all subsequent attempts by a "self" to conquer and colonize an "other." Todorov provides a graphic representation of the logic of superiority and inferiority by which Sepúlveda at Valladolid in 1550 opposed the Spaniards to the Indians and privileged the self over the other:

$$\frac{\text{Spaniards}}{\text{Indians}} = \frac{\text{adults (fathers)}}{\text{children (sons)}} = \frac{\text{men (husbands)}}{\text{women (wives)}} = \frac{\text{human beings}}{\text{animals (monkeys)}}$$

$$\frac{\text{forbearance}}{\text{savagery}} = \frac{\text{moderation}}{\text{violence}} = \frac{\text{soul}}{\text{body}} = \frac{\text{reason}}{\text{appetite}} = \frac{\text{good}}{\text{evil}} = \frac{\text{superior}}{\text{inferior}}$$

Although Todorov never once mentions the word *deconstruction*, in effect he deconstructs the oppositions conqueror/conquered and colonizer/colonized and exposes the metaphysical assumptions and logical (or ideological) biases that served Sepúlveda as convenient excuses in his effort to rationalize the subjugation of the Indians by the Spaniards. (In contrast to Derrida, however, Todorov does not imply that such invidious distinctions and intolerant practices are peculiar to the imperialistic West in the modern period. He admits that there are ample historical precedents for and parallels to this particular, although perhaps especially drastic, example of discrimination.) As an alternative to the logic of oppo-

sitions, Todorov recommends a logic of differences that would adhere to
the tenets of cultural relativism and, on the basis of impartial comparisons, result in "nonviolent communication" rather than violent confrontation between the self and the other. He advocates an attitude that
would neither assimilate the other as identical to the self nor alienate the
other as inferior to the self, but would simply appreciate (and respect)
the other as different from yet equal to the self. Todorov acknowledges
how difficult it is to realize this deconstructive ideal: "To experience difference in equality is easier said than done."[1]

As Christopher Norris defines deconstruction, it is "not simply a
strategic reversal of categories." It is an activity that "seeks to undo both
a given order of priorities and the very system of conceptual oppositions
that makes that order possible."[2] The objective is not only to reverse the
way the West has historically categorized certain phenomena but also to
expose the way it has arbitrarily prioritized (or privileged) some phenomena over others and uncritically utilized oppositional logic as a means to
that end. There is an affinity between the reversal of categories that Derrida advocates and the transvaluation of values that Nietzsche envi-
sioned, as well as the revolution of classes that Marx prophesied. For
example, Marx repudiates in no uncertain terms the ideological assumptions that he contends the capitalistic West has contrived to categorize
certain phenomena—in this case, classes. But he does not just reverse
the way the West, on the basis of the opposition greed/need, has historically privileged one class (the owners) over another (the workers). Although he adopts the oppositional logic of class conflict and exploits it for
rhetorical effect in the cause of revolution, he does so not in order simply
to subordinate the owners to the workers. He realizes that the reversal of
categories or revolution of classes is only a phase, although a necessary
one, in the struggle to establish a classless society in which the concepts
"owners" and "workers" would cease to have any significance (because
the workers would be the owners of the means of production)—a society,
that is, in which the oppositional logic of class conflict would no longer
serve any conceivable purpose. Marx proposes not to replace one order of
economic priorities with another (although he does tend to idealize the
proletariat) but to displace the entire system of conceptual oppositions
that validates the very existence of *any* order of economic priorities.
(Whether a communistic West would merely be a totalitarian West,
whether Marx is Utopian rather than scientific, is, of course, a serious
consideration but quite another matter.)

Derrida says explicitly and emphatically that a reversal of categories is a necessary (although not a sufficient) condition of any act of deconstruction.

> I strongly and repeatedly insist on the necessity of the phase of reversal, which people have perhaps too swiftly attempted to discredit. . . . To neglect this phase of reversal is to forget that the structure of the opposition is one of conflict and subordination and thus to pass too swiftly, without gaining any purchase against the former opposition, to a *neutralization* which in *practice* leaves things in their former state and deprives one of any way of intervening effectively.[3]

In a gloss on this passage Culler cautions that to dispense with the phase of reversal and to indulge in the casual expression of equalitarian sentiments amounts merely to a facile and naively ineffectual exercise: "Affirmations of equality will not disrupt the hierarchy. Only if it includes an inversion or reversal does a deconstruction have a chance of dislocating the hierarchical structure."[4] To experience difference in equality—rather than superiority and inferiority in opposition—may be the ultimate objective of deconstruction, but immediately and complacently to affirm that one phenomenon is equal to another is a premature gesture that serves no practical purpose. The result of such a declaration is not to displace the previous state of affairs (or order of priorities) but to keep it in place—and not to obtain any real advantage. It is to neutralize every effort to intervene and effect a radical alteration or dislocation in the oppositional or hierarchical structure. Deconstruction is thus an attempt not simply to reverse certain categories but to displace, to dislocate, or to shift (if ever so slightly and slowly) a historical structure and the logical system that has served as a convenient excuse for it. Todorov formulates this article of deconstructive theory and practice in characteristically eloquent style:

> I do not believe that history obeys a system, nor that its so-called laws permit deducing future or even present forms of society; but rather that to become conscious of the relativity (hence of the arbitrariness) of any feature of our culture is already to shift it a little, and that history (not the science but the subject) is nothing other than a series of such imperceptible shifts.[5]

According to Derrida, the West has employed oppositional (or conflictual) logic to privilege the spoken over the written, the serious over the frivolous, the factual over the fictional, the literal over the figural, the prosaic over the poetic, the referential over the reflexive, the masculine over the feminine, and so on and so forth. One term in the relation has had a positive, the other a negative, connotation. The West has regarded one term as primary and originative, the other as secondary and derivative, and has relegated the latter (the subordinate or merely supplementary term) to a condition of dependence on the former. One term has been the host, as it were, the other the parasite. Among the oppositions that Derrida deconstructs perhaps the most important is the opposition between the signified and signifier—that is, between the "concept" and the "image." (To define the signifier more or less exclusively as a sound-image, as Ferdinand de Saussure tends to do, is to adopt an untenably restrictive linguistic rather than a properly comprehensive semiotic perspective. There are just as many varieties of image as there are sensory media. As William Blake says, "Five windows light the cavern'd Man." In addition to sound-images, there are sight-images, taste-images, touch-images, and smell-images—hence the preference for the word *image,* which does not privilege one sensory medium over another.) The reason the opposition signified/signifier is so important to Derrida is that it is precisely this opposition that has served as a logical (or epistemological) justification for all the other oppositions that the West has employed to categorize phenomena. Thus, in order eventually to deconstruct these other oppositions, Derrida has initially to deconstruct the opposition signified/signifier. He argues that the relation between the signified and the signifier, between the concept and the image, is an arbitrary (or conventional) one. There is no necessary connection, that is, between the signified and a signifier; the connection is a purely discretionary one. There is no objective, transcendentally valid reason to relate a particular signifier to a particular signified and then to reduce the one to the other and declare that this signified, rather than that signified, is what the signifier "means" in a specific case.

To reduce the signifier to a signified and declare that this is what the signifier means is to privilege the signified over the signifier. But Derrida insists that "every signified is also in the position of a signifier."[6] He thus paraphrases what Charles Sanders Peirce concluded or conceded: that the process of signification is an infinite regression. In the semiotic jargon that Peirce devised, the signifier is the "sign," the signified the "interpretant." Peirce says that the sign is a representation. It represents something to somebody "in some respects or capacity." The sign "addresses somebody, that is, creates in the mind of that person an equivalent, or perhaps a more developed sign." (Why it might not create in the mind of that person a *less* developed sign Peirce does not say, although surely that is a possibility too.) "That sign which it creates," Peirce says, "I call the *interpretant* of the first sign." Not only by definition but also in fact, the interpretant is a sign that someone employs to interpret another sign (the signified is a signifier that someone employs to interpret another signifier). But if every interpretant is a sign, if every signified is (or occupies the position of) a signifier, then all that remains, in effect, is a series of signs or signifiers—one that regresses to infinity. Peirce acknowledges that the process of signification is logically illimitable (the only way to limit it is by an act of closure that arbitrarily arrests the process, and the only justification for such an act is purely pragmatic expedience): "So there is an infinite regression here. Finally the interpretant is nothing but another representation"—that is, another sign—"and as a representation, it has its interpretant again. Lo! another infinite series."

Culler attempts to deny, or at least to qualify, what this infinite regression logically entails. What it entails is that there is no interpretant (or signified) to which the series of signs (or signifiers) is ultimately reducible—that although there may be, in theory, a "final" interpretant (as Peirce says), there is none in practice. Culler asserts that the infinite regression does not necessarily imply "indeterminacy of meaning in the usual sense: the impossibility or unjustifiability of choosing one meaning over another." He contends that apparently unimpeachable criteria exist to determine what a signifier (or series of signifiers) means on a specific occasion, in a specific context, and he quotes Derrida in an effort to rebut the suggestion that no good reasons exist to relate a particular signifier to a particular signified:

> On the contrary, it is only because there may be excellent reasons for choosing one meaning rather than another that there is any point in insisting that the meaning chosen is itself also a signifier that can be interpreted in turn. The fact that the signified is also in the position of signifier does not mean that there are no reasons to link a signifier with one signified rather than another; still less does it suggest, as both hostile and sympathetic critics have claimed, an absolute priority of the signifier. . . . "The 'primacy' or 'priority' of the signifier," writes Derrida, "would be an absurd and untenable expression. . . . The signifier will never by rights precede the signified, since it would no longer be a signifier and the signifier 'signifier' would have no possible signified."[7]

There is, of course, no dearth of "reasons" that someone may adduce to rationalize the relation of a signifier to a signified and the reduction of the one to the other (or the reduction of a series of signifiers to a signified, the common denominator, as it were, by which all the signifiers are presumably divisible). But whether these are "good" (much less "excellent") reasons is quite another matter. By what criteria such reasons are good, bad, or indifferent Culler never says. In fact, to relate a signifier to one signified rather than another is, as Culler admits, a choice, and whether the reasons for the choice in a specific case are good or not is merely a matter of opinion. Every such choice is a value judgment that entails an exclusionary principle. To choose one signified rather than another and to insist that this is what the signifier means is to judge certain criteria more valuable than others. To express such a preference is preemptorily to exclude or summarily to dismiss from consideration other criteria that, from another perspective, might appear to be equally valid and that might complicate or even contradict the choice. To try to deny the inexhaustibility (if not the indeterminacy) of signification and the relativity of all criteria is to commit a fallacy and to conduct a futile exercise.

Derrida does, as Culler indicates, say that to attribute priority to the signifier over the signified would be to assume a preposterous and indefensible position. That a signifier is a signifier only in relation to a signified—that is, in relation to what it signifies, or means—is an analytic proposition that is "true" by virtue of the very definition of the word *signifier*. But if the reversal of categories is, as Derrida also maintains, a necessary phase in the act of deconstruction, then a reversal of the order of priorities that has previously subordinated the signifier to the signified serves a vital purpose, although a strictly strategic one. A phase of reversal that would, for a change, privilege the signifier over the signified would provide an opportunity for reflection, for a reconsideration of just what constitutes the true nature of the relation between the signifier and the signified. It is in this sense, and this sense only, that it is unobjectionable to attribute priority to the signifier over the signified. That the signified is (or is also) a signifier implies that there exists, at least for the duration of the phase of reversal, a purely differential relation between signifiers in a series rather than a simple oppositional relation between the signified and the signifier. These are signifiers in a regressive series, signifiers that, as Derrida indicates by means of the nonce word *différance*, "differ" one from another and infinitely "defer" the choice of a transcendental signified that would limit the process of signification by an act of closure that would arbitrarily arrest the process—the choice, that is, of a final interpretant that would interpret the series of signs in some ultimate sense, even (or especially) if this interpretant were one with polysemous implications. It is in this regard that Derrida proposes "dissemination" as an alternative to the polysemy of interpretation. (The "sem" in *polysemy* derives etymologically from *semeion*, or sign. In *dissemination* the "sem" refers to semen, or seed—but, by means of an ingeniously spurious etymological derivation on the part of Derrida, it, too, alludes to *semeion*. Thus Derrida puns on the infinitely regressive dispersion of the sign or seed. In contrast to interpretation, which is a sterile product, dissemination is a fertile process, a proliferation of signs or seeds that regress to infinity—to a "truth" that exists only at a purely hypothetical vanishing point where the parallel lines of signifier and signified presumably meet.) Derrida argues that there exists no signified that transcends the text (or series of signifiers), no signified that in imagination, intention, or experience thematizes or totalizes what the text means, with the result that the text ceases to express or represent any polysemous truth. This is why he says, in the imperative, "It is this hermeneutic concept of polysemy that must be replaced by dissemination."[8]

Deconstructive philosophy has, as Culler observes, not only evoked a sympathetic response but also provoked a hostile reaction. Some critics have regarded it simply as an application of the indeterminacy or uncertainty principle to texts, while other critics have regarded it as the institutionalization of an irresponsibility principle with insidiously nihilistic implications. In contrast to deconstructive philosophy, imaginal psychology has yet to excite much controversy (or much interest). Few critics know what imaginal psychology is, or, for that matter, who James Hillman, the principal proponent of imaginal psychology, is. Imaginal psychology is a depth psychology, a psychology of the unconscious. It derives from analytical (or archetypal) psychology but also departs from it, as well as from psychoanalysis. Formerly the director of studies at the C. G. Jung Institute in Zurich, Hillman is the author of at least ten books, among the most important of which are *Re-Visioning Psychology* (which he delivered as the Terry Lectures at Yale University), *The Dream and the Underworld,* and *The Myth of Analysis;* he is the editor of *Spring: An Annual of Archetypal Psychology and Jungian Thought;* he is the subject of an extensive interview with the aptly ironical title *Inter Views,* and he is the author of a psychological commentary on Kundalini, an account by Gopi Krishna of personal experiences with what Avalon (Sir John Woodroffe) called "the serpent power."

Although few critics yet realize it, there is a remarkable affinity

between imaginal psychology and deconstructive philosophy, between
Hillman and Derrida. (Hillman employs the term "imaginal,"[9] in contrast to the word "imaginary," which has the pejorative connotation of
"unreal." In this, he follows Jung, who emphasized that the imagination
is a "psychic reality" more ontologically and existentially immediate than
any physical reality.) It is not that Derrida has influenced Hillman—
quite the contrary—but rather that Derrida and Hillman have reached
similar conclusions by different and independent means. (Perhaps this is
evidence that what they have to say has validity.) Hillman even says that
he infers that "destructuralizing"[10] (by which he evidently means
"deconstructing") is an activity similar in purpose to what he means by
"revisioning": an effort to counteract the pervasive tendency to interpret
the image, that is, to reduce it to a concept—to what it "means" in hermeneutic terms. (In semiotic or deconstructive jargon, the image is, of
course, the signifier, and the concept, the signified.)

    According to Hillman, interpretation, as both Freudian and Jung-
ian analysts practice it, is invariably a reductionistic conceptualization of
the imagination. The interpretations that these analysts produce are utterly predictable scholastic exercises—a veritable monotony of concepts,
with the result that images cease to astonish. Analyzing, Hillman asserts,
has degenerated into allegorizing:

> The use of allegory as a defense continues today in the interpreta-
> tions of dreams and fantasies. When images no longer surprise us,
> when we can expect what they mean and know what they intend, it
> is because we have our "symbologies" of established meanings.
> Dreams have been yoked to the systems which interpret them; they
> belong to schools—there are "Freudian dreams," "Jungian
> dreams," etc. If long things are penises for Freudians, dark things
> are shadows for Jungians. Images are turned into predefined con-
> cepts such as passivity, power, sexuality, anxiety, femininity, much
> like the conventions of allegorical poetry.[11]

Although both Freudian and Jungian analysts might object that this is not
an accurate characterization but only a vulgar caricature, Hillman contends that formulaic interpretations are the rule rather than the exception. Freud devised the contextual method of "free association" as an
alternative to the cryptographic method of interpretation, which treated
the dream as a message in cipher from the unconscious and sought to
decode it by reference to a dictionary of typical (or even universal) sym-

bols. Although Freud allowed that there are some typical symbols, he cautioned that an analyst should never presume that he knows what a dream means but should instead induce the dreamer to interpret the dream by means of free association. According to Freud, this was the only way to allay the suspicion that a specific interpretation was simply an arbitrary construction on the part of the analyst. To the extent that Freudians and Jungians allegorize rather than analyze, they violate this fundamental principle. What concerns Hillman, however, is not just that analysts resort to an actual dictionary of symbols; it is that they rely at all on concepts in order to interpret, or define, images. Even free association culminates in an interpretation, a translation of images into concepts— into what the dream "really" means. As an alternative to free association, Jung proposed the comparative method of "amplification." But according to Hillman, amplification also tends to result in a reductionistic conceptualization of the imagination. In short, interpretation (whether by free association or by amplification) is an attempt at demystification. Hillman insists that the dreamer should experience the image rather than reduce it to a concept—rather than demystify, interpret, or translate it: "For a dream image to work in life it must, like a mystery, be experienced as fully real. Interpretation arises when we have lost touch with the images, when their reality is derivative, so that this reality must be recovered through conceptual translation."[12] (In deconstructive terms, analysts have, in effect, opposed the concept to the image and privileged the one over the other. They have regarded the concept as primary and originative, the image as secondary and, as Hillman says, derivative.)

Hillman would revision the oppositional logic that the iconoclastic West has habitually employed to categorize phenomena and reduce images to concepts. According to Hillman, "oppositionalism" is pervasive—ineluctably so; under the circumstances, the only appropriate (in fact, the only possible) response is not to accept oppositions uncritically (or unconsciously) but to revision them—that is, to displace, to dislocate, or to shift them by an act of reflection:

> This "ism," like any other, is an ideological frame imposed upon life by our minds and is usually unconscious to our minds. . . .
>
> We cannot move to another planet with another universe of discourse, or even to another cultural habit. Since we must remain where oppositionalism is in our very ground, the best we can do is enlighten ourselves about it . . . to shift oppositions, so that we may be less caught by them and more able to use them.[13]

Hillman mentions a number of oppositions that exert a subtle, even subliminal influence on analysts. Perhaps the most famous is the opposition ego/id, which Freud immortalized (or at least popularized) in the dictum, "Where id was, there shall the ego be." Ironically, this maxim is so memorable, at least in part, because Freud illustrated the concept with an image. The ultimate objective of analysis, he declared, is to reclaim land (the ego) from the Zuider Zee (the id). Freud thus privileged the ego over the id. In just this way, both Freudian and Jungian analysts have established an order of priorities that privileges the conscious over the unconscious, the rational over the irrational, the logical over the pathological, the normal over the abnormal. To Hillman, the most dubious value judgment of all is the one that privileges the conceptual over the imaginal.

An anecdote should suffice to illustrate the difference in attitude between Hillman and Jung (or, for that matter, between Hillman and Freud) in regard to images and concepts. In this instance, the image is a coiled black snake. Jung recounts the case of a patient, a young woman, twenty-seven or twenty-eight years old, who once consulted him:

> Her first words were when I had seated her, "You know, doctor, I come to you because I have a snake in my abdomen." "What?" "Yes, a snake, a black snake coiled up right in the bottom of my abdomen." I must have made a rather bewildered face at her, for she said, "You know, I don't mean it literally, but I should say it was a snake, a snake." In our further conversation a little later—that was about the middle of her treatment which lasted only for ten consultations—she said she had foretold me, "I'll come ten times, and then it will be all right." "But how do you know?" I asked. "Oh, I've got a hunch." And really, about the fifth or sixth consultation she said, "Oh, doctor, I must tell you, the snake has risen, it is now about here." Hunch! Then on the tenth day I said, "Now this is our last consultation. Do you feel cured?" And she said, beaming, "You know, this morning it came up, it came out of my mouth, and the head was golden." Those were her last words.[14]

Jung proceeds to interpret (in this case, to amplify by means of an ethnological parallel) this extraordinary image and to reduce it to an ordinary, if unfamiliar, concept. For Jung, the image of the coiled snake in the abdomen is a typical (or archetypal) symbol from the collective unconscious:

I told you the case of that intuitive girl who suddenly came out with the statement that she had a black snake in her body. Well now, that is a collective symbol. That is not an individual fantasy, it is a collective fantasy. It is well known in India. She had nothing to do with India, but though it is entirely unknown to us we have it too, for we are all similarly human. So I even thought in the first moment that perhaps she was crazy, but she was only highly intuitive. In India the serpent is at the basis of a whole philosophical system, of Tantrism; it is Kundalini, the Kundalini serpent. This is something known only to a few specialists, generally it is not known that we have a serpent in the abdomen. That is a collective dream or collective fantasy.[15]

In Kundalini yoga the snake in the abdomen rises up the spine through successive *cakras* until it finally emerges above the top of the head as the lotus with a thousand petals. That the snake in the abdomen of the young woman emerges from the mouth does not complicate matters for Jung. He argues that the young woman had an innate, intuitive knowledge of an ancient system of philosophy (or technique of meditation), and on that basis, he reduces the image to a concept: the serpent power. (For Freud, the image of a coiled snake in the abdomen of a young woman would probably have been a symbol of repressed sexuality.)

According to Hillman, whether the image is a coiled snake in the abdomen or a coiled snake in the corner, to reduce the image to a concept is to allegorize, not analyze:

We sin against the imagination whenever we ask an image for its meaning, requiring that images be translated into concepts. The coiled snake in the corner cannot be translated into my fear, my sexuality, or my mother-complex without killing the snake. . . . Interpretations and even amplifications of images, including the whole analytical kit of symbolic dictionaries and ethnological parallels, too often become instruments of allegory. Rather than vivifying the imagination by connecting our conceptual intellects with the images of dreams and fantasies, they exchange the image for a commentary on it or a digest of it.[16]

To interpret what the image means, Hillman says, is to misconstrue the purpose of analysis:

For instance, a black snake comes in a dream, a great big black snake, and you can spend a whole hour with this black snake talking about the devouring mother, talking about the anxiety, talking about the repressed sexuality, talking about the natural mind, all those interpretative moves that people make, and what is left, what is vitally important, is what that snake is doing, this crawling huge black snake . . . and the moment you've defined the snake, interpreted it, you've lost the snake, you've stopped it, and then the person leaves the hour with a concept about my repressed sexuality or my cold black passions or my mother or whatever it is, and you've lost the snake. The task of analysis is to keep the snake there, the black snake, and there are various ways of keeping the black snake . . . see, the black snake's no longer necessary the moment it's been interpreted, and you don't need your dreams any more because they've been interpreted.

But I think you need them all the time, you need that very image you had during the night.[17]

The reason why it is so important to keep the image is "because that image keeps you in an imaginative possibility." To lose the image, to reduce it to a concept that is a foregone conclusion—for example, "my guilt complex"—is to interpret the image in terms of "your ego system of what you know, your guilt," with the result that the dreamer now has an easy conscience because he presumes to know just what the image means. "You've absorbed the unknown into the known (made the unconscious conscious)," Hillman says, "and nothing, absolutely nothing has happened, nothing." For Hillman, the image is always more important than any concept: "I mean *The image is always more inclusive, more complex* (it's a complex, isn't it?) *than the concept.* Let's make that a rule. That's why 'stick to the image' is another rule."[18]

It was a great discovery, Hillman readily acknowledges, suddenly to realize, as Freud and Jung did, just how profound in implication the images in dreams and fantasies are. But then to attempt to ascertain only what these images might mean, as if the interpretation of dreams and fantasies were the sole reason for the very existence of these images, appears in retrospect, Hillman argues, to have been a questionable objective, a too restrictive one:

We have, since Freud, since 1900, this great *Traumdeutung,* where he said, "My goodness, look at the dreams!" The dreams—all these images in your dreams are significant, tremendously significant. And then Jung said, "All those images going on in psychotics are tremendously significant. The fantasies, the dreams, the images are going on forever in the collective unconsciousness. They're the background of art, they're the background of madness, they're the background of thought, the background of childhood thinking, the background of ritual . . . it's everywhere. The image, the imagination, is fundamental."

But then what they actually did was to make a move that we no longer want to do. Their move, that they both made, was to translate the images into crystallized symbolic meanings. That is, they took whatever they saw and didn't leave it where it was, but moved it into "this *means* that." I don't want to go into the details of their systems of translation. Put it another way—they brought up the material and then by the translation sent it back down again. Once you've translated the dream into your Oedipal situation or your omnipotence fantasy or your penis-envy or you've translated the big black snake into the mother, the Great Mother, you no longer need the image, and you let the image only say one thing, one word: Great Mother. Then it disappears. You don't want that black snake really any more. You want to work on your mother complex, change your personality and so on. . . . As somebody said about Jung, his whole myth was the myth of meaning. Now let's leave meaning, and the search for meaning, and the meaning of life.[19]

Freud and Jung could not leave the image well enough alone. They could not resist the urge to interpret it symbolically—that is, conceptually. In contrast, when Hillman insists that the image is more inclusive, more complex, than the concept, he emphasizes the particularity of the concrete image over the generality of any abstract concept. Interpretation is thus simplification, an exclusion of those imaginative possibilities that Hillman says are so much more important to the dreamer than any conceptual reduction. Rather than rely complacently on an interpretation that regards the image as a symbol and reduces it to a concept—to what it means—Hillman suggests that the dreamer should stick to the image, adhere to the "precise presentation"[20] of the image. Rather than immediately resort to a hermeneutic paraphrase of the image, the dreamer should attend to the phenomenological nuances, the unique sensuous qualities and activities, of the big black snake, reflect on them, and perhaps even elaborate on them (by means, for example, of the method of active imagination).

As an alternative to allegorizing, Hillman proposes "analogizing."

He defines analogy as "likeness in *function* but not in *origin.*" For example, the big black snake coiled in the abdomen or in the corner may be like a snake in the grass, a snake in the basket, a snake on the tree, or a snake on the cross; it may be a sleeping, dreaming snake or a waking, rising snake; it may be like a rattling, striking snake; it may be like a "cunning," "poised" snake (that is, a punning snake); it may be like a charmed serpent, a bruised serpent, a brazen serpent, a plumed serpent; it may be like the snakes of Medusa, of Laocoön, of Krishna, of Siva, of Clytemnestra, of Antony and Cleopatra, of Adam and Eve, of Aaron and Pharaoh, of Friedrich August Kékulé von Stradonitz and the benzene ring or Thomas Pynchon and the rainbow rocket; it may be like Quetzalcoatl, like Uroboros, or like Kundalini. It may have a function similar to any or all of these and other snakes (or, for that matter, to none of them), but a similar function does not, by any means, imply the same origin. "Analogies," Hillman asserts, "keep us in the functional operation of the image, in the patterns of similarities, without positing a common origin for these similarities." To posit such an origin is to allegorize rather than analogize: to regard the big black snake as a symbol, to reduce the image to a concept such as evil, sin, death, sex, birth, life, power, and so on. "The operative term is 'like,' " Hillman says. "This is like that."[21] (Not, as Freud and Jung said, this *means* that.)

Appropriately enough, Hillman describes what analogizing is like by means of an analogy:

> Analogizing is like my fantasy of Zen, where the dream is the teacher. Each time you say what an image means you get your face slapped. The dream becomes a Koan when we approach it by means of analogy. If you . . . "interpret" a dream, you are off the track, lost your Koan. (For the dream is the thing, not what it means.)
>
> Then you must be slapped to bring you back to the image. A good dream analysis is one in which one gets more and more slaps, more and more analogies, the dream exposing your entire unconsciousness, the basic matters of your psychic life.[22]

Hillman argues that the dreamer should submit to (and reflect on) an infinitely regressive number of slaps, analogies, and images—the more, the better—since the only alternative is an allegory, a concept:

> So the infinite regress should not bother us; it occurs even in empiricism when one tries to follow a sequence of ideas back to their "ori-

gin" in an observation of a "hard fact." Psychologizing by means of the infinite regress is also regressing toward the infinite, the God within. Each step in the process yields insight. It is like peeling the mystic's onion, but here not for the sake of an esoteric void at the core but for the sake of the perpetual movement inward.[23]

Whether the dream is more like a Koan or an onion, it is apparently an inexhaustible source of imaginative possibilities—if the dreamer and the analyst allow as much and respond to it with the proper sensitivity. If, however, they reduce a series of images to a concept, a series of analogies to an allegory, a series of similar functions to a common origin, they arbitrarily limit these possibilities.

Hillman does not propose to eliminate all concepts, even if that were possible. He admits that conceptual language, like oppositional logic, is a permanent fixture, a necessary feature, of contemporary discourse—although it is also, he cautions, one of the hooks and snares of the ego:

> Sure, I think in concept. . . . We're modern civilized people, we need our concepts. Of course, I don't mean throw out all conceptual language, but, generally speaking, conceptual language is where we're caught, where we are in the ego, where things are dead, where we go back to what is already made and finished and where the images can't reach us.[24]

What concerns Hillman is the assumption on the part of ego psychology (which is a conceptual rather than an imaginal psychology) that it is not only possible but also desirable, at every opportunity, to substitute concepts for images. (According to Hillman, to the extent that Freudian and Jungian analysts produce interpretations, they are all psychologists in the service of the ego—whether they realize it or not.) To conceptualize the image in this way is not to analyze, Hillman argues, but to allegorize: to obliterate all traces of the concrete phenomenological particularity of the image. Thus Hillman contends that conceptual psychology can result in *coagulation*, "so that before we know it we are strangled in a new typology—Gods and Goddesses as stereotypical models on a tight network for placing everything." But he also expresses an equally serious reservation about imaginal psychology. He concedes that it can result in *dissolution*, "so that all we do is move words around in an existential vacuum, anything as good as everything else in endless widespread analogies."[25] Although Hillman privileges the image over the concept (and employs polemical rhetoric in the process), perhaps this is only a phase of reversal, a strategy necessary to counteract the iconoclastic tendencies of analysts and to revision psychology imaginally: to remind analysts (who have forgotten or repressed the fact) that the concept needs the image just as much as—or more than—the image needs the concept.

Derrida and Hillman would reverse the logic of oppositions and the order of priorities that have privileged the signified over the signifier, the concept over the image. They would substitute dissemination or phenomenology for hermeneutics. This is not to say that there are no differences between Derrida and Hillman. But the differences are perhaps more semantic than theoretical or practical. For example, Derrida rejects the term "polysemy," while Hillman retains it. Hillman privileges the image over the concept because it implies multiple—or, he says, polysemous—imaginative possibilities.[26] If, as he seems to do, Hillman means a regressively infinite, logically indeterminate (in the strict sense of indeterminacy rather than merely what Freud meant by "overdetermination") number of such possibilities, then this difference between Derrida and Hillman is more apparent than real. Deconstructive philosophy and imaginal psychology are not reducible, the one to the other. But what Hillman would do for psychology is remarkably similar to (if not quite the same as) what Derrida would do for philosophy. What Derrida would deconstruct, Hillman would revision, imaginally.
(1985)

20 POETRY AND PSYCHE

Charles Boer

Charles Boer, professor of literature, poet, and current editor of the Jungian-archetypalist journal Spring, *presented this paper to the First International Seminar of Archetypal Psychology, a Hillman-inspired gathering. Boer traces a history of the poetic image, especially in its assumed relationship to psyche, in American poetry and criticism of the twentieth century. He cites the poet Charles Olson, and his belief in "objectism," which saw the objective world outside the mind as also "psyche (as imaginative and imagined)," as the person to credit for encouraging poetry to see that an image can and should be the basis for the act of knowing, not merely a subjective expression of the ego. Boer notes the difficulty of determining when a deep image in a poem has the ring of authenticity or is merely eccentric. However, his focusing of attention on the image has the effect of directly relating contemporary poetry, an obvious source of images, with the imaginal school of James Hillman and the archetypal psychologists who are re-visioning the Jungian concept of the archetype.*

Let me call your archetypalist attention to Charles Olson,[1] who was already talking about a poetry of soul (rendered first as "space") as early as 1948: "The measure of work now afoot is the depth of the perception of space, both as space informs objects and as it contains, in antithesis to time, secrets of a humanitas eased out of contemporary narrows."[2]

Specifically, Olson saw the realization of this "space" through a radical understanding of psychological analysis:

> It is time analysis be recognized as an opener not to cure but to cause a freeing of the human being both back into the ambiguity of himself and out into fable (dreams as the myth of the individual), sick or not—"L'humanité, c'est l'infirmité," and the sum of dreams the archetype source of the myth and faith of the race—not some norm of national advertised future health. Which brings me back to what I said at the beginning of these notes: all analysis is stuck on the rails of time. And an idea for a title to the proposition that man is prospective: PRIMORDIA.[3]

This is no old anything like "Jungianism" or "national advertised future health." As Olson moved his own writing and self out into fable, he moved out of *humanitas*. His work is not a humanism for our day but a poetry of soul, whose reach exceeds a humanist perspective altogether as the gods (inhumanly) take over (and in Olson's case, strange gods indeed). Even on his deathbed, he would write: "How far down one has to go / to get the gods which are."[4] His dissatisfaction with ego, and the poetry that comes of ego (which is to say, most poetry), is a key part of his essay on proprioception:

> "Psychology": the surface: consciousness as ego and thus no flow because the "senses" of same are all that sd contact area is valuable for, to report in to central. Inspection, followed hard on heels by, judgment (judicium, dotha: cry, if you must / all feeling may flow, is all which can count, at sd point. Direction outward is sorrow, or joy. Or participation: active social life, like, for no other reason than that—social life. In the present. Wash the ego out, in its own "bath" (os).[5]

For Olson, "the soul is proprioceptive." This means that it is neither in consciousness nor unconsciousness, but in a third place, "the body." Olson would locate soul physiognomically:

> This "demonstration" then leads to the same third, or corpus, thing or "place," the
>   *proprious*-ception
>   "one's own"-ception
> the "body" itself as, by movement of its own tissues, giving the data

of, depth. Here, then wld be what is left out? Or what is physiologi-
cally even the "hard" (solid, palpable), that one's life is informed
from and by one's own literal body—as well, that is, as the whole
inner mechanism, which keeps us so damn busy (like eating, sleeping, urinating, dying there, by deterioration of sd "functions" of sd
"organs")—that this mid-thing between, which is what gets "buried," like, the flesh? bones, muscles, ligaments, etc., what one uses,
literally to get about etc.

    that this is "central," that is—in this ½ of the picture—what they
call the SOUL, the intermediary, the intervening thing, the interrup-
tor, the resistor. The self.[6]

These are unusual reflections for a poet in or out of the American tradition in the 1950s and 1960s. Poetry and psychology, or even more rarely,
poetry and psyche, are not a common mixture in our literature. Poets
often say they avoid the psychologies (psychologists?) around them out of
fear (the "creative impulse" might become lost through analysis), loathing (so much "psychology" is simply insulting), boredom (the static systems of most psychologies contravene a poet's sense of movement), or
preoccupation (there are usually better games for poets to play than the
psychological game of "the four functions").

    Yet the psychological record of American poetry for the past twenty
years is discouraging testimony to the relationship of poetry and psyche:
our greatest poet drinking his tea out of peanut-butter jars in a Washington mental hospital; our official "greatest poet" taking the sleep cure at a
private mental hospital in Hartford; our most famous "confessional" poet
a suicide by oven gas in her London flat; our second most famous "confessional" poet a suicide by carbon monoxide in her suburban Boston
garage; our most famous alcoholic poet (and not a dubious distinction if
the *Dream Songs* are a compendium, as some say, of universal alcoholic
complaints) a suicide by a leap from a bridge over the Mississippi River;
and the list could be longer, as recent books delight in reminding us.

    Much of Olson's difference from these typical poets of his genera-
tion, and much of his interest in "psyche," is due to his unique sense of
"ego" in poetry. Of Pound, Olson writes, "The EGO AS BEAK is bent and
busted,"[7] and what has replaced it, William Carlos Williams's "blueberry
America . . . (Jersey dump-smoke covering same) also WENT (that is, Bill
with all respect, don't know fr nothing abt what a city *is*)."[8]

    Olson found his own way out of this dilemma by a radical reimagin-
ing of his own ego's role in the poem. Masked as the giant persona Maxi-

mus, Olson made a history of the city of Gloucester, Massachusetts, in verse (not, of course, *the* history of Gloucester, unless you like the poems more than the Essex County record-books).

I think he imagined that a poem (in the sense of the *Maximus Poems)* was already in some ways written before the poet brought himself to it, that the images of the poem already existed, separate from him, and that even the words of the poem found *him.* A poem, in its words and images, is already "out there" or "in there" (a distinction I think he saw mattered less and less). In this sense, he was not literally creating the words of his poems, or the images. In some ways, the images created him, found him the way words found him, compelling him to attend to them and to write their "story." It is image that makes the poet, who himself only makes a place for them or, to use that tired word, becomes their "vehicle."

In this perspective, the poem is already "right"; its images and words are already right. Everything is right except the ego of the poet approaching it (here I am applying a psychotherapeutic dictum of John Layard, but I think it was Olson's sense of ego, too). Thus, only the ego can spoil (improve?) things. The ego is ignorant, even irritable, and tampers with the poem's "results." And this ignorance can be so large if one is not careful that at first the ego thinks *he* is making all this up, this *poem.* He is convinced that *he* is writing the poem, is responsible not only for its "finish" but for its origins as well. The images of the poem are not from the unconscious, and the poet's role is not to awaken them (refine them, define them, or whatever). If we see the good old ego as "unconscious" too (an archetypal dictum of James Hillman), the images, if the poet is gifted, awaken *him.*

A new attunement to the function of image was the definitive mark of "modern" poetry at the beginning of this century. The first formal manifestation of what might be called the revolution of the image was the school called Imagism. Ezra Pound coined the word in 1912 to describe a poem by H.D. called "Hermes of the Ways." All Pound seems to have meant by this, originally, was H.D.'s own brand of laconic speech, light on adjectives and heavy on what was called "direct presentation." It was soon to become an actual "doctrine of the image." T. E. Hulme, Pound's philosophical mentor in 1909, had argued for the importance of images and against the weakness of "decoration" in verse. *Imagisme* was Pound's contribution (in pseudo-French) to the wonderful plethora of French "-ismes" then in vogue.

Hugh Kenner has listed some of these in his magisterial study, *The*

Pound Era: "Néo-Mallarméisme, the school of L'Abbaye, Néo-Paganisme, Unanisme (*aliter* Whitmanisme), L'Ecole de Grâce, Le Paroxysme, L'Impulsionnisme, Le Futurisme."[9] What a terrific *pluralism* of the imagination in 1900! To read such a list today, amid the paucity of styles and ideas in the practice of poetry, is to wonder how we lost so much.

F. S. Flint reviewed some of these schools in a sixty-page article in the August 1912 issue of *Poetry Review* titled "Contemporary French Poetry." His description of a group like the Impulsionnistes, who had their own review and a "Federation Impulsionniste Internationale," suggests the kind of thing that would soon be subsumed under the monolithic Imagist banner: " . . . the man whose sensitive system and cerebral organization are such that not only is he prone to meditation and knows the psychic instinct, but also feels the impulsion which urges him to fix his dreams, to realize his thought, he is the Poet, the creator (p. 179)." A case could be made for the influence of these spiritual and psychic literary movements on the developing European psychologies of their day, as a similar case might be made for the later parallel development of imagism and the role of the image in Freudian and Jungian psychology.

But even to quote Flint's description of the Impulsionniste movement is to hear groans from the modern poet's traditional hostility toward all things psychological and "the psychic instinct." Kenner makes a point of distinguishing Pound's *Imagisme* from all these other fin-de-siècle schools of poetry, with a pat on the back for Pound's sense of technique: " . . . we observe that Imagisme was named for a component of the poem, not a state of the poet, and its three principles establish technical, not psychic criteria. Psychic criteria, vainly hoping to distinguish poet from poet, are invoked in the decadence of a tradition, when 'poetry' has become as homogeneous as taffy (p. 179)." Perhaps. But now, in the long decadence of the Imagist tradition, poetry feels like taffy once more, and one cannot get it unstuck because there is no end of technically skilled writers of (interchangeable) verse.

Kenner would rescue Pound, correctly I think, from any charge of denigrating psyche for the sake of technique. He comments on the number of people who followed Pound's technical prescriptions for Imagism only to write trivial poems (most of the poets in *Des Imagistes,* he says): "All the confusion about Imagism stems from the fact that its specifications for technical hygiene are one thing, and Pound's Doctrine of the Image is another (p. 186)." The elusive Doctrine of the Image, which apparently escaped so many, is stated by Pound: "An 'image' is that

which presents an intellectual and emotional complex in an instant of
time (p. 185)." This was soon to be altered into a "Vortex," an image-
cluster "from which, and through which, and into which, ideas are constantly rushing."

There is a tendency, however, in all discussion of imagist poetics, to
leave psyche to the individual poet and make only *techne* a common working interest. And yet it is just here that our modern tradition, beginning
with Pound, spreads its peculiar chill over psyche. For while the poet is
allowed his own "psychic" world and all he wants of it, it is to remain
private. Psyche is private property. Soul is not seen as that bottomless
Heraclitean pit in which we all merge, submerge, or emerge with a host
of cataclysmic imaginal figures called, variously, dream, history, hallucination, illness, or fantasy. Psyche cannot be seen as anything so obviously
shared because such a collective notion smacks of intellectual sloppi-
ness—worse, it smacks of psychology! Modern poetry and its criticism,
rooted by Americans on British soil, have always kept an antiseptic distance from words like *psyche*.[10] Poets since Pound revere technique most
of all, then "feeling" or "perception." Some revere perception, then
feeling, and call the two technique. Others, perhaps the most old-fash-
ioned, revere feeling first, then technique, and do not worry at all about
perception. The larger notion of psyche rarely overarches these other
terms. For many poets, feeling is enough to account for psyche, which
thus dismisses out of hand any notion that psyche brings ideas as well.

It is no wonder that Pound tells us of his vast contempt for psychology. When asked at Saint Elizabeth's Hospital whether he thought Freud
or Jung "was better," Pound replied that he "couldn't distinguish between contents of the sewer."[11] For Pound, as for many lesser poets—
and their critics—there is no interest in psyche, or psychology. The role
of "image" in poetry is a technical one, much the same as the role of
meter.

Until Olson, in the 1950s, the attention to image in modern poetry
was more or less as Pound had formulated it, with Louis Zukofsky and
William Carlos Williams offering refinements. With Olson, however, a
leap was made for the first time beyond that earlier formulation, a leap
that would land outside mere technical discussions for once.

Although he was influenced by Pound—and Poundians begrudge
the influence[12]—Olson's work deepens the role of image in poetry psychologically. It does this in an ironic way, because it is the superficial,
unreflected sense of "lyrical ego"—all that most poets, Pound included,
seem to allow as psyche—that Olson set out to beat.

Olson shares Pound's routine sense of the image as the organizing, nondiscursive event of the poem. But as Charles Altieri has written, in an excellent article on their differences:

> Olson makes clear his difference from the symbolist proponents of the Romantic image by insisting on the image as the intensification of objective reality, not a transcending of it. Image does not, like symbol and allegory, refer beyond itself to conscious intentions and thus disperse energy away from the emerging present (*Human Universe*, 121). Instead, image gathers those energies, which might otherwise be dispersed into the independent fictive mind, within a single dynamic movement. Yet the movement must be more intellectual, more related to imaginative archetypes than it is with his objectivist masters. . . . [13]

Instead of "objectivism" (the Zukofsky-Williams refinement), Olson called his approach "objectism." The difference is more than merely replacing an adjective with a noun. For while it shares the former's detachment from subjectivity, it affirms a view of the world, of the "outside," of the body itself, as *psyche* (as imaginative and imagined), a view that so-called objectivists would never have accepted:

> What seems to me a more valid formulation for present use is "objectism," a word to be taken to stand for the kind of relation of man to experience which a poet might state as the necessity of a line or a work to be as wood is, to be as clean as wood is as it issues from the hand of nature, to be as shaped as wood can be when a man has his hand to it. Objectism is the getting rid of the lyrical interference of the individual as ego. . . . [14]

It is just here that modernists (subjectivists—subjectists?) have their grievance with Olson, thinking he was proposing some kind of "zombie-ism" because he was abandoning some tired old psychological notions about ego that nobody took seriously anyway. Altieri has answered their objections:

> Objectism does not, as Robert Bly claims, deny inwardness. Rather it seeks to go beyond myths that inwardness exists in some mysterious "ghost in the machine" where men function independently of natural energies . . . Olson comes to grips with the modern sense that human inwardness can no longer be relegated to an inner ghost

creating and reflecting upon private self-generated feelings. . . .
The task is to have natural law without behaviorist determinism, to
find the spirit within the letter; the method is imaginative participation in what all beings share by being alive.[15]

For Olson, image *is* natural law ("nature" as psyche). In one of his
earliest notebook jottings (1947), when he was first contemplating the
writing of *The Maximus Poems,* he put the logic of the image foremost
(*exactly* as an archetypal psychologist would do today): "Take next step
from Melville book and order things as a poet would the image, the intensity achieved by the juxtaposition of the material not in any logic of time
or classification but in the logic of the life of the thing as you see it."[16]

This faith in image is attested also by a curious dream Olson had in
which a strange voice told him the order of imaging. It is described in his
poem "ABCs(2)":[17]

what we do not know of ourselves
of who they are who lie
coiled or unflown
in the marrow of the bone

one sd:
of rhythm is image
of image is knowing
of knowing there is
a construct

If Pound is an imagist of humanist ego ("by the beak of his ego," as
Olson says Pound wrote his *Cantos*), Olson is an "objectist" of psyche.
For what Olson is advocating, with his unique sense of image and out-
wardness, is a form of direct realism[18] as it would apply to the writing of
poetry. He is advocating a poetry where perception is seen as unmediated (immediate) by a subjectivist ego. Image in this sense has nothing to
do with optics; it has everything to do with archetype and soul.[19] "Objectism" is an archetypal perspective. The poet, in this sense—outwardly,
physically, actually—works in a depth of image that exceeds anything
done "imagistically." Psychologically, *The Maximum Poems* are a quan-
tum leap from Pound's *Cantos*.

But they are still a disturbing leap (as Pound's own once was.) All
poets are now eccentric by profession. This is not because "the centre
cannot hold," so much as that no one would want to hold it anymore.

This makes poetry a notoriously difficult, even quizzical, subject, both to read and to write. It is almost impossible to differentiate among the poets whose eccentricity (uniqueness) offers depth and those whose eccentricity offers only surface. Technique is almost everywhere proficient and has become the most uninteresting of criteria. So-called psychic criteria are now of interest again, though not at all according to the old lights. It is Olson's great achievement, in a profusion of poems and essays, to have forced this issue, this "psychology" for poetry, on a reluctant audience. But most of us are still in the dark, and there is a long way to go before this new "space" is much recognized—if ever! We must learn an archetypal eye, if we are to see off-center.

(1979)

21 ARCHETYPAL DEPTH CRITICISM AND MELVILLE

Ralph Maud

The Canadian professor Ralph Maud provides an account, using Melville for his examples, of how to read a text according to principles suggested by James Hillman's imaginal, archetypal psychology. Maud interweaves theory and practice to demonstrate, under three headings—depth, image, and archetype—how archetypal psychology, with its task of "soul-making," can contribute to the criticism and teaching of literature.

"Depth" implies for Maud that the reader responds to the text not only with an active intellect but also with a developing individual soul: his demonstration here views Melville's "Bartleby" through the lens of Hillman's ideas on the proper uses of depression for healing and soul-making. The second heading, "Image," directs the reader to honor powerful images in the text, not merely by explicating or summarizing them, but by "reimagining the imagery," similar to the psychotherapeutic practice of active imagination encouraged in Jungian analysis (see Hillman's essay). The third heading, "Archetype," is also used by Maud to encourage a reader-critic to use his intuition as well as his intellect by measuring the text-image against his own imagination's ability to generate an image to match it.

In the last decade the aims of psychology have received a radical restatement in the works of James Hillman.[1] He has reintroduced classical notions of "the soul," that core of sensibility in us which recognizes and registers the meaningful; and he sees the task of psychology not as the strengthening of "the ego," nor as the individuation of "the self," but as the nurturing of "the soul." "Soul-making," as he terms it, is the intensifying of the significance of life in the face of death, and "the *deepening* of events into experiences . . . through reflective speculation, dream, image, and *fantasy*—that mode which recognizes all realities as primarily symbolic or metaphorical" (*Re-Visioning Psychology*, p. x). His overhauling of his discipline is based on "a psychology of image": "Here I am suggesting both a *poetic basis of mind* and a psychology that starts neither in the physiology of the brain, the structure of language, the organization of society, nor the analysis of behavior, but in the processes of imagination" (p. xi). Literary criticism cannot ignore a hand held out so collegially. Hillman borrowed the term "soul-making" from Keats.[2] My intention is to reappropriate it for literary studies with all the interest that has accrued to it while in Hillman's hands, and to do so under three headings: (1) depth; (2) image; and (3) archetype.

"What a person brings to the analytical hour," says Hillman, "are the sufferings of the soul" (*Suicide and the Soul*, p. 47). One thinks immediately, "Yes, that is what we also bring to the reading of a book." We sit down with a serious book prepared to give the author something of ourselves to work on: we move toward the reading experience with our sorrows, all our woe. Archetypal depth criticism takes from Hillman's psychology of soul-making the idea of depression not as a disability but as a necessary means of motion. Students of Milton are familiar with the concept of the fortunate fall. Dante enters the *Divine Comedy* depressed and makes a long underground journey. Ishmael's suicidal feelings launch him on a whaling voyage. Henderson leaves his pigs and goes to Africa. There are innumerable versions of the exile from Eden. "Do you not see," asked Keats in his letters, "how necessary a World of Pains and troubles is to school an Intelligence and make it a soul?" (2:102). No one rushes to read *Paradise Regained*. Indeed, the Christian emphasis on resurrection is a threat to the proper use of depression. Missionaries saw the risen god everywhere and wrote to James Frazer, so that he could ride his fertility tricycle around Cambridge. If three days was enough for Christ, and many another god, our being down, and staying down, is simply bad form (*Re-Visioning Psychology*, p. 98). And what about that other offense against expected behavior, the failure to have catharsis at the performance of a Greek tragedy? Shame on us; but quick purgation is annoying to anyone who feels the value of staying in the tragic mode. Aristotle's one sentence on this subject in the *Poetics* misrepresents the plays, which leave us with plenty of pity and fear for further soul-making.

We are indebted to James Hillman for a thorough reevaluation of depression as something to stay in: "The true revolution begins in the individual who can be true to his or her depression. Neither jerking one-self out of it, caught in cycles of hope and despair, nor suffering it through till it turns, nor theologizing it—but discovering the consciousness and depths it wants. So begins the revolution in behalf of the soul" (*Re-Visioning Psychology*, pp. 98–99). We shall be able to turn to Melville throughout this paper precisely because, in this sense, he is the revolutionary forebear of twentieth-century sensibility. He wrote in his review of *Mosses from an Old Manse* of the "great power of blackness" in Hawthorne "that so fixes and fascinates"; but he was able to move within his own blackness, especially in *Pierre,* capable of delineating its full depth. He is our renaissance man, since renaissances now come "out of the corner."[3] Bartleby the scrivener, whose affrontery undermines all normal preferences—why are we immediately on his side? We guess that he is the harbinger of something radically new, even though in the story he is the image of disintegration and death. Archetypal depth criticism would propose, following Hillman's line of thought, that it is especially because of his incurable pathology that Bartleby is a hermeneutic for us. "Only when things fall apart do they open up into new meanings; only when an everyday habit turns symptomatic, a natural function becomes an afflic-tion, or the physical body appears in dreams as a pathological image, does a new significance dawn" (*Re-Visioning Psychology*, p. 111). If we look again at Bartleby's wall we shall see something imaged there. Depression is prospective through its imagery.

The second tenet of archetypal depth criticism is that we should take the images of a literary work at least as seriously as a therapist takes the dreams of his patients. *A Wall Street office; outside the window, a block-ing wall; partitions inside, a screen, an inner office, an outer office; the offer of gingersnaps cut by a wall of refusal;* and the image that remains with me most strongly, *the office door barred one morning to its very owner.* To list the remembered ingredients of a story one has not read recently—it is as though one had dreamt it. It has been axiomatic in literary criticism that close reading precedes valid judgment. But in my experience of the liter-ary journals, a close reading often takes one, step by tedious step, away from where one instinctively knows the real value of the work hides. For all its good intentions, the rule has become, not a tool for fine work, but an instrument for boring. Can't we trust our memories more? I propose an alternative axiom for literary criticism: that what we actually remember without a careful, close rereading is probably what we should remember. *Dove sta memoria*—the rest is dross. Admittedly, the art of memory is not what it used to be, and rereadings will be needed, but they do not have to be constrictively corrective.

The analogy between literary criticism and dream-work is fruitful if one has a reasonable view of dreams and what to do about them. If we write down a dream at night and go back to it the next day or later, it is to reenjoy the images, to fantasize further on them, to remember how they spoke to us in the dream event, and to mull them over until we can hold on to the event as an experience. The psyche has supplied materials for a process that continues at intervals as long as the soul-making possibilities are present. Likewise, we return to some books time and again because we feel their shelf-life to be limitless; and if the life of a book is in its imagery, we will want to keep the images with us, as themselves, for as long as their power moves us. The main thesis of Hillman's latest book, *The Dream and the Underworld* (1979), is that dreams are not for our guidance in accordance with some system of interpretation, but for us to understand by a process of imaginative interplay.

> They are elaborations, linguistic and imagistic complexities, attesting to what Freud called "dream-work" *(Traumarbeit)*. Even the dumbest dream can astound us with its art, the range of its reference, the play of its fancy, the selection of its detail. If we follow our principle of likeness, then our response to the dream must go beyond the natural appreciation of dreaming it onwards. We shall as well have to respond with critical, imaginative appreciation, with a work that resembles its work. (p. 93)

This "work" suggests the alchemical model; the way to understand Bartleby's wall will be to have it in an alembic where the imagination can brood over it. Bartleby doesn't seem to mind his wall. What does it mean to have in a story (to have inside ourselves) a figure who does not mind walls? Well, a quick explication is not required; I am willing to wait for the image to "coagulate" and "intensify," to use Hillman's words in his latest book (p. 137). If one stuck on a label and called this "coffin" imagery, one would not be far wrong. But Bartleby deserves an expensive coffin, not a cheap one, one that has had a good long wake washed over it.

Literary criticism is conducted for profit, and the one piece of practical advice proferred here so far is most unbusinesslike. Soul-making could be called the principle of "slow turnover." But let us persist. What happens when one stays with an image for its soul-making possibilities? One must do something with it. *You wake at your normal time; you go to your office in the normal way. You have earned the right to some regularity in your life. But the key won't work this particular morning. Someone already inside won't let you in. You have made the mistake of acknowledging his right to be there. You have invented someone who won't let you remain comfortable. You have walled him in, but he makes you feel dispossessed. He is that something in you that wants walls, and is distressed by opportunities and riches. He is the dream of the lean kine; he is Biafra. As he makes small noises in your quarters, keeping you waiting, he is like a mouse retreating to its mousehole. He will seek prison, and die like a mouse in a bare cupboard. He must die, or else you will. So you let the accidie and famine in you die, in order to work and eat. This is your daily condition as you wait for famine to open your office to you. If he did not make you wait, you would not be able to reflect on these things.*

This is the kind of thing one does with an image in soul-making: one restates it. In recent issues of *Spring*, the annual journal of archetypal psychology, Hillman has been debating how one gets meaning from imagery without converting it into concept. The method he comes up with is verbal mitosis, letting the image speak "in multiple restatements."[4] *The key won't work. Work won't key. Waiting is a door to the inside.* The restatements can be on this level:

> When we shift the dream-words around, letting them play with other parts of speech, transformation takes place right in our ears. A dream is itself transformational because it transforms its own statements through polyvalence of its images. A dream is always deepening and differentiating itself. . . . We return to Freud's view that a dream is not a message, but is a self-satisfying narcissistic event. Because the dream's words are not concepts that refer, no dream can be interpretively translated to other referents. A dream can only be interpretively re-imagined, as one does with a piece of any other poesis. ("Further Notes," p. 175)

Let us follow up the implication here that creative writing—or the kind we find most interesting—is not harnessed to the ego, but is as guileless as Narcissus's day-dreaming. "The Grand Armada" chapter of *Moby-Dick* is a beautiful piece of poesis, in which Ishmael describes how his small boat is dragged through the circumference of a moving pod of whales into the smooth lake at the center. There he is entranced by the sight of mother whales and their infants, one of them only a day old: "He was a little frisky: though as yet his body seemed scarce yet recovered from that irksome position it had so lately occupied in the maternal reticule: where, tail to head, and all ready for the final spring, the unborn whale lies bent like a Tartar's bow."[5]

Now if this were a dream, we would not hesitate to see the frisky day-old infant whale as the dreamer himself. To reimagine this passage we can use one of the simplest devices of dream-work, the substitution of the first-person singular: my body seemed scarce yet recovered from that irksome position I had so lately occupied in my maternal reticule, etc. And a few sentences later on the page: my umbilical cord becomes entangled with the hempen one, so that I am thereby trapped. These confinement and entrapment images, reinforced by the larger scene of the encircled boat, reveal the true predicament of the protagonist. So I am suspicious when the narrator steps in to claim this as an image of his inner calm: "while ponderous planets of unwaning woe revolve around me, deep down and deep inland there I still bathe me in eternal mildness of joy" (p. 1209). I am suspicious that he is translating the poesis to other referents, and translating badly. This supposed "joy" has already been described in this chapter as "that enchanted calm" which "lurks"—an insidious word—"at the heart of every commotion" (p. 1206). In fact, the calm water is produced by a "subtle moisture thrown off by the whale . . . that smooth satin-like surface, called a sleek" (p. 1206). It is, in short, an oil slick Ishmael is caught in, from the body oil of the mothers.

There is a natural propensity to summarize experiences of reading. Amplification is a yeasty soul-making process, but there comes a time when one wants the mass to set, one wants a loaf. One enters then upon rather different soul-making work, the trials and pleasures of being intelligently reductive. Archetypal depth criticism recommends that the best conciseness is achieved by asking, not what the author did or how he or she did it, but who in the author caused the work, and to whom does it properly belong. What is happening in the "Grand Armada" passage, for instance, seems far too complicated to be summed up except by laying the whole thing on the sacrificial altar of the Terrible Mother, a well-attested archetype.[6] *Armada* is the feminine form of the past participle "armed." The secret about the mother-child serenity is the hidden constriction, the entrapment in the amour.

The method, then, is to bring out extra significance by reimagining the imagery, and during this rumination to intuit an archetype that seems to match the reality of the situation. What is an archetype? Every time

Jung addressed himself to any topic whatsoever he felt obliged to begin by explaining how archetypes have been discerned empirically from data given by the unconscious and confirmed by comparative mythology, and that they are categories intrinsic to the human mind and therefore provide organizing possibilities for any particular manifestations of the psyche.[7] Have the archetypes, or gods-as-archetypes, received more general assent in the decades since Jung's death? Probably not: there are too many stubborn agnostics around. Hillman feels that we should be at least "non-agnostic" (*Re-Visioning Psychology,* p. 167). We don't have to believe in the gods and archetypes religiously, only imaginally. When Ezra Pound in "Hugh Selwyn Mauberley" asks what god he should place a (tin) wreath upon, he is "non-agnostic." And when we try to think what would be a proper answer to his question, we are too. "What god—?" It was the question customarily asked at Delphi. Once you knew which god to turn to, you were on the right track. Similarly, in our polytheistic literary criticism, each genre will have its own kind of soul-making and a god who cares about doing things that way; each literary work will be a tribute to a god who has kinship with that particular mode. "What god—?" The answer will always spark debate on the merits of the comparison between the work's essence and the god's. This is an active way to be reductive.

Indeed, the gods have such a rich personal history and the archetypes such varied appearances in art and mythology that the reductive process is continually rebounding into amplification. It may seem easy and oversimple to tag the "Armada" passage with the Terrible Mother archetype, but that labeling is authenticated by a thick volume of Jung's collected works establishing and illustrating the archetypal battle of the hero's deliverance from the mother. Jung once said that *Moby-Dick* was the greatest American novel.[8] Though he did not elaborate, one of the novel's attractions must have been that it yielded up its hidden meanings so willingly when placed alongside all the parallel mythologems he had compiled for *Symbols of Transformation* (1912). I can happily refrain from attempting a major archetypal exegesis of *Moby-Dick* here because I believe Melville wrote a nineteenth-century novel which is our last great Saint George and the Dragon, and that Jung already, in effect, did the exegesis of it in that early book, a nineteenth-century theory of the hero and his archetypal struggle with the mother.[9] Furthermore, archetypal depth criticism is not likely to impress the reader by dwelling on a mother-son archetype that we have all to some extent outgrown. Hillman's essay "The Great Mother, her Son, her Hero, and the Puer," a milestone in post-Jungian thought, moves us toward a different assessment of "the heroic." The kind of initiation of youth which requires the overthrow of the previous generation is "anachronistic"; the fundamental task of the present, he says, is "becoming aware of the senex in all its archetypal significance and relating puer phenomena to it" (*Fathers and Mothers*, pp. 115–16). It is under the rubric of *senex-et-puer*, then, that I will exercise the criterion of "What god or archetype—?" We have a better vantage point than Jung for seeing not what *Moby-Dick* contained, but what it might have, and didn't.

Ishmael implies that the story is incomplete in its senex aspect when he says that Ahab's "larger, darker, deeper part remains unhinted" and proposes a journey like several classical models to consult with the father in the underworld: "Wind ye down there, ye prouder, sadder souls! question that proud, sad king! A family likeness! aye, he did beget ye, ye young exiled royalties; and from your grim sire only will the old State-secret come" (pp. 990–91). So one hidden god behind *Moby-Dick* is a broken Saturn, "throned on torsoes," deep beneath "vast Roman halls of Thermes" (p. 990). If only the wisdom of this real senex figure could have come up from the depths, the spoutings of Madame Leviathan might not have been so bewildering to "young" Ahab. For the crucial question is whether or not Ahab is senex at all. His John O'Gaunt beard may just be borrowed from Shakespeare along with his rhetoric. His scar might be an ever-open wound, as the pun in the word "livid" suggests, indicating a lifetime of unremitting puer hurt, and never becoming the healed wound of someone (in Hillman's words in an essay on Ulysses' Scar in *Puer Papers*) "whose soul can care for him" (p. 121). Every reader will recall the one moment in the "Symphony" chapter when Ahab at least *sounds* like a senex: "aye, aye! what a forty years' fool—fool—old fool, has old Ahab been! Why this strife of the chase? why weary, and palsy the arm at the oar, and the iron, and the lance? how the richer or better is Ahab now?" (p. 1374). But this mood passes in an instant, and Ahab's gaze fixes again on the cannibalistic sea and the path to his revenge. This obsession with the whale—has it been said often enough?—is a downright stupid thing for an intelligent grown man to get himself involved in. It surely should be seen as the hurt of a young man carried over imaginatively, but perhaps not successfully, to a fictionalized older man. *Redburn* provides the semiautobiographical prologue for *Moby-Dick*: "Talk not of the bitterness of middle-age and after life; a boy can feel all that, and much more, when upon his young soul the mildew has fallen; and the fruit, which with others is only blasted after ripeness, with him is nipped in the first blossom and bud. And never again can such blights be

made good; they strike in too deep, and leave such a scar that the air of
Paradise might not erase it" (p. 16).

Melville's swollen leg from the serpent sting in the paradise valley
of *Typee* is a curious presaging of Ahab's disability too. The loss Melville
suffered in youth is well-known. Redburn tells of it: the harsh reversal of
fortune which shattered the family upon the father's bankruptcy in business, followed by his mental breakdown and death. This catastrophe happened when Redburn/Melville was not yet thirteen, and induced in him
"demoniac" feelings, symbolized by an "insane desire" to destroy a
beautiful model sailing-ship made of glass with all its little glass sailors. I
see Ahab's scar as the perpetual sign of his having been struck by lightning at age twelve. He is fixed in the role of puer-hero revenging the
parental hurt. There seems to be no possibility of healing for Ahab; so he
will fight the "dragon," which is an essential aspect of himself in the role
of hero, to the death; he will fulfill Ishmael's jocular threat of suicide; he
will destroy the glass ship. I see Ahab's scar in contrast to that of Ulysses,
in the context provided by Hillman's essay "Puer Wounds and Ulysses'
Scar." In the case of Ulysses, "the senex urge to persist and endure takes
care of the puer spirit that is always ready to risk and die. Healing and
wounding alternate, or, as healed wound, tender scar, they present the
complex image of weak-strength, of soft-hardness. The scar remaining is
the reminder, the soft spot recalling the body to its tenderness. The scar
acts as a *memento mori,* recalling the Grandfather, and oneself as a Hunting Boy. That scar gets Ulysses through twenty years of unparalleled dangers" (*Puer Papers,* pp. 121–22). In Ahab's case Melville does not allow
into the picture anything like a grandfather or a hunting boy. There is no
healing, and his scar becomes a deformity. There is no transition "from
only-puer consciousness, wounded and bleeding, to *puer-et-senex* consciousness, open and scarred"(p. 122). Jung's *Symbols of Transformation*
gave us the mother-hero archetype by which to view *Moby-Dick,* and it
fits. Hillman's *Puer Papers* gives us the *puer-et-senex* archetype, and it
makes us wish *Moby-Dick* were more than it is.

Perhaps the above discussion is sufficient indication of how archetypal depth criticism might proceed in its dealings with an archetype.
The answer to the question "What god—?" here would be something
like "a Ulysses who never had a chance of getting home." Ahab leaves us
with such a negative that we should perhaps push through to *Billy Budd,*
which can be viewed as a long-awaited coda to *Moby-Dick* on the *puer-et-
senex* theme. Redburn took to Liverpool the diaries his father had kept on
a trip there many years before. They prove hopelessly out of date as a

guide. The very hotel his father stayed in has gone; the city will not speak to him of his father. Pierre's father is dead: "By vast pains we mine into the pyramid; by horrible gropings we come to the central room; with joy we espy the sarcophagus; but we lift the lid—and no body is there!"[10] Thus Pierre reports on his failure to find the royal sire. The Christ-figure in *The Confidence-Man* is mute, and we have to wait for Melville's final work of fiction for a senex who has speech and a puer who can listen.

Captain Vere himself undertakes to tell Billy Budd about the court martial's decision. The outcome is that Billy is satisfied with his lot, and just before he is hanged cries out, "God Bless Captain Vere!" This would seem to be a supreme triumph for the senex-puer relationship. Our father should be able to tell us that it is all right to die.

> It would have been in consonance with the spirit of Captain Vere should he on this occasion have concealed nothing from the condemned one—should he indeed have frankly disclosed to him the part he himself had played in bringing about the decision, at the same time revealing his actuating motives. On Billy's side it is not improbable that such a confession would have been received in much the same spirit that prompted it. Not without a sort of joy, indeed, he might have appreciated the brave opinion of him implied in his captain's making such a confidant of him.[11]

Melville does not risk verbatim speech here. We have to take the Augustinian flow and balance as a measure of the senex wisdom present, that a "something healing" (p. 119) has occurred. When Captain Vere leaves Billy, his face is "expressive of the agony of the strong" (p. 115); and when we next see Billy he is asleep: "Without movement he lay as in a trance, that adolescent expression previously noted as his taking on something akin to the look of a slumbering child in the cradle when the warm hearth-glow of the still chamber of night plays on the dimples that at whiles mysteriously form in the cheek" (p. 119).

This passage is a touchstone. If *Moby-Dick* is the "wicked book" that Melville said it was (in a letter to Hawthorne in 1851), if Ahab's vicious quest is the ultimate heroic puerility before a new epoch begins, then this passage is a test of whether or not we are ready to move with Melville into the next phase. Billy is gyved about the leg—that recurring symbol of puer hurt. But he does not bluster and cry vengeance like the old-style hero. Neither is he let off, like Isaac with Abraham, or Ishmael in *Moby-Dick*. He has not had to seek his father in frozen Tartarus; his captain was present and somehow helped him face death. Melville records that Billy was present as a grace at Vere's death, too. The framework of the senex-puer archetype enables us to accept the above passage, dimples and all. Those dimples, those "slight natural depressions," as the dictionary puts it, are part of a complete story, which is presented truly by someone who has earned the right to be a senex. As a customs inspector for twenty years, how many times a week was Melville lied to as Claggart lied? How many times a month did he have to make a stubborn bureaucratic decision that jeopardized someone's livelihood, as Captain Vere did? Billy was a composite of the Handsome Sailors of Melville's sea days, but Vere and their combined story waited on Melville's personal plenitude, when he could envision an older man in touch with innocence in a doomed military setting, and a youth in touch with his senex possibilities, attempting to redeem the father. Hillman gives us an image for Billy's "ascension" at the end in the Egyptian son-god, Horus:

> The Horus motif is paradigmatic for many such father-son situations, where the aim is not to overcome or slay the mother, but to redeem the father by surpassing him. The Goddess even encourages the puer ambition and is instrumental in senex-puer reunion. In this pattern the mother can be relatively secondary, while focus is upon the puer necessity: redeeming the father. In a young man's life, maybe any life, the puer represents the necessity of seeking the fathering spirit, the capacity to father. The Horus image of flying higher and further connotes a spiritual fathering.[12]

It has been the purpose of this article to inaugurate the adoption by literary studies of some of the interesting additions James Hillman has made to his own field. We have touched on the creativity in depression, the significance to be gained from reimagining the image, and the play of archetypes or gods-as-archetypes in a process that, following Hillman, we can call "soul-making," which is present in literary criticism as well as in literature and therapeutic psychology. Melville is a remarkably good case for study: his journey through depression is fascinating in its depths; his imagery is not fanciful but is given, dreamlike, by the landscape of the journey; and his works as a whole are so enigmatic that our technique of finding the personage behind them—the god or archetype—seems practically the only way to summarize them in order to keep their totality intact.

(1983)

JUNGIAN CONCEPTS IN CRITICAL PRACTICE

Part III

A. ARCHETYPES AND LITERATURE: THE TRICKSTER

Discovering and analyzing an archetypal symbol in a text is a staple of Jungian literary criticism, both in print and in the classroom. There is no dearth of essays dealing with the anima/animus, the wise old man, the hero, and many other archetypes besides the trickster. However, from the point of view of the literary critic, the trickster is especially interesting because there is so much material on this figure from a variety of disciplines—anthropology, folklore, and myth, as well as psychology. While myth critics readily make use of the concept of the archetype by comparing the pattern in one or more myths to that of, say, a literary character in the context of a story, they often balk at going beyond comparing of functions to a comparing of causes (see Campbell, chap. 6). But as these selections demonstrate—three by analyst/literary critics— clinical psychologists have amassed a substantial amount of experience, leading to a fairly high degree of confidence in their analysis, concerning the causes and effects within the dynamic psyche of the emergence of the trickster archetype. Thus, the reader may judge whether factoring the psychological description of the trickster into the sociofunctional descriptions provided by anthropologists and myth critics sheds more or less light on the range of subjects—from characters in works to creators and readers of works—which literary criticism must treat.

22 "TRICKSTER"

Andrew Samuels, Bani Shorter,
and Fred Plaut

This entry in the 1986 Critical Dictionary of Jungian Analysis *presents the contemporary Jungian psychological definition of the subject of the four selections in Part 3, section A. Illustrating these analysts' belief in the usefulness of Jung-and-literature as a resource for psychological study, Samuels refers several times to literary works to make clear his definition, as well as to Willeford's book of psychological literary criticism on the subject, from which the selection in Chapter 23 was taken.*

Trickster. When Jung first encountered the image of the Trickster, he was reminded of the tradition of carnival, with its striking reversal of hierarchic order and medieval observances, where the Devil appeared as "the ape of God." He found in the Trickster a striking resemblance to the alchemical figures of Mercurius, with his fondness for sly jokes and malicious pranks, the power to change shape, a dual nature (half animal/half divine), the urge for unremitting exposure to privation and torture, as well as an approximation to the figure of a savior. An altogether negative hero, the Trickster yet manages to achieve through his stupidity what others fail to achieve by concentrated effort.

As Jung discovered, however, the Trickster is both a mythical figure and an inner psychic experience. Wherever and whenever he appears, and in spite of his unimpressive exterior, he brings the possibility of transforming the meaningless into the meaningful. Hence, he symbolizes the propensity for enantiodromia; and, gauche, unconscious creature though he may be, his actions inevitably reflect a compensatory relationship to consciousness. "In his clearest manifestations," Jung writes, "he is a faithful reflection of an absolutely undifferentiated human consciousness, corresponding to a psyche that has hardly left the animal level" (*CW*, vol. 9, pt. 1, para. 465). He may be seen as inferior even to the beasts, because he is no longer dependent upon instinct alone; yet, for all his eagerness to learn, he hasn't achieved the full measure of human awareness. His most frightening aspect is probably not connected simply with his unconsciousness but also with his unrelatedness.

Psychologically, Jung saw the Trickster-figure as equivalent to the shadow. "The Trickster is a collective shadow figure, a summation of all the inferior traits of character in individuals" (*CW*, vol. 9, pt. 1, para. 484). However, his appearance is more than evidence of a residual trace inherited from primitive forebears. As in *King Lear*, his appearance owes itself to a dynamic existing in the actual situation. When the King wanders deranged as a result of his own arrogantly conscious blunders, his companion is the "wiser" Fool.

Nevertheless, for the Trickster-image to be activated means that a calamity has happened or a dangerous situation has been created. When the Trickster appears in dreams, in paintings, in synchronistic events, slips of the tongue, in fantasy projections and personal accidents of all kinds, a compensatory energy has been released. Recognition of the figure is only the first step in its integration, however. With the emergence of the symbol, attention is called to the original destructive unconscious state, but it is not yet overcome. And, since the individual shadow is an enduring component of the personality, it can never be eliminated. The collective Trickster-figure reconstructs itself continually, manifesting the energizing power and numinosity of all would-be savior images.

Jung's introduction to the Trickster-figure was Bandelier's *The Delight Makers*. He wrote his own commentary entitled "On the Psychology of the Trickster-Figure" as a contribution to the German edition of Radin's *The Trickster: A Study in American Indian Mythology* (1956). Willeford (1969) is generally regarded as having written the definitive work on the subject in contemporary analytical psychology.

23 THE FOOL AND HIS SCEPTRE

William Willeford

William Willeford was for many years both a professor of literature and a practicing Jungian analyst. His book on the Fool demonstrates how a Jungian approach can deepen and extend the traditional historical study of a literary symbol which is also a psychosocial archetype, by analyzing it in terms of the psychology of the audience's perennial response.

Willeford's critical method, introduced in section 1, is to explain the Fool by surveying and comparing many instances of its appearance; but what this not uncommon comparative approach means for Willeford becomes dramatically clear when he reads the literature of the Fool in light of his work in a psychiatric clinic, where "one becomes acquainted as a matter of life and death with irrational forces, their profundity, their contagiousness, and their power to create and destroy psychic and other structures (for example, the social structure of the family)." A sense of encountering boundary conditions, of a continuous interpenetration of literary criticism and psychological practice, gives Willeford's study an interesting and rare authority.

Section 2 first treats a skit by Buster Keaton and Charlie Chaplin from the film Limelight, and then a wild car ride sequence from W. C. Fields's film The Bank Dick. These selections display the psychological critic's ability to discover complex relationships between a popular art form's purely visual narrative and the viewing audience's response to it.

I. INTRODUCTION

The fools and instances of folly that I will discuss come from a variety of sources: records of folk festivals and court jesters, the fool literature of the late Middle Ages and early Renaissance, plays by Shakespeare and others, jokes, vaudeville and circus-clown skits, slapstick films, playing cards, paintings, and magazine cartoons. These have all been treated before in historical descriptions of fools and their kinds and in psychological studies of humor and laughter. In this study I will attempt to relate fools and instances of folly to a fundamental type, the fool of the title, and sketch the context of his folly and the functions it fulfills in art and life. This context includes the settings in which fools appear (for example, the circus or the court of a king) and the psychological sources of our response to fools (for example, hopes and fears, and patterns of thought and decorum that they may play with). In describing fools and folly in this way I am concerned with certain questions of "why?" that may still be profitably asked. *Why is the fool, as bumpkin, merrymaker, trickster, scourge, and scapegoat, such an often recurring figure in the world and in our imaginative representations of it? Why do fools from widely diverse times and places reveal such striking similarities? Why are we, like people in many other times and places, fascinated by fools?* These are really questions about what fools are in their effects upon us, about the interactions between the fool actor and the audience of his show. I pose these questions out of respect for an earlier conception according to which folly is one of the supreme facts about human nature, perhaps even about the world. I wish to trace our relations, conscious and unconscious, to the kinds of experience upon which that conception was based.

We have all seen circus clowns threatening to drag a spectator off with them; this business goes back at least to the Middle Ages, when theatrical clown-devils snatched at spectators as though to haul them into Hell-Mouth (for example, in the Towneley play *The Judgment*). Such clowning is probably much older still, and it is very common outside of Western Europe (for example, among the Pueblo Indians). We have all seen two circus clowns shaving a third with enormous razors and buckets of suds, a skit that has surely been presented in every modern circus. (One circus director grew so tired of it that he forbade it for a period of five years, only to have clowns then in his employ, the Fratellinis, flaunt his ruling and bring down the house.) Barbershop clowning appeared in the *commedia dell'arte* and in a number of English plays as early as Richard Edward's *Damon and Pithias* (1563); it also occurs in Marston's *The*

Dutch Courtezan (1603–4) and Ford's *The Fancies Chaste and Noble* (printed 1638), and it has been taken up by several film comedians, among them (with exquisite sadism) W. C. Fields. The temporal and spatial distribution of clownish threats to the audience and of the barber routine tells us nothing about why they are funny, but it tells us that they are relatively typical, in one way or another, of the bond between clowns and their audiences.

If we concern ourselves with the meaning of such clowning, with the reasons for its persistence or recurrence, with the way in which an individual clown takes it up, refines it, and makes it personal, and with its effects upon us, we are concerned with typical traits of fools and folly. The fool as a type—or, more narrowly, this or that type of fool—is drawn from elements reiterated in what fools have said and done, in their dress and manner, and in their procedures in making a show of folly. The description of the type concentrates our attention upon correspondences, variations, and contrasts among these elements, and this concentration of attention should deepen our conscious relationship to folly. One main reason for considering the fool as a type is heuristic: as we study formal relations among different fool figures we notice phenomena that we would otherwise overlook and raise questions that we would otherwise not raise. Another main reason for considering the fool as a type is interpretative: some of the forms that thus emerge are, one may reasonably believe, attributes of folly as an abiding possibility of human experience. If we are aware of these attributes of folly, we are able to place particular instances of it in the context of wider human interests and concerns. In doing so, we will finally reach a point where we experience folly as a reality that cannot be captured in a description, as it belongs too much to the basic texture of our lives. We will have respected the refusal of Erasmus's Mother of Fools to "expound myself by definition, much less divide myself. For it is equally unlucky to circumscribe with a limit her whose nature extends so universally or to dissect her in whose worship every order of being is at one."[1]

We worship folly by seeing it in people and in the world and by willingly displaying it in ourselves. This complex enterprise, which implies the roles of audience and fool actor, is basically symbolic, as should become clear in the course of this study. I am here using the word *symbolic* in a sense that was earlier common but is now much less so. Goethe conveys this sense when he writes, "Symbolism transforms the phenomenon into idea and the idea into image; in the image the idea remains infinitely effective and unattainable and even when expressed in all languages remains inexpressible."[2] In other words, the symbol contains an element that is ahistorical and transcendent, and this is the source of its deepest effect on us. Regarded psychologically, the symbol expresses a basic and a priori mode of psychic functioning and of adaptation to the world. (The maladaptation of most fools is also a kind of adaptation.) Insofar as folly is symbolic, it may be said, following C. G. Jung, to have an archetypal foundation. In his use of the term "archetype" Jung in turn follows various early writers, among them Irenaeus, who conjectured that "the creator of the world did not fashion these things directly from himself, but copied them from archetypes outside himself."[3] Applying this metaphor to the nature of the psyche, Jung writes that "what we mean by 'archetype' is in itself irrepresentable, but has effects which make visualizations of it possible, namely the archetypal images and ideas."[4]

In trying to understand materials that are symbolic in this sense we must, I believe, alternate between two processes of understanding: that of abstraction and that of what is in German called *Einfühlung*, a form of imagination by which we feel our way into the object in its manifold relations to the world and let it become part of our inner life.[5] In forming a concept of something that has an archetypal effect, we are drawing a distinction between what it is as a fact that may be known objectively and what it is as a content of subjective, personal experience. In doing this we are in some measure rendering it nonsymbolic, because we make a distinction between subject and object that is not present in our experience of the symbol. We cannot know what it is without being gripped by it, but we cannot form an unambiguous concept of the condition of being gripped or of the thing that grips us. Jung in many places describes the symbol under the aspect of the *coincidentia oppositorum*, the symbol forming a bridge between otherwise irreconcilable meanings. The psychic functions of abstraction and *Einfühlung* tend to be in one sense mutually exclusive, in another complementary, in the total workings of the psyche. Thus the ambiguous, even self-contradictory, nature of the symbol *as a content* has its counterpart in the ambiguity, and even self-contradiction, attendant upon our *understanding* of the symbol.

Empathic imagination (or *Einfühlung*) is, then, as necessary to an adequate understanding of symbolism as is intellectual judgment, since neither process can be reduced to the other. This necessity may be illustrated by an analogy from the realm of folly: we cannot describe a joke and its workings unless we get the point of it. If we do get the point of it, we were, while we laughed, inside the thing we wish to describe, and our description will have little meaning unless it conveys a lively awareness of that experience. Something that is deeply symbolic does not have a single point to get; rather, it presents us with facets behind which the effective core remains inaccessible. (No one succeeds in writing the last critical comment on *Hamlet*, and in every theatrical production of *King Lear* the Fool turns up in a different guise.)

To arrive at anything like an adequate understanding of a recurrent and powerful imaginative form, we must compare similar materials and analyze the psychic processes by which we (and others) relate to them and through them to the form. Similarity is, of course, not identity—the fool in a medieval play is not the same figure as a clown in a Pueblo Indian ceremony; and the psychological analysis of symbolism is limited by difficulties that I have already suggested. Nonetheless, the historical method characteristic of most of the good books that have been written about fool, and folly also encounters difficulties and also has limits. These are well described by J. I. M. Stewart, writing of Shakespeare: "It is only too probable that what [the historical critic] would have us accept as a criterion [of a Shakespearean performance] is simply what he conjectures was felt, expected, taken for granted. And thus, at the best, he will stop short just where the dramatist himself must be supposed to begin."[6] From that beginning Shakespeare went on to make something that reached to the depths of his audience. The same depths are alive in us, and our principal connection with Shakespeare's fools, and with many of the other fools to be met in the following pages, is through them.

I assume, then, that we may compare materials from different cultural and historical contexts, that we may find the similarities among them as impressive as the differences, and that we may be interested in the ways in which different but similar materials express basic psychic processes in different but similar ways. The nature of my own interest in fools and folly, and the focus of this book, may become clearer to the reader if I say that I am a student and teacher of literature and drama who has for several years worked as a psychotherapist in psychiatric clinics and in private practice. In a psychiatric clinic one becomes acquainted as a matter of life and death with irrational forces, their profundity, their contagiousness, and their power to create and destroy psychic and other structures (for example, the social structure of the family). There are moments when the atmosphere in a psychiatric clinic has much in common with the madhouses from which such clinics have developed. A madhouse contained people who were thought to be fools, as is suggested by the French *maison des fous* or "house of fools"; and modern psychologists are partly concerned with what was earlier known as folly.

The limited "explanation" of fools and folly to be found in these pages is thus primarily psychological rather than historical, anthropological, or sociological. Psychological and social phenomena are interrelated, and the psychological comments I make will often have a social implication.

II. ORDER AND CHAOS AND THE FOOL

Fertility rites of agriculture imply that there is an order in the world (spring comes after winter), that there are forces working against that order (the crops may be poor), and that man can help to ensure that the order will prevail (he mimes his involvement in the process of nature and his commitment to its order). The "contrary behavior" of clowns may also serve that order—a complex matter with which I shall continue to be concerned.

Fools are characteristically unperturbed by the ignominy that comes of being irresponsible. They have a magical affinity with chaos that might allow them to serve as scapegoats on behalf of order; yet they elude the sacrifice or the banishment that would affirm order at their expense. They reduce order to chaos in a way that makes a farce of the mythical pattern. They wrest life from the "destructive element" while ridiculing the ancient dream that victory over it is possible—and while ridiculing even more the idea that victory over it may be achieved through the observance of rules of conduct. Fools induce chaos by violating those rules. They may look on passively, innocently, even benignly, while the sympathetic magic that binds them to it works. Though they may seem innocently detached from it, it may be an active form of their folly. It may be overtly demonic, but it may also take a playful form, and it may emerge as the fool's guiding spirit in a transvaluation of values with him as its center. I have so far mentioned many fools who have attacked rules and by implication the whole principle of order. I wish now to illustrate these other forms of the fool's relation to order and chaos by scenes from modern films and vaudeville. I wish to show the persistence of concerns alive in ritual and of the fool's magic as a reality that again and again requires contemporary expression.

Folly is a disembodied and demonic force in a scene in Chaplin's film *Limelight* (1952), in which he and Buster Keaton are music-hall clowns performing a skit. Chaplin is a concert violinist accompanied at the piano by Keaton. As Keaton is getting ready to play, his sheets of music begin spilling from the piano, the confusion mounting and mount-

ing as though the music were possessed. His piano then starts to disintegrate, slowly and malevolently, and the strings snap and roll up until the
guts are an insidious snarl of wire. As the strings break one by one, weird
sounds erupt. As soon as Chaplin has begun to play his inanely showy
piece, one of his legs shrivels up and disappears into his trousers. He
stops, looks down startled, pulls the leg down with his hands till it
touches the floor, and begins playing again. The leg again shrivels up.
The audience howls with laughter.

It is, in fact, probable that we are laughing not only at their inappropriate and pedantic fussing but also at their heroic tenacity, at their dedication to the meaningful continuance of life. There is, as well, something
sinister about their heroism. Their participation in the human image, already slight because they are clowns, is violated further and further until
we must realize that it is not the human will that is in them enduring and
even holding its own against chaos; there seems, rather, to be a secret
collaboration between them and whatever is attacking them. They go on
being tormented as mice by a cat; if we were the mice, we would have
given ourselves up much sooner. The fact that the fools persist, without
succumbing to panic and running, makes us begin to suspect that a single
intelligence, like that of an unimaginable cat-mouse, is playing with us
through them, through their dilemma, and through their attempts to deal
with it.

■   ■   ■   ■

The magical force that induces chaos in the presence of the fool
often results in a transvaluation of values that could be the beginning of a
new order. This process is illustrated by a scene from W. C. Fields's film
The Bank Dick (1940). Fields drives a car at great speed while a bank
robber in the seat behind him points a gun at him; they are chased by
policemen on motorcycles. In the course of the pursuit, the controlling
mechanisms of the car begin to disintegrate. Unperturbed, Fields throws
away the gearshift and the brakes and passes the steering wheel to the
robber. The car careens madly but without accident, dodging obstacles,
until it finally comes to a halt at the very edge of a cliff. Fields steps out,
the criminal having passed out with fright, in time to be greeted as a hero
by the arriving police. The magical power that guides the car may be seen
as another form of that which horribly afflicted Chaplin and Keaton. That
this power belongs to the fool, or that he belongs to it, is shown by the
fact that Fields takes the astonishing course of events completely for
granted and that it ends in a triumph for him. In addition, the cliff over-

looks water with a sign labeling it "Lake Shosho-Bogomo," a product of the same mind, Fields's, that earlier in the film invented the disease "mogo on the gogogo": the fool's intelligence has plotted the course that the car takes as though by chance.

The nature of this power as a psychic reality becomes apparent if we regard automobile driving as an analogy for the functioning of the ego. Driving is not just an act of conscious thought or understanding but a very complicated interaction of conscious and unconscious functions. If a person is to drive well, his car must be in working order, he must know how to drive, he must have a clear idea of where he wants to go and how he wants to get there, and he must have a flexibility of understanding that will allow him to deal with unexpected events along the way. In other words, his driving is not just an act of conscious thought or will but a complicated interaction of conscious and unconscious, of voluntary and habitual functions.

The power of the automobile—the energy used by ego-functioning—may be assumed to derive from deep regions of the unconscious. More specifically, it may be assumed to derive from a constellation of archetypes, of transpersonal, unconscious factors that actively shape our experience. In Jung's view, the archetypes are sources of both instinctual energy and meaning. Unless a person experiences the constellated archetype on the symbolic level (as *Sinnbild* or "image of meaning"), he is immersed in its dynamism. This dynamism may animate states of subjective identity with the world; it may nourish projection, affect, and diffuse and obsessive sexuality; it may make objects unpredictable and adaptation to them extremely difficult; its effects—when meaning is inadequate—are largely destructive. A person's adaptation to the outer world may fail, as when he makes a wrong turn with his car into a one-way street; his adaptation to these inner factors may also fail, with the result that he may fall into magical modes of thought and behavior. The analytical psychologist Edward Whitmont sees magical phenomena as belonging to a field of energy derived from the archetype; he sees this field of energy as constituting a dimension of experience and a characteristic mode of psychic functioning.[7] This view implies a correlation between culture and the individual, between primitive peoples and modern Western individuals in states of regression, that may be too neat (for reasons I touched on in the previous section), but it is nonetheless suggestive when applied to personal psychology.

Fields can be imagined, then, as having fallen into such a magical field, with the dynamism of the archetypal constellation having usurped the controlling functions of ego-consciousness. The automobile is magical in that it continues to run despite its disintegration and finds its way among obstacles (thus implying a breakdown of the distinction between the intelligent subject and lifeless objects); the affect characteristic of strong connection with the archetypes appears in the war between the bank robber and the police. Fields's equanimity in the course of this perilous adventure is appropriate to the foolish characteristic of being only "as though the same as " oneself; what he *really* is—his folly—is at work in the disintegration of the car, in its precarious course despite this disintegration, and in the conflict between the forces of law and lawlessness. His role in the magical field is at first that of victim; then it becomes clear that he is its agent; and finally it allows him to triumph over both the criminal and the police as he—or it—makes fools of both of them.

Both the police and the criminal belong to an order based on certain rules of behavior and certain realities of power. In both culture and individual psychology, patterns of order tend to become rigid and sterile; they repeatedly need renewal. This tendency, too, is partly a matter of our relations to the unconscious. When the symbol or "image of meaning," the manifest content of the archetype, has crossed the threshold into consciousness, it is at first numinous; in time it loses its dynamism, which is also its capacity for provoking emotion. This loss is a natural part of the process by which rational meaning is formed and maintained in consciousness. "It is a fearful thing to fall into the hands of the living God" (Heb. 10:31); but the experience must lose its immediacy if it is translated into the discursive language of theology. However, the process of abstraction is necessary, as it splits the total experience of the archetype into one of a subject confronting an object and thus protects us from the archetypal dynamism.[8] But when the process of abstraction has gone too far, the repressed dynamism asserts itself. Life goes on even when it is meaningless; order must again and again be brought into relation with vital possibilities supplied by the unconscious. These are at first incomprehensible, but they may express what seem to be dispositions in the magical field.

Fields's wild car ride implies such a magical disposition. As we watch him, life avenges itself upon the colorless order that has been made of it, and folly avenges itself upon the nonfoolish values that have temporarily neutralized it. Chaos is spread throughout the normal world until the car halts at the edge of the cliff, as though the magical power that had guided it there were content to disappear again to the "outside," beyond the limits of conscious awareness. The result is a transvaluation of the

good and bad figures, the police and the robber, into fools who (as unwit-
ting butts of the folly that has possessed the car) must acknowledge the
superior power of the fool (as knave). This reduction of order to chaos in
which the magical power of the fool makes itself felt is related to that
effected by saturnalian revelers and primitive clowns.

It is striking how strongly inclined people are to believe the rational
constructions that, as individuals and groups, they make of the world.
Reason is often motivated by unconscious contents, as when scientists
explore and systematize owing to their emotional attitudes toward the
unknown and toward order; and ideas of what constitutes the proper form
of things facilitate action, as when our conception of our territory creates
the line at which we will act to defend it. Thus order invites belief, as
does that which violates it. However, one can argue skeptically that
knowledge of objective order is humanly impossible unless the psyche,
including the irrational, is granted the status of objective fact; but this
admission opens us to painful ambiguities that we had hoped to avoid
through our passion for reason. Thus people are also inclined to trim and
connive in their commitment to the order in which they believe. The
fool, deficient in normal understanding and in the normal appreciation of
order, readmits the magical power of chaos; he makes us surreptitiously
feel that a debt of honesty has been paid.

In his clowning the fool plays with some of the irrational hopes that
motivate the makers of order and some of the doubts that plague them. If
the world were different, we might find certainty in it; the unknown might
yield marvels, including a summer of golden plenty or a thought as perfect
as a crystal, instead of the threat of death. As things are, we may, like the
philosophical Jaques and like Hamlet in the guise of the morose clown, be
fool-victims in our inability to understand the world and ourselves and to
act nobly. But we may also, like the victorious fool-hero of the chase scene
in *The Bank Dick*, commit ourselves to the irrational flow of life. We may
feel that queer events (such as those that befall the car) are living traces of
a wholeness that is annulling, for a purpose, our customary distinctions
between order and chaos. That purpose transcends the train of the queer
events yet seems to inform them and to belong to the deeper nature of
things. The fool as magician-actor and "delight-maker" (as one kind of
Pueblo Indian clown was called) belongs to it, too.
(1969)

24 MAGNUS EISENGRIM: THE SHADOW OF THE TRICKSTER IN THE NOVELS OF ROBERTSON DAVIES

Russel M. Brown and Donna A. Bennett

These two Canadian professors of literature discuss the trickster figure not only in relation to Davies's Deptford Trilogy *(1970–75) but also in relation to Canada's shift in recent years from a tragic to a comic vision of life. The selection makes effective use of Jung's essay "On the Psychology of the Trickster Figure" to explain the significance of the occasionally bizarre actions of Davies's characters. Further, it follows Jung's essay in emphasizing the obscure but sometimes numinous figures, such as the anima or the wise old man, which may be hidden by, but are therefore in a relationship to, the trickster/shadow. It is an especial strength of these critics that they discover and describe not just the isolated archetype, but several archetypes interacting in dynamic combination, just as they do in real life. Surely, for literary criticism one of the strengths of a dynamic theory of personality should be that it accounts for character changes and character interaction, not simply the magnification of the single archetypal state of mind and its accompanying iconography. By following through the novels Davies's own sophisticated understanding of Jung, Brown and Bennett present an enlightening analysis not only of Davies's trilogy, but also of several key aspects of Jung's psychology.*

You see how it was: to him the reality of life lay in external things, whereas for me the only reality was of the spirit—of the mind, as I then thought, not having understood yet what a cruel joker and mean master the intellect can be.

Studies of Canadian literature have tended to characterize it as por-
traying man besieged by a hostile universe, as being filled with novels
whose characters are either damaged by the world or trapped in a stoical
struggle against it. In *Butterfly on Rock*, D. G. Jones—enlarging on Northrop Frye's notion of the garrison culture as the informing literary force in
Canada—describes the archetypal hero as Job, man suffering in a wilderness that is initially the literal one of the land but later becomes the community or is internalized within the self.[1] Similarly, Margaret Atwood's
Survival, though a more personal reading of Canadian literature, underlines analogous themes; the hero of Canadian fiction is a projection of the
Canadian identity: he is a victim struggling for "bare survival."[2] Ideally,
the best inhabitant of the world these critics perceive would be some sort
of saint (in fact, a great deal of attention has been paid to the figure of the
saint, both serious and ironic);[3] the truest gesture, the act of selfless
sacrifice.[4]

But this was Canadian literature in an older phase, a literature that
affirmed a tragic view of life in which man struggled and was destroyed,
frequently because of his own innate weaknesses and flaws. In the last
generation, however, and especially in the last decade, there has been a
loss of ability to accept a view of order in the universe that is necessary to
make a tragic pattern coherent or comprehensible. In its place a comic
vision has developed, one that tends to perceive an aleatory and absurd
world, not opposed to man but indifferent to him.[5] In such a world a new
pantheon of heroes must displace the old. For Canada this has especially
meant the appearance and positive depiction of a new kind of character
in its novels: the trickster, that figure which is opposed to the traditional
virtues upon which the old Canadian social ethic was built, virtues such
as prudence and dignity. Instead the trickster combines folly and guile,
cleverness and recklessness.[6]

Although the trickster is a figure relevant to contemporary literature in general, he is particularly interesting in a Canadian setting where,
compared to other literatures, he is a new arrival on the literary scene.
His presence in current fiction embodies a response to a relatively recent
loss of belief in a providential universe, while at the same time the extent
of his prominence is also an indication of an underlying sense of flux and
chaos that has, on the deepest level, troubled Canadian writers and disturbed the surfaces of their literary works since the last century. It is this
sense that has made "the problem of Job" a central topic, the problem of
reconciling man's experience of the universe with conventional wisdom.
The emergence of the trickster is significant because he represents not so

much an answer to as an escape from that problem: he is, as Stanley Diamond points out in a new edition of Paul Radin's classic study of the trickster, an anti-Job.[7]

The trickster as a positive figure made his first appearance in Canadian fiction of the 1950s, in books such as Ethel Wilson's *Swamp Angel*, where the eccentric ex-circus juggler Nell Severance acts to free the novel's protagonist from the socially defined traps of marriage and respectability. Mrs. Severance serves as a prototype for this kind of liberating trickster; Marian in Margaret Atwood's *The Edible Woman*, waiting for her wedding day, is "drifting with the current" that will drown her in meaningless nonbeing until she is carried into "an eddy of present time" by the parlous obliquity of the college student, Duncan; the protagonists of Margaret Laurence's Manawaka books are repeatedly being tricked into recognizing and acting on their freedom—Rachel, the victim of both Nick's lies and God's jests on her way to Vancouver at last; Stacey, frightened into action by the duplicity of Thor Thorlakson. When Sheila Watson's novel, *The Double Hook*, was published in 1959, it gave an added dimension to the development of the trickster in fiction by utilizing, and thereby calling attention to, the trickster mythology of the North American Indian. Watson's exploration influenced later writers, most notably Robert Kroetsch, who has frequently acknowledged his interest in the trickster and who has made him a central, rather than a secondary, character in his recent novels.[8]

Now, with the recent completion of Robertson Davies's new trilogy, we have in its portrayal of Magnus Eisengrim—the man who has been transformed from a small boy in Deptford, Ontario, into a "northern wizard"—the most fully developed fictional investigation of the trickster yet to appear. Davies's obvious interest in this figure was undoubtedly stimulated by his fascination with Jungian thought: "Freud was an enormous enthusiasm of mine before I was forty; after forty I came to examine the works of his great colleague Carl Gustav Jung, and I have been, over many years, reading and re-reading again the collected works of C. G. Jung."[9] This reading would have lead Davies to Jung's essay "On the Psychology of the Trickster Figure." Coincidentally, this would have put him in contact with the same Indian myth that attracted Watson and Kroetsch.[10]

The trickster figure, if he appeared at all in earlier Canadian fiction, was not seen in positive terms, but was rather viewed as either an embodiment of the threatening chaotic world against which man struggles, or as an individual who threatens social structures important to maintain. In Davies's first novels, the Salterton trilogy, which appeared in the fifties, this attitude may still be seen. Two of the books turn around jokes of a sort—the placing of a false engagement notice in a small-town paper (*Leaven of Malice*), the bitterly whimsical will of a dowager (*A Mixture of Frailties*)—but in both cases, though the outcome of the joke produces unexpected benefits, the joker is not forgiven: Bevill Higgin stands revealed as malicious, pathetic, and contemptible, while Mrs. Bridgetower is felt as a lingering malevolent presence that must be exorcised if a new generation is to begin. At the same time the trickster begins, in these novels, to be characterized with positive features as well. This may be seen, for example, in the character of Humphrey Cobbler, who appears in all three of the Salterton books, the jovial, antisocial, iconoclastic church organist whose antic behavior at Solly Bridgetower's party in *Tempest-Tost* brings into the open the hidden emotions of the men present and thereby allows events to progress to a satisfactory conclusion. It is Cobbler who opens *Leaven of Malice* with a lighthearted Halloween witch's Sabbath in the cathedral and who concludes *A Mixture of Frailties* with a "Joe Miller," a musical joke that juxtaposes the secular and the sacred.

It remained for Davies to develop the trickster beyond this relatively minor role only after he left behind his concern with the mannered society of Salterton for his growing interest in the individual states of consciousness around which he built his second trilogy: *Fifth Business* (1970), *The Manticore* (1972), and *World of Wonders* (1975). *Fifth Business* seems, at first encounter, to belong with Davies's earlier novels, for we are once more involved in the life a small Ontario town in this chronicle of three boys—Percy Boyd Staunton, Dunstable Ramsay, and Paul Dempster—growing up in Deptford. There is, however, more depth in Deptford than immediately meets the eye, and the novel's three principals mature into remarkable characters, the stuff of myth rather than of manners. As Ramsay says of them, "We have all rejected our beginnings and become something our parents could not have foreseen." Percy Boyd Staunton becomes "Boy" Staunton, the North American boy-man whom Davies makes into the epitome of the successful entrepreneurial capitalist ("one of the truly rich . . . one of those men whose personal income, though large is a trifling part of the huge mystical body of wealth that stands behind them and cannot be counted"). Dunstable Ramsay, renamed Dunstan after nearly dying in World War I, becomes a teacher and a famous historian who devotes his life to "explorations of the borderland between history and myth," finding himself at last in "the wondrous enclosed garden of hagiology." Paul Dempster's development and transformation is, of the three, the most unlooked for and the most striking. He vanishes from Deptford into the world of the circus, from which he eventually returns metamorphosed into Magnus Eisengrim, the trickster-magician who is the most fascinating and enigmatic character in the novel.

Most of *Fifth Business* describes the development of Ramsay and his interaction—which is an unacknowledged rivalry—with Boy Staunton. The central event of the novel takes place in the opening scene, when ten-year-old Boy throws a snowball which, missing Ramsay, strikes Mary Dempster and causes the premature birth of Paul. Paul disappears from the mainstream of events, while Ramsay becomes a friend and eventually the caretaker of Mrs. Dempster, a woman who loses touch with reality after the birth of her son, but who, Ramsay is convinced, is also a miracle-working saint. At the same time, Ramsay's continuing relationship with Boy, his "lifelong friend and enemy," comes to define the different worlds to which they belong and the roles to which they aspire: the material realm over which Boy seeks kingship, the world of the spirit in which Dunstan conducts a quest for sainthood.

The opposition between the two is also one of the past—represented by Dunstan's search for the wellsprings of history in myth and legend—and the present—incarnated in Boy who, in his perennial childhood and his fascination with the immediate benefits of modern technology, holds Ramsay's antiquarian preoccupations in contempt. This conflict, between life lived in the daily world of surfaces and the continued existence in man of deeply rooted primitive beliefs, is one that Davies pursues throughout *Fifth Business*. This is a contradiction which interested Jung as well, one he thought helped to account for the strength of the Indian trickster mythology. Relating anecdotes that demonstrate how individuals can simultaneously heed the calls of a primitive magical world and a modern one, he observes: "The conflict between the two dimensions of consciousness is simply an expression of the polaristic structure of the psyche, which like any other energic system is dependent on the tension of opposites" (*CW*, vol. 9, pt. 1, p. 483).[11]

Jung's conception of the relationship of the trickster to the psyche is a complex one. He suggests it in speaking further on the structure of the psyche in a way that is especially significant to us for the potential insight that it offers into the interrelationship of the three main characters of *Fifth Business*:

> The fact is, that this old trichotomous hierarchy of psychic contents (hylic, psychic, and pneumatic) represents the polaristic structure of

the psyche, which is the only immediate object of experience. The unity of our psychic nature lies in the middle, just as the living unity of the waterfall appears in the dynamic connection between above and below. Thus, the living effect of the myth is experienced when a higher consciousness, rejoicing in its freedom and independence, is confronted by the autonomy of a mythological figure and yet cannot flee from its fascination, but must pay tribute to the overwhelming impression. The figure works, because secretly it participates in the observer's psyche and appears as its reflection, though it is not recognized as such. It is split off from his consciousness and consequently behaves like an autonomous personality. The trickster is a collective shadow figure, a summation of all the inferior traits of character in individuals. And since the individual shadow is never absent as a component of personality, the collective figure can construct itself out of it continually. (*CW*, vol. 9, pt. 1, p. 484)

Jung's comments here need the context of his earlier essays. In "On the Nature of the Psyche" he describes the whole of the psyche as a kind of spectrum ranging from physical to spiritual. The lower portion of this spectrum, which arises out of the "organic material substrate," Jung variously identifies with the unconscious, with the instinct and its drives, and with emotions and sensations. The upper part of the spectrum, the supraconscious, is the realm of the spirit, of "feeling" in the Jungian sense of evaluation, and of the archetypes—which, by virtue of the way the psyche curves back upon itself, it furnishes to the lower level of the unconscious, thus becoming the source of images found in the collective unconscious. The psyche proper—which is associated with the ego, with the will, and with consciousness and cognition—lies between these two, not existing autonomously as they do, but rather deriving its existence from the way these other two psychic components overlap:

> The psyche is made up of processes whose energy springs from the equilibration of all kinds of opposites. The spirit/instinct antithesis is only one of the commonest formulations, but it has the advantage of reducing the greatest number of the most important and most complex psychic processes to a common denominator. So regarded, psychic processes seem to be balances of energy flowing between spirit and instinct. . . . (*CW*, 8:407)

This Jungian opposition is obviously the informing force behind Davies's depiction of Ramsay and Staunton. They are individuals who represent the psychic poles, each exemplifying the dangers of imbalance of which Jung warns:

> A poorly developed consciousness, for instance, which because of massed projections is inordinately impressed by concrete or apparently concrete things and states, will naturally see in the instinctual drives the source of all reality. It remains blissfully unaware of the spirituality of such a philosophical surmise, and is convinced that with this opinion it has established the essential instinctuality of all psychic processes. Conversely, a consciousness that finds itself in opposition to the instincts can, in consequence of the enormous influence then exerted by the archetypes, so subordinate instinct to spirit that the most grotesque "spiritual" complications may arise out of what are undoubtedly biological happenings. (*CW*, 8:407)

These are the extremes personified, on the one hand, by the materialistic, sexually driven Boy, "the quintessence of the Jazz Age," whose limited concept of the spirit is epitomized by the world-celebrating teachings of the Reverend Leadbeater, a man who sees God's beauty in the handful of gemstones he carries in his pocket, and, on the other hand, by the ascetic saint-seeking Ramsay, who grows old with "a whole great piece of . . . life that is unlived, denied, set aside." Separately, each lacks wholeness; together, they may benefit one another, providing the psychic wholeness that each lacks. They demonstrate Jung's dictum that, "although physical and spiritual passion are deadly enemies, they are nevertheless brothers-in-arms" (*CW*, 8:414).

Jung suggests that a lack of proper psychic balance is a particularly modern problem. The remedy he proposes in "On the Nature of the Psyche" provides the final needed gloss on the passage cited above from his essay on the trickster, and clarifies Paul Dempster's function in his guise as Magnus Eisengrim:

> Psychic processes . . . behave like a scale along which consciousness "slides." At one moment it finds itself in the vicinity of instinct, and falls under its influence; at another, it slides along to the other end where spirit predominates and even assimilates the instinctual processes most opposed to it. These counter-positions, so fruitful of illusion, are by no means symptoms of the abnormal; on the contrary, they form the twin poles of that psychic one-sidedness which is typical of the normal man of today . . . .

> This "sliding" consciousness is thoroughly characteristic of mod-
> ern man. But the one-sidedness it causes can be removed by what I
> have called the "realization of the shadow." . . . the growing aware-
> ness of the inferior part of the personality, which should not be
> twisted into an intellectual activity, for it has far more the meaning
> of a suffering and a passion that implicate the whole man. (*CW*,
> 8:408–9)

Eisengrim is the trickster and the shadow in the book. The sinister
projection of the once much abused child Paul, he has become a Wolf that
stands between a Boy and a Saint.[12] His transformation, described at
length in the concluding part of the trilogy, is the result of a psychic
journey into the inferno of a traveling circus, a voyage in which he exchanges innocence for mystery, eschews love for authority, and becomes
finally his own greatest creation. He is the reflection of the psyche of
which Jung speaks, produced in that crucial conjunction of matter and
spirit with which the novel opens. Davies's whole trilogy is ultimately
concerned with man's need for this trickster, along with his need to come
to terms with the shadow which the trickster represents.

One of the important things man must learn is that the shadow is
not to be dreaded or detested, that—as Jung several times points out—
the apparent inferiority and evil appearance of the shadow may be misleading. In the essay on the trickster Jung speaks of the positive aspects
of the shadow in a way that is again illuminating of Davies's use of the
figure:

> . . . the shadow, although by definition a negative figure, sometimes
> has certain clearly discernible traits and associations which point to a
> quite different background. It is as though he were hiding meaning-
> ful contents under an unprepossessing exterior. Experience con-
> firms this; and what is more important, the things that are hidden
> usually consist of increasingly numinous figures. The first thing we
> find standing behind the shadow is the anima, who is endowed with
> considerable power of fascination and possession. She often . . .
> hides in her turn the powerful archetype of the wise old man (sage,
> magician, king, etc.) (*CW*, vol. 9, pt. 1, p. 485)

A powerful anima does indeed stand behind the trickster-shadow in
Fifth Business, which suggests much about the structure of Ramsay's
quest. Mary Dempster serves as his anima and dominates the course of

his life: weighed upon by guilt-feelings about her apparent loss of reason after she takes the blow meant for him, distrustful of his own mother after a traumatic childhood encounter, Ramsay fastens upon Paul's mother with earnest devotion. Convinced that she has performed three miracles, he is led into his lifelong investigation of sainthood, seeking to understand not only the nature of saints but the source of the world's need for saintly figures.

Ramsay's pursuits carry him to the Jesuits of the Société des Bollandistes, where he meets Padre Blazon, the man who helps him understand the meaning of Mary Dempster:

" . . . she would never have got past the Bollandists, but she must have been an extraordinary person, a great lover of God, and trusting greatly in His love for her. As for the miracles, you and I have looked too deeply into miracles to dogmatize; you believe in them, and your belief has coloured your life with beauty and goodness . . . your life has been illuminated by your fool-saint, and how many can say so much?"

Padre Blazon is, of course, the Jungian old man, the sage that Ramsay finds hidden behind the anima. This theatrical, half-comic Jesuit, uncomfortably tolerated by the Bollandists "for his great learning and for what was believed to be his great age," shows Ramsay the limitations of the enquiries he has made thus far (and by implication of the life he has led) by teaching him of the other, the underground, aspects of sainthood. He concludes one of his lectures:

"But all this terrible talk about the saints is not disrespect, Ramezay. Far from it! It is faith! It is love! It takes the saint to the heart by supplying the other side of his character that history or legend has suppressed. . . . Mankind cannot endure perfection; it stifles him. He demands that even the saints should cast a shadow. If they, these holy ones who have lived so greatly but who still carry their shadows with them, can approach God, well then, there is hope for the worst of us."

This understanding of the dual aspect of Ramsay's beloved hagiography is but part of Padre Blazon's own search, for he professes himself "deep in the old man's puzzle, trying to link the wisdom of the body with the wisdom of the spirit until the two are one."

Thus Ramsay's preoccupation with Paul's birth allows him to fall under the domination of his anima; his quest for the meaning of her existence carries him to his sage; Blazon, in turn, sends him back to seek understanding of what has so far eluded the saint-ridden Ramsay: the nature of the shadow. It is this shadow, embodied in the trickster figure, that can join the pneumatic wisdom with the hylic, as Blazon knows. "At my age," he warns Ramsay, "you cannot divide spirit from body without anguish and destruction, from which you will speak nothing but crazy lies!"

Having rediscovered Paul once before (as Faustus Legrand, a magician in a small traveling show), Ramsay finds him again after his discussions with Blazon—now fully realized in his identity as Magnus Eisengrim. Traveling for a while with Eisengrim's troupe, Ramsay senses part of the answer to Blazon's "old man's puzzle" in the person of the beautiful Faustina. Eisengrim concludes each performance with a magical skit called *The Vision of Dr. Faustus*, which portrays the conflict between "sacred and profane love for the soul of Faust." His assistant, Faustina, portrays both female parts, the modest, domestic Gretchen and the erotic Venus, in a way that, for Ramsay, "conveyed unmistakably the message that beauty of spirit and lively sensuality might inhabit one body."

In the company of Eisengrim, Ramsay learns this lesson experientially as well—by spending a night of physical struggle and passion with Liesl, the grotesque woman who is the source of Paul's magic. From her he also learns the limitations of sainthood in the world in which man must dwell. "How can you really be good to anybody," she chides him, "if you are not good to yourself?" The failure of Ramsay's conception of saintliness is further underlined shortly afterward when he tries to communicate to the wandering mind of Mary Dempster the news that he has been in touch with her son: the result is disastrous, for he succeeds only in pushing her into a final and bitter madness from which she never recovers.

It is not in the company of his saint, but with her offspring, the trickster, who is the product of her self-destructive union with the rigorous puritan morality of her husband, Amasa, that Ramsay must find the resolution he seeks. This resolution takes place in the book's penultimate scene, one that brings the three principals together for the first time. In this climactic scene of revelation, we discover that the trouble-causing snowball was more potent than we had previously suspected, for it had carried a rock inside, an appropriate weapon for the material Boy.

Ramsay, acting for Boy as the "keeper of his conscience and keeper of the stone," has clung to this source of the past and vainly tries to impress Boy with its significance: " . . . for God's sake, get to know something about yourself. The stone-in-the-snowball has been characteristic of too much you've done for you to forget it forever!" But Staunton, a man without memory, living only in the present, has indeed forgotten the event and cannot understand the guilt that Ramsay expects him to feel.

Paul has also been asked to feel guilt about his mother's fate: his puritanical father implicates him for his very act of birth. But Paul, while understanding the nature of guilt (which Boy does not), refuses to accept its burden: " 'I was too young for the kind of guilt my father wanted me to feel; he had an extraordinary belief in guilt as educative force. I couldn't stand it. I cannot feel guilt now.' "

However, if Paul Dempster cannot feel guilt over his role in life's events, he nevertheless can join with Ramsay in extracting the final penance from Boy, helping to set straight what Dunstan calls their "moral bookkeeping" that ends *Fifth Business.* As Magnus Eisengrim, he does this by putting Boy in touch with his own shadow, with that unrecognized dimension of life which, as Liesl warns Ramsay, if unlived will take revenge on man and make a fool of him. Magnus grants Boy's inmost wish, the desire that Staunton has previously voiced ("I wish I could get into a car and drive away from the whole damned thing") and that Ramsay has already interpreted for him: "A truly mythological wish . . . you want to pass into oblivion with your armour on, like King Arthur." Following a final conversation with Eisengrim in which Boy at last articulates his terror of growing old and his distaste at having to play the public role the government is now offering him, he dredges from his subconscious images that of the abdication of the man once his greatest hero, the Prince of Wales. At the urging of Eisengrim to "do something symbolic" with the stone, Boy places it in his mouth and drives his Cadillac into the waters of the Toronto harbor.[13]

The synthesis of Eisengrim, Ramsay, and Staunton cannot hold, and Boy is destroyed by his encounter with the shadow. Eisengrim has, however, served as a catalyst, releasing both Ramsay and Staunton from their stasis so that Dunstan can speak at last, protest the unexpiated guilt, finally challenge Boy in a way that makes him realize that his reign has ended and that the time for fulfillment of his wish is at hand. The death of Boy Staunton only seems to end the potential for harmony between instinct and spirit, however. As *The Manticore* and, especially, *World of Wonders* make clear, a new triad replaces the old, with Liesl taking Boy's place as the representative of the material world. Staunton's death in 1968 marks the end of the material domination of the modern era which has neglected the demands of mind and spirit. Magnus's magical world displaces Boy's material one, but it draws its powers from Liesl's great wealth even as Eisengrim has gained his seemingly magical powers over the world of matter by mastering the secrets of the clockwork toys at Liesl's ancestral home. Liesl's home and Liesl's bed come, finally, to unite the three of them. The forces that could not be joined in *Fifth Business* (though even there we know that after the final events of the novel Ramsay seems to have accepted Liesl's invitation to come to Switzerland) are fully integrated in *World of Wonders*.

The Manticore, the book that stands between Ramsay's self-justifying narrative in *Fifth Business* and his history of Eisengrim in *World of Wonders*, acts as interlude—focusing not on Boy, but on Boy's son, David Staunton. A mythicized psychohistory, a fictionalized introduction to what Davies calls the "Comedy Company of the Psyche," it is a novelistic introduction to Jungian psychoanalysis. While in *Fifth Business* the division between physical and spiritual prevented the existence of a psychic center, in *The Manticore* David, who is the spiritual son of Dunstan as well as the physical offspring of Boy, *is* the rational, cognitive man who is out of touch with both body and soul. Not surprisingly, the first need his Swiss analyst identifies is his need to become acquainted with his shadow.

David discovers that he detests his shadow in himself and is repelled by those on whom he projects it. Eisengrim is one in whom David sees the shadow, and we learn that he felt a deep antipathy toward him when he attended (at the end of *Fifth Business*) one of his performances.

> "Shall I tell you why? Because he was making fools of us all, and so cleverly that most of us liked it; he was a con man of a special kind, exploiting just that element in human credulity that most arouses me—I mean the desire to be deceived . . . it's a kind of abject surrender, an abdication of common sense. I am a victim of it now and then."

Despite his dislike of the man, David is moved to shout a question to Eisengrim's oracular brazen head, receiving an answer that disrupts his life and begins his psychic quest.

David has chosen his profession of "criminal lawyer" (savoring the ambiguity of the term) because of the intensity of his desire to suppress the shadow, but paradoxically he finds himself defending it and working to prevent its prosecution. In the course of his analysis David learns to acknowledge his unpleasant shadow self, his frightening trickster nature; however, it is not until he leaves therapy and encounters Eisengrim, Ramsay, and Liesl that he is forced to go beyond intellectual comprehension and to confront his shadow directly.

To appreciate fully this climactic development of *The Manticore* in the context of the trickster myth, it is necessary to mention two anatomical anomalies that characterize the anthropomorphic Indian Trickster: an enormous phallus, which he carries in a box on his back, and vast quantities of intestines, which he keeps wrapped around his body. These two features suggest those facets of humanity, man's sexuality and his excretory needs, which he finds hardest to reconcile with his rational nature. They provide the basis for popular tales of Trickster's comic debasements: remarkable sexual escapades, including that of sending his penis swimming across a river to visit a chief's daughter, and scatological fables such as the widely occurring tale of the laxative bulb. (Trickster, eating of this bulb despite previous warnings, is forced to defecate so much that he must climb higher and higher into a tree for refuge, finally falling back into his own feces.) Davies, in *The Manticore*, and Kroetsch, in books such as *The Studhorse Man* and *Gone Indian*, may be thought of as dividing these two aspects of the trickster between them, for, just as the phallus is central to Kroetsch's books, so defecation is an important image in *The Manticore*, one that underlines David's search for psychic wholeness.

One of David's prominent childhood memories is of the humiliating treatments he underwent for constipation, an ailment he suggests is particularly prevalent in rural Canada, where "Farm people understandably dreaded their draughty privies in winter and cultivated their powers of retention." Such constipation becomes emblematic of the extreme self-restraint that individuals such as David have imposed on their feelings and instincts. Grandfather Staunton's crude remedy—"the harsh invading spike"—is a "forcing of Nature" that makes worse what it is meant to cure. Intended to make man's natural urges accord to some intellectually predetermined schedule, the weekly enemas become a ritual designed to purge David of his baser nature, administered by a man who is the antithesis of the Trickster. Instead of inspiring or expelling laughter, David's grandfather seems to consume it: "he did not blow laughter out, he sucked it in, with a noise that sounded like a snuk-snuk, snuk-snuk, snuk-snuk."

Taught by this elderly physician that man is full of poisons in need

of purgation, David has his association of defecation and depravity reinforced by an adolescent experience. Encouraged by a companion, Bill
Unsworth, to join in the wanton destruction of a summer home, he is
horrified when their rampage culminates in a scene that comes to seem to
him the emblem of man's potential for evil.

> He [Unsworth] jumped on the table, stripped down to his trou-
> sers and squatted over the photographs. Clearly he meant to defe-
> cate on them, but such things cannot always be commanded, and so
> for several minutes we stood and stared at him as he grunted and
> swore and strained and at last managed what he wanted, right on the
> family photographs.
> How long it took I cannot tell, but they were crucial moments in
> my life. For as he struggled, red-faced and pop-eyed, and as he ap-
> peared at last with a great stool dangling from his apelike rump, I
> regained my senses. . . . The destruction was simply a prelude to
> this. It is a dirty, animal act. . . .

It is because of this background that we fully appreciate the trick
that Liesl plays on David in the book's conclusion, a joke producing a
moment of sheer terror that causes David to lose control of his bowels. In
his abjection, David is reborn, released into feeling at last. In befouling
himself he gains a direct acquaintance with all that seemed vile in man,
yet he is still able, carrying this unpleasant awareness, to struggle out of
the cave into which Liesl had lured him and back to the light. There,
freed from the psychic paralysis which had disabled him, he is ready to
return home to Canada, to defend an individual on whom he had hitherto
unknowingly projected his own shadow.

By discovering a psychic unity within himself, David is also
brought, during his time spent with Ramsay, Eisengrim, and Liesl, to
perceive a unity in the world. Where before he has seen and despised
himself as literally a "devil's advocate," defending evil from good, crime
from the pursuit of justice, now he begins to understand the complex
kind of chess that his trickster-mentors play:

> "Each player plays both black and white. If the player who draws
> white at the beginning plays white on boards one, three, and five, he
> must play black on boards two and four. . . . you can't play the
> white pieces on all the boards. Only people who play on one, flat
> board can do that, and then they are in agonies trying to figure out
> what black's next move will be. Far better to know what you are
> doing, and play from both sides."

The desire to see the unity of a world made of up of black and white, good and evil, sun and shadow, is behind Ramsay's new interest in *World of Wonders*, that belated extension to his hagiography: his considerations regarding the nature of that arch-trickster, the Devil. (We are reminded that in *Fifth Business* Padre Blazon and Liesl recommend Ramsay's becoming acquainted with the Devil: "The Devil knows corners of us all of which Christ Himself is ignorant.") In the course of *World of Wonders*, one of the characters quotes Robert Louis Stevenson: "I hazard the guess that man will be ultimately known for a mere polity of multifarious, incongruous, and independent denizens." Although Paul Dempster's teacher and model, the actor Sir John Tresize, resists the suggestion that they "put the incongruous denizens on the stage," Davies does not resist, introducing them once more to his novel. Magnus Eisengrim, while completing his role in a film biography of the magician Robert Houdin, tells his life story to the three men responsible for the movie, men who divide between them the hylic, pneumatic, and psychic aspects of the mind: Kinghovn, the cameraman who is guided only by perception and who lives wholly in the material world ("Give me things! Give me the appearance of a thing"); Lind, the brooding Swedish director who gives artistic shape to the film and who lives with "one foot in Odin's realm"; and Roland Ingestree, the producer and guiding intelligence that holds the project together ("one of the New Men . . . committed to a theatre of ideas"). Ingestree does not immediately recognize Eisengrim, but as Paul Dempster's life story unfolds it is revealed that the two men were shaped by a common experience, their participation in Sir John's acting company—an experience that has left them paired in that vital antagonism of psyche and shadow.

Ramsay, in his meditation on the Devil, comes to view humor as one of his principal attributes. Liesl and Ingestree respond to him by describing the Devil as a joker whose jests may benefit mankind:

" . . . monotheism leaves no room for jokes, and I've thought for a long time that is what is wrong with it. Monotheism is too po-faced for the sort of world we find ourselves in. . . . Whereas the Devil, when he is represented in literature, is full of excellent jokes, and we can't resist him because he and his jokes make so much sense. To twist an old saying, if the Devil had not existed, we should have [had] to invent him. He is the only explanation of the appalling ambiguities of life. I give you the Devil!"

Following this speech of Ingestree's, Ramsay warns him that the Devil might be tempted to "throw a joke or two in your direction that would test your sense of humour." Before the novel is over, this sense of humor *is* seriously put to the test by Magnus Eisengrim.

Eisengrim is, in his concluding part of the trilogy, both more human (in his autobiographical recollections) *and* more diabolic (in his present persona). Becoming the devilish joker of which Ramsay was warned, he slowly springs a series of narrative jokes on Ingestree. His humor derives from his control of the tale he tells; in recounting this narrative he becomes not only trickster but true magician, the author-creator of events, the God and devil of his imagined universe.

> "[Eisengrim's] laugh troubled me," said Lind. "I am not good at humour, and I like to be perfectly sure what people are laughing at. Do you know what it was, Ramsay?"
>
> "Yes," I said, "I think I do. That was Merlin's laugh. . . . The magician Merlin had a strange laugh, and it was heard when nobody else was laughing. He laughed at the beggar who was bewailing his fate as he lay stretched on a dunghill; he laughed at the foppish young man who was making a great fuss about choosing a pair of shoes. He laughed because he knew that deep in the dunghill was a golden cup that would have made the beggar a rich man; he laughed because he knew that the pernickety young man would be stabbed in a quarrel before the soles of his new shoes were soiled. He laughed because he knew what was coming next."

The whole of Eisengrim's autobiographical revelation, his own knowledge of what was coming next, has several functions. It allows the reader to see how Paul Dempster was transformed into a shadow, a "fetch" (Eisengrim glosses this word as a supernatural double; it also means "trick"), a wolf, and a magical trickster. It provides Eisengrim with an opportunity to take a long-delayed revenge on an old opponent, the hyperrational man, Ingestree. Finally, it allows us to glimpse the vision—the "world of wonders"—that awaits the individual who fully integrates the mind and the shadow in a way that allows him to escape his "one-sidedness." Liesl identifies this integrated vision with a lost way of seeing the world:

> "You have read Spengler? No: it is not so fashionable as it once was. But Spengler talks a great deal about what he calls the Magian World View, which he says we have lost, but which was part of the

Weltanschauung—you know the world outlook—of the Middle Ages. It was a sense of the unfathomable wonder of the invisible world that existed side by side with a hard recognition of the roughness and cruelty and day-to-day demands of the tangible world. It was a readiness to see demons where nowadays we see neuroses, and to see the hand of a guardian angel in what we are apt to shrug off ungratefully as a stroke of luck. It was religion, but a religion with a thousand gods, none of them all-powerful and most of them ambiguous in their attitude toward man. It was poetry and wonder which might reveal themselves in the dunghill, and it was an understanding of the dunghill that lurks in poetry and wonder. It was a sense of living in what Spengler called a quivering cavern-light which is always in danger of being swallowed up in the surrounding impenetrable darkness."

"I don't talk about a Magian World View: I've no touch with that sort of thing. In so far as it concerns me, I live it. It's just the way things strike me, after the life I've lived, which looks pretty much like a World of Wonders when I spread it out before me, as I've been doing. Everything has its astonishing wondrous aspect, if you bring a mind to it that's really your own."

■   ■   ■   ■

(1976)

25 THE TRICKSTER IN THE ARTS

John Beebe

John Beebe is both a psychiatrist and a practicing analytical psychologist. He is the founding editor of The San Francisco Jung Institute Library Journal *and current coeditor of the* Journal of Analytical Psychology, *as well as a frequent commentator on the relationship of Jung's work to literature, film, and the visual arts. In this selection from one of his articles, Beebe explores the manifestations of the trickster archetype both in various stages of life and in certain masterpieces exhibiting what he calls a trickster quality. Using Henry James's* The Turn of the Screw *as a vivid example, Beebe relates this trickster characteristic to artist, artwork, and audience, and describes some of the ways in which it affects all three. Especially interesting is the analyst's perspective, which Beebe integrates into his doubly informed literary criticism.*

What I want to discuss here are the effects of certain works of art. Particularly, I have in mind works of art, like *Hamlet* or the Mona Lisa, which have a paradoxical, ironic, or ambiguous effect. Such works affect us rather in the manner of certain difficult people, who "get to us" with their unexpectedly unsettling impact. These works of art perplex or madden us as we try to comprehend what is being said or shown to us, yet all the while they appear to be pleading innocent of any such confusing intention. They just go on being themselves.

Indeed, the critical mountains that grow up around controversial works of art—the immense and troubled response that such works engender—remind me, as a psychiatrist, of the chain-reaction of emotional responses that certain psychotic individuals are capable of setting off.

I am thinking particularly of persons in the grip of a full-blown manic episode, whose effect on others resembles nothing else that one sees in the course of psychiatric work. When the diagnosis is going to be mania, a veritable trail of harried individuals follows the patient into the emergency room. They come in person, and by letter, and by phone, and their numbers, as well as the harried, exasperated quality of their responses, testify to the demonic impact of the possession at hand.

I think this effect closely resembles the impact of a difficult masterpiece upon its audience.

We get our word *mania* from the Greek word that begins *The Iliad*, *mainis*, meaning wrath or rage. The remarkable thing is the ability the unfortunately *mainis*-possessed manic patient has to put his wrath into other people, who are induced to act it out for him. In a textbook article I wrote: " . . . one way to recognize the manic patient is from the size and exasperation of his [concerned social system]. Many people will call the emergency room angry with the patient and with each other, each with a different idea of what must be done. The appearance of a *manipulated* [system of persons] at war with the patient and with each other is strong evidence of mania."[1]

Now to me, this sounds very much like the trickster[2] at work, reducing those around him to a state of bewilderment and helpless rage. Indeed, I have found it helpful to think of manic states as instances of possession by the archetypal trickster attitude. What interests me here, however, is the similar impact an ambiguous work of art may have upon its audience.

In using the analogy of a patient in a psychotic state to define the characteristic quality of a famous, but upsetting, work of art, I am trying to get across what Leon Edel has called "the madness of art,"[3] art's liability to be mad, and to drive others mad who are trying to understand it. A work of art, too, may emanate the spirit of the trickster.

For those who expect art to soothe, illuminate, or please, this quality of art is hard to accept, and it is difficult to see what the artist's motive in producing such a provocative, unsettling work may have been.

In the case of the manic patient, depth psychologists have usually postulated that the patient is unconsciously expressing his rage by acting it out on others. From the family histories of such patients, researchers have found that the individual, as early as childhood, accepted adult re-

sponsibility, adopting a conscience-ridden, nose-to-the-grindstone attitude quite prematurely in life, with all too considerate a response to the
needs and feelings of others. Of course, this can produce as a compensation a very large shadow of pent-up resentment, and it may be that the
psychosis functions to allow this shadow its day.

Critics, too, have speculated that the perpetrator of a maddening
work of art may have been in a state of rage at the time of its composition.
Henry James, for instance, made his first notebook entry recording the
germ of his idea for "The Turn of the Screw" just after the failure of
years of conscientious efforts to get himself accepted as a dramatist. The
opening-night London audience was so hostile to James's play, *Guy
Domville*, that the vengeful leading actor called the unsuspecting James
onto the stage to be booed and hissed by his public, certainly the worst
moment of James's working life.[4] "The Turn of the Screw," one of the
most confusing, deceptive, and reader-manipulating stories ever written,
may well be James's revenge upon that audience. Ironically, it has also
turned out to be his most widely appreciated work.

■   ■   ■   ■

I think that in a real masterpiece the activation goes far deeper than
the personal shadow, just as in a true psychosis the archetypal shadow is
activated. One's personal shadow is just not skilled to so demonic a degree at upsetting people, nor is it so difficult to integrate as is the shadow
that appears during a manic episode, or from deep within the structure of
an ambiguous masterpiece. A manic episode seems to be a centrifuge of
archetypal shadow imagery (which is why it is so notoriously difficult to
contain with psychotherapy alone), and so, too, is a great, dark work of
art, as it spins out its meanings (which explains why no single critical
response is ever adequate to it).

In both cases, as I have been hinting, there is an activation of the
trickster archetype. The only difference—but a very crucial one—is the
controlling ethical sense of the great artist who has unleashed the disturbance. This ethical sense does not seem to be present in the manic patient when he is out of control. Were it not for the seriousness of purpose
that is behind this ethical restraint, it would be possible (as many critics
actually have done) to dismiss the works I have been talking about as
aberrations of the creative spirit, or as harmless and amusing teases, un-
deserving of serious, sustained attention.

Once one goes beyond the obvious definition "one who tricks," the
trickster becomes an elusive concept. Jung thought of the trickster as a

personification of the archetypal shadow.[5] As such, the trickster arose between the Jungian analyst Jane Wheelwright and her dying patient, Sally, in the therapy Wheelwright describes in her book, *Death of a Woman*.[6] The trickster is important in the story because he emerges just as Sally begins to reach the borderline between this existence and the unknowable Beyond; the author therefore provides a definition in the glossary that accompanies her account.

> TRICKSTER. Image of the archetype of mischievousness, unexpect-
> edness, disorder, amorality, the trickster is an archetypal shadow
> figure that represents a primordial, dawning consciousness. Com-
> pensating for rigid or overly righteous collective attitudes, it func-
> tions collectively as a cathartic safety-valve for pent-up social
> pressures, a reminder of humankind's primitive origins and the falli-
> bility of its institutions. Frequently uniting the opposites itself, the
> trickster can have transformative powers as a transcendent symbol.
> Constellation of the archetype in an individual bogged down in the
> sterility of an excessively entrenched, well-ordered, or one-sided
> consciousness can provide access to creative possibilities in the col-
> lective unconscious, helping to restore psychic balance. Thwarting
> of conscious intentions, inner upheavals, outer mishaps, disrupted
> plans, are likely indicators that the trickster has been constellated.[7]

The concept of the "constellation" deserves some explanation, since it is important to understand better why an archetype like the trick-ster comes up at all. When an archetype is "constellated," it rises like the Big Dipper in the night sky, making its pattern of behavior apparent within the total functioning of the individual entity in whom or in which it appears. The archetypal constellation is even more like the star in the east which led the wise men to that place where an important new being lay. I accept Jung's idea that the archetype is constellated when it is needed, and not otherwise, and so it was in Jane Wheelwright's patient's life. The trickster showed up at the point of the patient's departure from life.

We see the trickster in another needed instance in the stage of in-fancy mothers know as the "terrible twos," when the developing toddler needs to test the limits of its mother's authority. He is also importantly present in normal preadolescence, when the limits of socialization as learned in the family and at school are tested. Indeed, before the trickster concept had been formulated by Paul Radin, Jung used to speak of a side of himself he called the "enfant terrible," the terrible child. (Unfortunately, this side is often unexpressed in childhood.)

Obviously, the trickster is important in adolescence; it's difficult to imagine anyone's becoming sexual without some experiencing of the trickster. And he comes again during the mid-life crisis, which, as so many recent movies have been showing us, is a time when the authority of spouse and career over one's life is apt to be challenged.

At each of these times, as often again before death, the trickster appears to give that extra bit of energy needed in order to step outside of one's frame and see one's life from a radically new perspective. He also provides the amount of treachery necessary to being disloyal to an old pattern and finding one's way into a new one. It is clear that the trickster is a great strain on others who are living around the developing individual at these times, and, worse, it is possible for a person to get stuck in a manifestation of the trickster and miss the purpose of the particular developmental stage. Such failures to integrate the trickster at these various stages play a large role in the development of borderline and sociopathic conditions, as well as in the psychological tangles that surface later in life. (I think this getting stuck in the trickster may be what occurs in manic-depressive psychosis. Lithium then seems to be required to get the trickster to release his stranglehold on the personality so that ongoing development may proceed without quite so much archetypal help.)

But even the strain produced by the trickster has its point, for each time the trickster appears, something about the individual and his social setting is revealed that wasn't apparent before. During adolescent turmoil, it is usual for both the parent and the child to learn something, so that Mark Twain's famous joke about his being impressed, after his own adolescence, with how much his father had learned, is as a comment double-edged because it is very probably true. One may say that when the trickster appears, a bit of fate unfolds, so that no one involved is quite the same.

The trickster also appears in order to help one combat adversity at times when one is forced to deal with an evil from outside of one's own nature. He is especially liable to be constellated when someone is in a state of disappointment that attends upon a loss, a failure, or a betrayal. *Hamlet* is thought to have been written after Shakespeare's only son, Hamnet, had died at the age of eleven. Melville experienced the commercial and critical failure, in turn, of his novels, *Moby-Dick*, *Pierre*, and *Israel Potter* before he took up his pen to write *The Confidence Man*, and this trickster work was to be the last piece of fiction he wrote for nearly thirty years. It may be that the turn to the trickster in art, like the turn to mania in life, is an alternative to feeling guilt over the rage that appears at such times of disappointment. The artist, like the patient, is provided a sulphuric alternative to leaden depression. For the artist, this alternative may be especially important if it keeps his creative fire from going out. But we cannot be sure that the trickster is merely a savior, for it is like him to set up a personal or a creative disappointment in order to emerge. In Melville's phrase, the trickster is "knave, fool, and genius."

When a work of art involves the trickster archetype, I think it is likely both to have a trickster subject in it and to be a trickster itself in the way the total work makes its audience react. The work is the concealed trickster, which tricks us into responding to the subject as well. I am concentrating in this discussion on the living trickster quality of the work itself, on all the ways in which the work works upon us, contriving to fascinate and upset us. Not least of these ways is the haunting anxiety that such a work can generate.

Jung points out that when we cannot evaluate an unconscious content with clarity, it tends to exert a fascinating quality. Often trickster individuals we meet in life exert a similar fascination, because we can't decide how we feel about them. They behave exactly like unconscious contents of our own, and in a sense they are, because we are not conscious enough to know how to deal with them. The trickster work of art exerts a similar fascination.

Often its trick is to get us into a double bind by making us think or feel two different things at once, all the while exerting a hypnotic fascination that makes us want to stay within this ambiguous field. This is the uncanny fascination of Billie Holiday's singing, and of Greta Garbo's acting. These great trickster performers had the ability to project two contradictory emotions at the same time behind a mesmerizing facade. The effect of their art was both divine and satanic.

The double bind stems directly, I think, from the duplex aspect of the archetype itself. Jung stressed this duplicity in his discussions of Hermes' Roman descendant, "the wily Mercurius," who became the alchemical trickster. It is an unsettling ambivalence, a splitting into two minds, that the trickster work is able to accomplish. This split can take place within a single individual or among members of a large audience. It is typical of the trickster, in art and in life, to split people into warring camps. Containing opposite feelings is what makes being a trickster so difficult. And perhaps the trickster is responding to some cultural double bind placed on him. As Gertrude Stein, who worked diligently at the effort to be a trickster artist, said, "it is *doubly* hard to be a poet in a late age."

The trickster kind of artist is inordinately concerned with the response of others to him, so that artists like Alfred Hitchcock, Greta Garbo, and Billie Holiday often have enormously complicated relations to their publics, which involve elaborate strategies for winning and retaining the confidence of others in the face of numerous violations and betrayals of public expectations. Their publicity becomes part of their art. I think this phenomenon goes with the archetype. The trickster seems to love most to win the confidence of those who would have every reason not to trust him.

■   ■   ■   ■

I think it is appropriate that the trickster was named from a myth found on American soil, for despite the worldwide distribution of the trickster mythologem within figures as disparate as Loki and Krishna, it is in America that the trickster has become a more or less conscious part of the national character.[8] This is clear not only in the tradition of southwestern humor from which Mark Twain emerged, but also in the northeastern figure of the clever Yankee Peddler, Sam Slick, who was admired for his shrewd deceptions whenever they managed to make him a buck. Today trickster elements in southwestern and northeastern United States cultures blend to define a national trickster style. Just as we have heard the southwestern accent of Woody Guthrie in the voice of Minnesota-born Bob Dylan, so Sam Slick operates out of the southwest today in the person of J. R. Ewing, the trickster hero of the television series *Dallas*.

Although the methods of the trickster artist can certainly be found in Leonardo da Vinci and Shakespeare, American artists have most consistently explored the possibilities of the trickster approach to art. We see this of course in our classic movies and jazz, as well as in our new wave of rock, but the trend is equally present in our classic and contemporary fiction. Our novelists fairly love to manipulate the reader through ambiguous and contradictory language, misleading narration, and other forms of deliberate mystification.

We find an ability to originate effects within the reader's or viewer's mind over and over again in trickster works. As one peruses "The Turn of the Screw," the governess's terrified quest for reliable information becomes the reader's. The longer one stares at the Mona Lisa, the more one takes on the state of ambivalent, tender amusement that seems to emanate from the subject. Such works deliver their impact by reworking the audience's mind in the image of their central characters. This is their tricksterish "originality," their capacity for originating tricksterish effects.

When a man's anima has failed to integrate the trickster, she tends to be at the trickster's mercy, and to become paranoid when she must respond to the shadow side of others. This is the dilemma of the governess in Henry James's "The Turn of the Screw." I feel justified in reading this as an anima story in part because of the way this trickster classic is framed. The story is presented as a ghost story told to the person who introduces the tale. That person claims that he heard it from a man named Douglas, who had originally read it aloud to an assembled company "with a fine clearness that was like a rendering to the ear of the beauty of his author's hand."[9] This author is the governess, and it is her diary he is reading. I think this woman's story, read by a man to produce a dramatic emotional effect, makes a good metaphor for an anima outpouring, and it is from this angle that I think the story has most to tell us.

Henry James was every bit as great a believer in consciousness as C. G. Jung, and almost as subtle a critic of forms of unconsciousness. This short novel, I feel, is James's bitterest attack on the sort of pseudoconsciousness that anima projection can create. Since, as Jung tells us, the anima is the projection-making factor in a man, one could call this diary that Douglas reads aloud a cautionary tale about the anima, demonstrating the dangers of living by her projections. But we can go a little further in understanding the psychological circumstances under which the anima makes her most dangerous projections by taking into account the characteristics of the tale itself along the lines I have been following in other works of art. For this tale is a trickster, which delivers its impact by drawing the reader into identification with the anima-figure governess, and her game of making projections. As Leon Edel observes:

> In the charged account of the governess, with her phantoms, her "certitude," her suppositions, which she turns into "fact," her "facts" which are mere suppositions, we recognize the materials of the witch-burners and executioners of old. Her narrative, with its consummate interweaving of paranoid fancy with circumstantial reality, is indeed capable of making readers pronounce the innocents guilty—as the testimony of Salem children long ago turned innocent men and women into sorcerers and magicians.[10]

Good critical reasoning does not put to rest the trickster cloud that hangs over the story and emerges whenever it is read again. The controversy continues, and the critical mountain grows, as it did more than a generation ago, when Edmund Wilson aroused a storm of controversy by suggesting, in what was called a "Freudian" interpretation of the story, that the ghosts were the governess's projections. Reading this story, as one critic has observed,[11] is a little like being driven mad. One becomes overrun by a trickster which will not let one off the hook. One sometimes wonders whether the evil that the governess senses is somehow altogether objectively present, and some critics have argued that the governess acts with integrity. I do not think they are right, but with its endless and unfathomable ambiguities, the story is indeed a great trickster which forces us to recognize the fallibility of our understanding in the face of the unknown. It is this fallibility which the governess herself tragically cannot accept, preferring the certainty of a paranoid solution that leaves the evil outside her. She substitutes her theory of what is going on for the dilemma of not being able to know. And the reader is shaken to realize, as he rereads the story, how much he too has filled in the blanks and gaps in his knowledge with suppositions. He is left with the uneasy feeling that he, too, might have tried too hard to save the child and inadvertently but ruthlessly killed him.

The governess figure, with her network of moods, opinions, and projections, is an image of the anima that has failed to integrate the trickster; she perceives the trickster as a lurking danger from outside, requiring efforts at suppression. The more such an anima resists, the more the unaccepted trickster is constellated, and in the end he overruns the psychological field. When the anima is overrun by the trickster, her instinctive responses are poisoned, and she becomes a dangerous trickster herself, capable of inducing paranoia. I feel that the manipulation of the reader exerted by the story expresses the very power of the trickster which this kind of anima figure refuses to recognize. The strength of that power is the final impression that the tale leaves on its reader when he is finally able to put the story aside.

"The Turn of the Screw" was, in Henry James's personal development, like a nightmare in the individuation process, a release from the spell of unconsciousness by means of a terribly vivid example of it. For me, the unconsciousness in the great novelist was only partly derived from the hunger for popularity that earlier led him to foist the undeveloped play that preceded "The Turn of the Screw" upon the public. Behind that, as Leon Edel has demonstrated in his fine biography of James, lay an earlier failure of development. In James's youth, he failed, in contrast to his popular brother William, to experience his trickster side in company with other boys. Because he had not realized the trickster part of himself that demanded some rough exchange with others, he miscalculated both the dark side of his audience (which ruthlessly insisted on being entertained) and the anger of the actor who needed a better vehicle through which to entertain them. Arriving backstage only at play's end, in fatuous hope of triumph, James allowed himself to be made a fool of by the very trickster element that he had up to now avoided. The audience cried, "Author! author!" and the aggrieved actor led James in mock triumph onto the stage. The audience proceeded to boo and hiss him. It was a humiliating defeat for the sensitive author, but it provided his own belated initiation into the trickster. He was at last experiencing in his own life a theme that had long intrigued him: the end, through betrayal, of innocence.

As I have mentioned, it was just after this experience that James made his first notebook entry recording his idea for "The Turn of the Screw." The bitter trauma, I feel, joined the issue of the trickster for James as a creative personality. All the work that he wrote after it includes a grasp of the shadow that has rarely been equaled in fiction, ensuring him the fame that had eluded him in the theater. Never again was his anima so naive, or his calculation so off. James's own midlife crisis was then at an end, and "The Turn of the Screw," which he finished a few years later, represents the final disgorgement of his youthful failure to integrate the trickster.

We experience, through trickster works of art, the onesidedness of whatever exists in us to threaten the ongoing development of consciousness, and we are forced into a duplex mode that rethinks our basic suppositions. Particularly, we experience the limits of our own trusting upstandingness, when this favorable result of good mothering experience has begun to threaten our understanding. If in a work of art the trickster succeeds in shocking or confusing us out of our complacency, he does this that we may see anew and thereby manage to survive the world.
(1981)

B. JUNG'S PERSONALITY THEORY: PSYCHOLOGICAL TYPES AND THE INDIVIDUATION PROCESS

The selections presented in this section—Radford and Wilson on literary character, Atkinson on psychological type and the textual unconscious, and Messer on alchemy and individuation—illustrate the many possible applications for literary criticism offered by Jung's theory of personality dynamics and development.

The first selection, by Radford and Wilson, presents a theoretical discussion of the possibilities before applying some of them to the fiction of Patrick White. Michael Atkinson discusses Jung's theory of personality type and its uses in "reading" patterns both in fictional character and in reader response to a genre. Richard Messer shows how Fowles's novel *The Magus* uses alchemical symbolism very effectively to convey the mysterious unity underlying the differentiation typical of life's developmental stages. Other selections in the book also address these matters, including Drew, Hinz and Teunissen on Lawrence, and Pratt, in Part I.

26 SOME PHASES OF THE JUNGIAN MOON: JUNG'S INFLUENCE ON MODERN LITERATURE

F. L. Radford and R. R. Wilson

In this selection, taken from an essay surveying a number of modern writers, Commonwealth and Continental, whose work has been influenced by Jung's psychology, two Canadian critics focus on the Australian novelist Patrick White to generate an illuminating discussion of the importance of Jung's theory of personality as a psychological model for twentieth-century literary concepts of "character." They argue that Jung's greatest influence on modern literature is through his powerful models both of personality type and personality development, including the related concepts of the individuation process and of the relationship of the archetypes and the persona to character, as elaborated in Psychological Types *and elsewhere. Jung's models enabled creative writers "to make the concept of the Unconscious both actively significant in characterization and envisionable in reading." Radford and Wilson distinguish between literary "character" and psychological "personality," and insist on the inseparability of the literary character from the artistic presentation that makes him/ her "envisionable in reading" to the twentieth-century audience. Thus their essay not only illuminates many of the possibilities writers have discovered for character depiction in Jung's psychology but also warns against a common misapplication of psychology to literature.*

This paper confronts a double elusiveness. It attempts to add something to the continuing discussion of that slippery literary term "character," and it seeks to clarify an aspect of G. G. Jung's tentacular influence upon literary creation. The two considerations are tightly linked. An analysis of "character" must ultimately touch upon the function of a psychological model that has given shape to the particular characterization. Such models are inferable from the text (much as one might infer a historical or social background) and are seldom self-evident. Nonetheless, they are significant elements of the text's implicitness; no thorough analysis of character can fail to deal with them. Jung's influence lies precisely in having provided modern literature with the strong outlines of a determinate psychological model.

Clearly, models vary greatly from one writer to another, as they do from one culture or period to another: those that emerge from a Renaissance text, with their emphasis upon hierarchy, the upward and downward of reason and sense, are quite unlike those of the nineteenth century where, normally, a character's psychology is threaded upon the lucid consciousness of rational decision. The various psychological models that shape characterization in modern literature have brought into focus aspects of the human psyche that previously had been ignored or imperfectly formulated. In these terms, nothing more pertains to the problem or "character" than the strategies by which the concepts of an unconscious and of unconscious motivations have been incorporated into literature. Here Jung's influence is strikingly apparent. He has shown more than one author how to make the concept of the unconscious both actively significant in characterization and envisionable in reading.

Considered in its essential terms, character is a problem in conceptual structure.[1] Characters are discontinuous and void. Students of literature often overlook the obvious fact that only what is given belongs to characterization, and that little is given. Characters, as William H. Gass has put it, "are mostly empty canvass."[2] They have attributes (though not by any means the same ones), such as language, gestures, appearances, motivations, ideas, mental processes, associated imagery, symbols, signatures, and so (complexly) forth, but none of this adds up to much until they are organized. There must always be, as Martin Price argues, an "inevitable artifice."[3] No one has adequately analyzed character who thinks (in Gass's words again) that "traits make character like definitions do a dictionary."[4] One needs to search out the principle of organization (or artifice) upon which the series of attributes hangs together, from which it derives coherence and becomes (and only then becomes) a figure, the image of a human person, a character. One such principle, perhaps the most important, certainly the most inevitable, is the psychological model. No character can be shaped other than in terms of an idea of that which it figures.

In modern literature, psychological models have commonly been derived, though seldom rigorously, from psychoanalysis. The impact of psychoanalysis upon literature has been massive (it may be seen in the thriller as well as in virtually all surrealistic productions), but its peculiar force has been to provide the postulate of unconscious mental processes. Modern literature contains a wide range of narrative methods for suggesting unconscious motivation, plural or ambiguous motives, and symptomatic analyses of otherwise unknown motives. Thus there is a generalized, eclectic psychoanalytic system that runs through a large number of this century's literary works: it is far from uniform, and it does not correspond to the actual conceptual system of any particular psychoanalysis as a whole. One might infer from an extensive reading of modern literature the broad conceptual outlines (though in a confused state) of psychoanalysis. Some of the elements of this generalized psychoanalytic system that function, often deeply implicitly, in characterization are: an unconscious (or unconscious mental acts), instinctual drives, the psychic demand for drive reduction, the mechanism of repression, psychic conflict between the opposed demands of drive reduction and repression, self-censoring psychic powers, the existence of an internal embodiment of external values (a superego), and the diagnostic potential of symptoms, errors, word association, and dreams. It should go without saying that in any work of literature the concepts of this generalized system may not reflect the order of importance that Freud, or any other psychoanalyst, might have given them.

Jung's particular influence has been wide and diverse. In specific literary works it is often conflated with that of Freud or later theorists such as Laing (as in some of Doris Lessing's writing where characters dream archetypes, following a Jungian prescription, but experience sexual repression and the devastating consequences of the father image, much as Freud might have recommended, and respond to social repression, including that of their families and their psychotherapists, in ways indicated by Laing). Indeed, there are few pure examples in literature of either Jung's or Freud's influence. Nonetheless there are a number of works in which Jung's influence, even though often in an admixture with other psychoanalytic concepts (in the shifting structure of the generalized psychoanalytic system), is strongly pronounced.

In the application of Jungian theory, as in most other methods of criticism or analysis, literature divides itself into two main parts—that for

which the method works and that for which it does not. One cannot see
that much is to be gained by the application of Jungian (or, for that matter, Freudian or Marxian) analysis to *Pride and Prejudice*. A devoted Jungian might insist that Elizabeth is an anima who brings Darcy to a more
accurate perception of himself and his values, and that Wickham is the
shadow that he must confront before he can complete the integration of
his fragmented personality. But the effort is one that directs us away from
what is worth knowing about Jane Austen and her art. And we might
suspect the sanity of anyone who insisted that Mrs. Bennet is a manifestation of the Magna Mater, however much we might agree that she is a
terrible mother. By contrast, *Wuthering Heights* drives us toward Jung for
illumination. If Jane Austen creates an intense sense of character and
value precisely by means of subtle nuances of minor activities, it is difficult to imagine Brontë's Catherine and Heathcliff engaging in casual day-
to-day activities: they are archetypes embodied, albeit embodied in vitally memorable characters. The observer, Lockwood, confronts these
images of the forces within almost as an Austen character transported to
Brontë's world. If we take Wickham and Lydia as the Heathcliff and
Catherine of *Pride and Prejudice,* the difference is underlined. One could
readily imagine Jung himself turning to *Wuthering Heights* as evidence
that the archetypes are not his invention but a priori images of the human
psyche, supplying much raw material for fictional creation, whether in
dream, fantasy, or literature.

In modern literature, Jung's influence shows most emphatically in
the significance that has been attributed to myth and in the stressing of
certain aspects of his psychological theory, such as the concept of the
archetype and the problem of individuation, which have only a tangential
significance within the generalized psychoanalytic system. Jung's interpretation of myth as both a universal (and interconnected) body of concepts *and also* a projection of inherent mental activities, themselves also
universal, provides the first touchstone of his influence. His view of myth
as possessing psychological roots—and thus projecting a correspondence
between the interior and the exterior, the individual and the universal—
has affected many aspects of modern culture, including literature. It may
be seen, for example, in the work of Hesse and Mann, in Miguel Asturias
(and perhaps in other Latin American writers), in Lessing, and in Lawrence, Patrick White, and Robertson Davies.

Specific concepts from Jung's psychological theory, beginning at
least with Hesse's *Demian,* have been widely adapted to the purposes of
literary characterization. Jung's more flexible understanding (than

Freud's) of instinctual drives, his concept of autonomous complexes, the power he attributes to the complexes of "splitting off" into independent personalities, the effects of the archetypes (in desire, dreams, and creativity), and the way in which he establishes individuation as man's fundamental psychic task are all aspects of his theory that reflect divergence from Freud. It is important to bear in mind that Jung's influence on characterization began relatively early. Not only did Hesse, in early works such as *Demian* and *Steppenwolf,* employ explicit conceptual detail from Jung's theory (aspects of which remain evident in his later work, such as *The Glass Bead Game*), but Thomas Mann also used Jungian concepts both to universalize his narratives and to thicken the psychological underpinnings of characterization. The episode in *The Magic Mountain,* for example, where Hans Castorp, lost in a blizzard, has a hallucinatory vision of Hellenistic order and then awakes asking himself how it could be possible to dream life outside one's personal experience, unmistakably illustrates the literary exploitation of Jung's theory. Hans poses recognizably Jungian questions: where do mythic visions, more encompassing than individual life, come from? are dreams only individual or are they, finally, anonymous and communal? The works that respond to Jungian analysis are on a continuum of which one extreme is what might be called the representation of "raw" archetypes, such as the characters of comic books or the more simpleminded science fiction of the type of *Star Wars.* Here Jungian analysis may serve primarily the sociological purpose of explaining the immense popular appeal of artistically crude works. Of course, there is always the possibility that the detection of Jungian archetypes will be claimed as evidence for artistic importance, but calling raw hamburger steak tartare does not make it haute cuisine. Toward the other end of the continuum are works that create out of the raw materials of Jungian theory a genuine artistic structure of complex character, approximating the intricacy and variety in which Jung purports to find those materials in the real human psyche. These works, in turn, divide into two main categories: those in which the character is primary and the archetype serves to give depth and universal significance; and those in which the archetype is primary and the character serves to give it body. One might say that the archetype serves the function of endoskeleton or exoskeleton, respectively.

Of the three works mainly under discussion [in the orginal essay], the characters of *Women in Love* are the most fully achieved in vivid independent life. The detection of governing archetypes serves principally to show hidden connections that universalize what might seem highly idio-

syncratic and that reveal the tight structure of a novel sometimes attacked for being loosely structured. In *The Aunt's Story* a highly
individualized central figure moves from being a character of the type of
Jane Eyre, relatively easily defined in traditional terms, to one rendered
protean by the flickering projections of her own psyche. In *Fifth Business*
all of the characters are intentionally placed on a continuum of individuation, from total domination by the persona to domination by archetypal
projections, with only the narrator achieving an integrated personality
through the reabsorption of the governing archetype of the mother into
his own psyche. D. H. Lawrence, Patrick White, and Robertson Davies
do not exhaust the scope of Jung's impact, but they do illustrate it with
particular clarity. Lawrence's work shows clearly the Jungian sense of
mythic significance, at once universal but psychologically rooted. White's
novels, at least those of his middle period beginning with *The Aunt's Story*,
exhibit explicit, if highly deformed, uses of the key concepts of Jung's
theory with regard to the actual workings of the human psyche. Davies's
most recent writings provide a remarkable instance of the sophisticated
intertwinings of the mythic and psychological aspects of Jung's thinking.
With these examples in mind, the two questions of Jung's influence and
the nature of characterization will have received, at least, a partial answer.

■   ■   ■   ■

. . . Patrick White's writings suggest the high degree of sophistication which a psychological model strongly influenced by particular aspects of Jung's theory may possess. To claim that White's psychological
model is complex, and his characters in their reflection of this model similarly complex, is only to assert, in a fairly obvious way, that a great deal
has been available to him and that he has used this knowledge well. Typically, the characters in much modern fiction are more various, more differentiated, and more integrated along distinct levels of thought (but not
"better" or more convincing, perhaps) than in previous fiction. For example, the irrationality of characters in modern fiction, such as White's, can
be linked to a theory of unconscious activities. Literary characters have,
no doubt, always behaved irrationally, but it is one thing to ascribe this
kind of behavior to an intervention from outside or to a failure of rationality and quite another to treat irrationality as the unavoidable end-product
of unconscious urges. In part, White builds characters upon the tension
that can obtain between irrationality and reason, compulsion and volition, unconscious and conscious mental acts. Thus his psychological

model shows a human nature that is at once more complex, with greater depths and seemingly more mystery, *and* more open to rational explanation than could be the case in those ancestral novels in which the characters reason astutely in the full light of consciousness. Man's demons, though powerful and great, are functions of himself. That thought lies encoded in all White's characters and, as much as any single thing, it gives clear evidence of the radical influence upon literature of Jung's theory.[5]

Like so many characters in modern literature, White's suffer various psychic dysfunctions: they go insane in ways that are clinically familiar and the etiology of which can be made partially explicit; and they are driven by obscure, even plural and conflicting, motivations that might once have appeared as evil, demonic, or (at best) irrational but which, in the context of their characterization, are seen to follow upon sufficient causation and to exist as inseparable aspects of a total personality. White's characters possess memories that work unpredictably upon the surface of consciousness yet are governed by rules (of vividness, of reaction, of intervention) that are evident to an outside point of view. They dream, create (musicians, painters, writers, actors, and dancers recur), and act violently, often murderously so, all in accordance with the directives of an expansive, form-giving unconscious. From as early as Ernest Moriarty in *Happy Valley* (1939) to Jack Chance in *A Fringe of Leaves* (1976) and including most of the major characters in the intervening fiction, White's characters have shown a marked capacity for violence (even Theodora Goodman, in *The Aunt's Story*, takes up a knife against her mother), but it is a violence that invariably reveals a line of causation, an origin in the depths of the character's being that is open to understanding, and which functions as an objective mode of compensatory fantasy. It is also a frequent prelude to radical self-transformation. Violence, then, like creativity, occurs in White's fiction as an aspect of a potentiality other than itself and as a part, perhaps inherent, of human personality. In itself this should suggest that White's psychological model is complex, rich, indebted to the generalized psychoanalytic system, and, in particular, informed by several of Jung's key concepts.

One key Jungian concept that White employs more skillfully than perhaps any other modern writer—more flexibly than Hesse, more complexly than Robertson Davies—is that of the persona. White makes the persona of the character a part of its definition, but he also makes the awareness of having a persona a part of the characterization. Almost all of White's characters are partially developed around the contrast between the inside and the outside of their actions. In some cases, this contrast is vast, in others it is extremely narrow; but it is almost always present. His characters often develop intense complexities behind an exterior of apparently simple roles; others (his "villains") allow their interior potential to wither in an effort to impose an unreal permanence upon their social roles. All of White's characters perceive that they possess both an interior reality and an exterior role, but while some develop inwardly, accepting the need for a persona ironically, or tentatively, others develop outwardly only, fashioning their mask into an inflexible illusion while, within, they shrivel to unfeeling ash.

Theodora Goodman in *The Aunt's Story* is a good example of the first class of character. Theodora develops a labyrinthine interior being behind a seemingly simple mask. She is seen to possess almost bewildering powers of imaginative participation in the lives of others (even the nonhuman others), of understanding and empathy. Yet all this works quietly behind the appearance of an unassuming, undistinguished spinster. She is persistently seen as ugly, thin, sallow, yellow, and "slommacky." The actual Theodora (as opposed to the phenomenal Theodora seen by the other characters: "this thing a spinster which, at best, becomes that institution an aunt")[6] is utterly unlike the persona. What is more, she is aware of the contrast between her actuality and her persona, and this awareness contributes significantly to her characterization.

On the other hand, White's less appealing characters normally harden the persona's contours in trying to give permanence and substantiality to their social roles or in trying to fulfill what seems to them as the frightening responsibility of their own potentiality. These characters (like Horrie Last in White's story "Down at the Dump") often construct masks of civic and personal rectitude that restrict them, in the face of grief or emotional exigencies, to a few moral clichés. But behind these rectitudinous masks there is nothing except a sterile, unresponsive wasteland. Similarly, the infamous Mrs. Flack and Mrs. Jolly in White's *Riders in the Chariot* have made themselves personae that are as respectable as their inner beings are stunted and unfeeling. And in *The Aunt's Story,* Theodora's simple mask and inner complexity are set in contrast to the complex persona and sterile inner self of her mother, Mrs. Goodman, as well as to those of several minor characters in the second section of the novel, the "Jardin Exotique," such as Mrs. Rapallo and Weatherby. Indeed, it is a contrast of great structural fruitfulness, since it runs pervasively through the novel, involving all the other characters from Theodora's sister and brother-in-law to the dumbfounded Americans in the last section. Certain characters, such as Major Sokolnikov, the musician Moraïtis, and the children Lou, Katina, and Zack, reiterate Theodora's own imbalance between simple mask and intricate self, but most seem only to restate the contrasting imbalance first indicated by Theodora's mother. On the one hand, there are characters, like Mrs. Goodman, who have exchanged their capacity to feel, to experience love, kindness, and compassion, for a role, a mode of seeming; on the other, there are characters who are not persona-ridden and who, like Theodora, retain their powers of feeling and their ability to grow inwardly.

Beneath the persona there is consciousness, and beneath that there is the perplexing maze of the unconscious in which disparate, but interconnected, functions surge and ebb. This rigorous choreography of unconscious activities indicates the degree to which White's implicit psychological model reaches beyond that evident in most modern fiction. For White, the unconscious is neither the dark nexus of instinctual motivations (as, say, in Lawrence or Faulkner) nor the sink of repressed experience (as in O'Neill, Aiken, or Anderson). It is an active, smoldering magma of creative imagination. White embodies this concept in several ways: the recurring artist figures in his fiction, the explosive eruptions of compensatory violence, hallucinatory projections, and dreams. Only Doris Lessing (particularly in the Jungian *Golden Notebook*) has succeeded as well as White in using dreams as a strategy of characterization. Dreams in White's fiction are typically revelatory, explanatory, and integrative. Hence they tend to accord with the theory of dreams found in Jung's psychology, in that they are, above all, purposeful, organic products of the psyche, as well as infused with recognizable archetypal content. It may be said that, in general, the concept of the unconscious plays a fundamental role in all characterization in White's fiction. In whatever form it takes, the unconscious thrusts forward creatively (extending, anticipating, and even giving shape to actual experience), providing the ground both for an abrupt explosion of numinous self-realization and for a capacity to share empathetically in others' lives. Thus, White's use of the concept of the unconscious in characterization, though distinctly literary, unmistakably reflects Jung's central ideas on the subject.

As early as his short story "The Twitching Colonel," White's fiction has contained reiterated images of fire, or brass balls containing fire, or shards of glass, of marbles and chandeliers, all images of multiple refracted light that symbolize the explosive potential of a character's interior being to burst forth, actualized and confident, to astonish others. In *The Aunt's Story*, Theodora, whose symbols are the volcano and the rolling filigree ball filled with fire, emerges interiorly from within herself through a series of projections. It is an explicitly disciplined series that, in itself, is highly instructive with regard to White's use of Jung's ideas: Theodora begins with empathetic understanding of animals (a worm is the initial object of her empathy), shows a capacity to feel at one with other humans, develops a power to share imaginatively in the lives of others, begins to project her fantasy life upon others, allows her fantasies to intertwine with those of others, and finally creates, within the terms of her experience, an ideal male figure who consoles and advises her. The final stage may represent a collapse into madness, as some of White's critics have thought, or an assertion of supreme self-transcendence, as others have argued. It is, in either reading, an intensely Jungian moment in which an aspect of Theodora's unconscious splits off into an autonomous entity and speaks, reflexively, to her.

The kind of experience that Theodora shares—where, for example, she *becomes* Sokolnikov's sister escaping and then being shot in the pine forests of revolutionary Russia or the furniture in Wetherby's brick house in Birmingham—demands a psychological model that contains the underlying patterns of potential experience and predicates an intuitive capacity to feel similarity and to assume identity arising from this unconscious potential. This radically empathic experience might be called, in the phrase that Jung borrowed from Lévy-Bruhl, *participation mystique:* valid interpersonal understanding that operates outside of, and appears to deny, normal rational and analytic categories. Theodora's responses to others (first seen in her childish feeling for a worm curled in a rosebud) cannot be adequately explained, either in terms of their diversity or their intensity, solely on the basis of ordinary analytic categories, such as a simple repression/fantasy formula. White's model includes that mechanism, but it goes much further: it allows for the abruptly new, the creative, in experience. Thus Theodora's final act in the novel is her objectification of a fantasy embodying everything that she has previously perceived to be wise and meaningful. Holstius emerges from her unconscious, determined in the detail of his experience by her memories of important men in her life, such as her father and The Man Who Was Given His Dinner, but more than any of them singly, or even the combination of their traits. In some respects Holstius resembles the archetype of the unconscious that Jung referred to as the animus—that is, the ideal form of male personality that every female carries (Jung thought) in her unconscious. As an archetype, the animus is a form of possible experience (as is the anima for men) available to every woman. Whether or not "animus" accurately describes Holstius's function in *The Aunt's Story,* it cannot be far off; certainly he is not merely, as at least one critic has supposed, the owner of the cabin in which Theodora madly sets up housekeeping.[7] Holstius is a projection, a fantasy-product, but he is not trivially hallucinatory. Arising from Theodora's unconscious, he is a psychologically integrative force. He represents the attempt of her unconscious to deal with a crisis in her life, a crisis in fragmentation.

This points to a final, and supremely important, aspect of the complex model behind White's characterization. His characters experience the need to integrate the diverse levels of their selves, to become, in a word (Jung's), *individuated.* For a character in White's fiction, life is confronted as a problem, an exercise in the integration of diversity. Some fail to solve the problem (which is always at once universal and painfully individual) and become like Horrie Last or Mrs. Goodman, shrunken, narrowed, self-delimited. Others do achieve solutions in the shape of continued development, actualization of possibilities, a capacity to respond, and the formation of a self that, when it is seen for what it is, appears brightly numinous. When White's characters do achieve individuation, they seem to transcend those around them, and, more easily than they inspire devotion, they may be feared and hated. (Thus Theodora is seen, at the end, by the American onlookers as just "a crazy Annie.") Individuation is exceptional, perhaps rare, in fiction as in life, but White's psychological model proposes that it is always possible. And in this solution to the endlessly recurring Hydra-riddle of how one learns to be oneself, White is perhaps most essentially Jungian.

■　■　■　■

In all of the novels discussed the surface actions of characters and their relations to one another are governed by the working of archetypes that symbolize deep forces of the psyche, much as Jung sees similar images at work in the actual human psyche. The kind of integration of these forces, which in turn permits the achievement of true individualization, is explicitly achieved by Ramsay (as it had been by Hesse's Emil Sinclair in *Demian)* but is only implicitly achieved by Lawrence's Birkin and Ursula (or by Mann's Hans Castorp). Other characters fail in one degree or another, but the achievement of integration is seen to be the ideal. In White, the question is more problematical and characters are developed whose archetypal projections overwhelm reality, leading them into states of creative conflict that transcend integration. (The ending of *The Aunt's Story,* for example, may indicate Theodora's failure at individuation or her self-transcendence, but it can scarcely represent, given the presence of the split-off, autonomous Holstius, integration.) But in all cases, the peculiarly poetic nature of Jung's analysis of the psyche offers the writer a convenient model (a structure of characterization, in effect) for the indication of underlying psychological significance and for the multiple layering of character demanded by modern concepts of personality.

As we stressed in the introduction to this paper, the identification of a work of fiction with a psychoanalytic system which it may seem to embody is rarely a simple matter: works of fiction are more than, and can be only minimally interpreted as, systematized exempla. One suspects that it must be uncommon for an artist to begin with a psychological theory and then turn from it to the creation of character, even in cases like those of Hesse and Davies where the artist's commitment to a particular system is evident. Hazlitt denied that a "preconcerted theory of character" could account for the effects of characterization in Shakespeare,[8] and one must suppose that this is commonly the case, at least where characterization is powerful. It is much more likely that the artist exists in an intellectual ambiance where a particular way of looking at the human psyche is, or is becoming, dominant. The complex of theories concerning the nature of the unconscious that sprang into being early in this century created such an ambiance, and artists worked within it. The artist may then intuit the necessity of expressing some view of the psyche in order to create what can be perceived as psychological completeness in his age (and perhaps only for his age). In turn, this is likely to become part of the complex of form and content that defines his art as modern for his times.

The kind of psychological model discussed in this paper is essentially a critical construct—that is, an interpretative inference from the literary work much as one might infer from the evidence of the work a social theory, or even a social geography. Such constructs offer explanations and postulate necessary preconditions, but they are not biographical and they do not speak directly to the labyrinths of the creative process. The value of theory to the artist seems to be of two kinds: on the one hand, it offers a convenient model for the shaping of character in its requisite new form and, on the other, it provides a validation of the artist's insights, at least in so far as these entail the forms that will bear the most significance in his own times. The immense appeal of Jung as a source of validation lies in the fact that his system also validates the traditional methods of art in the use of image, legend, myth, and allusion generally. Jung's model also accounts for the concept of multiple facets in personality and allows for the protean, metamorphic change within personality that appeals to the modern sense of the impermanence of absolutes and (perhaps paradoxically) the depths beneath surfaces: Jung points the artist toward, as a common source of all creation, the deep pool of the human unconscious. It is here that Jung's appeal goes beyond that of Freud, whose strict confinement of the psyche within a set mold (after childhood, at least) also confines the artist to certain rigid patterns of personality such as those which occur again and again in the works of Eugene O'Neill and Sherwood Anderson, where outcome is always foreseeable. In contrast, the Jungian model, as seen through the writers discussed in this paper, proves to be itself metamorphic, multiplexly adaptable, and fruitful.

(1982)

27 TYPE AND TEXT IN *A STUDY IN SCARLET:* REPRESSION AND THE TEXTUAL UNCONSCIOUS

Michael Atkinson

Michael Atkinson relies primarily on Jung but draws as well upon Freud and deconstructive criticism to discuss how a text might be governed by an unconscious element that acts like the unconscious does in a personality, providing hidden motivation to explain behavior at the conscious level. Atkinson uses this concept to examine not only Watson, Holmes, and other characters in Arthur Conan Doyle's first archetypal Sherlock Holmes mystery, but also the subgenre itself. His analysis makes extensive and quite sophisticated use of Jung's theory of psychological types, especially the personality's four functions (two pairs of opposites) of thinking and feeling, sensing and intuiting. Atkinson shows the importance of the so-called inferior function (undeveloped, hence more entangled with, and therefore an entrance into, the unconscious), both in a character's behavior and in the text's reception by the reader. His idea of characterizing whole texts by psychological type echoes Beebe's description of a trickster-text. Also, he discusses how the presence of the four functions, in combination with the developmental process known as individuation, influences the indirect manner in which elements rise from the oceanic chaos of the unconscious into consciousness, creating patterns of emergence which a novelist might capture in his fiction to powerful effect.

A Study in Scarlet, the first tale in the Sherlock Holmes canon, is a key story in more ways than one. It is a strong paradigm, setting forth in a single fiction many of the essential strokes and maneuvers that structure the tales to follow. But it is also deeply flawed, inconsistent (to a fault) in its most paradigmatic gestures. Yet, with narratives as with the human psyche, it is the inconsistent moment, the faltering or false gesture—the slip—that so often gives us the clue leading to the heart of the matter, the obscured motivation, the repressed feeling. And so it is with this short novel. Its most conscious literary strategies are subverted or qualified in a dramatic way by other elements of the text itself, which point to the functioning of what we might accurately call its textual unconscious.

For the text itself, and not just the characters within it, is structured along psychological lines and exhibits in an exemplary way the dynamics of psyche. And appropriately enough, the telling fault is one of the most frequently remarked and least understood features of the tale.

First, the conscious pleasures. For readers today, *A Study in Scarlet* bristles with an excitement and an echoic richness that it could never have had for its original readers, a kind of unearned increment bestowed upon it by all the later Sherlock Holmes stories. The text is electric with the sense of primacy and the pleasure that comes with seeing the beginnings of things that could not know their own flowering. Here we witness the first of the Holmesian deductions of an individual's past from his present appearance—"Been in Afghanistan, I perceive"—and watch the conversion of Watson from bemused skeptic to wholehearted admirer and chronicler. Here, too, we see the establishment of 221-B Baker Street, still free of the peculiar marks and traces that the subsequent adventures and emerging eccentricities of Holmes himself will leave on it: a blank site, ready to house the rest of the canon and bear its scars and imprints. The Baker Street irregulars (how quickly assembled and named) appear here. And we see the first tentative evidence of Holmes's drug addiction: "such a dreamy, vacant expression in his eyes, that [Watson] might have suspected him of being addicted to the use of some narcotic, had not the temperance and cleanliness of his whole life forbidden such a notion." (What a feeling of readerly gratitude, that this dismissed suspicion was retrieved and actualized in future stories.) And we have the pleasures of Watson's narration, this story "Being a Reprint from the Reminiscences of John H. Watson, M.D., Late of the Army Medical Department." His attentive sight, which gives us the facts; his faltering insight, which allows the reader to slip ahead of him on the trail Holmes runs; his sense of astonishment, a chorus to our own: all are here—though certain of Watson's moral qualities await development in future stories. And here, too, we find a demonstration of Holmes's faith in the practice of "analytic reasoning," reconstructing the path back from the effect to its causes, the process so frequently invoked to punctuate and bring satisfying closure to his episodes of detection.

Put on the spot, most of us would agree that the two chief sources of delight in the Holmes stories are those last mentioned—the strategic filter of Watson's narration (we not only feel its rightness here, but we know that later experiments in doing without it were quite unsuccessful) and Holmes's art of analytic reasoning back through the webs of causality to the sources of things. But these very causes of our richest pleasure are precisely the flawed elements in this founding story, oddly and seriously skewed—disrupted in a way that is richly revealing.

For there is a flaw in the text, at which both consistent narration and analytic reason come up short. Nothing so trivial as a question of Doyle's shuffling (losing track of, not caring about) the elapsed time in which the events take place (a feature of several tales). And nothing so sly as a Derridean teasing of the text against itself, to bring down the whole edifice like a house of cards. No; rather there is a curious disjunction in the telling—both in Watson's framing and Holmes's retrospection—which marks the narrative and which at the same time holds a key to its essential strategies. It may be more productive to think of this not as a flaw, but as a fault, in the geological sense: a meeting of and a rift between plates of story in the text, plates which grind against each other, releasing tremors that send cracks through the narrative, revealing the strata of its structuration, splitting its characters, fracturing its prose style, and effacing the sustaining tensions between its ethical polarities.

The surface manifestation of the fault or fissure is clearly evident: it is the oft-remarked and occasionally lamented seam between the first and second halves of the novel. Part 1 is established as a reprint from Watson's reminiscences, and conforms to the conventions it establishes by having Watson narrate the sequence of events of the London crime, from the moment it first comes to his and Holmes's attention through the arrest of the perpetrator. But Part 2, on the other hand, begins with an account of the events in America that resulted in the crimes the pair were engaged in solving. We see the sources of the crime in the actions of persons long dead by the time of its enactment through a powerful, omniscient, and distinctly unWatsonian eye (so different is the vision that Jack Tracy has made a clever tentative attribution of its authorship, like that of the second part of *The Valley of Fear*, to Doyle rather than Watson [p. 108]).

The point is not simply that there is a narrative inconsistency—no need for the rigid pedantry of the beginning fiction workshop here—but that the information in the Mormon melodrama, which, however bathetic, is the emotional foundation of the novel, *never reaches the principals, Watson and Holmes,* in the course of the story. Everything that Holmes and Watson discover and respond to has its roots in the events that unfold and play themselves out in the great blank plains of the American West. The Mormon melodrama entirely motivates the later action. Yet Holmes, who prides himself on getting to the sources of things, is not cognizant as he solves the crime of anything earlier than some postconjugal jealousy in Cleveland, in which Hope shadows the men who will in London become his victims.

In the human psyche, that which motivates action and shapes character but remains unknown to the actor and buried in the unexplored past we call the unconscious. And as Holmes himself, presaging the analytical psychologists, tells us, it is indeed often the inconsistent moment that opens the door to the inner chamber—offers the thread, the clue we may follow to the core of the psyche, the unconscious motivation from which action springs. What I want to explore here is the way in which the Mormon melodrama serves as a textual unconscious for the novel as a whole, motivating and defining the workings of the text itself and the characters in it, compensating for the excesses of professed conscious attitudes, transforming and qualifying conscious purpose and intent, yet remaining, except for a few traces, unknown and uncomprehended. In the interpolated narrative, we have both the motivation for the crime and the erasure of its evil. It speaks not only of the Americans' motivations, but of Holmes's. And this split in function tallies with and alerts us to other splits in the text of *A Study in Scarlet*—splits in voice, splits in characterization, splits in the codes that define the meanings of actions, and splits in the psyches of individual characters themselves. . . .

■ ■ ■ ■

"Some facts should be suppressed."

Clearly, two very different types of tales are joined together to form this one short novel. Differences of character, ethos, style, and theme diverge from the rift in the text and yet form one complete fiction, the parts of which relate to one another through their very conflict, thrust and counterthrust, as do elements, forces, traces in the human personality. The work of Carl Jung and his followers in developing a comprehensive theory of personality types will be of particular use in understanding the psyche, the "personality" of this text, the dynamic by which the unconscious and conscious interact to shape, sharpen, and blunt one another.

It was to comprehend the source and pain of his break with Freud that Jung began work on his theory of personality types, a study that would bear rich fruit in the years to come. From this work, the clinical terms "introvert" and "extrovert" became part of the universal psychological parlance. Even more important for the practice of psychiatry, and for the understanding of those different from ourselves, were Jung's concepts of the two pairs of antithetical personality functions: thinking and feeling, and sensation and intuition. Like much intellectual work begun in the pain of personal loss, this theory of psychological types resonates with the tension of opposite forces, and etches with great clarity the functions and the purposes they serve.

Briefly, the theory runs like this. There are four ways in which an individual can orient him- or herself toward the world—through thinking, feeling, sensation, or intuition. Each of us uses all these functions to a greater or lesser degree. In his briefest formulation of the different functions, Jung says that *"sensation* (i.e., sense perception) tells you that something exists; *thinking* tells you what it is; *feeling* tells you whether it is agreeable or not; and *intuition* tells you whence it comes and where it is going" (*Man and His Symbols,* p. 49). But each individual typically utilizes one of these functions far more characteristically, and more reliably, than the others—to such a degree that it comes to form the style of his personality and relation with the world. This predominance establishes the person as a thinking type, a feeling or sensation type, or an intuitive. The thinking type excels at ordering experience conceptually, analyzes and categorizes with ease. Flow charts and diagrams, outlines and logical schemas come naturally to thinking types, producing logical hierarchies which (they would claim) reflect the way the world is ordered. They make good planners, engineers, and lawyers, are better at managing systems than other people, and often express little emotion. Our culture values them highly, and they often rise to positions of power within it. Our official hope that third world countries will be led not by passionate crusaders but by technocrats is a measure of our public trust in the thinking type.

The feeling type also orders and prioritizes experience, but on quite a different basis. He will have a strong sense of right and wrong; moral evaluation does not have to be pondered but will be immediately obvious to the feeling type. The emotional and ethical realities of the situation will be what he most clearly and readily grasps and articulates.

Feeling types prefer people-centered jobs: sales, health care, pastoral work, journalism. Dedication, tenacity, and loyalty mark their characters.

The sensation type will have a natural eye for details, large and small, important and seemingly insignificant, that elude others. In fact, his lack of a penchant to prioritize is one of his greatest strengths. The visual artist, the designer, the accountant, the warehouse supervisor, the massage therapist, the dancer are likely to be dominant in sensation. The intuitive type has the knack for seeing the implications and possibilities of the situation. Though the data may seem inconclusive or aimed in a particular direction, he often has a contrary hunch, a "feeling," an inkling that despite appearances, or in the absence of evidence, things are going to turn out in a certain way. Successful stockbrokers as well as psychics and palm readers are among those who rely most strongly on intuition. Theoreticians and research scientists almost always have intuition as a first or second function (think of Einstein's pronouncement that his theory of relativity "did not come from the rational mind" and Kekule's discovery of the structure of the benzene ring after dreaming of the archetypal snake biting its tail). And of course intuition runs high in the creative arts.

What makes the theory of psychological types particularly interesting is that it not only accounts for the different ways in which people mainly perceive and respond to their world, the world we all share from our differing perspectives, but that it offers a model as well for the contrary forces in the *internal* psychic economy of a given personality. For the functions are paired in opposition, thus:

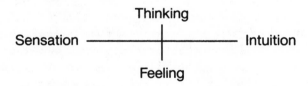

This simple diagram is intended to illustrate the polarities of the functions as they operate in the individual psyche. What is above is most available to consciousness: what is below, least. The configuration just given here illustrates the case of the thinking type. For her, who bases her personality naturally around thinking, intuition and sensation are also more or less available, though secondary, and feeling is most distant from consciousness, most unconscious, most difficult to utilize in a skillful and

differentiated way. Thus the thinking type will most often have trouble
with feeling (e.g., the stereotype of the uncaring or amoral scientist).
Simple rotation of the diagram indicates the case of the other types. If,
say, intuition is the dominant and uppermost, then feeling and thinking
may be more or less available, and sensation—dealing with the concrete
world of facts—will often be crude and bumbling at best.

It is only with great difficulty that the maturing person can integrate the inferior function into the fabric of daily life, because it is what is
most unnatural. It is split off from our normal functioning, and lives a
kind of second-rate, often unacknowledged life of its own in our psyches.
The inferior function may be ignored; or conversely, in a time of great
psychological growth or change, a crisis of personality, it may come to
seem the most important part of life precisely because it offers so much
new ground for exploration and development. The inferior function is
also significantly associated with the shadow, the name Jung gave to the
counterpersonality that each of us harbors. This is the part of ourselves
which we deny, neglect, even despise; we are quicker to see it in others
than ourselves. Underdeveloped, clumsy, inept, or inappropriate in its
expression, it thus has the potential to disrupt or undermine our conscious lives and strivings. The feeling of the thinking type will tend to be
crude and undifferentiated when it does emerge: moments of bathos, or
even a lifetime of misery can result: consider the maudlin feeling that
takes over and brings to ruin the professor in *The Blue Angel*. The thinking
of the feeling type often comes out in similarly crude and undifferentiated ways: consider the feeling type who adheres in a doctrinaire way to a
few simple ideas which, by a Procrustean forcing, explain the world to
him—viz. Ezra Pound. Similarly, the down-to-earth, practical, matter-
of-fact sensation type may find himself taken over by fervently held extremes of cultish and theosophical mysticism: Doyle himself in seance.
The sensation function of the intuitive is usually equally inept: consider
the common inability of intuitives and visionaries to manage the concrete
details of daily life (Marx, unable to feed his family) or their tendency to
give themselves over to physical excesses in, say, food, sex, or pain.[1]

I have of course chosen extreme characterizations for the sake of
bold relief. But they will serve the purpose well, for the lines in *A Study in
Scarlet* are crisply drawn. What I want to utilize here is the notion that
there is a psychological economy for texts as well as for individual people,
for whole fictions as well as for the characters that inhabit them. Jungian
typology can reveal the ground, and even the appropriateness, of some
textual problems, as well as clarify and explain the workings of a number

of motifs in both sections of this particular text. While my goal here is to consider the psychological configuration of the entire tale, and its effect upon the reader—not just to put the hero on the couch—the psychology of the protagonist is a good place to begin.

Sherlock Holmes is, of course, preeminently a thinking type. He has, however, a good command of the auxiliary functions, sensation and intuition. By an act of will, he usually suspends temporarily the thinking type's penchant for ordering and hierarchizing so that he may take in all the physical details of scene or person without, for the time, ranking them in importance, thus avoiding the mistakes usually made by his fellow investigators, when such representatives appear on the scene. And though he usually calls it logical inference, he uses guesswork, or intuition, to a larger degree than he would admit. (Watson's tan and wound could with equal likelihood have been acquired in South Africa as Afghanistan, for example.) But it is the thinking which comes so naturally to him, and which he finally allows to come into play, that organizes the perceptions and intuitions into the rational schemata that display the patterns of the crime for all to see. It is the leap from suspended thinking to thinking with a vengeance that so marks the coda of each tale with readerly satisfaction, as we see at last the elegant act of thought by which he joins all the links in the causal chain.

But it is not just the smooth functioning of the superior and auxiliary functions that offers itself for our scrutiny and delectation. The repression of feeling in the character of Holmes himself is so marked, and so consistent, that the perfection of its very squelching provides a complementary tension and source of literary delight—especially since it is compensated elsewhere in the text. So demented is Holmes's feeling function that in our first report of him we hear of his beating the corpses "in the dissecting rooms with a stick . . . to verify how far bruises may be produced after death." It is scientific interest rather than personal involvement that motivates him. The blood test he is so excited to discover relates to none of the cases he has been involved in so far. And at most, he expresses only a passing concern for legal justice; here and later, he is unconcerned when it is muted. Holmes pursues cases on the basis of their interest, not the magnitude of the crime or the extent of injury done.

The repression of feeling ramifies itself in all aspects of his work. Holmes claims pride in tracing events back to their sources, but expresses no interest in limning in what emotions drove Jefferson Hope to his murders. He even yawns during Gregson's description of the passionate domestic row between Drebber and the Charpentier household, though of course his lack of interest might conceivably have been feigned did it not so perfectly fit the pattern. The irrational and supernatural are equally unremarked. When he hears Hope tell of the shades of Lucy and Ferrier guiding him forward to the scene of the murder, and of the theologically grounded game of pharmaceutical roulette, he expresses no interest or astonishment, not even disbelief. Moral concerns, irrational phenomena, and guiding passions are only marginally present to him. This is perhaps most forcefully symbolized by his *not even hearing* the interpolated narrative, the history of passion and grief from which the crimes sprang.

Though feeling seems entirely repressed or absent from Holmes's consciousness, it is strongly present in *A Study in Scarlet* as a whole. The name of the novel aptly embodies the split unity. Here, as in other narratives, in dreams, in personal prejudices, and in cultural biases, the unrecognized, repressed, or disowned tendency is projected onto the other, the outer representative of the shadow. Just as the expansive and visionary Gatsby, who intuits a fresh green world of possibility, is brought down by Tom Buchanan and George Wilson, representatives of the sensation function at its rawest or most degraded; just as bookish Ishmael is restored by savage and loving Queequeg; as Jekyll is haunted by the hidden Hyde; as Hitler accused the Jews of designs for international domination; so here, too, we have a case of the projection of the inferior function onto another character, whose narrative, whose values, and whose deeds erupt into the consciousness of the principal character with a crude force he would like to deny.

Jefferson Hope carries the burden of the feeling function in this novel, a weight later assumed with greater delicacy and finesse—and greater integration—by Holmes's companion Dr. Watson. Here that feeling is primitive, undifferentiated, and overwhelming, as the inferior function is in eruption. There are not sixty crimes that punctuate Hope's life with interest, but one that dominates it with passion. It transforms him. He does not so much pursue the righting of a wrong as become the very vengeance itself. It is his life. Jefferson Hope leaves humanity behind and becomes a Fate, a nemesis to the perpetrators of the twenty-year-old crime. So complete is his identification with the course of his justice, that he calls his stabbing Joseph Strangerson, who resisted the poison test, an act of "self-defence." Also significant is the absence of anything elegant or intellectual about his method of pursuit: once he takes it up, it is characterized by unswerving dedication and loyalty to feeling rather than by thought and ingenuity. Patience and hard work are the hallmarks of his dogged trek. And so totally does he become his vengeance that, once it is wreaked, he expires with it. Such is the characterological balance or compensation for Holmes's complete suppression of feeling.

Holmes and Hope have been our focus for the time, but it is important to see that it is not just a question of two opposite characters, but an interpenetration of two different texts grounded in different psychological functions. The valorizing codes that emanate from their protagonists also characterize the tale types, the other characters, even the prose styles. The portion of the novel that Watson narrates could scarcely find a more appropriate label than the tag Poe gave to his own stories of detection: it is a tale of ratiocination. The values the frame tale espouses are essentially, even militantly, rational, qualified only by an occasional shudder of feeling from Watson. Though the other detectives and Holmes play at mutual condescension, they share the allegiance to the values of rational inference. That Lestrade and Gregson should find the crime "a puzzler" rather than an outrage or a horror is perhaps to be expected from men who deal with the effects of violence on a daily basis, but it is worth remarking that they are no more curious than Holmes is about its emotional roots and passion-filled history.

The interpolated narrative, the textual unconscious, on the other hand, is in every sense a tale of feeling: a sentimental romance. The events, from the initial discovery of the two waifs, through the blossoming of the flower of Utah and her rescue by Hope on horseback, to her being cast into the harem of the elder's son and dying of a broken heart, and thence to Jefferson Hope's unswerving vow of revenge—all are the stockest elements of romance, literary boiler plate. Both Lucy and John Ferrier are grounded in feeling from the beginning, in their care for each other in the face of death, and both later respond with indignant hearts to the moral affront to feeling that polygamy presents to them. Further, the American saga is rooted in certainties of faith, from the opening childlike piety of Lucy, through the resistance to the perversion of faith that Mormonism stands for in this story, to Jefferson Hope's conviction that in his vengeance he is carrying out the justice of God—all this in contrast to Holmes's skeptical empirical positivism. The interpolated narrative is the moral center of the tale, and its center of feeling. The entire chain of events springs from it. Yet since this is in its conscious purpose a tale of ratiocination, it is psychologically appropriate that the emotional center is repressed and inferior. There is plenty of emotion here, but it is *feeling as Holmes would characterize it:* crude, destructive, bathetic. Thus it is appropriate, too, that Holmes neither embraces, accepts, or even rejects the sentimental tale's moral feeling. Repressed, it simply does not exist for him, even at the textual level.[2]

The split between the two portions of *A Study in Scarlet* is also evident on the stylistic level. The narrative prose of the frame tale and its dialogue are essentially polished, urbane, as is appropriate to a fiction that embodies and advertises the thinking function. The style of the interpolated romance places it firmly at the bathetic end of the sentimental spectrum. The crude American dialogue, especially evident at the beginning of the Mormon melodrama, is the dialectical opposite of the urbane musings of the Londoners. Here is a fair taste.

> "Then mother's a deader too," cried the little girl, dropping her
> face in her pinafore and sobbing bitterly. . . .
> "I guess that's about the size of it."

And it is not only the dialogue that draws from the sentimental tradition; Doyle's prose style fluctuates here, but it often offers a deep and saccharine draught of conventionally bathetic sentiment: "On such occasions, Lucy was silent, but her blushing cheek and her bright happy eyes showed only too clearly that her young heart was no longer her own. . . . " So the stylistic differences in the two parts of the text reinforce the other divergences, pervasively marking the rift between superior and inferior function even more dramatically.

The opposition and interaction of the two narratives could be diagrammed thus:

Part 1—Frame Narrative—Dominant Superior Function Governs

Textual Consciousness

Tale of Ratiocination	Thinking Valued	Legal Justice	Immediate Past & Present	Urbane Style
Sentimental Romance	Feeling Valued	Divine Justice	Remote Past	Bathetic Style

Textual Unconscious

Part 2—Interpolated Narrative—Repressed Inferior Function Governs

Immediately evident are the multiple ways in which the two stories
are distinguished; but equally significant are the ways in which values
from the textual unconscious impinge upon the conscious attitude of the
frame narrative. Several effects are indicated here. First, the cause of
legal justice is entirely subverted by the simple narrative event of Jefferson Hope's dying when and as he does. The law does not exact its price
for the crime, and its perpetrator's serene death from an overfull heart
reads as well as a beatification as it does as a penance or punishment.
Better. There is no integration of these attitudes, but simply the muting
of the conscious by the unconscious. This mooting of legal justice presages Holmes's emerging nonchalance toward such questions; and though
no concept of divine justice arises in his consciousness, we do see in the
later stories a civilized version of revenge in the settling of scores that
motivates Holmes in contest with such figures as Moriarty and John Clay.
The effect of the central issue in one set upon that of the other is most
dramatic, but the peripheral ones have their effects as well, in a strength
that diminishes with their distance from the center.

The death of Jefferson Hope is, of course, mediated by the narrative and the active voice of Watson, who adds to the facts his own feelings
and implicit judgments on the issue of the crime, which have telling effects both for this story and for later additions to the canon. Watson's
increasingly important role as a bearer of the feeling function, reacting to
(even against) Holmes's indifference to emotion, is seeded here. Later
he brings to the tellings stronger feelings about suffering, injustice, and
even love. (In the very next short novel, *The Sign of Four*, Watson falls in
love in such a way that the success of his romance depends on the failure
of Holmes's rational scheme to restore a treasure to Mary Morstan; justice is replaced by love.) In *A Study in Scarlet*, Watson's role as a bearer of
feeling is less clearly and consistently set forth, but it appears rather
clearly when he (alone among the Londoners) dallies with the code of
faith long enough to surmise that Hope's death had summoned him "before a tribunal where strict justice would be meted out to him," leaving it
for the ambivalent reader to decide whether that justice would be beatification or damnation, though heavily prejudicing the case with his vision
of Hope's peaceful visage.

Watson's judgment is essentially iconic, and is a feeling-based
counterpart of Holmes's own method of reading appearances. It has a
parallel in the first part of the book when Watson felt a rush of "gratitude
for him who had removed [the] owner . . . [of] the distorted, baboon-
like countenance of the murdered man . . . from the world." This iconic

reading of the moral significance of Drebber's visage is the other side of the Janus-coin imprinted with Hope's countenance, and the two faces frame the pair of histories we are offered, and deny and confirm the very notion of history itself. For although traditionally the morally legible icon has been used to synopsize stories, spatialization and synopsis are the contraries of history, which is based in causally ordered time and is thus, despite Aristotle, closely related to reason. Watson reacts to both faces as moral icons without knowing the histories of either man. His judgment is based on an immediately intelligible feeling, not reason or history (fact and time). It is the opposite and the parody of Holmes's carefully deductive reading of appearances, and its effect is to bring the moral feeling values of the Mormon melodrama into the main narrative wholesale, without, however, knowledge of the sequence of events that have grounded and valorized them. Icons, like the images from the unconscious, unexplainable but difficult to dismiss, are finally based in a transcendental and nontemporal ground. Here, the feeling values and the ethical codes of the romance from the remote past have been imported, though now rootless, into the frame narrative through the medium of Watson's feeling.

The fact that the history of the Mormon melodrama is never heard by the principals of the story, except in the truncated, erasure-filled, and self-deprecating account Hope gives at the police station, is ample indication that the sentimental romance itself barely impinges on the consciousness of the tale. The sentimental and bathetic style, too, is mainly abandoned by Hope himself, as if he recognized that only the valorizing code of its plot type could grant it real intelligibility, legitimacy. The noble motives of the sentimental romance are fundamentally discarded as the raison d'être for what now appear mainly as a sordid series of crimes, a double ethical vision that Holmes only recognizes half of, and one about which the reader is left distinctly ambivalent. Only Watson's spontaneous concessions to feeling allow these unrooted traces of sentimental style and plot their presence in the frame narrative. But they leave their mark.

■   ■   ■

" . . . *a most incomprehensible affair* . . . "

To this point we have mainly been concerned with the psychic split in the text's two narratives, the ways in which the textual unconscious impinges upon the narrative frame of which Holmes and Watson are aware, and the effect that has on the values consciously espoused there. But if we turn to the inner dynamics of part 2, we find within its confines an equally dramatic psychological paradigm at work. As the events of Utah move out of their remoteness in time and place toward eruption onto the London scene, they form a significant parallel to the universal processes by which the contents and dispositions of the unconscious move toward consciousness.

That all mental life begins in undifferentiated totality and proceeds toward consciousness by differentiation is a tenet on which all schools of depth psychology agree. Primary mentation is undifferentiated; the infant does not distinguish between sleeping and waking, fantasy and reality, self and other. All is one in the oceanic totality, the original fullness.[3] The first division seems to be generated by the threat of privation, which would be death for the helpless infant. Repletion and want slowly become reified in the distinctions between infant and parent, self and other, dream and waking. The parent is particularly ambiguous, benign as provider, malign as withholder of food, warmth, and affection. From this, the distinction between the good and bad parent arises. Either parent can be the figure of provision or privation. And, for the male child (let us focus on his case here, since the fiction with which we are dealing is male-centered), the polarity also affects the oedipal triangle, with the father possessing the female prize against the desires of the growing boy, intensifying a split perception in the child between the father protector and the father possessor/depriver, against whom murderous hostility comes to be directed.

Concomitant with the complexities of the self/parent distinction, other distinctions within the self emerge: first the body/mind dichotomy; and within the mind, the differentiation of the personality I call my own from the thoughts and feelings I reject (and often project onto others) — i.e., defining the ego by creating the shadow, alluded to earlier. From these initial divisions stem all the this/that, me/world distinctions that create and define our perceived social and psychological environment. At each level, an original unconscious unity is divided by an act of differentiation, which has the effect of casting the conscious individual personality into sharper relief, and of limiting it more severely.

A work of literature can gain great power by duplicating in a displaced or symbolic way structures and processes that are fundamental to the human psyche. *The Metamorphosis, Moby-Dick, Frankenstein, The Sound and the Fury*—a work at any level of seriousness or excellence can symbolically incorporate elements of these primary processes, producing not

so much a shock of recognition as a subliminal undercurrent of resonance. And so it is with *A Study in Scarlet*, which embodies in its textual
unconscious some of the most basic psychological paradigms, the ones
outlined above.

Part 2 begins on the blank stretches declining from the Sierra
Blanco, a vast and indistinct desert that might well serve as an image of
the initial unconscious itself—the primary psyche, unlimited and undifferentiated, awaiting the marks and traces of difference and choice that
create, that are, human consciousness. When we first discover Lucy and
John Ferrier, they are alone on that large, blank landscape, about to lapse
into earthly nonbeing. . . .

■ ■ ■ ■

" . . . a most extraordinary case . . . "

What is so extraordinary is that in creating this tale in which
Holmes would first come to consciousness, his and our own, Doyle has so
thoroughly mimed—here as nowhere else—the coming to consciousness
of psyche generally, and the dynamics by which consciousness and the
unconscious interact. Some of the strokes may seem crude in light of
later stories, but the pattern is clear and effective. The psychology of his
fascinating protagonist, in which so many find such delight, is everywhere
ramified in the details and structure of the text, which reach far beyond
his own person, his knowledge, even his will to know. It was a consciousness that Doyle would find burdensome in time, but one for which readers have been continuously grateful. *A Study in Scarlet* serves as a
founding myth of a subculture that is one of the broadest in English letters, a beginning that could not know its end.

(1987)

28 ALCHEMY AND INDIVIDUATION IN *THE MAGUS*

Richard E. Messer

Richard Messer is a professor of literature and creative writing; he has read widely in Jung's psychology and the related work of Neumann, Hillman, et al. Further, he has had the experience of a Jungian analysis. His essay opens up John Fowles's complex novel by following through the implications of reading it as "an alchemical parable," with the stages of the alchemical process corresponding to the stages of the individuation process described by Jung. Messer identifies and explains the psychological meaning of many of the typical symbols of the alchemical process, so that readers who are unfamiliar with the subject still may understand some of its uses in literary criticism. For further discussion of Jung's writings on alchemy and their importance for literary criticism, see the Frye selection "Forming Fours" in Part 1.

Generally, *The Magus* has been seen as a kind of existential detective story, but from a psychological standpoint it may be viewed as an alchemical parable. Nicholas Urfe, the protagonist, searches unknowingly for himself, for union with those darker aspects of his psyche that will make him whole and aware of his portion of personal freedom. Blindly, he seeks a psychic transformation. To understand the nature of this transformation and its significance one must turn to the concepts of the ancient alchemists as they are understood by the depth psychologist Carl Gustav Jung.

From his extensive study of alchemy, Jung concluded that "There is no doubt that the goal of the philosophical alchemists was higher self development" (*CW*, 13:189). Jung believed that alchemy represented the processes of psychic transmutation which he called individuation, whereby unconscious contents are crystallized and synthesized into consciousness so the self is made whole. Studying the ancient texts, analyzing thousands of his patients' dreams and fantasies, Jung concluded that the process described by the alchemists goes on in the unconscious of many moderns, especially those who have entered a mental cul-de-sac (such as Nicholas Urfe). The process can be fostered by someone initiated in its secrets, and that is essentially what Maurice Conchis, the magus, does in his dealings with Nicholas.

Conchis calls his operation the God Game, not alchemy. But the God Game and alchemy have the same goal, follow the same general processes, and progress by means of identical symbols and archetypes. Traditionally, the alchemical process divides into four parts. Each, as Heraclitus[1] stated, is accompanied by its own characteristic color, element, and quality: *Melanosis* (blackening), *Leukosis* (whitening), *Xanthosis* (yellowing), and *Iosis* (reddening) (*CW*, 13:179). By the fifteenth century, the third stage, yellowing, had been omitted, and thus will not be considered in this analysis.

Descriptions of the alchemical process were always couched in complex rhetoric and arcane symbols but, to oversimplify, we may say it begins when the material to be transmuted, the *prima materia*, is isolated in an egg-shaped retort. It is then broken down into its basic elements. Of these elements fundamental opposites are formed, which must be united. In the next stage this union is dissolved as the *materia* is washed and whitened. In the last stage, the reddening, intense heat transmutes the white to gold. Thus the gold or lodestone is achieved (*CW*, 12:218).

As the *prima materia* of the God Game, Nicholas's psyche undergoes the same changes. In what follows I shall draw parallels between the above description of the alchemical process and what happens to Nicholas, but these parallels will quickly break down unless one keeps in mind that "in alchemical symbolism the stages and imagery of an inner process of transformation were being expressed in pseudochemical language."[2] The events and process of alchemy represent projections of the alchemist's unconscious. The alchemist's work was a voyage, not so much into the nature of matter as into the depths of his own psyche, and what he encountered in the depths were archetypes of the collective unconscious (*CW*, 12:220–21).

Nicholas's voyage begins when he is isolated on the island of Praxos. The height of the *Melanosis* occurs when he feels life is so sterile and meaningless that he attempts suicide. Conchis initiates the transitional, life-affirming phase of the *Melanosis* by enticing Nicholas to his villa, Bourani, and stimulating his interest in the mysterious girl Lily. For Nicholas, the *Leukosis* is a matter of differentiating his attitudes toward love and sexuality, death and spirituality. He must come to terms with his narcissism, his self-pity, and his cynicism. The *Iosis* will set forth the task of integrating into consciousness what he has learned of the darker side of his psyche. He must do this by establishing feeling relationships with others while realizing that his actions are choices enabled by his freedom. Thus he will accomplish the alchemical opus, the marriage of the king and the queen, or what Jung calls the transcendent function.

Maurice Conchis, Nicholas's guide on this arduous journey, is well suited for his role. Nicholas first describes Conchis as "saurian as well as simian,"[3] which relates him to Thoth, the chief god of Egyptian alchemy. Later, he sees him as a spider and as a transvestite, both of which are embodiments of Hermes Trismegistus and Mercurius. Time and again Nicholas feels that Conchis radiates an air of brooding omniscience and sinister ambiguity. All these characteristics earn him the title of magus and archetypal status as Mercurius or the Wise Old Man; throughout the novel he functions as a symbol of the self.

Before he meets Conchis, Nicholas is filled with unacknowledged guilt and unhappiness over the end of his love affair with Alison; he feels he is in a *gabbia,* which he describes as a black cage constructed of "light, solitude, and self-delusions" (p. 58). After his abortive suicide, he says he could not pull the trigger because to do so would have been a mere aesthetic gesture. But what actually stopped him was the pure song of a distant girl tending goats. It evokes a childlike part of himself that, beyond all his cynicism, can still find joy in simply being alive. It is through this tenuous childlike quality that the *Melanosis* leads him, not to death, but to Bourani, to Conchis and his world of potentially resurrecting mystery and illusion.

Nicholas speaks of Bourani (meaning "skull") as Tartarus, but just as Tartarus was an early projection of the unconscious, so Bourani and the events that take place there become a projection of Nicholas's unconscious. All that Nicholas encounters there, the artworks, the stories, the people, the masques, are mythic and dreamlike. As he is drawn into the labyrinth of mystery at Bourani, Nicholas's rational grip on reality loosens.

Having lured Nicholas to Bourani, Conchis begins the symbolic process of alchemy and individuation that Jung has described in *Archetypes of the Collective Unconscious* as "an experience *in images and of images.* Its development usually . . . presentś a rhythm of negative and positive, loss and gain, dark and light. Its beginning is almost invariably characterized by one's getting stuck in a blind alley . . . its goal is, broadly speaking, illumination or higher consciousness. . . . (*CW 9,* pt. 1, 2d ed., p. 38). Nicholas, in the midst of the blackening, exchanges his cage of empty "light" for the illuminating darkness of Bourani. Conchis guides Nicholas to illumination of his attitudes toward love and sexuality by presenting him with a series of images in the magical circle, the mandala, described by Aniela Jaffe as a prime archetype of Western and Eastern alchemy.[4] According to Jung, the mandala is a symbolic means of containing the chaotic psychic elements, and therefore reflects inner conflicts.

The mandalas of Nicholas's own unrecognized sexual attitudes that he must confront in the course of the novel range from purely physical to the virginally ideal. He encounters the following mandala images at Bourani: photographs of breasts and nipples in *The Beauties of Nature*; a clock with a rosy cupid in its center; a round snuffbox, inside the cover of which two satyrs and a nymph are depicted in an obscene pose; and, between cupid and satyrs, an oval photograph of the mysterious Lily, symbolically representing aspects of both extremes.

Following this overture of images, Conchis presents images to Nicholas mainly through narratives of his life and through masques, which metaphorically dramatize the narratives. These images drive Nicholas to analyze his conscious attitudes and force him to *experience* unconscious contents. Thus, as in alchemy during the *Melanosis,* the basic elements of the *prima materia,* Nicholas's psyche, are separated and constellated. The narratives and masques fall into two opposite groups: those concerning war or science and those concerning love or the supernatural. The masques overall symbolize Nicholas's one-sided, predatory masculinity. He cannot achieve an integrated self, a masculinity beyond superficial codes of what a man should be, until he comes to know and accept the feminine side of his psyche, represented by Lily. Lili, Lilie, and the Lily Maid were names often given to the alchemical opus, or to its feminine side.

Conchis's first story expresses the terror, humiliation, and revulsion he felt during a charge across a World War I battlefield. That evening Nicholas is roused from sleep by the strains of "Tipperary" floating up from the woods. On his way to the window to discover the music's source, he is overwhelmed by the stench of muck and rotting corpses. Later,

Conchis refines the point made by both narrative and masque as he speaks to Nicholas about the American notion of "a man's world," saying such a world is "governed by brute force, humorless arrogance, illusory prestige, and primeval stupidity." He adds, "Men love war because it is the one thing that stops women laughing at them. In it they can reduce women to the status of objects. That is the great distinction between the sexes. Men see objects, women see relationships between objects. . . . It is an extra dimension we men are without, and which makes war abhorrent to all real women—and absurd" (p. 373).

Conchis amplifies his point about objects with the second narrative and masque. He tells of Alphonse de Deukans, a rich eccentric who collected a veritable museum of beautiful, rare objects from every epoch and country. Deukans's object-world is destroyed by a chauffeur whom he fired for bringing a real woman into the house. After Conchis's story, Nicholas peers into the darkness outside Bourani and sees several spotlighted figures. A satyr pursues a nymph, lunges for her, but, at the sound of a note from Apollo's horn, is transfixed by an arrow from the bow of Artemis, played by Lily. This narrative and masque symbolize Nicholas's attitude toward women, whom he has collected like so many notches on a pistol grip. But he has not gone unpunished. The masque reflects his conquest of Alison and the resultant suffering while foreshadowing what he will suffer at the hands of Lily, whom he also tries to add to his collection.

Lily and her roles are variations of the anima archetype. From the time she meets Nicholas on the beach onward, she is linked continually to sea imagery; she is like a nixy, a water spirit, a virginal mermaid. She is also a Circe, or Melusina. The archetype behind the Circe figure is the devouring mother, and one of the tasks Nicholas faces during the *Melanosis* is to avoid being "eaten," that is, overwhelmed by destructive elements in the unconscious. At one point Lily turns to him wearing a green and black oriental dragon mask, saying: "I have come to gobble you up!" (p. 201). Often the Melusina and the Wise Old Man archetypes merge in the individuation process, just as Conchis and Lily often seem to represent different phases of one personality. As Nicholas pursues Lily and pulls away one of her masks to find that she is "really" Julie, he comes closer to knowing the feminine side of his psyche, and the whitening begins to emerge from the blackening stage.

The images of *Leukosis* are consistent with previous imagery in that they pertain mainly to water, fishing, and the sea. (Earlier, in the midst of the blackening, Nicholas describes himself as a "fish in stale water" [p. 52].) A metaphoric microcosm of the water imagery occurs just before the whitening stage begins, when Conchis takes Nicholas fishing. Instead of live bait, Conchis uses a piece of white cloth to catch a small octopus. "You notice," he says, "reality is not necessary. Even the octopus prefers the ideal." Asking Nicholas how he likes the sea, "the world below," he replies, "Fantastic. Like a dream." Conchis answers, "Like humanity. But in the vocabulary of a million years ago" (p. 134). Retrospectively commenting on this scene, Nicholas says of Conchis: "For him the sea was like a gigantic acrostic, an alchemist's shop where each object had a mysterious value—an inner history that had to be deducted, unravelled, guessed at" (p. 135).

The sea symbolizes the unconscious and objects connected with it function as archetypes of the collective unconscious. At one point Nicholas drones that no man is an island, but Conchis retorts that *all* men are islands, suggesting that consciousness itself is like an island that has risen from the sea of the unconscious. Lily functions in the same way as the white bait Conchis dangled before the octopus. Catching her, Nicholas is hooked. Fish and Fisherman, she draws to consciousness those contents of Nicholas's psyche which he has repressed or ignored, but which could be his salvation.

The water imagery of *Leukosis* recurs when Alison and Nicholas meet in Athens for a brief holiday. After climbing Mount Parnassus, they go for a swim in a jade green pool near its base and then make love. This scene is the culmination of the *Leukosis*. What Nicholas has learned from his experience with Lily and Conchis takes effect. Feeling and intellect, Luna and Sol, feminine and masculine, are integrated for a moment as he realizes he loves Alison. But he denies his knowledge and chance for salvation by returning to Bourani to pursue Lily. When he gets close to her, Anubis, the black dog-headed man, appears and spits in his face. He swims in the sea to wash himself. Shortly afterward, he meets Lily to consummate their affair and bathes with her as he had with Alison, but at the moment of consummation Anubis and another black figure rush in and subdue him. A hypodermic injection from Conchis sends him into "a deep mine of black rage" (p. 478). Nicholas has betrayed his hard-won knowledge of love and is betrayed in return; the union of opposites has occurred and is now dissolved. The *Iosis* begins.

Conchis's story of Henrik Nygaard, the Norwegian mystic who talked to God and was said to have had a "pillar of fire" in his mind, foreshadows the transition into *Iosis*. For Nicholas the fire essential to the final stage of the alchemical opus will consist of two emotions, anger at

Lily and grief at Alison's apparent suicide. His anger manifests itself only after Lily betrays him; it reaches a fierce crescendo during the trial scene that follows.

Throughout this scene images of black, white, and red predominate; the narratives and the masques all flow together to form one ritualistic drama, a kind of alchemical theater of cruelty as defined by Artaud.[5] The trial is performed in a huge underground cistern, which approximates a giant alchemical retort, as well as being a microcosm for Bourani, or the unconscious. Nicholas is bound, gagged (which prevents his habitual physical interference with psychic revelation), and installed on a throne above which is painted an eight-spoked mandala. Before him parade thirteen hideous masked figures. Each figure removes its mask to reveal a white-coated technician who stands before Nicholas and psychologically vivisects his personality. The scene reaches a peak when he is untied, given a whip, and told that he is free to lash the bare back of Lily, who lies stretched on a rack nearby. Nicholas realizes that this scene parallels an episode from Conchis's life. During the Second World War, the commander of the German forces occupying Praxos made Conchis choose between executing a captured member of the Greek resistance or going before a firing squad himself, along with eighty villagers. Conchis, though he survived, chose death. In doing so he asserted his personal freedom. Nicholas, though he is boiling with outrage, also chooses not to strike.

The drama, however, is not over. Nicholas, bound again, must undergo the final reddening, which Conchis calls the beginning of "disintoxification." Everyone leaves, and in the darkened cistern Nicholas is forced to watch a pornographic movie called "The Fabulous Whore Io," starring Lily and Joe, the Negro who had earlier played the part of Anubis. Afterward, in the light, atop a sumptuous altar in front of him, Lily and Joe genuinely make love.

Alchemically, this event represents the *conjunctio,* the marriage of opposites, the incestuous hierogamous. It is out of this symbolic union in alchemy that the lapis, or philosopher's stone, is born. Confronting the sexual relationship between Lily and Joe forces Nicholas to withdraw his projections from Lily and admit his suppressed attitudes toward sexuality. He begins to realize that sex can express both physical desire and deep tenderness and love, and have equal validity in a relationship; Lily and Joe do love each other.

During the process of synthesis (in which the white, Lily, must blend with the red, his outrage, to form the gold, illumination) it is not surprising to find Nicholas thinking of Alison and grieving, actually admitting his responsibility for her supposed suicide and the failure of their relationship. Throughout his ordeal, he clung to the thought of Alison. Her memory was like "a tiny limpid crystal of eternal nonbetrayal—like the light in the darkest night" (p. 441). Later, when Conchis and his crew have disappeared, leaving Nicholas abandoned on a hillside, he again grieves for Alison and experiences a sensation like a line of fire eating its way through him (p. 487). Only then does he understand that all of his relationships with women have been poisoned by his cowardice and selfishness.

As Nicholas accepts this, he sees that he has lived his life as though he were playing to an audience in his mind, sometimes being ingratiating, sometimes sulking or storming in petty defiance. He now understands that no one is watching, that he is not a victim and can participate creatively in the constitution of reality. But the insight is momentary, because the realization that he is truly free overwhelms him with ecstasy and terror. At this point the disintoxification peaks; the reddening subsides to a steady fire. Conchis has made him aware of his incomplete selfhood, but Nicholas must finish the process himself by consciously unraveling the experience he has undergone and thereby regaining Alison, whose "suicide," he discovers, was a trick.

He feels that something is expected of him, "some Orphean performance that would gain me access to the underworld where she was hidden . . . I had apparently found the entrance to Tartarus. But that brought me no nearer to Eurydice" (p. 555). Clearly, Nicholas "Orfe" is a kind of Orpheus figure. At the end of the novel he assumes the role consciously. He descends again into Tartarus, finds his Eurydice, but does not look back. The novel ends as he walks away from Alison trusting her to follow. He walks, he says, "Fiercer than Orpheus." Whether or not Nicholas's psyche is actually differentiated to the point where he may grasp the alchemical secret of the transcendent function is left an open question at the end of the novel.

Nonetheless, Nicholas, having completed the alchemical transmutation, experiences the archetype of the child, that of hermaphrodite. The masculine qualities in his psyche are now complemented by corresponding feminine qualities. When the novel opened, Nicholas was a representative twentieth-century Orpheus living on a desolately rational plane. Actually, he did not wish to "live"; contact with life's painful intellectual and emotional ambiguities overwhelmed him, and since he spent his time avoiding all that was spontaneous or numinous, he could not believe in God, or man, or love. Early in the novel, he saw himself as "a conjuror with his white rabbit." But his form of magic was a stage magician's cheap trick. He used it to produce the "solitary heart" as a means of seducing romantic young women. His emotional con-game was the opposite of Conchis's God Game, and it demonstrated one of Nicholas's major problems: he constantly confused love and sex. He was afraid of love yet felt guilty about treating sex as mere appetite.

Nicholas's journey through the underworld of Bourani gave him a clearer view of the problems, though it did not solve them. Conchis's alchemy helped transmute his psyche to the point where he could understand that love is only possible when one understands what freedom is. Early on, Conchis tells Nicholas, "The novel is dead. As dead as alchemy" (p. 92). When one finishes *The Magus* one realizes that he was referring to the traditional novel, with its neat beginning, middle, and end, and to the world view that produced it. Alchemy seen merely as the forerunner of modern chemistry is dead, but true alchemy is quite alive in modern man's unconscious; its gold is real. As Norman O. Brown says in a similar vein in *Love's Body:* "The goal cannot be the elimination of magical thinking or madness; the goal can only be conscious magic, or conscious madness; conscious mastery of these fires."[6] The magus has given Nicholas the symbolic consciousness of the alchemist; he has helped him create a bridge between present-day consciousness and the natural, instinctive wholeness of primeval times; and he has given him a knowledge of freedom and its terrible joy.

(1976)

C. JUNG AND GENDER CRITICISM

Gender criticism, both theory and practice, has generated much discussion among Jungians. Historically, Jung and his followers (e.g., Erich Neumann's *The Great Mother: An Analysis of the Archetype*) expounded upon the feminine principle in the psyche, and its accompanying imagery in art and literature, as being of great importance for both the individual and society (see Robert Bly's Great Mother essay in *Sleepers Joining Hands,* discussed by Atkinson in Part 1). The feminist movement has brought both praise for Jung and a critical rethinking of the role of the feminine as he described it. This sure sign of the field's vitality is clearly evident in many selections in this book.

In Part 1, both Gelpi and Pratt address the subject in the course of demonstrating its power for literary criticism. The first essay of this section, Karen Elias-Button's analysis of the presence of the Dark Mother archetype in contemporary women's poetry, discusses how writers are exploring and re-visioning the archetypal image to fit the context of life today. Albert Gelpi's essay on H. D. and Adrienne Rich begins with a statement of his "archetypal-feminist" approach and an acknowledgment of his debt to Jung in previous criticism. Annis Pratt's selection explains and illustrates many of the uses of the archetypal gender approach to literature that she outlined in her "Spinning" essay in Part 1, offering the perspective both of a feminist archetypal literary theorist and a practicing teacher-critic of women's literature.

29 JOURNEY INTO AN ARCHETYPE: THE DARK MOTHER IN CONTEMPORARY WOMEN'S POETRY

Karen Elias-Button

Karen Elias-Button combines a commitment to feminism with her knowledge of contemporary women's poetry to discuss several issues important for Jungian literary criticism. The most obvious one is whether the traditional Jungian conception of the feminine, whether found in Jung's description of the anima or in literature's symbolic representations of the various aspects of the Great Mother archetype, is a patriarchal, condescending image that the feminist movement cannot accept. But underlying this controversial issue is one more fundamental to Jungian psychology: what is the status of any archetype, essentialist and unchanging or to some degree existential and imaginal? If the latter, as Hillman and his followers in the imaginal school believe, then contemporary women's poetry becomes as important a source as the ancient myths for archetypal images of the goddess, serving as "a metaphorical model toward a definition of the feminine in women's own terms." Elias-Button follows this line of inquiry and discovers in poems by Anne Sexton, Sylvia Plath, Robin Morgan, May Sarton, and Adrienne Rich two major reasons for refashioning the Dark Mother in today's terms. Elias-Button justifies this work in Jungian terms, declaring that the poetry is a form of self-discovery as well as redefinition for both poet and her audience, and that its refigured images of the Dark Mother can help everyone to assimilate into consciousness new definitions of the feminine.

In recent articles,[1] Naomi Goldenberg has constructed a feminist critique of Jungian theory, pointing out ways in which Jungian categories (anima/animus, eros/logos) perpetuate patriarchal hierarchies. She also warns those who are tempted to use archetypes in the service of feminist thinking that defining women's experience in terms of absolute, unchanging patterns will necessarily limit that experience. The separation and hierarchical arrangement of these two realms, the primary absolute and the secondary experiential, have served within the patriarchal system to justify women's inferior position: women are (and should remain) inferior because they partake of the Eternal Feminine, by definition an absolute and at the same time inferior condition.[2]

Archetypes, Goldenberg argues, can also function, however, within *feminist* systems in similarly destructive ways. Focusing on the archetype of the Great Mother in one or more of her various guises, for example, could result in a distortion or reduction of lived experience. Susan Griffin, poet and feminist, makes the same point in her poem "The Great Mother."[3] Here Griffin presents the mother-goddess as a ridiculous deus ex machina who comes parachuting out of a helicopter and appears to the speaker just as she is about to throw herself "down a ravine" from despair. While claiming to know the speaker's every thought before it is spoken, the goddess proceeds to put into the speaker's mouth questions she would never have asked, and then to answer them by evasive pulling-of-rank: " 'Because,' she said, '*that* is another mystery.' " The mother-goddess has been reduced here to a talky sentimentalist whose healing powers are grossly inadequate in the face of contemporary human needs. Faith in such a figure, Griffin implies, would necessarily inhibit truthful expression of experience and perception.

Women have three options, Naomi Goldenberg concludes, when faced with the problem of archetypes: to accept the patriarchal definition of the feminine, to search for female archetypes, or to redefine the term. As a first step toward the process of redefinition, she suggests that women "equate image with archetype" and thus break down those hierarchies of mind so inimical to them.[4]

I would like to contend in this paper that some women, in the poems they are currently writing, are indeed working toward such redefinition. It is true, of course, that others would like to do away with the concept of archetype altogether. Susan Griffin, for example, focuses some of her most powerful poems on the devastating effects that imposed (often male) mythological systems have on women's sensibilities. She seems, therefore, concerned with *de*mythologizing, divesting patriarchal myths of their power and efficacy in order to allow women's experience to surface and be heard. This is in itself a valuable enterprise: to express and assert women's lived experience as valuable in its own right, without moving beyond it into the realm of (possibly) meaningless abstractions. Simone de Beauvoir writes in this regard:

> An existent *is* nothing other than what he does; the possible does not extend beyond the real, essence does not precede existence; in pure subjectivity, the human being *is not anything*. He is to be measured by his acts. . . . if one considers a woman in her immanent presence, her inward self, one can say absolutely nothing about her, she falls short of having any qualifications.[5]

In this view, then, women should move beyond the condition in which their essentiality is imposed upon them by the patriarchy by asserting that such essentiality does not exist.

And yet, it seems to oversimplify the reality of women's lives to say that they share only the existential condition of victimization by the patriarchy. Indeed, women are discovering that it is becoming possible to define "the feminine," beyond its relation to the Other (specifically, the male), in their own terms.[6] And in this process, they are finding that some mythological concepts can be recovered and redeemed in the service of this self-discovery.

Many women, as Goldenberg points out,[7] have become interested in the idea of "matriarchy" and in exploring its possible ramifications. Jane Alpert, for example, claimed in her article "Mother Right: A New Feminist Theory,"[8] that society should be reshaped in the image of the matriarchy and that, by virtue of being mothers, women must assume social and economic control. Barbara Deming, in her reply to Alpert,[9] argued that reverting to matriarchal thinking perpetuates the stereotype of sexual superiority; in truth, stated Deming, rather than asserting power over the Other, both sexes must come to accept their essential androgyny.

It is my contention, however, that both of these theories depend too much on their relation to masculinity: Alpert's, in the *opposition* to masculinity of matriarchy; Deming's, in the *incorporation* of masculinity within androgyny. If we look to the "age of matriarchy" for the roots of a specifically *feminine* consciousness (feminine now, not as a complement to the masculine, but in its original sense, "of or pertaining to women"), we should find there, not a societal system ready for immediate transfer, but the figure of the goddess herself, prepared to serve as a *metaphorical* model toward a definition of the feminine in women's own terms.

■ ■ ■ ■

The figure of the goddess, as we know, emerged during the neolithic age as a fertility deity who represented and was responsible for the yearly decay and renewal of the earth, and within whose being all lived out their existence and found their eventual rest. The goddess thus represented in her own person the creative life process, which includes the forces of light and life as well as their necessary underside, the forces of darkness and death. According to Jungian thinkers, the archetype of the Great Mother also has its negative underside. This dark aspect of the Mother, whose effects are seen as damaging, even paralyzing, to the developing consciousness, has found its way into male mythology and psychology as the female dragon, the Stoner Mother, the castrating terror, whose powers must be permanently destroyed to enable the (male) "hero" to attain maturity.[10]

It is the dark or terrible mother who appears so frequently (as Medusa, as Kali, as the Erinyes) in contemporary women's poetry. She appears there, I believe, for two reasons.

1. The dark mother as representative of the difficulties of the mother-daughter relationship. Within recent years, women have begun to investigate the importance of the mother-daughter relationship in the development of the feminine personality. Nancy Chodorow, for example, in her article, "Family Structure and Feminine Personality,"[11] asserts that because the prevailing patterns of child-rearing for both males and females involve intensive primary contact with a mother-figure, this relationship exerts a decisive influence on personality development. For the male, whose gender identity must eventually replace his primary identification with the mother, masculinity often appears to him as "that which is not feminine or involved with women."[12] This negation of the mother-figure is reflected in male mythology in Neumann's idea that the developing consciousness (represented, for instance, by Perseus) must overcome the fascination of the unconscious (Medusa) in order to reach maturity.

For the female, however, as Chodorow points out, role identification with the mother does not necessitate a rejection of the earlier situation. Under favorable conditions, this fact may benefit women, giving them a sense of security which males lack. But often the nature of this relationship militates against differentiation, leading to difficulties (for mothers as well as daughters) with

boundary confusion or equation of self and other, for example, guilt
and self-blame for the other's unhappiness; shame and embarrass-
ment at the other's actions; daughters' "discovery" that they are
"really" living out their mothers' lives in their choice of career;
mothers' not completely conscious reactions to their daughters' bodies as their own (overidentification and therefore often unnecessary
concern with supposed weight or skin problems, which the mother is
really worried about in herself); etc.[13]

For various reasons (such as the fact that within Western culture so much
emphasis is placed on child-rearing), Western daughters in particular
have difficulties differentiating themselves from their mothers and are
involved in problems of infantile dependence.

The difficulty of establishing identity for women is further apparent, I believe, in the fact that the mother's body comes to represent not
only the childhood the daughter is deserting but also the adulthood she is
moving toward and must eventually adopt. In an article commemorating
Mother's Day, Martha Weinman Lear has written:

> Liberation. Extrication. Our mothers grow old and we watch them
> becoming us, and ourselves becoming them, and whom do we extri-
> cate from what? And how? And do we pass this dear, murderous
> entanglement on to our daughters with the family silver? Often I
> wonder if this is not some ultimate form of liberation: the most pain-
> ful, and the most elusive.[14]

This situation is reflected, interestingly, in the poetry of Anne Sexton and Sylvia Plath. In her poem, "Housewife,"[15] Anne Sexton states,
"A woman *is* her mother. / That's the main thing," and in her brilliant
poem "The Double Image,"[16] she describes a set of portraits of herself
and her mother which have been hung opposite each other in the
mother's house:

> And this is the cave of the mirror,
> that double woman who stares
> at herself, as if she were petrified
> in time—

Sylvia Plath, in "The Disquieting Muses,"[17] also associates the terrors of
paralysis with the mother-daughter relationship. Here the terrible
mother appears in the guise of a dark triple-goddess ("three ladies /

Nodding by night around my bed, / Mouthless, eyeless, with stitched bald head"), whose attentions to the speaker are ultimately stultifying:

> Day now, night now, at head, side, feet,
> They stand their vigil in gowns of stone,
> Faces blank as the day I was born,
> Their shadows long in the setting sun
> That never brightens or goes down.

Although these are her "Godmothers," her "Muses," they stand vigil, in this stopped universe, as if at a deathbed. Dressed themselves in "gowns of stone," their influence, like that of the mythic Medusa, will paralyze and destroy. Thus, both Plath and Sexton use the archetype of the terrible mother in its traditional sense to reflect a perilous mother-daughter entanglement and the need for disengagement and escape.

2. The dark mother as representative of female powers women are beginning to claim. Other, more contemporary women poets are employing the archetype of the dark mother to women's advantage by turning it on its head. Unlike earlier poets such as Plath and Sexton, who merely apply the traditional archetype to women's situation, these poets are doing two additional things: claiming the archetype's content as women's own, and "dissolving" its formal properties. The relationship to the Medusa-figure expressed by these poets is no longer that of a dependent, vulnerable child to an all-powerful mother who can cause barrenness and emotional death. Instead, these poets are removing from the dark mother her patriarchal, almost deterministic connotations; no longer does she reflect either a theological (the god[dess] as transcendent power) or social (the goddess as grasping mother) situation that women feel powerless to change. If women do see this figure as one aspect of the prepatriarchal Great Mother, it is not in the traditional, reverential sense, but rather as an immanent, accessible force. The goddess, as metaphor, now represents the dark but necessary side of our own creative possibilities.

In her poem, "Monster,"[18] Robin Morgan performs the very act of seizing the power of this image and making it her own. Here the poet's little boy, whose "Hair, oh pain, curls into fragrant tendrils damp / with the sweat of his summery sleep," is nevertheless still a "White. Male. American." who sees his mother through the eyes of a little Freud:

> But just two days ago on seeing me naked for what must be the five-
> thousandth time in his not-yet two years, he suddenly thought of

the furry creature who yawns through his favorite television program; connected that image with my genitals; laughed, and said, "Monster."

Gradually, as the poem progresses, the poet's pain at the imposition of such labels turns into a force she determines to use in the service of "a revolution / so total as to destroy maleness, femaleness, death," a force which, by the end of the poem, she has accepted as her own power: "I am a monster. / And I am proud."

Thus, Robin Morgan performs the difficult task of assimilating this image; May Sarton, likewise acknowledging this figure, sees her as playing an inherent part in the creative act. In her poem "The Invocation to Kali,"[19] Sarton invokes the terrible mother in the person of the Hindu goddess, Kali, who represents, at first, the "raging demands" of poetry: a "brute power," both beast and god, "that cannot be tamed." Although she can think at times only of murdering this "terrible god," the poet realizes that "Kali, the destroyer, cannot be overthrown; / We must stay, open-eyed, in the terrible place." For Kali represents not only the demands of poetry but also the underside of every act of creation:

Every creature is born out of the dark.
Every birth is bloody. Something gets torn.
Kali is there to do her sovereign work
or else the living child will be stillborn.

Women, then, as we have seen in these poems, are beginning to realize the necessity of incorporating the mother's dark powers rather than destroying or escaping them. These powers, formerly associated with emotional castration, figure importantly now in the creation of new self-definitions, which include not only the recognition of anger but also the understanding that every creative act is somehow rooted in the dark and that our own further development is contingent upon recognizing these sources within ourselves.

■ ■ ■ ■

I have already examined briefly some of the ways in which contemporary poets are attempting to dissolve the archetype's formal properties. To show how Adrienne Rich has accomplished further work in this direction, I would like to conclude by examining two of her poems. In her article "When We Dead Awaken: Writing as Re-Vision,"[20] Rich speaks of the abysmal gap between traditional literary mythologies and a woman's sense of her own complex reality:

> A lot is being said today about the influence that the myths and images of women have on all of us who are products of culture. I think it has been a peculiar confusion to the girl or woman who tries to write because she is peculiarly susceptible to language. She goes to poetry or fiction looking for *her* way of being in the world, since she too has been putting words and images together; she is looking eagerly for guides, maps, possibilities; and over and over in the "words' masculine persuasive force of literature" she comes up against something that negates everything she is about: she meets the image of Woman in books written by men. She finds a terror and a dream, she finds a beautiful pale face, she finds La Belle Dame Sans Merci, she finds Juliet or Tess or Salome, but precisely what she does not find is that absorbed, drudging, puzzled, sometimes inspired creature, herself, who sits at a desk trying to put words together.

Thus, aware of the dangers women must experience in attempting to fight through this mythic landscape, Rich is nevertheless excited by the possibility that, through the very act of writing (when employed as "revision"), women will begin to discover "the challenge and promise of a whole new psychic geography to be explored."

We can observe such a psychic geography, devoid now of the traditional mythic landmarks, slowly taking shape within Adrienne Rich's poetry. In "Diving Into the Wreck,"[21] she explores the old consciousness, seen here as a drowned ship, the remnant perhaps of a former war, and investigates its relationship to herself. The poem takes on the aspect of a ritual as the speaker dresses herself in a costume which, because of its very absurdity, effectively removes her from the expectations of society and prepares her for an arduous descent. The ritualistic elements are further pointed up as the speaker is forced by her flippers to "crawl like an insect down the ladder" as she moves, in a kind of initiation rite, from an easy mode of being in the world to those transformations which will allow her to move and be "in the deep element."

But this is not a ritual whose prescriptions she is mindlessly carrying out; rather, this process is her own, created by her as she moves through it step by step. Thus, she is careful to emphasize that it is "the thing itself and not the myth" she has come for. She wants her own perceptions of this wreck, not its story.

There is more to this experience, however, than careful observation. Just as she has had to learn to breathe and move differently in this new element, so the discovery she makes involves her own further transformation. The sea, she says, "is not a question of power," and she has had to leave behind her the old rules of aggressive competition in order to learn to "Turn (her) body without force / in the deep element." Now, coming upon the wreck, the speaker moves beyond her old identity and becomes an anonymous being who is, at the same time, the wreck itself. The speaker and the wreck, now identical, have suffered damage, she discovers, but still carry obscure but precious cargo, and by means of a further transformation, which now includes the reader, the poet implies that her discovery is common psychic territory, an inheritance. Equipped with knife and camera to excise and record, she asks us to realize that the mythologies we have inherited are a kind of legacy against which we may measure and judge ourselves but which will never ultimately define us: "a book of myths / in which / our names do not appear."

The process Adrienne Rich previews and outlines in "Diving Into the Wreck" develops further, in her most recent poems, as she continues to dissolve the barriers between her experience as an individual woman and the collective experience of women in general. She increasingly places her own perceptions within the context of an evolving women's consciousness, finding there new sources of energy, of creative power. "We are still laboring under the burden of patriarchal definitions of femininity, of femaleness," she has said in an interview. "So I think attention has got to be paid by women to what it means to be a woman. Just simply. What *we* think it ought to mean, what *we* think it has meant, *our* interpretations replacing patriarchal interpretations. I want to put my energy into that."[22]

In "From an Old House in America,"[23] the poet returns presumably to an old summer house filled with memories of the past and uses this experience to explore what it means to live the life of an American woman. She devotes the first six sections of the poem to a description of those tangible remnants of the past which provoke memories of lives lived out according to the old formulas. But these are dead memories, and instead of expending her energies trying to bring them back to life, she decides to concentrate instead on the revitalization of woman's experience: "the undead to watch / back on the road of birth."

But the life-history of American women has been painful. Just as African women, on their way to this country, gave birth on slave ships, chained to the bodies of the dead, so American women in general have lived their lives enslaved by dead ideas: women as "witches," as "breeding wenches," woman as "wheatfield" and "virgin forest." And the poet makes it clear that it is the patriarchal "fear and hatred" of women which is responsible for these destructive mythologies.

The poet's sensibilities, however, maintain a double edge. She sees, entangled among the sharp "spines of nightmare," a "simpler herb," a "dream of tenderness":

> because the line dividing
> lucidity from darkness
> is yet to be marked out

Thus, at the end of the poem she invokes the Erinyes, those ancient matriarchal fury-figures whose purpose it is, on the one hand, to pronounce sentences on these centuries of misuse, but on the other to "speak tenderness" as well: "if still you are on your way / still She awaits your coming." The mother-goddess appears here as the ultimate female force who calls us to our own growth, a process the poet has prefigured in an earlier section in which she sees women escaping the bonds of restrictive definition in order to discover our own free forms. These forms, though manifested in individual terms, participate in and are presided over by a female presence:

> If it was lust that had defined us—
> their lust and fear of our deep places
>
> we have done our time
> as faceless torsos licked by fire
>
> we are in the open, on our way—
> our counterparts
>
> the pinyon jay, the small
> gilt-winged insect
>
> the Cessna throbbing level
> the raven floating in the gorge
>
> the rose and violet vulva of the earth
> filling with darkness

yet deep within a single sparkle
of red, a human fire

and near and yet above the western planet
calmly biding her time.

It is interesting that each of these images includes within its own circumference certain opposing qualities. The first four are images usually associated with flight and release, and yet each includes a sense of connectedness as well. The pinyon jay, for instance, known for its swift flight, also feeds characteristically on the ground, "walking or running with head held high."[24] The insect, carrying its own brilliance on its wings, is nevertheless subject to cyclical process. And the Cessna and raven, both designed to soar, maintain connection to the earth. The earth, commonly associated with an unredeemable "female" heaviness, is here given its full, female equation, but its darkness is not oppressive but regenerative, harboring within itself "a human fire." Finally, the poet uses Venus, "the western planet," to epitomize the inclusion of both immanence and transcendence within the female experience. Just as Venus, here the embodiment of female power, expresses itself within our present lives, so the planet also locates itself at the same time above, calmly awaiting our coming.

Women, then, as is apparent in the poetry of both Susan Griffin and Adrienne Rich, are finding it necessary to develop critical tools that will make it possible for them to escape the restrictive, indeed destructive, confines of patriarchal mythology. They are no longer willing to live out the roles imposed upon them by a system that defines woman's place only in relation to itself and its own needs. While poets such as Susan Griffin equate the concept of archetype with this system and thus proclaim the necessity of discarding archetype altogether, others such as Adrienne Rich are using the concept in new ways, seeing an image of the inclusiveness of female experience, for example, in the Erinyes who speak judgment and tenderness at the same time. The plurality of these figures is significant, for women do not find efficacy, Rich implies, so much in the personification of individualized deities as in those forces, critical as well as creative, which women are working to discover within themselves. The rituals that women are inventing in this process of self-discovery are constructed as they go along, according to their own needs, and thus arise from individual (and collective) necessity, not from with-

out. And as women draw closer to the sources of their own individual creativity, they are also finding that these sources are shared, and that a new psychic geography, a woman's landscape, is gradually taking shape. Thus, the symbols they are finding to structure this new world, taken often from their rediscovery of matriarchal mythology, include shared, archetypal qualities as well as uniquely imagined and experienced particulars. The journey of this archetype, which is really a journey women themselves are discovering and creating at the same time, moves toward the realization of their own powers, their own myths, their own beginnings: "we are in the open, on our way—".
(1978)

30 ARCHETYPAL PATTERNS IN WOMEN'S FICTION

Annis V. Pratt

This selection from Pratt's book on the subject not only presents a clear state-ment of the three major archetypal patterns she has found to be typical of women's fiction, but also cites in detail the sources in myth and history from which these patterns emerge. Further, Pratt makes the argument that these ar-chetypal patterns, rightly understood, constitute a "buried feminine tradition," which women writers have turned to again and again in order to imbue their writing with a sense of inner freedom that belies their fiction's surface acquies-cence to the conventions of a patriarchal culture. This selection provides an important underpinning for Pratt's essay in Part I.

. . . Women's shared experience *as women* endows their fiction with a degree of continuity, abundance of analogue, and uniformity of concern sufficient to elucidate a single work by reference to the field of the woman's novel as a whole. Not only does this tradition span nearly three centuries in Britain and America; its narrative and symbolic struc-tures reflect an even more ancient, unresolved tension between feminine power and feminine powerlessness in the history of human culture. We have surveyed the relationship between aspects of women's fiction and various descriptions of the role of women in primitive and prehistoric societies. With the field as a whole in mind, it is also possible to see a relationship between the rise of women's fiction in the last several centu-

ries and three interrelated repositories of archetypal materials: the De-
meter/Kore and Ishtar/Tammuz rebirth narratives, the grail legends of
the later Middle Ages, and the cluster of archetypal and ritual materials
constituting the Craft of the Wise, or witchcraft.

· · · ·

The archetypal patterns that we have seen in women's fiction constitute signals from a buried feminine tradition that conflict with cultural
norms and influence narrative structures. One of the difficulties that
women writers experience is the fact that woman's ego, or persona, her
social being, exists from day to day in a world not only deaf to such buried
messages but filled with contrary materials. An author's normative values
derive from the subconscious realm, where memories and dreams of day-
to-day life are engendered; when she wants to describe her unconscious
world, she cannot adapt material from culture but must delve into a region whose patterns are less likely to conform to socially available myths,
religions, and rituals than to seem puzzling, encoded, and hieroglyphic.
Rarely brought to consciousness in any socially acceptable form, these
materials are, to use Laura Willowes's term, "dynamite in one's boots,"
full of potential for celebration and growth but also, because they are so
strongly repressed, for explosion.

My first inkling that women's fiction contained links to archetypal
systems from the ancient past was based on apparently random coinci-
dences between isolated textual and mythological motifs. I wondered
why Harding's definitions of virginity, mature Eros, and androgyny
should correspond so closely to desirable qualities described in novels of
Eros and rebirth; why, when Woolf dealt with the unconscious, she used
so many leitmotifs from grail legends; and why so many images, motifs,
and symbols analogous to witchcraft appeared in stories and novels by
women. It gradually became clear that women's fiction could be read as a
mutually illuminative or interrelated field of texts reflecting a preliterary
repository of feminine archetypes, including three particularly important
archetypal systems—the Demeter/Kore and Ishtar/Tammuz rebirth
myths, Arthurian grail narratives, and the Craft of the Wise, or witchcraft.

The principal archetypes that recur in women's fiction—the green-
world epiphany, the green-world lover, the rape trauma, enclosure, and
rebirth—find counterparts in these three complexes of ritual and narrative,
which Carl Jung, Emma Jung, Jean Markale, Jane Ellen Harrison, Margaret
Alice Murray, and Joseph Campbell all perceive as archetypal repositories
of uniquely feminine and androgynous import. The Demeter/Kore narra-

tive, as we saw in the previous chapter, is of particular importance to women, uniting the feminine generations. The psychological effect of participating in the Eleusinian mysteries, suggests Carl Jung, is to "extend the feminine consciousness. . . . An experience of this kind gives the individual a place and meaning in the life of the generations, so that all unnecessary obstacles are cleared out of the way of the life-stream that is to flow through her. At the same time the individual is rescued from her isolation and restored to wholeness. All ritual preoccupation with archetypes ultimately has this aim and this result."[1] Jung's understanding of the personal enhancement resulting from formalized reenactment of such archetypes suggests a parallel theory of the effect of women's fiction upon an audience, a subject that I shall briefly touch upon in concluding this study. His recognition that the Demeter/Kore narratives have particular appeal to women also extends to a suggestion that they derive from feminine materials alien to the patriarchy: "In fact, the psychology of the Demeter cult has all the features of a matriarchal order of society, where the man is an indispensable but on the whole disturbing factor."[2] The disturbing element in this archetype, as in women's fiction informed by the rape-trauma pattern, is Pluto's abduction and rape of Persephone; Demeter overcomes this disturbance, however, by rescuing her daughter.

The archetypes of the green world and the green-world lover so characteristic of women's fiction may derive from two sets of ancient rituals celebrating the death and rebirth of the seasonal year. Both the Demeter/Persephone and the Ishtar/Tammuz narratives (also the Aphrodite/Adonis and Isis/Osiris stories) underline ancient feminine rituals celebrated in preclassical and classical times. Both sets of narratives have uniquely feminine overtones, and the rites that derive from them have had a perennial appeal to women. Jane Ellen Harrison remarks that the Demeter/Kore (Persephone) celebrations at the end of September were "almost uncontaminated by Olympian [patriarchal] usage," deriving from pre-Hellenic practices in Thrace and Crete.[3] Carl Jung concurs that "in the formation of the Demeter/Kore myth the feminine influence so far outweighed the masculine that the latter had practically no significance. The man's role in the Demeter myth is really only that of seducer or conqueror."[4] With other scholars allocating the origin of rape narratives to the conquering of pre-Hellenic villages by the invading Aryan and Semitic tribes,[5] it seems clear that such rituals deal with a widespread usurpation of feminine power. The story of the abduction of Persephone by Pluto, of her mother's grief (Demeter herself was tricked and raped twice, once by Poseidon and another time by Zeus), Demeter's devastation of vegetation, her quest for her daughter, and the triumphant rebirth of both Persephone and the green world, make up the Eleusinian rites.[6] (These rites were part of secret oral traditions, and thus our understanding of them is pieced together from a medley of contemporary and historical accounts.)

The ritual of following the road that Demeter took in her grief and her triumph creates a transformation or rebirth of the personality in the participant; although male initiates existed, the transformational power derived from the relationship of women to each other. In the four rebirth texts that I considered in the previous chapter, the reuniting of daughter with mother plays a similar role to the transformation of the hero's personality: Lily discovers and absorbs the power of Mrs. Ramsay, Lillian attempts to reconcile her inner "Madonna" and child, Atwood's hero is able to assimilate the green-world figure of her dead mother into her own powers of maternity and rebirth, and Martha Quest becomes a beneficent and life-saving woman after her mother's final visit and death. In other novels the quest of the mother for the daughter leads to the rebirth of the mother: the plot of Kay Boyle's *The Underground Woman* (1973), for example, is based on the loss, locating, and letting go of a daughter, an experience that brings the hero to herself at the denouement; Lessing's *Memoirs of a Survivor* (1975) uses a similar pattern, that of an older woman coming to terms with a girl who is left in her care and who is taken away in a kind of interplanetary apotheosis; and E. M. Broner's *Her Mothers* (1975) is structured on the hero's quest back into her own daughterhood and forward through Europe, Israel, and California in search of her missing daughter.

The mothers and daughters in women's fiction seem also to be enacting the various aspects of the triple goddess, who was virgin, maternal figure, and old woman at one and the same time. The third figure in the triad, who has often been gynophobically perceived as "devouring mother" or "crone," represents the wise older mother's knowledge of the best moment to fledge or let go of her children, a moment that, if precipitous or delayed, can lead the maternal element to become destructive. She also controls death and rebirth. The fully matured feminine personality comprehends all three elements and can bring any one of them into play at any time. A novel that is structured according to the Demeter/Kore archetype, like the Eleusinian mysteries, comprises a story of the rejuvenation of the mother in the personality of the daughter and of the daughter in the personality of the mother.

The archetype of the green-world lover seems related to the dying god in the stories of Aphrodite and Adonis, Ishtar and Tammuz, Isis and Osiris. These goddesses have lovers who die and whom they restore to life: Ishtar (as in the parallel case of Isis and Osiris) through a perilous journey, and Aphrodite through the mediation of Zeus. In both cases, the goddess's love for her consort gives her the power of rebirth, his return being celebrated in rituals appealing primarily to women. Jessie Weston notes of the Tammuz and Adonis figures that the hero can be released from death only through feminine power, and that in many of the rituals based on these stories women accompany a figure of their god, tearing their hair in their grief for him and celebrating his return with wild dances. "The most noticeable feature of the ritual was the prominence assigned to women," remarks Weston. "It is the women who weep for him and accompany him to his tomb. They sob wildly all night long; this is their god more than any other, and they alone wish to lament his death and sing of his resurrection."[7] Other feminist scholars have pointed out that cults of Isis and of Dionysus were not only openly permitted to women throughout Greek and Rome history but were considered a proper feminine activity, however wild and ecstatic the celebrations. They provided an outlet for women to celebrate their eroticism, power, pride, and joy, an outlet that also typifies both grail and witchcraft narratives. Although such figures as Emily Brontë's Heathcliff and Charlotte Brontë's Rochester contain elements of the dying-god archetype, he is more often an imaginary figure projected from within the hero's psyche, like Willa Cather's Corn God in *O Pioneers!* or the lovers dreamt of but never brought to life in Woolf's *Night and Day* and Chopin's *The Awakening*. In women's fiction the hero himself is more likely to become a "dying god" of feminine eroticism, punished by madness, death, or ostracism, or falling victim sexually to her opposite, the gothic rapist, hideous husband, or unsuitable suitor.

Jessie Weston suggests a number of links between the dying-god narratives and rituals and the popular grail legends of the High Middle Ages, and one need not go at length into the scholarship explaining such a continuity to recognize in the Celtic Breton culture from which the grail legends derive many elements of feminine authenticity. The feminine eroticism evident in the cults of Osiris, Tammuz, Adonis, and Dionysus provided women with a chance to celebrate with each other a licensed rebellion against marital fidelity. Celtic women, according to Jean Markale, enjoyed a higher degree of freedom over their own bodies than women in patriarchal systems, a freedom based on their ability to control segments of the communally owned property and cattle. Among the Celtic peoples settled in Britain, Ireland, and Wales at the time of the

Anglo-Saxon invasions (and who later joined with the Normans to defeat them) infidelity was condoned, divorce easy, women warriors and queens powerful, and a number of goddesses revered and worshiped.

Both Emma Jung and Jean Markale argue that the grail legends contain rebellions against the institution of matrimony and other patrilinear norms. "Mythologically," remarks Markale, "the Quest for the Grail is an attempt to re-establish a disciplined sovereignty, usurped by the masculine violence of the despoiling knight, while the kingdom rots and the king, the head of the family . . . is impotent." Restoration can be achieved only by "the appointed successor, the nephew of the wounded king."[8] His qualities, in Emma Jung's description, are less rigidly "masculine" than androgynous: he must achieve compassion, the ability to ask the wounded king what ails him; this impotent king, whose lands have been laid waste by the Rape of the Maidens of Logres, is that key figure in all matrilinear systems, Perceval's mother's brother.[9] We are dealing, clearly, with the rape-trauma archetype and with an archetypal quest to restore a kingdom punished for violating women. The Breton materials are full of stories of women exiled to islands, "submerged princesses" forced underwater or into underground "fairy grottoes" or castles by usurping males.[10] Typical narratives of this type are those involving the island of Avalon, where Arthur was taken after his death, and islands of immortal women sought by the hero in the medieval prose poem "Voyage of Bran." Ladies of the lake, fairy queens, elf maidens, and mermaids are all archetypes expressing the repression of powerful women. "In the ever more prevalent symbolism of a magical Beyond and land of the dead," remarks Emma Jung, "there is a psychological expression of an extraordinary stirring of the unconscious, such as does happen from time to time, especially in periods when the religious values of a culture are beginning to change."[11] The grail as container of beneficence, feeder of the tribe, and locus of rebirth predominates in this material as still another archetype of feminine power. As "mother pot," "magic cauldron" (with which Persephone can regenerate the dead heroes and heal the sick), golden bowl of healing, etc., this archetype expresses women's generative and regenerative powers and corresponds to the sacred vessels of the vestal virgins and to Demeter's *Cista Mystica,* or magic basket.[12]

The disruptively feminist element in the grail material may have been responsible for the gradual denigration of women in the Arthurian legend. Whereas in much of folklore, fairy tales, and earlier accounts Morgan la Fée was an admirable warrior-goddess or -priestess and Guinevere a respected queen indulging in socially acceptable extramarital behavior, by the fifteenth century writers like Malory were interpreting them as figures of horror, treachery, and adultery. Some of the Celtic standards for feminine eroticism seem to have found their way into the courtly love tradition under the patronage of Eleanor of Aquitaine, who tried the cases of true lovers at her court and forbade them to be married; but even within her lifetime her teachings were invaded by misogynistic repudiations. Perhaps the veneration of the Virgin Mary—who, as Magna Mater, Stella Maris, Our Lady of the Vineyards, Our Lady of the Barley, Our Lady of the Caves, etc., amalgamated qualities of pre-Christian virgins alien to the Roman Catholic conception of chastity—represents a weakened survival of the goddess into the Middle Ages. "Apart from a tendency to restore the ancient mother goddess in the guise of the Virgin Mary," writes Markale, "there have been a great number of heresies within Christianity itself that have sought to implement the female rebellion."[13] Scholars of witchcraft like Trevor-Roper, Gerald Gardner, and Mary Alice Murray have noted the correspondence between places where large numbers of witches were tried and loci of heresies—places like Wales, Cornwall, the Channel Islands, the Isle of Man, and Ireland in the British Isles, and the Pyrenees, Vosges, and Ardennes on the Continent, marginal to the centers of patriarchal power.[14]

The Craft of the Wise, or witchcraft, in its herbal lore and healing, fertility dances around a horned god, and belief in reincarnation, "mother pots," or cauldrons, seems to constitute a variation on the dying-god, Celtic, and grail archetypal repositories. The witches acted as midwives, advisors, and healers to their villages, gathered in colleges located on islands or in the mountains, controlled considerable property, and were particularly concerned with the feminine reproductive cycle. The witch cult persisted in England throughout the Roman occupation and was popular in Norman England during the eleventh through the thirteenth centuries (some think that most Normans, and all of the Plantagenets, were members of covens),[15] and only with the Renaissance and Age of Reason was it subjected to a patriarchal backlash so virulent that between the fourteenth and eighteenth centuries churchmen and scholars, undoubtedly motivated by its subversive feminine element, killed perhaps as many as nine million individuals.

■　■　■　■

As a result, "secrecy and fear of discovery necessarily wiped out the open scholarship of the ancient matriarchal colleges and sacred islands. . . . Those who were herbalists let their gardens go to seed. Those who kept the ancient matrifocal law did so within the confines of their homes, but publicly joined the throngs of enslaved female chattels and swaggering masters."[16] Contemporary witches and scholars of witchcraft have suggested that the testimonies exacted under torture reflect less of the witch cult itself than the phallocentric and rabidly gynophobic imaginations of the "witch doctors" and judges.[17] The true Craft of the Wise, meanwhile, was passed down orally through the generations to the present.

■　■　■　■

I believe that the novel performs the same role in women's lives as do the Eleusinian, dying-god, and witchcraft rituals—a restoration through remembering, crucial to our survival. "If women say again and again that society denies them clear paths to fulfillment," writes Patricia Meyer Spacks, " . . . they also affirm in far reaching ways the significance of their inner freedom. . . . That escape through writing declared possible by Anaïs Nin and Anna Wulf emblemized an even larger kind of escape, through imagination."[18] Women's "escape through imagination" is not escapist but strategic, a withdrawal into the unconscious for the purpose of personal transformation. The deadlocks in women's fiction that many feminist critics deplore result from women's powerlessness in Western culture, but women authors present them in such a way that their novels become vehicles for social change.

Without pretending to survey the field of the reader/text relationship, which is central to much modern critical theory, I would like to suggest that the restorative power of women's fiction consists in a dialectical relationship between novel and audience. Women's fiction may indeed be suspended between two poles of desire, deadlocked between contrary forces rarely resolved within an individual text, and hence polar or dichotomous rather than dialectical. The process that dialecticians characterize as *aufheben*—to negate, absorb, and transcend—is rarely completed in an individual novel; even in those few instances when heroes emerge as fully developed personalities, their social future is uncertain. I perceive the woman's novel as a symbolic vehicle indicating a meaning or import that it does not itself contain. In negating gender behavior, absorbing or integrating "masculine" and "feminine" roles into those few fully mature characters, it points toward transcendence or synthesis. The woman's novel asks questions, poses riddles, cries out for restitution, but remains in itself merely rhetorical, an artifact or idea rather than an action. As in the archetypal rituals of Demeter and Kore and of the dying god, Persephone is always being raped and restored, the god always dying and being reborn. The synthesis, or final element, of the dichotomy between loss and restoration does not occur within the individual novel, or even in the field as a whole, but in the mind of the reader, who, having participated in the narrative reenactment, must put its message into effect in her own life.

■   ■   ■   ■

It seems to me, then, that the archetypal patterns in women's fiction provide a ritual experience for the reader containing the potential for personal transformation, and that women's novels constitute literary variations on preliterary folk practices that are available in the realm of the imagination even though they have long been absent from day-to-day life. A woman knitter once wanted to learn to spin her own wool and found the directions in the handbook on spinning hard to follow. When she actually picked up her spindle and began to wind the threads through it and to twirl it in rhythm, she found that her fingers already seemed to know how to perform motions arcane to her conscious mind. She coined the term *unventing* for this rediscovery of a lost skill through intuition, a bringing of latent knowledge out of oneself, in contrast to "invention" from scratch.[19] Following this model, I would term the writing and reading of women's fiction a form of "unvention," the tapping of a repository of knowledge lost from Western culture but still available to the author and recognizable to the reader as deriving from a world with which she, at some level of her imagination, is already familiar.

To put it another way, for three centuries women novelists have been gathering us around campfires where they have warned us with tales of patriarchal horror and encouraged us with stories of heroes undertaking quests that we may emulate. They have given us maps of the patriarchal battlefield and of the landscape of our ruined culture, and they have resurrected for our use codes and symbols of our potential power. They have exaggerated the worst attributes of the "male" and the "female" enemy so that they become laughable paper dragons. They have provided us moments of epiphany, of vision, when we can feel rising from our depths a quality that altogether transcends the gender polarities destructive to human life. They have dug the goddess out of the ruins and cleansed the debris from her face, casting aside the gynophobic masks that have obscured her beauty, her power, and her beneficence. In so doing, they have made of the woman's novel a pathway to the authentic self, to the roots of our selves beneath consciousness of self, and to our innermost being.

(1981)

31 Two Ways of Spelling It Out: An Archetypal-Feminist Reading of H.D.'s *Trilogy* and Adrienne Rich's *Sources*

Albert Gelpi

Albert Gelpi has discussed elsewhere both H.D. (in his A Coherent Splendor) and Adrienne Rich (in a book written with his wife, the feminist critic Barbara Charlesworth Gelpi). Here he links the two in terms of a common commitment to a poetry of self-definition, especially in regard to the role of the masculine in the authors' lives. Gelpi conjoins the historical and the psychological in his definition of the masculine—both the men the women knew and the animus in their psyches. At the essay's beginning, he describes his use of Jung's psychology in literary criticism and his position on the archetypes of gender (animus/anima) in the continuing culture versus psyche debate among Jungians within the feminist movement.

   Gelpi uses two different critical techniques in this essay and proves that both are very compatible with his archetypal-feminist analysis. For H.D., he uses a close reading to follow the wordplay of a poet building symbols through allusion and subtle accretions—a process very much like an analysand's amplification of the meaning of dream images through the work of what Jungians call active imagination. For Rich, the critic makes greater use of biographical and historical information. Gelpi notes that whereas H.D. "sublimates and encodes" the biographical in her wordplay, imagery, and mythic allusions, Rich displays her life and history in her work and then intensifies it into poetry.

In proposing archetypal readings of H.D.'s *Trilogy* and Adrienne

Rich's *Sources*—two long poems of self-definition yet expressive of different phases in women's consciousness, pivotal in the careers of their creators—I am responding, through exemplary texts, to objections that a number of feminist theorists have registered against archetypal psychology. Most Jungian as well as Freudian commentary has been presented from a male perspective, even when the Jungian or Freudian happens to be female. For example, Jung posited the animus as equally crucial for the woman's psychological development as the anima is for the man's; yet both his own speculation on the subject and his wife Emma's essay "Anima and Animus" deal at length with the anima but leave the animus, and thus women's psychology, a postulated but largely unexplored matter. Similarly, most archetypal literary critics, female as well as male, have treated male writers; and when contemporary feminists have taken up archetypal criticism at all, it has almost always been to express their suspicion or hostility, because notions like anima and animus tend to absolutize and perpetuate gender stereotypes that have kept men dominant and women oppressed in society.

The configuration of the anima or animus is critical to the Jungian schema. The anima is the image, in the psyche of the man, of those qualities, tendencies, and capacities within himself which he perceives and experiences, or has been acculturated within his society to perceive and experience, as "feminine": emotion, intuition, passion, compassion. In the same way, the animus images within the woman's psychic life the range of traits and potentialities which she associates, or has been acculturated to associate, with the "masculine": reason, will, control, order.

In Jungian theory, the lifelong process of individuation requires the resolution and integration of polar aspects of the psyche. In that dialectic the animus or the anima presents to the woman or the man aspects which at first she or he experiences, or has been acculturated to experience, as "other," but which for that very reason must be integrated into a developing self-identity. In the life of dream, fantasy, and imagination the anima or animus comes to mediate the whole gamut of possibilities, from the body's sexuality and materiality to the spirit's intimations of the absolute. At times "he" or "she" may appear the negating agent of the shadow, fomenting violence and havoc, and at other times can shine forth as a god or goddess, the image of the fully realized self. In the process of individuation, therefore, the animus or anima constitutes the decisive point of engagement, transition, and possible resolution with the "other" or seeming "other." Although contention with the anima or animus may be fraught with reversals and betrayals as well as rescues and epiphanies, the process is seeking a reconciliation of polarities into an integrated self, symbolized at times by a hierogamy or syzygy, at times by the apparition of a deity in the same gender as the dreamer or imaginer.

Although anima and animus do refer not to actual men and women but to psychic dynamisms, the feminist concern about the validation of gender stereotypes is nonetheless relevant, for our associations with the anima or animus not only affect an individual's relations with actual women and men but are affected by those relations and by the prevailing norms of the cultural ideology. Nevertheless, I feel that one can work as a feminist to change patriarchal values and structures and still accept the authenticity of anima and animus not as metaphysical absolutes but as psychological factors whose images are, to some extent at least, culturally and historically conditioned but are actually operative in the psyche and need to be engaged and integrated. Jung himself admitted that the archetypes and their valences were not fixed but could change gradually over a period of time. But always the dramas of our inner life, whether in dreams or more consciously in art, must be taken on their own terms, because they are telling truths about ourselves that cannot be blinked away; any prospect of altering the story they tell and the values they reflect depends, not upon falsification or repression, but upon expression and transformation. Though Adrienne Rich would not call herself a Jungian, the force of her feminist critique derives in good part from the fact that she sees the will to change and the politics of change counterpointed and complemented by an awareness of the presence of history and past experience, a recognition of the depth of sources as well as resources.

In the practice of literary criticism I have found archetypal psychology useful in understanding the creative process and, specifically, have often found the animus or anima a way of understanding a poem and an entire poetic career. I have dealt with Walt Whitman and Ezra Pound, T. S. Eliot and Wallace Stevens, as poets whose work turns on their complex and different relations with the anima, and I have found it equally revealing to see the relation to the animus as a crux in the work of Emily Dickinson, Denise Levertov, Sylvia Plath, and, as in the emphasis of this essay, H.D. and Adrienne Rich.

I

Hilda Doolittle received H.D. as her nom de plume in 1912 from Ezra Pound, when he declared her the most perfect Imagist poet. Her Imagist poems, concise and finely chiseled, at once chaste and passionate, at once intense and controlled, at once Greek-classical and romantic, established her early reputation. The three long poems that make up *Trilogy* represent a later phase of her career. They were conceived amid the catastrophic destruction of London in World War II, as Nazi bombers crossed the Channel in waves night after night for a year to blitz the city and its civilian citizens. The first poem in the sequence, *The Walls Do Not Fall*, was written in 1942 just after the blitz, and the other two, *Tribute to the Angels* and *The Flowering of the Rod*, were written in two creative outbursts in May and December 1944, during the Allied campaign that ended the war in Europe. Though they were not published together till after H.D.'s death, they were written as a sequence, each poem consisting of forty-three sections of varying lengths written in unrhymed pairs of lines.

The impulse informing all H.D.'s writing is the effort to define her own identity as an individual and as a woman, up to her very last poem, completed within weeks of her death in 1961, entitled "Hermetic Definition." This effort is to the end played out, complicated, and resolved, through her relation to the masculine—to the men in her life and to the animus—as both protagonists and antagonists in her psychic drama. *Trilogy* initiates the last, great period of H.D.'s work by enacting the phases of that parthenogenesis: in *The Walls Do Not Fall*, through H.D.'s identification with male gods and scribes of antiquity; in *Tribute to the Angels*, through identification of herself with the Virgin Scribe (her astrological sign was Virgo); in *The Flowering of the Rod*, through identification of herself with the Virgin Mother.

The first poem in this process of self-mothering and self-birthing is an invocation to a number of male figures from Greek and Egyptian mythology, Judaism, and Christianity. The men advance and recede, blend in and out of one another, constellated around the figure of Hermes. In her notebooks, H.D. referred to the men she loved as "initiators" because in various ways they inspired and confirmed and corresponded to her own animus powers as poet and visionary. From adolescence she was drawn to poetry and mysticism as expressions of the central mystery of the psyche and the universe. In her own experience, as well as in her reading of history and art, men seemed to attend to this mystery and offer the techniques for construing it.

In blitzed London, powerfully evoked in the opening section of *The Walls Do Not Fall*, H.D.'s instinctive reaction to the eruption of world war is to withdraw into the psyche as protective shell. Section 4 uses the metaphor of the shellfish, whose cunning is tough enough to survive the crushing jaws of violence:

I sense my own limit.
my shell-jaws snap shut

....

so that, living within,
you beget, self-out-of-self,

selfless,
that pearl-of-great price.

That section had begun with the statement that "there is a spell . . . in
every sea-shell." The word "spell" punningly connects "magic" and
"language," and in the spell of the words the secreted self survives, is
nourished and reborn. Hence the shellfish becomes "egg in egg-shell,"
and the poem goes on to reiterate imagery of female gestation—cocoon,
jar, alchemical crucible—to generate the pearl of great price: "self-out-
of-self, / selfless."

What aroused the poem and roused H.D. out of her shell was a letter
from an American friend who doubted the power of the spell, the efficacy of
the poet, before violence and holocaust: "so what good are your scribblings?" H.D. told another friend that she had begun *The Walls Do Not Fall*
"in a sort of exhilaration of rage" as a "vindication of the writer, or the
'scribe.' " In section 9 she summons Hermes against the blitz:

Thoth, Hermes, the stylus,
the palette, the pen, the quill endure,

though our books are a floor
of smoldering ash under our feet. . . .

And again on the next page:

so what good are your scribblings?
this—we take them with us

beyond death; Mercury, Hermes, Thoth
invented the script, letters, palette;

the indicated flute or lyre-notes
on papyrus or parchment

are magic, indelibly stamped
on the atmosphere somewhere,

forever; remember, O sword,
you are the younger brother, the latter-born,

your Triumph, however exultant,
must one day be over,

in the beginning
was the Word.

Thoth is the Egyptian predecessor of the Greek Hermes, as Mercury is his Roman avatar. But why is Hermes H.D.'s god and animus? In the pantheon Hermes plays many roles: he is "psychopompos," the messenger of the other gods and the mediator-guide of the underworld, the realm of the unconscious; he is magician, mercurial agent of change, and the planet Mercury rules her sun sign, Virgo; he is heroic explorer of the unknown; he is a healer, and his staff, the caduceus, is the sign of the medical profession; he is a word-magician as well, the inventor of the hieroglyphs, the prime scribe or writer. Behind Hermes the scientist-doctor stand, in H.D.'s own life, her father, Dr. Charles Doolittle, who studied the stars as a professor of mathematics and astronomy, and Sigmund Freud, who, as her analyst in the thirties, had unriddled her psyche. Behind Hermes the scribe stood Pound and D. H. Lawrence and Richard Aldington. The shared initial letter of the names Hilda and Hermes signifies that the animus holds the key to her hermetic definition as poet and mage and healer. So now Hilda summons Hermes in the war not to fight but to write, so that by a punning sleight of hand his Word / her Word can subdue Mars's Sword: *"in the beginning / was the Word."* With the last phrase Hermes, as scribe of Amenhotep, becomes overlaid with John as Jesus' scribe, and the word "Amen" repeatedly puns to connect the pharaoh-god with the Christos.

The birth symbolically projected in the middle sections of the poem continues to blend Christian and Egyptian, Greek and Jewish references. The palimpsest of associations requires citing the whole of section 21:

Splintered the crystal of identity,
shattered the vessel of integrity,

till the Lord *Amen,*
paw-er of the ground,

>   bearer of the curled horns,
>   bellows from the horizon:
>
>   here am I, Amen-Ra,
>   *Amen*, Aries, the Ram;
>
>   time, time for you to begin a new spiral,
>   see—I toss you into the star-whirlpool;
>
>   till pitying, pitying,
>   snuffing the ground,
>
>   here am I, Amen-Ra whispers,
>   *Amen*, Aries, the Ram,
>
>   be cocoon, smothered in wool,
>   be Lamb, mothered again.

Lord Amen Ra Ram is the archetypal father, the paw-er with power; but in the course of these few lines he becomes mother-cocoon and, with the pun on "smother / mother" becomes the newborn son: the Lamb as Lord, the Lord as Lamb. Then the "I" of Amen-Ra's whispered prayer subtly elides in section 22 into the poet's own voice, praying now to the father for her to gestate in his womb as "re-born Sun" / Son:

>   Now my right hand,
>   now my left hand
>
>   clutch your curled fleece;
>   take me home, take me home,
>
>   my voice wails from the ground;
>   take me home, Father:
>
>   pale as the worm in the grass,
>   yet I am a spark
>
>   struck by your hoof from a rock:
>   *Amen*, you are so warm,

       hide me in your fleece,
       crop me up with the new-grass;

       let your teeth devour me,
       let me be warm in your belly,

       the sun-disk,
       the re-born Sun.

Sun / Son is Helios and Christos, is Hermes, is Thoth, is Osiris, the
brother-husband-son of Isis. The final sections of the poem pun repeatedly on the names of Osiris and Isis, and those echoes portend the
ultimate union that would resolve polarities in the psyche and in the war-
torn world: "Oh, Sire, is this the path? . . . O, Sire, is this the waste? . . .
O, Sire, / is this union at last?" Having demonstrated the power of the
scribe in the time of war, the spell of the poem can conclude with the
suggestion that since the walls of London do not fall but still stand, *"possibly we will reach haven, / heaven."*

       Tribute to the Angels was written two years later, H.D. told a friend,
during "a wonderful pause just before D-Day," the Allied assault on
Nazi Europe which turned the tide of the fighting in the European theater; this augur of peace produced, in a frenzy of inspiration, "a sort of
premature peace poem." The epiphany that generated this Easter poem
came to H.D. on a London bus when she caught a glimpse of an apple
tree that had been incinerated in the blitz blossoming again in a bombed-
out city square. Picking up where the previous poem left off, *Tribute to the
Angels* begins with the scribe-mages, Hermes and Saint John of the Revelations, but pretty quickly the references to Hermes lead to Aphrodite,
and the Christian references lead to Mary. In Jungian terms, the animus
leads to and unlocks the secret of her womanhood.

       H.D. participated in almost daily seances during the war years and
had become very much interested in angelology, particularly through the
books of Robert Amberlain. In this poem the invocation of the archangels
attendant upon the throne of the Lamb in Revelations—first Raphael,
then Gabriel, Azrael, and Uriel—climaxes in an amazing revelation of
the archetypal feminine, at once Mary and Venus / Aphrodite. Here is
section 8:

       Now polish the crucible
       and in the bowl distill

a word most bitter, *marah,*
a word bitterer still, *mar,*

sea, brine, breaker, seducer,
giver of life, giver of tears;

now polish the crucible
and set the jet of flame

under, till *marah-mar*
are melted, fuse and join

and change and alter:
mer, mere, mère, mater, Maia, Mary,

Star of the Sea,
Mother.

The evocation of the feminine archetype in the middle sections of the
poem (roughly sections 15 through 23) leads to the revelation of the fifth
angel, Annael, identified by H.D. with the Hebrew Anna or Grace and
with the Mohammedan Venus (she appears at first in a syzygy with
Uriel), and to the association of Annael with the "half-burnt-out apple-
tree / blossoming" miraculously in the city square. Then, out of nowhere, a personal revelation: "I had been thinking of Gabriel, / . . . how
could I imagine / the Lady herself would come instead?" And the dream
apparition persists more strongly even after the dreamer awakens:

Our Lady of the Goldfinch,
Our Lady of the Candelabra,

Our Lady of the Pomegranate,
Our Lady of the Chair;

we have seen her, an empress,
magnificent in pomp and grace,

and we have seen her
with a single flower

> or a cluster of garden-pinks
> in a glass beside her. . . .

The incantatory catalogue of images of the Lady from Renaissance and Pre-Raphaelite paintings continues for pages, but H.D. goes on to the oracular declaration that the universally recognized Lady is not the Madonna or the *Bona Dea,* or rather that the universally recognized Madonna-goddess represents the achieved and apotheosized self:

> . . . she is not shut up in a cave
> like a Sibyl; she is not
>
> imprisoned in leaden bars
> in a coloured window;
>
> she is Psyche, the butterfly,
> out of the cocoon.

What's more, the Lady's character is defined when she is linked with the sixth archangel, Michael, "regent of the planet Mercury" and thus a manifestation of Hermes. The self imaged here is neither the lover nor the mother but the virgin scribe. This Lady does not hold the divine Son ("the Child was not with her"; "the Lamb was not with her") but a book, in fact the very poem we are reading:

> She carried a book, either to imply
> she was one of us, with us,
>
> or to suggest she was satisfied
> with our purpose, a tribute to the Angels. . . .

The tribute ends with the invocation of the seventh archangel, Zadkiel, as "Zeus-pater or Theus-pater, / / *Theus,* God; God-the-father, father-god / or the Angel god-father, / / himself, heaven yet at home in a star," but then the vision of the various angels fuses alchemically into an image that seems mysterious, even anticlimactic, but anticipates the third poem of *Trilogy:* "a cluster of garden-pinks . . . a face like a Christmas-rose." For this poem does not exhaust the revelation; the virgin scribe's final book is yet to be written: "the pages, I imagine, are the blank pages / of the unwritten volume of the new."

H.D. imagines and writes that volume as the concluding poem of *Trilogy*, entitled emblematically *The Flowering of the Rod.* The rod is the tree in the London square, and Hermes' caduceus, and Christ's cross or rood; and just as the archetypal revelation of the masculine scribe opened the way to that of the virgin scribe, so now the virgin scribe reveals the full feminine archetype. If *Tribute to the Angels* is a spring flowering, this is a Christmas flowering. *Tribute* had said it would be "a tale of a Fisherman / a tale of a jar or jars." The Fisherman is of course Jesus, and the female vessels are the two jars of myrrh belonging to Kaspar the mage. The first jar he presented to the newborn Child in His mother's lap at Bethlehem; the second, according to legend, he gave to Mary Magdalene years later, and she used it to anoint her Lord before His crucifixion. Just as the jars are twinned, so are the Marys, the courtesan and the virgin; but here the oppositions are inverted: the courtesan becomes chaste, and the virgin gives birth.

The mystery of Mary is the key to the poem. H.D. inverts the chronological order of Jesus' birth and death in her telling of the story, in order to move from the Magdalene to the Madonna. In the first episode the aged Kaspar is impelled, against his inbred patriarchal misogyny, to accede to the Magdalene's plea for the second precious jar of myrrh, as a result of her revelation of the matriarchal mystery. This mystery extends back through history and beyond to Eve and beyond Eve to Lilith and even before Lilith to the nameless mother from the lost paradise of Atlantis: the ur-mystery exfoliating through the cycles of generation. It is from the matriarch of Atlantis that we all come, and to her we all return; she enfolds and unfolds Paradise, lost and regained.

In the Magdalene, Kaspar glimpses the Madonna Mary or the second Eve, through whom, in the Christian myth, Spirit entered history in the Son so that death might issue in resurrection. The metamorphosis is reiterated in the puns on Mary's name throughout the tale, as H.D. spells out the transformation: "through my will and my power, Mary shall be myrrh . . . (though I am Mara, bitter) I shall be Mary-myrrh . . . *I am Mary, the incense-flower of the incense-tree, / myself worshipping, weeping, shall be changed to myrrh.*" The youngest of the Magi, Kaspar knelt not before the nameless Jahweh but before God's Word, incarnate of the Mother; he brought myrrh to Mary-mère. In the final section of *The Flowering of the Rod* the masculine is offspring and adoring witness to the Virgin-Mother:

> But she spoke so he looked at her,
> she was shy and simple and young;

she said, Sir, it is a most beautiful fragrance,
as of all flowering things together;

but Kaspar knew the seal of the jar was unbroken,
he did not know whether she knew

the fragrance came from the bundle of myrrh
she held in her arms.

The poems of *Trilogy* disclose a series of archetypes that reveal a deepening sense of H.D.'s selfhood: the scribe, the virgin with the book, the Madonna with Child. The tremendous revelation the poem has made possible is that through the power of poetry the wars within and the wars without are contravened; H.D. survives the strife and emerges whole: "self-out-of-self, / / selfless, / that pearl-of-great-price"; "Psyche, the butterfly, / out of the cocoon." The parthenogenesis is complete as poet H.D. is virgin-mother, self-born. The bundle of myrrh in Mary's arms is both the child and the poem: the child in the poem, the Word of the poem, the poem of the Word, the poem as child. Moreover, her survival is not merely personal; like Mary in Christian theology, she is the representative of humankind.

II

H.D. is an important poet for Adrienne Rich, and *Trilogy* is a poem of particular interest and resonance for her; lines from *Tribute to the Angels* serve as epigraph for *The Dream of a Common Language* (1978). Both women were daughters in middle-class families with powerful professorial fathers: Dr. Doolittle, an astronomer at the University of Pennsylvania; Dr. Arnold Rich, a pathologist at the Johns Hopkins Medical School. But the symbiosis between them must acknowledge difference as much as continuity. The cultural, temperamental, social, even economic differences are enormous. H.D. was an expatriate in monied circles of the international literary elite. But Rich's radical feminist politics complicate but, if anything, deepen her sense of connection with her place and time; *Sources* appeared in a volume entitled *Your Native Land, Your Life* (1986). Moreover, Rich has deliberately eschewed the hermetic and occult, metaphysical claims and mystical intimations; her poem called "Transcendental Etude" (1966) remains grounded in the here and now. In prefacing her most recent selected poems, *The Fact of a Doorframe,* with the following declaration, she might have been framing the contrast with H.D.: "I have never had much belief in the idea of the poet as someone of special sensitivity or spiritual insight, who rightfully lives above and off from the ordinary general life." The poem was never a "spell" for Rich; mythification seemed mystification, and over the years the metaphysical conceits and literary allusions that her early poetry featured increasingly gave way to or were integrated into the immediacies of direct statement.

At the same time, what links these poets (and links them both to Emily Dickinson) is a ferocious commitment to the life of consciousness in language as the instrument for discovering and constructing their identities as women and as poets in specific historical situations. The point is not simply that H.D. is mythic and Rich is autobiographical and political. The intent and reference of H.D.'s mythologizing was compulsively autobiographical: the psychological tangle of her relations with her father and mother and with those she loved—Pound, Aldington, Lawrence, Bryher—unraveled within the cataclysms of modern history. As I have shown in the H.D. chapter of *A Coherent Splendor,* even the recasting of the Greek and Trojan characters in her late anti-epic *Helen in Egypt* is still rehearsing and resolving the autobiographical riddle. Without theorizing about sexual politics in explicitly feminist terms, her poetry from the Imagist *Sea Garden* to *Helen in Egypt* and *Hermetic Definition* has contended with the masculine as oppressor and liberator. Rich's feminism pursues a more ideologized interpretation of the correlation between the psychological and the political in a patriarchal society than H.D. developed or found in her culture. Nevertheless, on its own terms *Sources,* like *Trilogy,* is a poem of parthenogenesis in which the masculine—the men in her life and the animus in her psyche—function, again but differently, as liberator and oppressor.

Autogenesis, birthing one's self, is a theme in Rich's poetry from as far back as *Snapshots of a Daughter-in-Law* (1958–60) and *Necessities of Life* (1962), which begins: "Piece by piece I seem / to re-enter the world." The second section of *Sources* begins by cautioning against any recourse (like H.D.'s) to magic ("I refuse to become a seeker for cures"), but projects the poem as a self-birthing:

> Everything that has ever
> helped me has come through what already
> lay stored in me. Old things, diffuse, unnamed, lie strong
> across my heart.

Sources evolved in twenty-three sections between August 1981 and August of the following year; the sections are of varying length, written often in pairs of unmetered lines (like *Trilogy)*, sometimes in verse paragraphs, occasionally in prose. Again as in *Trilogy,* the progress of the poem, drawing up, defining, and naming the sources of identity "already . . . stored in me" is not linear but looping and circular. It expands to contract, it focuses to open out; its revelations are at once cumulative and climactic; its returns make the point of origin a full circle.

"Sixteen years," the first phase of the first section, indicates the first turning back and turning in. She is returning to the Vermont house that occupies a special place in her life and has served in the past as an imaginative matrix—last time in the long poem "From an Old House in America," written in 1974. So it has not been literally sixteen years since she has been back to Vermont. What period, then, is she demarcating so self-consciously? As we shall see, without reverting to H.D.'s magic, the poem achieves an unexpected mandala, circling back to the squaring of square. Sixteen years from the composition of the poem in 1981–82 takes her back to 1965–66, back to what stands now as a decisive turning point in her life: her departure from New England—a poet not yet forty but already acclaimed, wife of the economist Alfred Conrad, mother of three sons—to live with her family in New York. The intervening years had brought change and trauma, both public and private, political and psychological: the Vietnam War and New Left politics, the struggle for civil rights, the Conrads' involvement in demonstrations of protest and solidarity, her husband's suicide, her sons' adolescence, her teaching in the open-admissions program at the City University of New York, her radicalization as a feminist and a lesbian. Where did those changes leave her as woman and poet?

The imagery of the first section also indicates a submersion in her earlier poetry as well as her life. The New England landscape recalls such poems as "Autumn Sequence" (1964), "From an Old House in America" (1974), and "The Spirit of Place" (1980); the vixen in the second verse paragraph is carried forward from "5:30 A.M." (1967) and "Abnegation" (1968); the queen anne's lace in the third verse paragraph repeats the description of the flower in "The Knot" (1965). Allusions from the earlier poetry thread through the text, reenforcing our awareness that Rich is concentrating her previous life toward a new clarification. She had begun dating her poems in the fifties in order to track the progress of her consciousness. In "Planetarium" (1968) she had written "seeing is changing," and in "Images for Godard" (1970), "the moment of change is the only poem." And she summed up the purpose of her poetry when she gave the autobiographical essay "When We Dead Awaken" the subtitle "Writing As Re-Vision"—that is, as change and metamorphosis.

So now it has been sixteen years since she saw the vixen in 1965 as "an omen / to me, surviving, herding her cubs," but that vixen is now "long dead." That phrase begins to reverberate, initiating the principal drama of *Sources:* the poet's confrontation with the two men, both dead, who had shaped her life as a woman and a poet: her father and her husband. A pair of poems from 1972 addressing her husband after his suicide are called "For the Dead" and "From a Survivor." The "twilight" world of the vixen may even recall the "twilight" in which the poet bids farewell to her dying father in "After Dark" (1964). The vixen raises the question of the poet's plight: survival or death. In the end, can the dead awaken? They are beyond metamorphosis. Since the course of her life had been bound to the dead, can she survive them and re-vise?

The essay "When We Dead Awaken," in *On Lies, Secrets, and Silence,* tells of her being reared by Dr. Rich as a prodigy and educated by him from the books in his library to be a poet: "So for about twenty years I wrote for a particular man, who criticized and praised me and made me feel I was indeed 'special.' " By the time she returned to him in *Sources,* she had for years identified as patriarchal oppression the paternal authority she learned from and learned to resist: "I saw myself, the eldest daughter raised as a son, taught to study but not to pray, taught to hold reading and writing sacred: the eldest daughter in the house with no son, she who must overthrow the father, take what he taught her and use it against him." Marrying Conrad soon after graduation from Radcliffe, against her father's vehement opposition, liberated Rich from "that most dangerous place, the family home." And if she soon found herself at the center of her own "family home" (also described in "When We Dead Awaken" and in *Of Woman Born*), Conrad encouraged her career and sought to help her open spaces in the domestic routine for poetry. In turn she addressed him as spousal partner in poems like "A Marriage in the 'Sixties" (1961)—"Dear fellow-particle" and "twin"—and "Like This Together" (1963)—"Sometimes at night / you are my mother . . . Sometimes / you're the wave of birth. . . . " Moreover, the poets who influenced her development even after she left her father's library were principally men. Echoes of Yeats, Frost, Stevens, Auden punctuate the early poems; Auden chose her first book for the Yale Younger Poets Award; Robert Lowell, Randall Jarrell, and John Berryman became admiring peers.

Rich's sense of intelligence and verbal mastery as masculine qualities had strong autobiographical reenforcement, as it did for H.D., and
expressed itself in a number of dialogues with her animus as the source of
her identity and poetic power. "Orion" (1965, sixteen years before
Sources) sums up in seven stanzas an identification with her animus:

> Far back when I went zig-zagging
> through the tamarack pastures
> you were my genius, you
> my cast-iron Viking, my helmed
> lion-heart king in prison.
> Years later now you're young
>
> my fierce half-brother, staring
> down through that simplified west
> your breast open, your belt dragged down
> by an oldfashioned thing, a sword
> the last bravado you won't give over
> though it weighs you down as you stride
>
> and the stars in it are dim
> and maybe have stopped burning.
> But you burn, and I know it;
> as I throw back my head to take you in
> an old transfusion happens again:
> divine astronomy is nothing to it.

In these early stanzas Rich treats Orion with ironic humor—the Viking in
cast-iron armor, Richard the Lion-Heart imprisoned in the night sky, the
swaggering adolescent with his phallicized sword—but there can be no
doubt about her envious empathy. Orion is both other and self: her "genius" and "half-brother," invulnerable to such soft feminine virtues as
pity; and Rich's note to the poem, indicating that a few phrases echo
Gottfried Benn's essay on the plight of the modern artist, underscores the
fact that the animus-figure represents her capacity as poet.

In the concluding stanzas, "indoors" is the domestic setting for the
wife-mother to "bruise and blunder," for breaking faith with herself, for
emptiness (the man finding her eyes vacant) and alienation (the woman
turning away from her image in the mirror) and fragmentation (the children "eating crumbs of my life"). Her own sense of being walled into the

house may make her see Orion with his back to the celestial wall; nevertheless, she chooses, in her imagination and for the sake of her imagination, his situation over hers. She escapes the house and opens herself to receive the "transfusion" of her twin's ego, more potent than "divine astronomy." His masculine privilege still laces her empathy with irony ("You take it all for granted"), but her incandescent identification with him gives her a "starlike eye" (a transcendent perspective and insight as well as identity). By the end of the poem her potent glance matches his, spear for sword, as she finds words for her "speechless pirate."

So now, sixteen years later, casting back to see whence she has come in order to see where she stands, Rich must confront the masculine again. In the third and fourth sections of *Sources*, a voice that seems hers but speaks in italics with her father's challenging and rebuking tone, presses on her the question of sources: *"From where does your strength come, you Southern Jew? / split at the root, raised in a castle of air?"; "With whom do you believe your lot is cast?"* The psychology and politics of gender are inseparable from the psychology and politics of race and class, of historical and geographical circumstance. Split at the root between a father Jewish in name but not in faith and a nominally Christian mother, alienated from both southern and New England values, Rich ponders the dilemma of her identity in the widening historical gyre: the oppression of women by men, of the poor by the privileged, of blacks by Klansmen, of Indians by Yankees, of the Jews by the Nazis.

Rich's Jewishness, particularly in the shadow of the Holocaust, poses the problem of identity most acutely. What is it for a woman, a radical feminist and lesbian, to be a Jew? Can she separate Jewish culture, Jewish history, from traditional Jewish faith? What is it for a nonbelieving Jew to participate in secular, patriarchal WASP culture? How can she weigh the oppression of Jewish patriarchalism toward women against the anti-Semitism that caused the Holocaust, continues to oppress Jews, men and women alike, and make deracination the price of assimilation into WASP society? In her husband she found a Jew of a different kind and social class from her father, but no more a believing and observing Jew than her father: in fact, in the end, a man whose alienation led to his death. So now she sees the two of them, whom she used to think were antagonists, tragically kin: both deracinated Jews whose sense of identity as men was defined and compromised by the anti-Semitism of their culture.

As the poem tells us, she had been brooding over her Jewishness since adolescence, and the issue presses in now, insisting on clarification.

The phrase "split at the root," which sounds like a knell throughout *Sources,* echoes her statement of the dilemma in the 1960 poem "Readings of History":

> Split at the root, neither Gentile nor Jew
> Yankee nor Rebel, born
> in the face of two ancient cults,
> I'm a good reader of histories.

Simultaneously with the writing of *Sources,* Rich was also exploring her Jewishness in an essay entitled "Split at the Root," written for the lesbian-feminist collection *Nice Jewish Girls.* Where the essay fills in the autobiographical narrative behind the poem, the poem seeks to push beyond the irresolution at the end of the essay. Through the course of the poem Rich's identity begins to take root, paradoxically, in her admission of and separation from both father and husband, and specifically in her rejection of their deracination. She does not think but *feels* her way past the paradoxes and contradictions of her situation. Her psychological probe reaches past paradox, past the empowering and constricting contentions with the masculine, to a founding sense of self as a Jewish woman. From the integrity of that perspective—"now, under a powerful, womanly lens . . . I can decipher your suffering and deny no part of my own." The acknowledgment of suffering, and of the cause of the suffering, with an unsparing love, attains a searing, healing clarity in the three prose sections of *Sources,* beyond the formal decorum of verse: the direct address to her dead father in section 7, and to her dead husband in sections 17 and the penultimate 22.

No discursive commentary can convey the concentrated catharsis of those encounters in the space opened by the ruminations of the surrounding verse passages. But those recognitions and relinquishments and self-recognitions ground Rich sufficiently to enable her to move on: "without faith" but "faithful," convinced at least that there is "something more" to being a Jew than custom, and so "wearing the star of David / / on a thin chain at my breastbone."

The painful recovery and redefinition allows the poem to speak more and more distinctly with the accents of a "woman with a mission, not to win prizes," as her ambitious father intended for her poetic career, "but to change the laws of history." This daunting ambition makes her describe herself in section 20 in the transpersonal, archetypal third person: "she is gripped by a blue, a foreign air, / a desert absolute: dragged by the roots of her own will / into another scene of choices." But the archetypal energies of the self that Rich is drawing on here enable her to conclude forcefully, even prophetically, in the first person. From that vantage she looks backward and forward in the last lines and locates her self in the sources and resources she intuited at the beginning "already / lay stored in me" embryonically; acknowledging her dead husband at the end of the poem's gestation, she stands free. The prose passage that ends *Sources* indicates not a conclusion but a renewed commitment to the difficult process of definition and construction. Through the power of womanhood reiterated in the first-person pronoun she assumes responsibility to and for "your native land, your life":

> I have wished I could rest among the beautiful and common weeds I
> can name, both here and in other tracts of the globe. But there is no
> finite knowing, no such rest. Innocent birds, deserts, morning-glo-
> ries, point to choices, leading away from the familiar. When I speak
> of an end to suffering, I don't mean anesthesia. I mean knowing the
> world, and my place in it, not in order to stare with bitterness or
> detachment, but as a powerful and womanly series of choices: and
> here I write the words, in their fullness: powerful; womanly.

Trilogy and *Sources* have required different kinds of commentary, but as poems of self-definition they have much in common. The crux for both is an engagement with the animus, and in both poems that engagement—more beneficent for H.D., more conflicted for Rich—issues in metamorphosis: the emergence of the self from the cocoon. Nevertheless, in spelling the myth differently the poems thereby spell a somewhat different myth. In the crucible of language H.D. sublimates and encodes autobiography into hieroglyphic symbol; Rich concentrates pressure on autobiographical facts to the point of revelation and release. *Trilogy* enacts autogenesis in archetypal robes; *Sources* performs it in person. (1990)

APPENDIX A: JUNG'S WRITINGS ON LITERATURE

The starting point for a thorough investigation of the history of publication of all Jung's work is volume 19 of *The Collected Works*, the *General Bibliography of C. G. Jung's Writings*, compiled by Lisa Ress with Collaborators, 1979. This volume indexes works, translations, and "subsequent revisions and/or expansions thereof, with reciprocal cross-references," through 1975, arranged by language (nineteen are represented). It cites the contents of both the original German and the subsequent English editions of Jung's *Collected Works*, coordinated on facing pages, with cross-references to the immediate predecessor of each work; finally, it lists Jung's extensive body of Seminar Notes. This book has a number of uses: one can identify exactly what was or was not available to a writer in his native language at any given time; one can trace backward to the Ur version of a work, to assess the nature and importance of changes; one can discover introductions that were influential in guiding the reader's response to Jung's work (e.g., Beatrice Hinkle's introduction to *Psychology of the Unconscious*, her 1916 translation of Jung's 1912 German book, which, after Jung's extensive revisions of 1952, was retranslated for the 1956 English *CW*, 5, and is now known as *Symbol of Transformation*).

Jung's *Psychology of the Unconscious*, in the Hinkle edition, remained in print from 1916 through 1972, and was a very important source of Jung's psychology for the English-speaking world. It represented Jung's break from Freud and provided many examples of Jung's method of amplifying the symbols of a patient's dreams by comparing them with similar archetypal motifs in literature and myth. It emphasized his belief in a correspondence between poetry's symbols and those of myth and dream. Jung believed that symbols not only accompanied but could actually cause and direct dynamic shifts in personality, an idea that had an instant and powerful appeal for artists and critics alike.

Psychological Types, or The Psychology of Individuation, the 1923 translation by the British psychiatrist H. G. Baynes of Jung's 1921 German work, indicates in its title two of Jung's signature concepts: psychological types of personality and the individuation process of personality development. This work was quickly recognized as significant (Herbert Read in 1925 called it Jung's best work). It made extensive use of literature in its argument, discussing the German poet Schiller's essay "On the Aesthetic Education of Man" as a source for Jung's own theory of personality types. Further, it presented whole sections on "The Problem of Types in Poetry" and "The Problem of Typical Attitudes in Aesthetics." Finally, where *Psychology of the Unconscious* had related art's symbols to the individual psyche, *Psychological Types* discussed the relationship of art and its symbols to society at large, and to historical periods.

H. G. Baynes and his wife, Cary Fink Baynes, translated two important works published in 1928. *Contributions to Analytical Psychology* contained fourteen essays from a variety of sources, about half previously unpublished in English, the rest scattered in journals. One of these, "On the Relation of Analytical Psychology to Poetic Art," originally translated by H. G. Baynes in 1923 for *The British Journal of Medical Psychology* from Jung's 1922 lecture in Zurich, distinguishes Jung's approach from Freud's on the question of the relationship of the artist's psyche to his art, and thus of psychology to literary criticism; it was reprinted in *CW*, 15, *The Spirit in Man, Art, and Literature*. The second translation of 1928, *Two Essays on Analytical Psychology*, though not addressed specifically to literary matters, nevertheless is important for its general reputation as a very good presentation of Jung's basic ideas.

The year 1930 saw the first English publication of the essay "Psychology and Poetry," translated by Eugene Jolas for his journal, *transition*. This essay was retranslated and retitled in 1933 as "Psychology and Literature" for the very popular book of essays *Modern Man in Search of a Soul*, trans. H. G. Dell and C. F. Baynes. Under the latter title the essay is reprinted in *CW*, 15.

In 1932 Jung published in Berlin's *Europäische Revue* a twenty-one-page essay titled "Ulysses." It was reprinted in Spanish a year later, then republished with the addition of a forenote in a 1934 book published in Zurich. Not until 1949 was it printed in English, and then only for private circulation as "Ulysses, a Monologue" by the Analytical Psychology Club of New York in its journal, *Spring 1949*. Only in 1953 (erroneously cited as 1952 in *CW*, 15) did it achieve anything approaching general circulation, in the journal *Nimbus*, as "Ulysses: A Monologue." Since then, it has been retranslated and published as "Ulysses: A Monologue" in *CW*, 15, *The Spirit in Man, Art, and Literature*. Many critics have brought an archetypal approach to Joyce's work, though none has had Jung's unique perspective on its author, as consulting analyst to Joyce's schizophrenic daughter, Lucia.

APPENDIX B: SELECTIONS EXPLAINING JUNGIAN CONCEPTS

A number of selections in this book provide material useful for understanding the basic terms of Jung's psychology. Indeed, one goal of the book has been to present an interdisciplinary description/definition of important terms, both from the psychologist's and the literary critic's point of view. Not only the historical development of Jung's psychology, but also the antipathy of its author toward the rigid thinking so often associated with schools of thought, argue for a descriptive approach to the problem of explaining concepts and terminology.

Both disciplines have provided helpful source material. The concise explanation of terms by the analyst and critic Joseph Henderson, substantially buttressed by Jaffé's excerpts from Jung's *Collected Works,* was the foundation for the Glossary following the Notes. Samuels's 1986 *Dictionary of Jungian Analysis* provides descriptive definitions of four key terms. Authors offering a more comprehensive discussion of concepts are analysts Jacoby, who reviews at length Jung's writings on literature, and Maduro and Wheelwright. From the literary critics come analyses of key terms at specific historical moments (Frye, Baird, Willeford, Adams). And Philipson adduces numerous quotations from Jung's works as the basis for his philosophical/literary analyses of Jung's concept of the symbol.

NOTES

CHAPTER 1

1. T. S. Eliot, *The Dial*, November 1923.

2. Bronislaw Malinowski, "Magic, Science, and Religion," in *Science, Religion and Reality*, ed. Joseph Needham (London: The Sheldon Press, 1926), p. 69.

3. Freud, *Totem and Tabu*, p. 260.

4. Ibid., p. 268.

5. T. S. Eliot, *The Listener*, March 30, 1932.

6. C. G. Jung, *The Integration of the Personality*, trans. S. M. Dell (London: Kegan Paul, 1940), p. 25.

7. C. G. Jung, *Psychological Types, or The Psychology of Individuation*, trans. H. G. Baynes (London: Kegan Paul, 1923), p. 272.

8. C. G. Jung, "On the Relation of Analytical Psychology to Poetic Art," in *Contributions to Analytical Psychology*, trans. H. G. Baynes and C. F. Baynes (London: Kegan Paul, 1928), p. 247.

9. See, particularly, *The Psychology of the Unconscious*, trans. B. M. Hinkle (London: Kegan Paul, 1921), which contains Jung's own theory of the meaning of the Oedipus complex.

10. C. G. Jung, *Two Essays on Analytical Psychology*, trans. H. G. Baynes and C. F. Baynes (London: Baillière Tindall and Cox, 1928), p. 268.

CHAPTER 3

1. C. G. Jung, *Modern Man in Search of a Soul*, trans. W. S. Dell and Cary F. Baynes (New York: Harcourt, Brace and Co., 1933), pp. 159, 160–61.

2. C. G. Jung, *The Psychology of the Unconscious*, trans. Beatrice M. Hinkle (New York: Dodd, Mead and Co., 1931), pp. 360 et passim.

3. *Modern Man in Search of a Soul*, p. 165.

4. Jolande Jacobi, *Complex/Archetype/Symbol in the Psychology of C. G. Jung*, trans. Ralph Manheim (New York: Bollingen Series 57, published by Princeton University Press, 1959), p. 60.

5. "The Problem of Types in Poetry," in C. G. Jung, *Psychological Types, or the Psychology of Individuation*, trans. H. Godwin Baynes (New York: Harcourt, Brace and Co., 1923), p. 262.

6. C. G. Jung, "Mind and Earth," in *Civilization in Transition*, vol. 10 of *The Collected Works of C. G. Jung*, trans. R. F. C. Hull; ed. Herbert Read, Michael Fordham, and Gerhard Adler; exec. ed. (from 1967), William McGuire, 20 vols. Bollingen Series 20 (Princeton, N.J.: Princeton University Press, 1964), p. 31. Hereafter cited as *CW*.

7. C. G. Jung, *Psychology and Religion: West and East*, vol. 11 of *CW* (1958), p. 50.

8. C. G. Jung, "Concerning the Archetypes and the Anima Concept," in *The Archetypes and the Collective Unconscious*, vol. 9, pt. 1, of *CW* (1959), p. 69, n. 27.

9. C. G. Jung, "On the Nature of the Psyche," in *The Structure and Dynamics of the Psyche*, vol. 8 of *CW* (1960), pp. 213–14.

10. I refer to critical studies, in vogue earlier in this century, which belong to a school inspired by German literary studies of "Einflusse."

11. In the work of Stevens, see, in particular, "Chocorua to Its Neighbor" and "The Auroras of Autumn."

12. Joseph Campbell, *The Hero with a Thousand Faces* (Princeton, N.J.: Princeton University Press, Bollingen Series 17, 1968), p. 382.

13. Jung's regard for *Moby-Dick* is well known: he called it "the greatest American novel." See *Modern Man in Search of a Soul*, p. 154.

14. "The Problem of Types in Poetry," p. 326.

15. Ibid., p. 335.

16. *The Enchafed Flood* (New York: Random House, 1950), p. 76.

17. Campbell, *Hero with a Thousand Faces*, p. 12.

18. Jung, *Psychology of the Unconscious*, p. 35.

19. Ibid., p. 480.

20. Ibid.

21. In my study of Stevens, *The Dome and the Rock* (Baltimore: Johns Hopkins University Press, 1968), I have demonstrated the seasonal passages of the poetry. After the study was published, I became aware that I should have admitted some of the premises of Jung under discussion here.

22. Jung, *Modern Man in Search of a Soul*, p. 167.

23. Ibid., pp. 156–57.

24. Ibid., p. 169.

25. Ibid., p. 171.

26. Jung, "The Problem of Types in Poetry," p. 238.

27. Jung, *Modern Man in Search of a Soul*, p. 158.

28. Jung, "Some Meanings of Myth," in *Myth and Mythmaking*, ed. Henry A. Murray (New York: George Braziller, 1960), pp. 108–9.

29. See Jacobi, *Complex/Archetype/Symbol*, p. 85.

30. Jung, "The Problem of Types in Poetry," pp. 229–30.

31. Ibid., p. 231.

32. Note, for instance, his observation on the return of a pagan "licentiousness . . . exemplified by life in our large modern cities." *Psychology of the Unconscious*, p. 258.

33. Northrop Frye, *The Anatomy of Criticism* (Princeton, N.J.: Princeton University Press, 1957), p. 6.

34. Ibid., p. 7.

CHAPTER 4

1. C. G. Jung, "The Type Problem in Aesthetics," in *Psychological Types*, CW, 6:296–97.

2. Erich Neumann, *Art and the Creative Unconscious*, trans. Ralph Manheim, Bollingen Series 61 (New York: Pantheon, 1959), pp. 89–90.

3. Ibid., p. 91.

4. Ibid., p. 94.

5. Ibid., p. 100.

6. Ibid., p. 105.

7. Thomas Mann, *Doctor Faustus,* trans. H. T. Lowe-Porter (New York: Knopf, 1948).

8. Otto Rank, *Beyond Psychology* (Camden, N.J.: Haddon Craftsmen, 1941).

9. Ira Progoff, *Death and Rebirth of Psychology* (New York: Julian Press, 1956).

10. Aniela Jaffé, "Symbolism in the Visual Arts," in C. G. Jung and M.-L. von Franz, *Man and His Symbols* (New York: Doubleday, 1964).

11. Joseph Campbell, *The Masks of God,* vol. 4 of *Creative Mythology* (New York: Viking, 1968), p. 567.

12. Rosemary Gordon, "Symbols: Content and Process," *Journal of Analytical Psychology* 12, no. 1 (January 1967): 30–32.

CHAPTER 5

1. C. G. Jung, *Memories, Dreams, Reflections* (New York: Random House, 1963), pp. 154–55.

2. Ibid., p. 150.

3. Ibid., p. 151.

4. Ibid., p. 363.

5. E. Jones, *The Life and Work of Sigmund Freud,* 3 vols. (New York: Basic Books, 1955), 2:140.

6. Jung, *CW,* 6:485.

7. Ibid., 9, pt. 1, p. 5, n. 9.

8. Ibid., 6:474.

9. Jung, *CW,* 6:475.

10. Ibid., p. 476.

11. Jung, *CW,* 11:330–31.

12. Jung, *CW,* 7.

13. W. Dement, "Psychophysiology of Sleep and Dreams," in *American Handbook of Psychiatry,* 3 vols. (New York and London: Basic Books, 1959–66), 3:290–332.

14. Jung, *CW,* 8:253.

15. Jacobi, *Die Psychologie von C. G. Jung: Eine Einführung,* 4th rev. ed. (Zurich: Rascher, 1959), p. 127.

16. (1) "On the Relations between Analytical Psychology and Literature"; (2) "Psychology and Literature"; (3) "Ulysses"; all in *CW,* 15.

17. Quoted by W. F. Otto, in *Theophania* (Hamburg: Rowohlt Taschenbuch, 1959), p. 107.

18. Goethe, *Conversations with Eckermann* (New York: E. P. Dutton, 1960).

19. R. M. Rilke, *Sämtliche Werke,* 6 vols. (Wiesbaden: Insel-Verlag, 1955–66), 1: 655.

20. (Frankfurt am Main: Fischer, 1967).

21. See, for instance, W. Muschg, "Psychoanalyse und Literatur-wissenschaft," in *Pamphlet und Bekenntnis* (Olten: Walter-Verlag, 1968).

22. W. Emrich, "Wertung und Rangordnung literarischer Werke," in *Sprache im technischen Zeitalter* 12 (1964): 983.

23. W. Muschg, *Tragische Literaturgeschichte* (Bern: A. Francke, 1953), p. 262.

CHAPTER 6

1. Ovid *Metamorphoses* 8.203–6, trans. Horace Gregory (New York: The Viking Press, 1958), pp. 211–12.

2. C. G. Jung, *Analytical Psychology, Its Theory and Practice* (New York: Pantheon Books, 1968), pp. 11–14.

3. Ibid., pp. 21–25.

4. Ibid., p. 8.

5. Ibid., pp. 40–41.

6. James Joyce, *Ulysses* (Paris: Shakespeare and Company, 4th printing, 1924), p. 552; reprint (New York: Random House, 1934), p. 574.

7. Innocentii III, *Epistolae*, bk. VII, no. 75, in Migne, *Patrologia Latina*, 215: 355–57.

8. T. S. Eliot, *Collected Poems 1909–1962* (New York: Harcourt, Brace and World, 1963), p. 55.

9. *Bṛhadāraṇyaka Upanishad* 5.2.

CHAPTER 8

1. *The Poems of Emily Dickinson*, ed. Thomas H. Johnson (Cambridge, Mass.: Harvard University Press, 1955).

2. Albert Gelpi, *The Tenth Muse: The Psyche of the American Poet* (Cambridge, Mass.: Harvard University Press, 1975), pp. 247ff.; see also Albert Gelpi, *Emily Dickinson: The Mind of the Poet* (Cambridge, Mass.: Harvard University Press, 1965), pp. 109–15.

3. *Prose Works 1892*, ed. Floyd Stovall (New York: New York University Press, 1963), 1:250.

4. *The Letters of Emily Dickinson*, ed. Thomas H. Johnson and Theodora Ward (Cambridge, Mass.: Harvard University Press, 1958), 2: 474. For volcano poems, see *Poems*, 3: 1141, 1153, and 1174.

CHAPTER 9

1. That psyche (like the cosmos) is numerically and rhythmically organized is one of the principal tenets of the *Timaeus*; that the heart, too, is so organized we learn from ancient medical writers—cf. W. B. Stanford, *The Sound of Greek* (Berkeley: University of California Press, 1967), pp. 36–37: "Galen, quoting an earlier medical writer, says that there is a similarity between the systolic and diastolic beats of the pulse and the arsis and thesis of a metrical foot. . . . [W]hatever Galen's exact meaning may be, his statement emphasizes the fact that even in our bloodstream there is both stress and time. Our pulse beat is a built-in measure of rhythm."

CHAPTER 10

1. C. G. Jung and A. Jaffé, *Memories, Dreams, Reflections*, trans. R. Winston and C. Winston (New York: Pantheon, 1961).

2. S. Leavy, "A Footnote to Jung's 'Memories,' " *Psychoanalytic Quarterly* 33 (1964): 567–74.

3. *CW*, 7, §183. For more on the daimon as allotter of fate, see B. C. Dietrich, *Death Fate and the Gods* (London: Athlone, 1967), pp. 18, 57.

4. Cf. R. Grinnell, "Reflections on the Archetype of Consciousness—Personality and Psychological Faith," *Spring 1970* (Zurich/New York: Spring Publications, 1970), pp. 30–39.

5. "The Study of Images I," *The Collected Poems of Wallace Stevens*, p. 463.

6. Cf. R. F. C. Hull, "Bibliographical Notes on Active Imagination in the Works of C. G. Jung," *Spring 1971* (Zurich/New York: Spring Publications, 1971), pp. 115–20, for a full list of passages.

7. *CW* 14, §707 ff. (part 6, 6, "Self-Knowledge").

8. That self-knowledge is endless is not only Heraclitean (the soul is without end) and Socratic (self-knowledge is ultimately the study of dying, as well as of the Divine—*First Alcibiades* 127d ff., also where *self* is interpreted as *soul*), it is also Judeo-Islamic, where "Know Thyself" means, fundamentally, knowledge of God (*Homo imago Dei*): "He who knows himself knows his Lord." Cf. A. Altmann, "The Delphic Maxim in Medieval Islam and Judaism," in his *Studies in Religious Philosophy and Mysticism* (London: Routledge, 1969), pp. 1–40, with rich notes. In keeping with this tradition I have in this paper consistently understood the Delphic "self" as "soul,": *nefesh, nafs, nafashu, psyché, anima.*

9. Jung's discussion in the last part of the *Mysterium Coniunctionis* concerning self-knowledge and active imagination returns continually to Mercurius, who seems thus to be both the secret (hermetic) "knower" and the object of the knowing (*CW*, 14, §§705 to end).

10. Wolfgang Giegerich, "Ontogeny = Phylogeny?" *Spring 1975* (New York/Zurich: Spring Publications), p. 118.

11. My "On Senex Consciousness," *Spring 1970* (New York/Zurich: Spring Publications), pp. 146–65. Also on Saturn from the psychological viewpoint, see A. Vitale, "Saturn: The Transformation of the Father," in *Fathers and Mothers: Essays by Five Hands* (New York/Zurich: Spring Publications), pp. 5–39.

12. Patricia Berry, "An Approach to the Dream," in her *Echo's Subtle Body* (Dallas: Spring Publications, 1982).

13. Fowler, *Critical Terms*, see s.v. "Hero."

14. On Saturn and reduction, see P. Berry, "On Reduction," in *Echo's Subtle Body*, and my "The 'Negative' Senex and a Renaissance Solution," *Spring 1975* (New York/Zurich: Spring Publications), pp. 88ff.

15. Annabel M. Patterson, *Hermogenes and the Renaissance: Seven Ideas of Style* (Princeton, N.J.: Princeton University Press, 1970).

CHAPTER 11

A NOTE ON CITATIONS

All current editions of *Lady Chatterley's Lover* are textually corrupt, and since the definitive text is not yet complete, we quote from the Florence edition of 1928, which Lawrence supervised. For the convenience of readers, however, we cite page numbers of the Grove Press "Black Cat" edition, widely available in America.

The following abbreviations of frequently cited sources are used throughout the chapter:

CL   *The Collected Letters of D. H. Lawrence.* Edited by Harry T. Moore. 2 vols. New York: Viking, 1962.

FLC   Version 1 of *Lady Chatterley's Lover,* published as *The First Lady Chatterley.* New York: Dial, 1944. Reprint. London: Heinemann, 1972.

JTLJ   Version 2 of *Lady Chatterley's Lover,* published as *John Thomas and Lady Jane.* London: Heinemann, 1972; New York: Viking, 1972.

LCL   Version 3 of *Lady Chatterley's Lover.* Florence: Orioli, 1928. Reprint. New York: Grove, Revised Black Cat Edition, 1982.

Phoenix   *Phoenix: The Posthumous Papers of D. H. Lawrence.* Edited by Edward D. McDonald. 1936. Reprint. New York: Viking, 1972.

Phoenix II *Phoenix II: Uncollected, Unpublished, and Other Prose Works by D. H. Lawrence.* Edited by Warren Roberts and Harry T. Moore. New York: Viking, 1970.

1. The distinction is Leslie Fiedler's, although he phrases it as the difference between "archetypal literature" and "literature about archetypes." See "Archetype and Signature," in *Art and Psychoanalysis,* ed. William Phillips (Cleveland and New York: Meridian Books, 1963), pp. 454–72.

2. Robert Graves, *The Greek Myths* (Harmondsworth: Penguin, 1975), 1:68.

3. D. H. Lawrence, *Apocalypse* (New York: Viking, 1966), p. 47; hereafter cited in the text as *A.*

4. D. H. Lawrence, *Women in Love,* ed. Charles L. Ross (New York: Viking, 1982), pp. 66, 239, 213.

5. Although another essay would be required to do full justice to the topic, of more than passing interest here is Mr. Noon as a portrait of H. G. Wells, who was legendary for the triangular configurations of his sexual relationships and an author with whom Lawrence shared a common background and with whom he felt a degree of competitiveness. It can be conjectured that, despite Lawrence's remark to Blanche Jennings that Wells's *The War of the Worlds* was "not worth reading" (*CL,* 54), his description of the sexual triangle as a "tripod" recalls for us the mechanical tripods of the Martians in that novel which enable them to overcome earth's stronger gravity and *almost* conquer England. More to our purpose, however, is that after their defeat on Earth the Martians apparently succeeded in invading Venus, leaving the narrator to conclude: "It may be that in the larger design of the universe this invasion from Mars is not without its ultimate benefit for men; it has robbed us of that serene confidence in the future which is the most fruitful source of decadence." See *The War of the Worlds* (New York: Lancer Books, 1967), p. 251.

6. D. H. Lawrence, *Fantasia of the Unconscious,* in *"Psychoanalysis and the Unconscious" and "Fantasia of the Unconscious"* (New York: Viking, 1960), pp. 210–12; hereafter cited in the text as *FU.*

7. D. H. Lawrence, *The Plumed Serpent* (New York: Viking Books, 1959), p. 463.

8. D. H. Lawrence, *Etruscan Places* (New York: Viking, 1957), p. 123.

9. For a detailed discussion of the essential generic differences between the

three versions, see Evelyn J. Hinz, "Pornography, Novel, Mythic Narrative: The Three Versions of *Lady Chatterley's Lover*," *Modernist Studies* 3, no. 2 (1979): 35–47.

10. Our attention was drawn to this specific change by Michael Squires, who, however, argues for an autobiographical explanation of its significance. See "New Light on the Gamekeeper in *Lady Chatterley's Lover*," *D. H. Lawrence Review* 11, no. 3 (Fall 1978): 234–45.

11. Oriented toward "proletarian" fiction, Kingsley Widmer finds this change "morally" well-taken but lacking in "plausibility." See "The Pertinence of Modern Pastoral: The Three Versions of *Lady Chatterley's Lover*," *Studies in the Novel* 5 (Fall 1973): 302.

12. See Mark Spilka, "Lawrence Versus Peeperkorn on Abdication; or *What Happens to a Pagan Vitalist When the Juice Runs Out*," in *D. H. Lawrence: The Man Who Lived*, ed. Robert B. Partlow, Jr., and Harry T. Moore (Carbondale: Southern Illinois University Press, 1980), pp. 105–20, 274–76. Spilka's approach is not mythic, however, but Freudian.

13. For a provocative discussion of how critics who adopt the "fertility myth" approach distort the meaning of many of Lawrence's works, see Charles Rossman, "Myth and Misunderstanding D. H. Lawrence," in *Twentieth-Century Poetry, Fiction, and Theory*, ed. Harry R. Garvin (Lewisburg, Pa.: Bucknell University Press, 1977), pp. 81–101.

14. See Keith Sagar, *The Art of D. H. Lawrence* (Cambridge: Cambridge University Press, 1966), pp. 193–96.

CHAPTER 12

1. Lewis Thomas, *The Medusa and the Snail* (New York: Viking, 1979), p. 39.

2. C. G. Jung, *Psychological Reflections* (New York: Harper & Row, 1953), p. 94.

3. Ibid., p. 97.

4. See Annis V. Pratt, "Archetypal Approaches to the New Feminist Criticism," *Bucknell Review* 21, no. 1 (Spring 1973): 3–14.

5. See, for example, Lillian Robinson's "Dwelling in Decencies: Radical Criticism and the Feminist Perspective," *College English* 32, no. 8 (May 1971): 879–89.

6. Naomi R. Goldenberg, *Changing of the Gods: Feminism and the End of Traditional Religions* (Boston: Beacon Press, 1979), p. 62.

7. Ann Bedford Ulanov, *The Feminine in Jungian Psychology and in Christian Theology* (Evanston, Ill.: Northwestern University Press, 1971), p. x.

8. See Emma Jung and Marie-Louise von Franz, *The Grail Legend* (New York: Putnam's, 1970); M. Esther Harding, *Woman's Mysteries: Ancient and Modern* (New York: Bantam, 1971), and Marie Louise von Franz, *Problems of the Feminine in Fairy Tales* (Zurich: Spring Publications, 1972).

9. June Singer, "The Age of Androgyny," *Quadrant* 8, no. 2 (Winter 1975): 92, and letter to the author, September 25, 1976.

10. Naomi R. Goldenberg, "A Feminist Critique of Jung," *Signs* 2, no. 2 (Winter 1976): 448.

11. Medusa is one example. See Annis V. Pratt, " 'Aunt Jennifer's Tigers': Notes Toward a Preliterary History of Women's Archetypes," *Feminist Studies* 4, no. 1 (Feb. 1978): 163–94.

12. Maud Bodkin, *Archetypal Patterns in Poetry* (London: Oxford University Press, 1973), p. 305. Bodkin strongly dislikes the psychological dependence of Dante on the "Mother-Imago": "Within my own experience it is only as I relate the dialogue and description of the vision to the movement of the poem in its completeness that I can pass beyond the feeling of revulsion against what seems the dominance in the mind of Dante of the Mother-Imago" (p. 178). Although she does not attribute her revulsion to any realization that such an obsession has less appeal (in the form of sublimated love for the spiritualized feminine) for women than for men, she states that "the attempt to trace the form assumed in poetry by the archetypal images of man and woman suggested the inquiry whether one could find in the poetry of women writers any imaginative representation of man, related to the distinctive inner life of a woman in the same manner as an image of woman appearing in poetry shows relation to the emotional life of man" (pp. 290–91).

13. See Annis V. Pratt, *Archetypal Patterns in Women's Fiction* (Bloomington: Indiana University Press, 1981), chap. 8.

14. C. G. Jung and C. Kerényi, *Essays on a Science of Mythology: The Myth of the Divine Child and the Mysteries of Eleusis*, trans. R. F. C. Hull (Princeton, N.J.: Princeton University Press, 1950), p. 177; and as quoted in C. Kerényi, *Eleusis—Archetypal Images of Mother and Daughter*, trans. Ralph Manheim (New York: Schocken, 1971), pp. xxi–xxxii.

15. Jean Bethke Elshtain, "Feminist Discourse and Its Discontents: Language, Power, and Meaning," *Signs* 7, no. 3 (Spring 1982): 618.

16. The researcher's name was Dr. Rosalinde Schindler, at Wayne State College of Lifelong Learning.

17. Carol Christ, "Spiritual Quest and Women's Experience," *Anima* 1, no. 2 (Spring 1975): 6.

CHAPTER 14

1. M. Kettner, "Some Archetypal Themes in Homosexuality," *Proceedings of the Fifteenth Annual Joint Meeting of the Northern and Southern California Societies of Jungian Analysts* (San Francisco: C. G. Jung Institute, 1967), pp. 34–35.

2. Cf. M. Fordham, *New Developments in Analytical Psychology* (London: Routledge & Kegan Paul, 1957), and E. Osterman, "The Tendency Toward Patterning and Order in Matter and in the Psyche," in J. Wheelwright, ed., *The Reality of the Psyche* (New York: G. P. Putnam's Sons, 1968), pp. 14–27.

3. M. Fordham, *Children as Individuals* (New York: G. P. Putnam's Sons, 1969), p. 96.

4. J. Jacobi, *Complex/Archetype/Symbol in the Psychology of C. G. Jung* (Princeton, N.J.: Princeton University Press, 1959).

5. J. Perry, "Reconstitutive Process in the Psychopathology of the Self," *Annals of the New York Academy of Sciences* 96 (1961): 853–76.

6. Jung, vol. 5 of *CW* (1911, 1956); and vol. 9, pt. 1 (1940), pp. 113–50.

7. J. Henderson, *Thresholds of Initiation* (Middletown, Conn.: Wesleyan University Press, 1967).

8. Cf. *CW*, vol. 9, pt. 1, pp. 151–81; R. Maduro, "Journey Dreams in Latino Group Psychotherapy," *Psychotherapy: Theory, Research and Practice* 13, no. 2 (1976): 148–77; M.-L. von Franz, *The Problem of the Puer Aeternus* (New York: Spring Publications, 1970).

9. F. Fordham, *An Introduction to Jung's Psychology* (Baltimore: Penguin Books, 1953), p. 53.

CHAPTER 15

1. H. Ellenberger, *The Discovery of the Unconscious* (London: Allen Lane; New York: Basic Books, 1970); E. Neumann, *The Origins and History of Consciousness* (London: Routledge & Kegan Paul, 1954); J. Hillman, *Re-Visioning Psychology* (New York: Harper & Row, 1975); and M. Williams, "The Indivisibility of the Personal and Collective Unconscious," in *Analytical Psychology: A Modern Science*, ed. M. Fordham et al. (London: Heinemann, 1973).

2. R. Money-Kyrle, *Collected Papers*, ed. D. Meltzer (Strath Tay, Perthshire: Clunie Press, 1978); A. Samuels, *Jung and the Post-Jungians* (London and Boston: Routledge & Kegan Paul, 1985).

3. R. Sheldrake, *A New Science of Life* (Boulder, Colo., and London: Shambhala, 1981).

4. R. Otto, *The Idea of the Holy* (1917; London: Oxford University Press, 1923).

CHAPTER 17

1. In his *Eleusis: Archetypal Image of Mother and Daughter*, trans. Ralph Manheim (New York: Pantheon, 1967), pp. xxvi–xxvii.

2. Ibid., p. xxxii.

3. "The Structure of the Psyche," *CW*, 2d ed., 8:152.

4. "Psychology of the Child Archetype," *CW*, 2d ed., vol. 9, pt. 1, pp. 152–53.

5. For myths as traditional tales, see G. S. Kirk, *The Nature of Greek Myths* (Harmondsworth: Penguin, 1974), pp. 27–28. For a relatively adequate definition of myth, see Lauri Honko, "The Problem of Defining Myth," in *The Myth of the State*, ed. Haralds Beizais (Stockholm: Almqvist, 1972), pp. 7–19; reprinted in *Sacred Narrative: Readings in the Theory of Myth*, ed. Alan Dundes (Berkeley: University of California Press, 1984), p. 49.

6. See, for example, "The Structural Study of Myth," in *Structural Anthropology*, vol. 1, trans. Claire Jacobson and Brooke G. Schoepf (New York: Basic Books, 1963), pp. 206–31; *The Savage Mind* (Chicago: University of Chicago Press, 1966); "The Story of Asdiwal" and "Four Winnebago Myths," *Structural Anthropology*, vol. 2, trans. Monique Layton (New York: Basic Books, 1976), pp. 146–210.

7. Kerényi, *Eleusis*, p. xxviii.

8. *Art and the Creative Unconscious: Four Essays*, trans. Ralph Manheim (Princeton, N.J.: Princeton University Press, 1959), pp. 108–9.

9. Kerényi, p. xxxii.

10. Kirk, *Nature of Greek Myths*, p. 278.

11. Ibid., pp. 277–86.

12. In "Der ursprüngliche Mythos im Lichte der Sympathie von Mensch und Welt," in his *Mythos und Welt* (Stuttgart: Ernst Klett, 1962), pp. 230–66.

13. Goethe quoted and briefly discussed by Otto in "Die Sprache als Mythos," *Mythos und Welt*, p. 284; my English translation.

14. In "Ordo Amoris," *Selected Philosophical Essays*, trans. David R. Lachterman (Evanston, Ill.: Northwestern University Press, 1973), p. 122 (italics in Lachterman's ed.).

15. Otto, *Mythos und Welt*, p. 284.

16. See Joseph F. Rychlak, *Introduction to Personality and Psychotherapy: A Theory-Construction Approach* (Boston: Houghton-Mifflin, 1973), p. 4.

17. *Images and Symbols: Studies in Religious Symbolism*, trans. Philip Mairet (1961; New York: Search-Sheed, 1969), p. 59.

18. Polanyi and Prosch, *Meaning*, pp. 124–25.

19. Eliade, *Images and Symbols*, p. 59.

20. For Zeus and Hera, see Homer *Iliad* 14.346ff.

21. *CW*, 2d ed., 8:211–12.

22. *The Idea of the Holy: An Inquiry into the Non-Rational Factor in the Idea of the Divine and Its Relation to the Rational*, 2d ed., trans. John W. Harvey (London: Oxford University Press, 1950), pp. 25–30.

23. See Matthew Fox's Introduction to *Breakthrough: Meister Eckhart's Creation Spirituality in New Translation*, trans. M. Fox et al. (Garden City, N.Y.: Doubleday, 1980), p. 44.

CHAPTER 18

1. Ira Progoff, *Jung's Psychology and Its Social Meaning* (New York: Grove Press, 1953), p. 281.

2. Ibid., p. 187.

3. Sigmund Freud, *Beyond the Pleasure Principle* (New York: Liveright, 1950), p. 72.

4. Edward Glover, *Freud or Jung?* (New York: Meridian Books, 1957), p. 173.

5. Ernest Cassirer, *An Essay on Man* (New Haven: Yale University Press, 1944), p. 25 (italics mine).

6. Glover, p. 174.

7. Ibid.

8. William York Tindall, *The Literary Symbol* (Bloomington: Indiana University Press, 1955), p. 6.

CHAPTER 19

1. Tzvetan Todorov, *The Conquest of America*, trans. Richard Howard (New York: Harper & Row, 1984), pp. 153, 182, and 249.

2. Christopher Norris, *Deconstruction: Theory and Practice* (London and New York: Methuen, 1982), p. 31.

3. Jonathan Culler quotes this passage from *Positions* in *On Deconstruction: Theory and Criticism after Structuralism* (Ithaca, N.Y.: Cornell University Press, 1982), pp. 156–66. Culler notes that for some inexplicable reason the English translation of the French edition of *Positions* omits the first sentence of this passage.

4. Ibid., p. 166.

5. Todorov, *Conquest of America*, p. 254.

6. Culler quotes this passage in *On Deconstruction*, p. 188.

7. Ibid., p. 189.

8. *Dissemination*, trans. Barbara Johnson (Chicago: University of Chicago Press, 1981), p. 262.

9. Hillman derives the term "imaginal" from Henri Corbin. See Corbin, "*Mundus Imaginalis*: or the Imaginary and the Imaginal," *Spring* (1972), pp. 1–19.

10. Hillman, *Inter Views* (New York: Harper & Row, 1983), p. 57.

11. Hillman, *Re-Visioning Psychology* (New York: Harper & Row, 1977), p. 8. According to Hillman, the interest in symbology on the part of both Freudian and Jungian analysts is an excessive, even obsessive, preoccupation: "When I am asked, as it often happens in the discussion following a lecture, 'Why don't you speak of symbols?' . . . I usually reply with a confession: I come from Zurich; for the past quarter-century I have lived in a world of symbols. They no longer hold my attention. Everyone in Zurich speaks of symbols, looks them up, writes theses on them . . . and I too have worked on them. This is because it is said by the Zurich school that one cannot understand psychic materials, dreams especially, without a knowledge of symbols."

The concern with symbology is not, as Hillman observes, a vice peculiar to the Zurich school; it is also a shibboleth of the Vienna school—as proof he quotes the passage from *The Interpretation of Dreams* where Freud insists that a knowledge of symbols is a necessary supplement to the method of free association ("An Inquiry into Image," *Spring* [1977], p. 62). It is Erich Neumann in *The Great Mother* who perpetrates what is perhaps the most egregiously reductionistic unintentional parody of the symbological method. In *The Dream and the Underworld* (New York: Harper & Row, 1979), Hillman notes that for Neumann virtually every "female figure and image become 'symbols' of the 'Great Mother.' " Hillman comments: "If one's research shows results of this kind, i.e. where all data indicate one dominant hypothesis, then it is time to ask a psychological question about the hypothesis" (p. 216n.).

12. *The Dream and the Underworld*, p. 123.

13. Ibid., pp. 74–75. "The logic of oppositions and all their kinds (contradictories, contraries, polarities, complementaries), whether the opposites are formal only or material as well, and then whether the pair of terms together are exhaustive, all this, as well as the metaphysical structure of dualism that seems both to require and imply oppositional logic," Hillman says, is a vast subject, but one with special relevance for depth psychology, which was "conceived by Freud and even more by Jung in terms of opposites" (p. 75).

14. *C. G. Jung Speaking*, ed. William McGuire and R. F. C. Hull (Princeton, N.J.: Princeton University Press, 1977), pp. 309–10.

15. Ibid., pp. 322–23.

16. *Re-Visioning Psychology,* p. 39.

17. *Inter Views,* pp. 53–54.

18. Ibid., p. 54.

19. Ibid., p. 58.

20. "An Inquiry into Image," p. 68.

21. Ibid., p. 86.

22. Ibid., p. 87.

23. *Re-Visioning Psychology,* pp. 153–54.

24. *Inter Views,* pp. 56–67.

25. "An Inquiry into Image," p. 85.

26. See "Further Notes on Images," *Spring* (1978), pp. 152–82. For more on polysemy in imaginal psychology, see Paul Kugler, *The Alchemy of Discourse: An Archetypal Approach to Language* (Lewisburg, Pa.: Bucknell University Press, 1982), pp. 89–95 and 109–12.

CHAPTER 20

1. For a biography of Olson, see Charles Boer, *Charles Olson in Connecticut* (Chicago: Swallow Press, 1975).

2. "Notes for the Proposition: Man Is Prospective," *Boundary 2,* vol. 2, nos. 1/ 2 (Fall 1973): 2.

3. Ibid., p. 4.

4. Boer, p. 136.

5. "Proprioception, in *Charles Olson: Additional Prose,* ed. George Butterick (Bolinas: Four Seasons Foundation, 1974), p. 17.

6. Ibid., p. 18.

7. "Mayan Letters," in Charles Olson, *Selected Writings,* ed. Robert Creeley (New York: New Directions, 1966), p. 83.

8. Ibid., p. 84.

9. *The Pound Era* (Berkeley: University of California Press, 1971), p. 179.

10. A grand, if radical, exception would be Christopher Caudwell's classic Marxist study, *Illusion and Reality* (London: Macmillan and Company, 1937). For Caudwell, however, the psyche is an "illusion" for poets, because "the instincts *unadapted* are blind and unfree. . . . Thus, knowing the essence of this bourgeois illusion to be a special belief concerning 'individualism' or the 'natural man,' which in turn derives from the conditions of bourgeois economy, we cannot be surprised that the bourgeois poet is the lonely man who, apparently turning away from society into himself, by so doing expresses the more strongly the essential relations of contemporary society. Bourgeois poetry is individualistic because it expresses the collective emotion of its era" (p. 71). Caudwell views psyche (and poetry) through the literalizing and single-minded lens of Marxist theory, and the results are predictable. But at least he has a view of psyche and its relationship to poetry!

11. Michael Reck, *Ezra Pound; A Close-Up* (New York: McGraw-Hill, 1967), p. 80.

12. "About Olson, Pound would only say irritatedly that he was concerned with abstractions, not with verse (probably referring to Olson's theoretical essays about poetry)" (ibid., p. 87).

13. Charles Altieri, "Olson's Poetics and the Tradition," in *Boundary 2*, vol. 2, nos. 1/2 (Fall 1973): 179.

14. Cited in ibid., p. 178.

15. Ibid., p. 179.

16. "As of Form," in *The Journal of the Charles Olson Archives*, no. 5 (Spring 1976): 22.

17. Charles Olson, "ABCs(2)," *Archaeologist of Morning* (New York: Grossman Publishers, 1970).

18. Peter Kugler and I have addressed the question of direct realism, and its implicit revision of many traditional psychological notions, in "Archetypal Psychology Is Mythical Realism," in *Spring 1977*. We show there (following James Gibson and James Hillman along different but converging routes) how perception is an unmediated process that constantly picks up information from what we call "the environmental unconscious." A direct realist view of psyche is our way of stating Olson's "abstractions" on poetry, his unparalleled vision of an imaginative participation in "what all beings share by being alive."

19. In 1953, Olson, as Rector of Black Mountain College in North Carolina, decided to conduct an "Institute" on what he called "The New Sciences of Man." Among others, he invited Jung to attend. Jung sent regrets that he was too ill to travel but asked his colleague Marie-Louise von Franz to represent him for the occasion, which she did. As preparation for the students, Olson gave a series of lectures on the subject, including what he considered his own specialty, "The Science of Image." The title derived from lengthy ruminations on Jung and Kerényi's *Essays Toward a Science of Mythology*. Olson felt disturbed by the title and finally wrote to the poet Robert Creeley that the concept of mythology as a "science" was "crap." The real science, he decided, was a "science of the image." These lectures are now available in *The Olson Journal*, ed. George Butterick, no. 10 (Fall 1978), which can be obtained from the University of Connecticut Library, Storrs, Connecticut.

CHAPTER 21

1. The three chief titles, all currently available as Harper Colophon paperbacks, are: *The Myth of Analysis*, first given as lectures at the Eranos meetings of 1966, 1968, and 1969 (Evanston, Ill.: Northwestern University Press, 1972; paperback, 1978); *Re-Visioning Psychology*, delivered as the 1972 Dwight Harrington Terry Lectures at Yale University (New York: Harper & Row, 1975; paperback, 1977); and *The Dream and the Underworld*, first developed in lectures during 1972–73 (New York: Harper & Row, 1979). Spring Publications of Zurich and Dallas publishes *Spring: An Annual of Archetypal Psychology and Jungian Thought*, ed. James Hillman, and a number of his works, including: *Suicide and the Soul* (2d ed., 1976); *Loose Ends—Primary Papers in Archetypal Psychology* (1975); (with Marie-Louise von Franz) *Lectures on Jung's Typology* (1971); (with others) *Puer Papers* (1979); (with others) *Facing the Gods* (1980); and (with others) *Fathers and Mothers* (1973).

2. Hillman, *Re-Visioning Psychology*, p. ix; see also his essay "Peaks and Vales" in *Puer Papers*, p. 58. Keats wrote, in a letter of April 21, 1819: "Call the world if you Please 'The vale of Soul-making' Then you will find out the use of the

world" (*The Letters of John Keats 1814–1821*, ed. Hyder Edward Rollins [Cambridge, Mass.: Harvard University Press, 1958], 2:102).

3. In *Re-Visioning Psychology* Hillman writes: "We misapprehend the Renaissance by seeing it as a turbulent tribute to Gods of love, light, life, and nature. . . . Renaissance psychology never lost touch with disintegration and death. Revival emerges from the threat to survival and is not a choice of something preferable. Revival is forced upon us by the dire pathologizing of psychic necessities. A renaissance comes out of the corner, out of the black plague and its rats, and the shades of death within the shadow" (pp. 206–7).

4. "Further Notes on Images," *Spring* (1978), pp. 152–82, quotation on p. 157. See also "An Inquiry into Image," *Spring* (1977), pp. 62–88, and "Image-Sense," *Spring* (1979), pp. 130–43.

5. *Redburn, White-Jacket, Moby-Dick* (New York: Library of America, 1983), p. 1208. Subsequent references to *Moby-Dick* and to *Redburn* will be to this edition, whose text is that of the Northwestern-Newberry edition of *The Writings of Herman Melville,* ed. Harrison Hayford, Hershel Parker, and G. Thomas Tanselle (Evanston and Chicago, Ill.: Northwestern University Press and The Newberry Library).

6. See especially C. G. Jung, *Symbols of Transformation* (Princeton, N.J.: Princeton University Press, 1967); for instance, "Horus' fight is the typical fight of the sun-hero with the 'whale-dragon' who, as we know, is a symbol of the Terrible Mother, of the voracious maw, the jaws of death in which men are crunched and ground to pieces" (p. 251).

7. Hillman in *Re-Visioning Psychology* is clearly orthodox in his statement on archetypes: "Archetypal psychology envisions the fundamental ideas of the psyche to be expressions of persons—Hero, Nymph, Mother, Senex, Child, Trickster, Amazon, Puer and many other specific prototypes bearing the names and stories of the Gods. These are the root metaphors. They provide the patterns of our thinking as well as of our feeling and doing. They give all our psychic functions—whether thinking, feeling, perceiving, or remembering—their imaginal life, their internal coherence, their force, their necessity, and their ultimate intelligibility" (p. 1281).

8. "Psychology and Literature," in *The Spirit in Man, Art, and Literature* (Princeton, N.J.: Princeton University Press, 1966), p. 88.

9. This rather obvious fact seems altogether to have escaped the notice of Edward F. Edinger, whose *Melville's Moby-Dick: A Jungian Commentary* (New York: New Directions, 1978) suffers thereby. When Martin Leonard Pops deals with the Mother archetype in *The Melville Archetype* (Kent, Ohio: Kent State University Press, 1970), he relies on Erich Neumann's redaction of Jung rather than on Jung himself.

10. *Pierre,* ed. Harrison Hayford, Hershel Parker, and G. Thomas Tanselle (Evanston and Chicago, Ill.: Northwestern University Press and The Newberry Library, 1971), p. 285.

11. *Billy Budd Sailor,* ed. Harrison Hayford and Merton M. Sealts (Chicago: University of Chicago Press, 1962), p. 115.

12. *Fathers and Mothers,* pp. 76–77. The contrast of this use of Horus with Jung's (see n. 6 above) is a further illustration of the revision Hillman has been making in Jungian thought.

CHAPTER 23

1. Desiderius Erasmus, *The Praise of Folly*, trans. Hoyt Hopewell Hudson (Princeton, N.J.: Princeton University Press, 1941), p. 10.

2. *Maximen und Reflexionen*, no. 1113.

3. *Adversus haereses* II.7.5.

4. *The Structure and Dynamics of the Psyche*, trans. R. F. C. Hull, *CW*, vol. 8, Bollingen Series XX (New York: Pantheon, 1960), p. 214, par. 417.

5. The distinction is applied to esthetics by Wilhelm Worringer in his *Abstraktion und Einfühlung: Ein Beitrag zur Stilpsychologie* (Munich: R. Piper, 1911). It is explored more broadly by Jung in his *Psychological Types*, trans. H. G. Baynes (New York: Pantheon, 1923), especially in chapter 7, pp. 358–71.

6. *Character and Motive in Shakespeare: Some Recent Appraisals* (New York: Longmans, Green, 1949), p. 42.

7. Edward Whitmont, "The Magical Dimension in Transference and Counter-Transference," in Gerhard Adler, ed., *Current Trends in Analytical Psychology* (London: Tavistock Publications, 1961), pp. 180–81. The analogy between ego-functioning and driving an automobile was suggested by Whitmont in a discussion.

8. Ibid., pp. 183 and 180.

CHAPTER 24

1. D. G. Jones, *Butterfly on Rock* (Toronto: University of Toronto Press, 1970); see especially pp. 5–8 and the chapter called "The Problem of Job" (pp. 83–110). For Frye's discussion of the garrison culture, see "Conclusion to a *Literary History of Canada* in *The Bush Garden* (Toronto: Anansi, 1971), especially pp. 225–26.

2. Margaret Atwood, *Survival: A Thematic Reading of Canadian Literature* (Toronto: Anansi, 1972), passim.

3. See Stephen Scobie, "Scenes from the Lives of the Saints: A Hagiography of Canadian Literature," *Lakehead University Review* 7 (1974): 3–20.

4. See Donald Stephens, "Lilacs out of the Mosaic Land: Aspects of the Sacrificial Theme in Canadian Fiction," *Dalhousie Review* 48 (1969): 500–509.

5. See Robert Kroetsch's comments in Russel M. Brown, "An Interview with Robert Kroetsch," *University of Windsor Review* 7 (Spring–Summer 1972): 1–18.

6. A full definition of the trickster, a term borrowed from anthropology, lies beyond the limits of this essay; indeed, there is some debate as to how this mythic archetype is best defined. An immensely influential book is Paul Radin's *The Trickster: A Study in American Indian Mythology* (London: Routledge & Paul, 1956), which contains the Winnebago trickster cycle, along with commentary by Radin, C. G. Jung, and Karl Kerényi. See also: Norman O. Brown, *Hermes the Thief* (New York: Random House, 1969); Max Linscott Ricketts, "The North American Trickster," *History of Religion* 5 (1966): 327–50; and Laura Makarius, "Le Mythe du Trickster," *Revue de l'Histoire des Religions* 175 (November 1969): 17–46.

7. Stanley Diamond, "Introductory Essay" in Radin, *The Trickster* (New York:

Schocken, 1972), p. xi. Diamond's entire essay is relevant, providing an extended comparison between the trickster myth and the Book of Job.

8. Ethel Wilson, *Swamp Angel* (Toronto: Macmillan, 1954); Margaret Atwood, *The Edible Woman* (Toronto: McClelland & Stewart, 1969); Margaret Laurence, *A Jest of God* (Toronto: McClelland & Stewart, 1964), and *The Fire Dwellers* (Toronto: McClelland & Stewart, 1969); Sheila Watson, *The Double Hook* (Toronto: McClelland & Stewart, 1959); Robert Kroetsch, *The Studhorse Man* (Toronto: Macmillan, 1969), and *Gone Indian* (Toronto: New Press, 1975).

9. "Robertson Davies: The Bizarre and Passionate Life of the Canadian People," in Donald Cameron, *Conversations with Canadian Novelists* (Toronto: Macmillan, 1973), 1:35.

10. Kroetsch specifically encountered the trickster myth in Radin's book; see interview (n. 5 above), p. 6. Jung's essay, translated into English as "On the Psychology of the Trickster Figure," first appeared in Radin's book and is reprinted in *CW*, vol. 9, pt. 1, *The Archetypes and the Collective Unconscious*.

11. Parenthetical references are to volume and paragraph numbers of *CW*.

12. In the concluding scene of *Fifth Business*, Eisengrim explains that his name was given him by Liesl: "It comes from one of the great northern beast fables, and it means Wolf." Near the end of *World of Wonders*, Liesl explains further: "I was acquainted with the great beast-legends of Europe, and in Reynard the Fox, you know, there is the great wolf Eisengrim, whom everyone fears, but who is not such a bad fellow, really."

13. Most of these details are not revealed until *World of Wonders*. At the end of *Fifth Business*, the reader is led to presume that Eisengrim's part in Staunton's death may have been much more significant, that he may even have used hypnosis to convince Staunton to fulfill his self-destructive fantasy. In *World of Wonders*, Eisengrim rather disingenuously denies all responsibility while relating the details of his final conversation with Staunton.

CHAPTER 25

1. John Beebe, *Psychiatric Treatment*, ed. C. P. Rosenbaum and J. E. Beebe (New York: McGraw-Hill, 1975), p. 100.

2. Paul Radin, *The Trickster: A Study in American Indian Mythology, with Commentaries by Carl Kerényi and C. G. Jung* (New York: Philosophical Library, 1956).

3. Leon Edel, *The Life of Henry James: The Treacherous Years: 1895–1901* (New York: Avon Discus Books, 1978).

4. Ibid., p. 84.

5. C. G. Jung, "On the Psychology of the Trickster Figure," in Radin, pp. 195–211.

6. Jane Wheelwright, *Death of a Woman* (New York: St. Martin's Press, 1981).

7. Ibid., p. 286.

8. Warwick Wadlington, *The Confidence Game in American Literature* (Princeton, N.J.: Princeton University Press, 1975), pp. 9–23.

9. Henry James, "The Turn of the Screw," in *The Two Magics* (New York: Macmillan, 1898), p. 15.

10. Edel, *Life of Henry James*, p. 205.

11. Susan Harvey, "One Fine Ignorance: The Experience of Reading Henry James," unpublished MS.

CHAPTER 26

1. For discussions of "character" as a critical and theoretical term in literary studies, see R. R. Wilson, "On Character: A Reply to Martin Price," *Critical Inquiry* 2, no. 4 (Autumn 1975): 191–98; "Approaching a Theory of 'Character,' " (review article), *Humanities Association Review* 27, no. 1 (Winter 1976): 32–46; "The Bright Chimera: Character as a Literary Term," *Critical Inquiry* 5, no. 4 (Summer 1979): 725–49.

2. William H. Gass, *Fiction and The Figures of Life* (New York: Alfred A. Knopf, 1970), p. 45.

3. Martin Price, "The Other Self: Thoughts about Character in The Novel," *Imagined Worlds: Essays on Some English Novelists in Honour of John Butt*, ed. Maynard Mack and Ian Gregor (London: Methuen, 1968), pp. 292–93.

4. Gass, p. 36.

5. Jung's influence upon White has been much discussed (and occasionally denied) in the past dozen years or so. The first major attempt to deal with this possible line of influence was A. P. Reimer's essay, "Visions of the Mandala in *The Tree of Man*," *Southerly* 1 (1967), reprinted in *Ten Essays on Patrick White*, ed. G. A. Wilkes (Sydney: Angus and Robertson, 1970), pp. 109–26. In her *The Mystery of Unity: Theme and Technique in the Novels of Patrick White* (Montreal: McGill-Queen's University Press, 1972), Patricia A. Morley stresses White's *familiarity* with Jung's concepts without trying to determine whether Jung was actually a *source* (pp. 9–11; cf. p. 90). Peter Beatson, in his *The Eye in The Mandala: Patrick White: A Vision of Man and God* (London: Paul Elek, 1976), methodologically assumes the primary relevance of Jung's work to an understanding of White's (pp. 10–11; esp. p. 117). More recent critics have placed an even greater emphasis upon the significance of Jung's influence. See especially, David Tacey, " 'It's Happening Inside': The Individual and Changing Consciousness in White's Fiction," in *Patrick White: A Critical Symposium*, ed. R. Shepherd and K. Singh (Adelaide: Centre for Research in the New Literatures in English, 1978), pp. 34–40. However, it should be remembered that not all of White's critics do agree about the extent of Jung's influence, and some would prefer to deny it altogether. This latter position appears to be White's own: in 1975 he remarked, in a letter to David Tacey, that he had not read any Jung "till about the time when [he] was writing *The Solid Mandala*" but that thereafter he could "honestly say" that Jung became an influence, whereas "anything Jungian in *The Aunt's Story* can only have come out of the unconscious." (See David Tacey, "Patrick White: Some Misconceptions About Jung's Influence," *Australian Literary Studies* 11, no. 2 [October 1979]: 245). Nonetheless, students of literature will recall Lawrence's apothegm concerning authors and tales.

6. *The Aunt's Story* (London: Eyre and Spottiswoode, 1948), p. 10.

7. Morley, p. 66.

8. William Hazlitt, "On Shakespeare and Milton," in *Lectures on the English Poets* (1818); reprinted in W. J. Bate, ed., *Criticism: The Major Texts*, rev. ed. (New York: Harcourt Brace Jovanovich, 1970), p. 308.

CHAPTER 27

1. The classic account of the four types is given in Jung's *Psychological Types*. Although the subsequent literature on the subject is voluminous, perhaps the most useful additional volume is *Jung's Typology*. In it, Jung's coworker and friend Marie-Louise von Franz presents several lectures on "The Inferior Function." Rather than focusing, as Jung did, on the attitude generated by the dominant function, von Franz characterizes the inferior function of each type and explores the way it impinges on his or her behavior.

2. The Mormon melodrama does eventually come to his attention. After the case was closed and the account written, Holmes did give minimal notice to the narrative of the events that had occurred in the American West, and his opinion of its appropriateness is a classic statement of his attitude toward feeling in general. At the beginning of *The Sign of Four*, Holmes makes his own evaluation of *A Study in Scarlet*, and we can be virtually certain that his remarks are addressed to part 2, which, in a deft act of literary revisionism not present in the original text, is now attributed to, and accepted by, Watson.

> "I glanced over it," said he. "Honestly, I cannot congratulate you upon it. Detection is, or ought to be, an exact science, and should be treated in the same cold and unemotional manner. You have attempted to tinge it with romanticism, which produces much the same effect as if you worked a love-story or an elopement into the fifth proposition of Euclid."
>
> "But the romance was there," I remonstrated. "I could not tamper with the facts."
>
> "Some facts should be suppressed, or, at least, a just sense of proportion should be observed in treating them. The only point in the case which deserved mention was the curious analytical reasoning from effect to causes, by which I succeeded in unravelling it."
>
> "I was annoyed at this criticism of a work which had been specially designed to please him. I confess, too, that I was irritated by the egotism which seemed to demand that every line of my pamphlet should be devoted to his own special doings."

That Holmes only "glanced over it" indicates that if he is at last aware of the facts, he has still rejected their feelingful impact on consciousness. It also puts the written text in a special light, since that is the only vehicle by which he could have heard of the events. His remarks on proportion and manner indicate that he found the style as well as the content inferior. His literary opinions and his modus operandi both favor the suppression of feeling that governs his whole conscious ego.

3. Synoptic comments by Freud on the oceanic feeling and subsequent differentiations may be found in the opening chapters of *Civilization and Its Discontents*. Erich Neumann, Jung's favored student, offers the most comprehensive and

detailed account in *The Origins and History of Consciousness,* especially sections A of Part 1 and Part 2.

WORKS CITED

Doyle, Arthur Conan. *The Complete Sherlock Holmes.* Garden City, N.Y.: Doubleday, 1930.

von Franz, Marie-Louise, and James Hillman. *Lectures on Jung's Typology.* Dallas: Spring, 1984.

Freud, Sigmund. *Civilization and Its Discontents.* Trans. and ed. James Strachey. New York: Norton, 1961.

Jung, Carl G. *Psychological Types.* Trans. R. F. C. Hull. Princeton, N.J.: Bollingen, 1971.

Jung, Carl G., et al. *Man and His Symbols.* New York: Dell, 1964.

Neumann, Erich. *The Origins and History of Consciousness.* Trans. R. F. C. Hull. Princeton, N.J.: Bollingen, 1970.

Tracy, Jack. *The Encyclopedia Sherlockiana.* Garden City, N.Y.: Doubleday, 1977.

CHAPTER 28

1. John Fowles, *The Aristos* (New York: New American Library, 1975), p. 215. Speaking of this work, a book of philosophy elaborating upon many of the tenets in his novels, Fowles says that Heraclitus provided "the original impetus and many of the ideas" for it.

2. Aniela Jaffé, *From the Life and Work of C. G. Jung* (New York: Harper & Row, 1971), p. 57.

3. John Fowles, *The Magus* (New York: Little, Brown and Company, 1965), p. 58. All further references to the novel will be cited in the text.

4. Jaffé, p. 60.

5. Antonin Artaud, *The Theatre and Its Double* (New York: Grove Press, 1958). Chap. 3, pp. 48–67, on "The Alchemical Theatre," offers many interesting insights into and further revelations about alchemy as it relates to *The Magus.*

6. Norman O. Brown, *Love's Body* (New York: Random House, 1966), p. 254.

CHAPTER 29

1. See Naomi Goldenberg, "Feminism and Jungian Theory," *Anima* (Spring 1977), pp. 14–17; and "A Feminist Critique of Jung," *Signs* 2, no. 2 (Winter 1976): 443–49.

2. See, for example, Erich Neumann, *The Origins and History of Consciousness* (New York: Harper and Brothers, 1954), pp. xxii, 125, 139, where he equates the feminine with nature, darkness, and the unconscious.

3. Susan Griffin, *Like the Iris of an Eye* (New York: Harper & Row, 1976), pp. 77–80.

4. Goldenberg, "A Feminist Critique," pp. 448–49.

5. Simone de Beauvoir, *The Second Sex* (New York: Bantam Books, 1952), p. 241.

6. See, for example, Carol Christ, "Some Comments on Jung, Jungians, and the Study of Women," *Anima* (Spring 1977), pp. 66–69.

7. Goldenberg, "A Feminist Critique," p. 448.

8. Jane Alpert, "Mother Right: A New Feminist Theory," *Ms. Magazine*, August 1973, pp. 52–55, 88–94.

9. Reviewed in *Ms. Magazine*, November 1974, p. 37.

10. See Neumann, pp. 54–95, passim.

11. Nancy Chodorow, "Family Structure and Feminine Personality," *Woman, Culture and Society*, ed. Michelle Zimbalist Rosaldo and Louise Lamphere (Stanford, Calif.: Stanford University Press, 1974), pp. 43–66.

12. Ibid., p. 50.

13. Ibid., p. 58.

14. Martha Weinman Lear, "Mother's Day: Bittersweet," *The New York Times Magazine*, May 11, 1975, p. 13.

15. Anne Sexton, *All My Pretty Ones* (Boston: Houghton Mifflin, 1962), p. 48.

16. Anne Sexton, *To Bedlam and Part Way Back* (Boston: Houghton Mifflin, 1960), pp. 53–59.

17. Sylvia Plath, *The Colossus and Other Poems* (New York: Vintage Books, 1968), pp. 58–60.

18. Robin Morgan, *Monster* (New York: Vintage Books, 1972), pp. 81–86.

19. May Sarton, *Collected Poems (1930–1973)* (New York: W. W. Norton, 1974), pp. 316–20.

20. Adrienne Rich, "When We Dead Awaken: Writing As Re-Vision," *College English* 34, no. 1 (October 1972): 18–25.

21. Adrienne Rich, *Poems: Selected and New, 1950–1974* (New York: W. W. Norton, 1975), pp. 196–98.

22. Barbara Charlesworth Gelpi and Albert Gelpi, eds., *Adrienne Rich's Poetry* (New York: W. W. Norton, 1975), p. 122.

23. Rich, *Poems*, pp. 235–45.

24. Henry Hill Collins, Jr., *Complete Field Guide to American Wildlife* (New York: Harper & Row, 1959), p. 169.

CHAPTER 30

1. C. G. Jung, "The Psychological Aspects of the Kore," in *Archetypes and the Collective Unconscious, CW*, 9, pt. 1, p. 188.

2. From C. G. Jung and C. Kerényi, *Essays on a Science of Mythology: The Myth of the Divine Child and the Mysteries of Eleusis*, trans. R. F. C. Hull, Bollingen Series 22 (Princeton, N.J.: Princeton University Press, 1969), p. 177.

3. Jane Ellen Harrison, *Prolegomena to the Study of Greek Religion* (Cleveland and New York: Meridian Books, 1966), p. 120.

4. "The Psychological Aspects of the Kore," p. 184.

5. Further documentation can be found in Merlin Stone, *When God Was a Woman* (New York: Dial Press, 1976), chap. 4, pp. 62–102, and in Jean Markale, *Women of the Celts*, trans. Gordon Cremonesi (London: Cremonesi Publications, 1975).

6. My principal sources are Harrison's *Prolegomena* and C. Kerényi, *Eleusis: Archetypal Images of Mother and Daughter,* trans. Ralph Manheim, Bollingen Series 65:4 (New York: Schocken Books, 1977).

7. *From Ritual to Romance* (Garden City, N.Y.: Doubleday/Anchor Books, 1957), pp. 37, 43, and 47. Sarah Pomeroy, in *Goddesses, Whores, Wives, and Slaves: Women in Classical Antiquity* (New York: Schocken Books, 1975), also discusses the centricity of the dying-god motif to rites celebrated through Greek and Roman history by and for women.

8. Markale, pp. 197–98.

9. "It also turns out," confirms Emma Jung, "that the hermit is a brother of Perceval's mother and of the rich Fisher's father. In the matriarchal order of society the mother's brother is granted the standing of a godfather." In Wolfram von Eschenbach's grail narrative, she explains, "it is also significant that the guardian of the Grail is Parzival's mother's brother, or else his grandfather or forebear on his mother's side." Emma Jung and Marie-Louise von Franz, *The Grail Legend,* trans. Andrea Dykes (New York: G. P. Putnam's, 1970), pp. 226, 73–74.

10. Markale, chap. 3.

11. Jung and von Franz, p. 25.

12. Edward Davies, a nineteenth-century scholar of Celtic lore, identifies the sacred vessel with a caer, or magically enclosed place, "and the same caer is described as an island," which the bard Taliesson portrayed as containing nine damsels presiding over a cauldron "in a quadrangular sanctuary, within a sacred island" (*The Mythology and Rites of the British Druids* [London: J. Booth, 1809], p. 154). In the first century A.D., Strabo wrote that "in an Island close to Britain, Demeter and Persephone are venerated with rites similar to the orgies of Samothrace." Quoted in Margaret Alice Murray, *The Witch-Cult in Western Europe* (London: Clarendon Press, 1921; rpt. Oxford University Press paperbacks, 1971), p. 21.

13. Markale, pp. 170–71.

14. See H. R. Trevor-Roper, *The European Witch-Craze of the Sixteenth and Seventeenth Centuries and Other Essays* (New York: Harper, 1967).

15. "Witchcraft: The Art of Remembering," p. 43, n. 3.

16. Ibid., p. 44. See also Gerald B. Gardner, *Witchcraft Today* (London: Rider and Company, 1954), p. 34, and Trevor-Roper, pp. 93, 145, 161.

17. This is Trevor-Roper's particular thesis; see *The Witch-Craze,* pp. 91–93.

18. Patricia Meyer Spacks, *The Female Imagination* (New York: Knopf, 1975), p. 411.

19. Elizabeth Zimmerman, *Knitter's Almanac* (New York: Scribner's, 1974), pp. 75–76.

GLOSSARY OF JUNGIAN TERMS

T*his glossary has been compiled from the work of several authoritative Jungian analysts; sources are indicated at the conclusion of each entry, and it should be emphasized that the brief definitions here are buttressed in the original sources by further paragraphs and even pages of discussion. Also, since there continue to be disputes within the Jungian camp on the evolving meaning of terms, the reader is best advised to consult several sources, and to read beyond their glossaries (Jung's own "Definitions" in* CW, *6, pp. 408–86) to get the most complete sense of a term's meaning. Finally, some entries include cross-references to other entries or to helpful selections in the text, such as the chapters by Maduro and Wheelwright and Samuels.*

Joseph Henderson. "Glossary." In *Cultural Attitudes in Psychological Perspective.* Toronto, 1984. Hereafter (HEN).

Aniela Jaffé, "Glossary" (including many direct quotations from Jung's *Collected Works*). In *Memories, Dreams, Reflections by C. G. Jung.* Recorded and edited by Aniela Jaffé. Translated by Richard and Clara Winston. Rev. ed. New York, 1973. Hereafter (JAF).

Frieda Fordham, "Glossary." In *An Introduction to Jung's Psychology,* 3d ed., 1966. Reprinted London, 1979. Hereafter (FOR).

Aniela Jaffé, "Technical Terms." In *C. G. Jung: Word and Image,* edited by A. Jaffé. Bollingen Series 97:2. Princeton, 1979. Hereafter (W&I).

ACTIVE IMAGINATION. The process of coming to know the images from the unconscious by reimagining them through some other medium, such as painting, poetry, drama, sandplay, etc. *See* Chap. 10, Hillman.

ALCHEMY. The older form of chemistry, which combined experimental chemistry in the modern sense with general, symbolic, intuitive, quasi-religious speculation about nature and man. Onto the unknown *materia* were projected many symbols that we now recognize as contents of the unconscious. The alchemist sought the "secret of God" in the unknown substance and thereby embarked on procedures and paths of exploration which resemble those of the modern-day psychology of the unconscious. This science, too, found itself confronted with an unknown objective phenomenon: the unconscious (W&I). *See* Chap. 2, Frye, "Forming Fours," and Chap. 28, Messer.

AMPLIFICATION. Elaboration and clarification of a dream-image by means of directed association and of parallels drawn from the human sciences (symbology, mythology, mysticism, folklore, history of religion, ethnology, etc.) (JAF).

Anima (Latin, "soul"). The unconscious, feminine side of a man's personality. She is personified in dreams by images of women ranging from prostitute and seductress to spiritual guide (Wisdom). A man's anima development is reflected in how he relates to women. Identification with the anima can appear as moodiness, effeminacy, and oversensitivity. Jung calls the anima "*the archetype of life itself*" (HEN). See Chap. 14.

Animus (Latin, "spirit"). The unconscious, masculine side of a woman's personality. Identification with the animus can cause a woman to become rigid, opinionated, and argumentative. More positively, he is the inner man who acts as a bridge between the woman's ego and her own creative resources in the unconscious (HEN). See Chap. 14.

Archetypes, Archetypal Images. Irrepresentable in themselves, their effects appear in consciousness as the archetypal images and ideas. These are universal patterns or motifs that come from the collective unconscious and are the basic content of religions, mythologies, legends, and fairy tales. They emerge in individuals through dreams and visions (HEN). See Part 2, Section A.

Collective. Psychic contents that are not unique to one individual but common to many (e.g., Archetypes, Instincts). When these contents are unconscious, they are termed the *collective unconscious* (FOR).

Complex. An emotionally charged group of ideas or images. At the "center" of a complex is an archetype or archetypal image (HEN).

Constellate. Whenever there is a strong emotional reaction to a person or a situation, a complex has been constellated (activated) (HEN).

Ego. The central complex in the field of consciousness. A strong ego can relate objectively to activated contents of the unconscious (i.e., other complexes), rather than identifying with them, which appears as a state of possession (HEN).

Extroversion. Attitude-type characterized by concentration of interest on the external object (JAF). Opposite of Introversion attitude-type.

Feeling. One of the four psychic functions in every personality. It is a rational function that evaluates the worth of relationships and situations. Feeling must be distinguished from emotion (HEN). See Chap. 27, Alkinson.

God-Image (God Imago). A term derived from the Church Fathers, according to whom the *imago Dei* is imprinted on the human soul. When such an image is spontaneously produced in dreams, fantasies, visions, etc., it is, from the psychological point of view, a symbol of the self (q.v.), of psychic wholeness. *See* Chap. 3, Baird.

Hierosgamos. Sacred or spiritual marriage, union of archetypal figures in the rebirth mysteries of antiquity and also in alchemy. A typical example is the alchemical conjunction of sun and moon (JAF).

Individuation. The conscious realization of one's unique psychological reality, including both strengths and limitations. It leads to the experience of the Self as the regulating center of the psyche (HEN).

Inflation. A state in which one has an unrealistically high or low (negative inflation) sense of identity. It indicates a regression of consciousness into unconsciousness, which typically happens when the ego takes too many unconscious contents upon itself and loses the faculty of discrimination (HEN).

INSTINCT. An unconsciously determined impulse or action which is collective (FOR).

INTROVERSION. Attitude-type characterized by orientation in life through subjective psychic contents (JAF). *See* EXTROVERSION.

INTUITION. One of the four psychic functions (along with feeling, sensation, and thinking). It is the irrational function which tells us the possibilities inherent in the present. In contrast to sensation (the function that perceives immediate reality through the physical senses), intuition perceives via the unconscious, e.g., through flashes of insight of unknown origin. See Chap. 27, Atkinson.

LIBIDO. Psychic energy (FOR).

MANDALA (Sanskrit). Magic circle. In Jung, symbol of the center, the goal, or the self (q.v.) as psychic totality; self-representation of a psychic process of centering; production of a new center of personality. This is symbolically represented by the circle, the square, or the quaternity (q.v.) (JAF). *See* Chap. 2, Frye, "Expanding Eyes."

MYTH. See ARCHETYPES. *See* Chap. 15, Samuels et al., "Myth."

NUMINOSUM. Term for the inexpressible, mysterious, terrifying, directly experienced, and pertaining only to divinity (JAF). *See* Chap. 15, Samuels et al., "*Numinosum.*"

OBJECTIVE PSYCHE. Replaces and enlarges Jung's earlier term "collective unconscious"; see Chap. 14, Maduro and Wheelwright.

PARTICIPATION MYSTIQUE. A term derived from the anthropologist Lévy-Bruhl, denoting a primitive, psychological connection with objects, or between persons, resulting in a strong unconscious bond (HEN).

PERSONA (Latin, "actor's mask"). One's social role, derived from the expectations of society and early training. A strong ego relates to the outside world through a flexible persona; identification with a specific persona (doctor, scholar, artist, etc.) inhibits psychological development (HEN).

PERSONAL UNCONSCIOUS. Repressed memories, wishes, emotions, etc., and subliminal perceptions of a personal nature (FOR).

PROJECTION. The process whereby an unconscious quality or characteristic of one's own is perceived and reacted to in an outer object or person. Projection of the anima or animus onto a real woman or man is experienced as falling in love. Frustrated expectations indicate the need to withdraw projections in order to relate to the reality of other people (HEN). See Chap. 14.

PSYCHE. A necessary postulate defining the subject matter of psychology and, as such, including the conscious and the unconscious (FOR).

PSYCHOSIS. The invasion of the conscious by unconscious contents, so that the ego is partially or completely overwhelmed. What is commonly known as insanity (FOR).

PUER AETERNUS (Latin, "eternal youth"). Indicates a certain type of man who remains too long in adolescent psychology, generally associated with a strong unconscious attachment to the mother (actual or symbolic). Positive traits are spontaneity and openness to change. His female counterpart is the PUELLA, an "eternal girl" with a corresponding attachment to the father-world (HEN).

QUATERNITY. "The quaternity is an archetype of almost universal occurrence. There are always four elements, four prime qualities, four colours, four castes, four ways of spiritual development, etc. So, too, there are four aspects of psychological orientation [Ed., the four functions]. . . . The ideal of completeness is the circle or sphere, but its natural minimal division is a quarternity" (Jung, *CW*, 11: 167; quoted in JAF). *See* Chap. 2, Frye, "Forming Fours."

REPRESSION. The more or less deliberate withdrawal of attention from some disagreeable experience, causing it to be expelled from consciousness so that it cannot be recalled at will (FOR).

SELF. The central archetype; the archetype of order; the totality of the personality. Symbolized by circle, square, quaternity (q.v.), child, mandala (q.v.), etc. " . . . the self is our life's goal, for it is the completest expression of that fateful combination we call individuality" (Jung, *CW*, 7, par. 404, quoted in JAF). *See* INDIVIDUATION. M. Fordham and others believe Self to be superordinate to the other archetypes.

SENEX (Latin, "old man"). Associated with attitudes that come with advancing age. Negatively, this can mean cynicism, rigidity, and extreme conservatism; positive traits are responsibility, orderliness, and self-discipline. A well-balanced personality functions appropriately within the puer-senex polarity (HEN).

SHADOW. An unconscious part of the personality characterized by traits and attitudes, whether negative or positive, which the conscious ego tends to reject or ignore. It is personified in dreams by persons of the same sex as the dreamer. Consciously assimilating one's shadow usually results in an increase of energy (HEN). *See* Chap. 22, Samuels et al., "Trickster."

SOUL. "If the human [soul] is anything, it must be of unimaginable complexity and diversity, so that it cannot possibly be approached through a mere psychology of instinct (*CW*, 4:331–32). . . . It would be going perhaps too far to speak of an affinity [between God and the human soul]; but at all events the soul must contain in itself the faculty of relation to God, i.e., a correspondence, otherwise a connection could never come about. This correspondence is, in psychological terms, the archetype of the God-image (q.v.)" (*CW*, 12, par. 11, quoted in JAF). *See* Chap. 10, Hillman.

SYMBOL. The best possible expression for something essentially unknown. Symbolic thinking is nonlinear, right-brain-oriented; it is complementary to logical, left-brain thinking (HEN). *See* Chap. 18, Philipson.

TRANSCENDENT FUNCTION. The reconciling "third" which emerges from the unconscious (in the form of a symbol or a new attitude) after the conflicting opposites have been consciously differentiated, and the tension between them held (HEN).

TRANSFERENCE AND COUNTERTRANSFERENCE. Particular cases of projection, commonly used to describe the unconscious emotional bonds that arise between two persons in an analytic or therapeutic relationship (HEN).

UNCONSCIOUS. " . . . everything of which I know, but of which I am not at the moment thinking; everything of which I was once conscious but have now forgotten; everything perceived by my senses, but not noted by my conscious mind; everything which, involuntarily, and without paying attention to it, I feel, think, remember, want, and do; all the future things that are taking shape in me and will sometime come to consciousness: all this is the content of the unconscious" *(CW,* 8:185).

" . . . we also find in the unconscious qualities that are not individually acquired but are inherited, e.g., instincts as impulses to carry out actions from necessity, without conscious motivation. In this 'deeper' stratum we also find the . . . archetypes. . . . The instincts and archetypes together form the 'collective unconscious' " *(CW,* 8:133–34).

"The deeper layers of the psyche lose their individual uniqueness as they retreat farther and farther into darkness. 'Lower down,' that is to say as they approach the autonomous functional systems, they become increasingly collective until they are universalized and extinguished in the body's materiality, i.e., in chemical substances. The body's carbon is simply carbon. Hence 'at bottom' the psyche is simply 'world' " *(CW,* vol. 9, pt. 1, p. 173; JAF).

UROBOROS. The mythical snake or dragon that eats its own tail. It is a symbol both for individuation as a self-contained, circular process, and for narcissistic self-absorption (HEN).

LIST OF BIBLIOGRAPHIES

Further resources for the study of Jung-and-literature include a number of bibliographies. The most comprehensive is:

Meurs, Jos van, and John Kidd. *Jungian Literary Criticism, 1920–1980: An Annotated, Critical Bibliography of Works in English (With a Selection of Titles After 1980).* Metuchen, N.J., and London: Scarecrow, 1988. This excellent book presents 902 entries, provides an author and subject index (in itself a Jung-and-literature literacy test), and briefly describes fourteen other sources for bibliographical searching.

Other useful bibliographies include:

Vincie, Joseph F., and M. Rathbauer-Vincie. *C. G. Jung and Analytical Psychology: A Comprehensive Bibliography.* New York: Garland, 1977. Arranges entries by year of publication through 1975.
Catalog of the Kristine Mann Library of the Analytical Psychology Club of New York. 2 vols. Boston: G. K. Hall, 1978.
Kiell, Norman, ed. *Psychoanalysis, Psychology, and Literature: A Bibliography.* 2 vols. 2d ed. Metuchen, N.J.: Scarecrow Press, 1982.
Duncan, Joseph E. "Archetypal Criticism in English, 1946–1980." *Bulletin of Bibliography* 40, no. 4 (1983): 206–30.
Natoli, Joseph, and Frederick L. Rusch. *Pyschocriticism: An Annotated Bibliography.* Westport, Conn.: Greenwood Press, 1984.
Dyer, Donald R. *Crosscurrents of Jungian Thought: An Annotated Bibliography.* Boston and London: Shambhala Publications, 1991. This work describes 780 books by Jung or about his ideas.

Various computer databases, such as *Dialog Information Services* and *BRS Information Technologies,* provide powerful opportunities to generate specialized bibliographies through searches across disciplines by single or combined words, whether occurring in titles or in footnotes.

Grateful acknowledgment is made to the publishers and individuals who have granted permission to reprint the following works, in part or in their entirety:

Adams, Michael Vannoy. "Deconstructive Philosophy and Imaginal Psychology." *Journal of Literary Criticism*, 2, no. 1 (June 1985): 23–39. Reprinted in *Deconstruction: A Critique*, ed. Rajnath. London: Macmillan, 1989. Reprinted by permission of Michael Vannoy Adams.

Atkinson, Michael. "Robert Bly's *Sleepers Joining Hands:* Shadow and Self." *Iowa Review* 7, no. 4 (1976): 135–53. Reprinted by permission of Michael Atkinson.

———. "Type and Text in *A Study in Scarlet:* Repression and the Textual Unconscious." *Clues* 8, no. 1 (1987): 67–99. Reprinted by permission of Popular Press.

Baird, James. "Preface," *Ishmael*. Baltimore: The Johns Hopkins University Press, 1956. Reprinted by permission of The Johns Hopkins University Press.

———. "Jungian Psychology in Criticism: Theoretical Problems." In *Literary Criticism and Psychology*, ed. Joseph P. Strelka. *Yearbook of Comparative Criticism*, vol. 7 (University Park and London: The Pennsylvania State University Press, 1976), pp. 3–30. Copyright 1976 by The Pennsylvania State University. Reproduced by permission of the publisher.

Beebe, John. "The Trickster in the Arts." *The San Francisco Jung Institute Library Journal* 2 (Winter 1981): 22–54. Reprinted by permission of John E. Beebe III, M.D.

Bennett, Donna A. *See* Brown, Russel M., and Donna A. Bennett.

Boer, Charles. "Poetry and Psyche." *Spring* (1979): 93–101. Reprinted by permission of Charles Boer.

Brown, Russel M., and Donna A. Bennett. "Magnus Eisengrim: The Shadow of the Trickster in the Novels of Robertson Davies." *Modern Fiction Studies* 22, no. 3 (Autumn 1976): 347–63. *Modern Fiction Studies*, copyright 1976 by Purdue Research Foundation, West Lafayette, Indiana 47907. Reprinted with permission.

Campbell, Joseph. "The Fashioning of Living Myths." In *Myths, Dreams, and Religion*, ed. Joseph Campbell. New York: E. P. Dutton, 1970. Reprinted by permission of ARC: The Society for the Arts, Religion, and Contemporary Culture.

Drew, Elizabeth. "The Mythical Vision." In *T. S. Eliot: The Design of His Poetry*. New York: Charles Scribner's Sons, 1949. Reprinted with permission of Charles Scribner's Sons, an imprint of Macmillan Publishing Company. Copyright 1949 Charles Scribner's Sons; copyright renewed © 1977 William H.

Brownell. UK and Commonwealth rights by permission of Eyre & Spottis-woode, an imprint of Octopus Publishing Group.

Elias-Button, Karen. "Journey into an Archetype: The Dark Mother in Contemporary Women's Poetry." *Anima* 4, no. 2 (1978): 5–11. Reprinted by permission of *Anima*.

Fordham, Frieda. "Glossary," *An Introduction to Jung's Psychology*, 3d ed. (London: Penguin Books, 1966). Copyright © Frieda Fordham, 1953, 1959, 1966; reproduced by permission of Penguin Books Ltd.

Frye, Northrop. "The Archetypes of Literature" (in the "My Credo" series). *The Kenyon Review* 12 (Winter 1951): 92–110. Reprinted by permission of the Helen Heller Agency, Toronto.

———. "Expanding Eyes." *Critical Inquiry* 2, no. 2 (1975–76): 199–216. Reprinted by permission of The University of Chicago Press.

———. "Forming Fours." *The Hudson Review* 6, no. 4 (Winter 1954): 611–19. Copyright © by the Hudson Review, Inc.; reprinted by permission.

Gelpi, Albert. "Emily Dickinson and the Deerslayer: The Dilemma of the Woman Poet in America." *San Jose Studies* 3, no. 2 (1977). Reprinted by permission of Albert Gelpi.

———. "Two Ways of Spelling It Out: An Archetypal-Feminist Reading of H.D.'s *Trilogy* and Adrienne Rich's *Sources. The Southern Review* 26, no. 2 (Spring 1990). Reprinted by permission of the author.

Henderson, Joseph L. "The Artist's Relation to the Unconscious." In *The Analytic Process: Aims, Analysis, Training,* ed. Joseph B. Wheelwright. The Proceedings of the Fourth International Congress for Analytical Psychology, published for the C. G. Jung Foundation of New York. New York: Putnam, 1971.

———. "Glossary," in *Cultural Attitudes in Psychological Perspective.* Toronto: Inner City Books, 1984. Reprinted by permission of Inner City Books.

Hillman, James. *Healing Fiction.* Barrytown, N.Y.: Station Hill Press, 1983. Copyright © by James Hillman; reprinted by permission.

Hinz, Evelyn, J., and John J. Teunissen. "Culture and the Humanities: The Archetypal Approach." *par rapport* 1, no. 1 (1978): 25–29. Reprinted by permission of Evelyn J. Hinz and John J. Teunissen.

———. "War, Love, and Industrialism: The Ares/Aphrodite/Hephaestus Complex in *Lady Chatterley's Lover.* In *D. H. Lawrence's "Lady": A New Look at Lady Chatterley's Lover,* ed. Michael Squires and Dennis Jackson. Athens, Ga.: University of Georgia Press, 1985. Copyright © by the University of Georgia Press; used by permission.

Jacoby, Mario. "The Analytical Psychology of C. G. Jung and the Problem of Literary Evaluation." In *Problems of Literary Evaluation,* ed. Joseph P. Strelka. *Yearbook of Comparative Criticism,* vol. 2 (University Park and London: The Pennsylvania State University Press, 1969), pp. 99–128. Copyright 1969 by The Pennsylvania State University. Reproduced by permission of the publisher.

Jung, C. G. *The Collected Works of C. G. Jung.* 20 vols. Edited by Herbert Read, Michael Fordham, and Gerhard Adler; executive editor (from 1967) William McGuire. Translated by R. F. C. Hull, except as otherwise noted. Bollingen Series 20. New York: Pantheon Books for Bollingen Foundation, 1953–60; Bollingen Foundation, 1961–67. Princeton, N.J.: Princeton University Press,

1967–79; London: Routledge & Kegan Paul, 1953–78. Fair use gratefully acknowledged.

——. "Glossary" in *Memories, Dreams, Reflections,* recorded and edited by Aniela Jaffé. Trans. Richard Winston and Clara Winston. New York: Pantheon, 1961. Translation copyright © 1961, 1962, 1963 by Random House, Inc. Reprinted by permission of Pantheon Books, a Division of Random House, Inc.; British Commonwealth rights by permission of Harper Collins Publishers Limited.

——. "Chronology" and "Technical Terms: Alchemy." In *Word and Image,* ed. Aniela Jaffé. Bollingen Series 97:2. Princeton, N. J.: Princeton University Press, 1979. Copyright © 1979 by Princeton University Press. Excerpts, pp. 221–25 ("Chronology"), p. 226 ("Technical Terms: Alchemy"), reprinted by permission of Princeton University Press.

Maduro, Renaldo J., and Joseph B. Wheelwright. "Analytical Psychology." In *Current Personality Theories,* ed. Raymond J. Corsini. Itasca, Ill.: F. E. Peacock Publishers, Inc., 1977. Reprinted by permission of the publisher.

Maud, Ralph. "Archetypal Depth Criticism and Melville." *College English* 45, no. 7 (November 1983): 695–704. Copyright 1983 by the National Council of Teachers of English. Reprinted with permission.

Messer, Richard E. "Alchemy and Individuation in *The Magus.*" *Cauda Pavonis* 2, no. 2 (Fall 1976): 2–8. Reprinted with permission of the author.

Olney, James. "*The Rhizome and the Flower.*" *The Perennial Philosophy—Yeats and Jung.* Berkeley: University of California Press, 1980. Copyright © 1980 The Regents of the University of California; reprinted by permission.

Philipson, Morris. "Symbolism and Epistemology" and "Jungian Aesthetics." In *Outline of a Jungian Aesthetics.* Evanston, Ill.: Northwestern University Press, 1963. Reprinted by permission of Morris Philipson.

Pratt, Annis V. *Archetypal Patterns in Women's Fiction.* Bloomington: Indiana University Press, 1981; Hemel Flemstead, Hertfordshire, England: The Harvester Press, 1981. Reproduced by permission of the publishers.

——. "Spinning Among Fields: Jung, Frye, Lévi-Strauss and Feminist Archetypal Theory." In *Feminist Archetypal Theory: Interdisciplinary Re-Visions of Jungian Thought,* ed. Estella Lauter and Carol Schreier Rupprecht. Knoxville: University of Tennessee Press, 1985. Copyright © 1985 by the University of Tennessee Press. Reprinted with permission.

Radford, F. L., and R. R. Wilson. "Some Phases of the Jungian Moon: Jung's Influence on Modern Literature." *English Studies in Canada* 7, no. 3 (1982): 311–32. Reprinted by permission of *English Studies in Canada.*

Raine, Kathleen, "C. G. Jung—A Debt Acknowledged." *Harvest* 34 (1988–89): 7–22. Reprinted by permission of Kathleen Raine.

Samuels, Andrew, Bani Shorter, and Fred Plaut. *A Critical Dictionary of Jungian Analysis.* London: Routledge, 1986. Reprinted with permission of Routledge.

Teunissen, John J. *See* Hinz, Evelyn J., and John J. Teunissen.

Wheelwright, Joseph B. *See* Maduro, Renaldo J., and Joseph B. Wheelwright.

Willeford, William. *The Fool and His Sceptre.* Evanston, Ill.: Northwestern University Press, 1969. Reprinted by permission of Northwestern University Press.

——. *Feeling, Imagination, and the Self.* Evanston, Ill.: Northwestern University Press, 1987. Reprinted by permission of Northwestern University Press.

Wilson, R. R. *See* Radford, F. L., and R. R. Wilson.

Blake, William, 34, 37, 71, 122, 167–76, 224, 236
Bly, Robert, 83–102, 255
Bodkin, Maud, 160, 224
Boehme, 122, 170, 171
Bollingen Foundation, 168
Boyle, Kay, 370
Broner, Esther, 163, 370
Brontë, Charlotte, 371
Brontë, Emily, 371
Brown, Norman O., 193, 351
Buddha, 96

Campbell, Joseph, 26, 46, 47, 57, 75–82, 193, 195, 368
Canadian literature: national psyche in, 286–87
Cassirer, Ernest, 3, 23, 220, 221
Cather, Willa, 53, 371
Chaplin, Charlie, 275, 280–81
Character, literary: animus and, 324–25; depiction of unconscious motivation in, 323–24; dreams and, 323; individuation and, 325; influence of Jung's model of personality upon, 315–27; and persona, 321–23; and type, 335–36
Child archetype, 305; analysts' exposition of, 184–85
Chodorow, Nancy, 358
Chopin, Kate, 371
Christ, Carol, 166
Coleridge, Samuel Taylor, 9, 50
Cooper, James Fenimore, 103, 108–10
Criticism, literary. See Archetypal literary criticism; Feminist archetypal literary criticism; Imaginal literary criticism; Jungian literary criticism; Myth criticism
Culler, Jonathan, 232, 235, 237, 238, 239
Cupid, 193

Daedalus, 76, 77
Daimon: in Yeats and Jung, 120, 129, 130–31; as personified images of interior vision, 130–32
Dante Alighieri, 71, 73, 160
Davies, Robertson: and Jungian influence, 386; and trickster, 285–301, 318, 320, 321
Deconstruction: and imaginal psychology, 129, 231–39
Delphi, 41
Demeter-Kore archetype, 203, 368, 369,

370, 371, 374; and feminine rebirth pattern, 155, 160, 162. See also Persephone; Mother, Great
Demming, Barbara, 357
Derrida, Jacques, 231–39; and James Hillman, 240, 248
Devil: as trickster, 299–300
Dickinson, Emily, 103–17, 378, 388
Didion, Joan, 161
Dionysus, 371
Doolittle, Charles, 381
Doolittle, Hilda (H.D.), 103, 116, 252, 376–94
Edel, Leon, 303, 309, 310
Einstein, Albert, 333
Eliade, Mircea, 193, 208
Eliot, George, 161
Eliot, T. S., 94, 116, 193, 195, 197, 378; and Grail Legend, 81–82; and mythical vision, 9–20
Ellenberger, Henri, 189
Elshtain, Jean, 165
Elusinian Mysteries: and myth and ritual, 203, 369, 370. See also Demeter-Kore; Persephone
Empedocles, 122, 123, 127
Erinyes, 364
Eve, 386

Father, 91
Faulkner, William, 323
Faust, 32, 68, 130
Feminine: archetypal, 383–87; and Dark Mother, 358–61; Eternal, feminist critique of, 157, 356; preliterary feminine archetypes, 367–75; triple goddess of, 370; and Great Mother, 84–85. See also Anima
Feminist archetypal literary criticism: and androgyny, 159–60, 368; and anima, 156; critique of Jung, 153–59; and feminine archetypes, 367–75; and feminist politics, 165; objections to Jung discussed, 377–78; and women's quest-myth, 159–63
Ferenczi, Sándor, 61
Fiedler, Leslie, 193, 197
Fields, W. C., 275, 277, 281–84
Flint, F. S., 253
Fool: as American myth, 308; and anima, 309–11; and chaos, 280–81; creative transvaluation of values by, 280–84;

Jaffé, Aniela, 130, 346
Jarrell, Randall, 390
Jesus Christ, 30–32, 381, 386
John, Saint of the Revelations, 383
Jolas, Eugene, 396
Jones, D. G., 286
Joyce, James, 57, 58, 71, 78, 80, 82, 94, 197, 396; and individuation, 76–77
Joyce, Lucia, 396
Jung, Carl Gustav: and alchemy, 29–32, 344, 346; animus, neglect of, 377; and archetypes, 15–17, 181–89; and art, source of, 13–14; attraction of, for non-Jungians, 167; concepts in selections, xi; and feminine archetypes, 368–69; and Frazer, 27–28, 29; and individuation process, 18–19, 313–14; and literature, 42, 264, 315–27; and *mundus imaginalis*, 169–71; and personality theory, 78–79, 313–14, 332–34; and polarities in psyche, 46–47, 333–34; and psychological types, 331–34; publications on literature and psychology, 65–72; and religion, 45–46, 172; and ritual, 369; and sexism, 155–56, 356; and symbolic language, 173–74, 215–22; and Yeats, 118–28. *See also* Jung and Freud; Jungian literary criticism
—and Sigmund Freud: Jung's break with Freud, 60–61, 130–31, 133, 154–55, 181–82; fiction and psychoanalysis, 131; libido theory, 26, 43–44; and life's stages, 47–48, 287; and literary criticism, 13–17, 28, 223–24, 317–19, 327; monism or dualism in systems of, 219–22; on myth, 13–14, 190; on "racial memory," 183
—Works: *Archetypes of the Collective Unconscious*, 346; *Man and His Symbols*, 56, 332; *Modern Man in Search of a Soul*, 169; *Mysterium Coniunctionis*, 133; "On the Nature of the Psyche," 61; "On the Psychology of the Trickster-Figure," 274, 287; "On the Relation of Analytical Psychology to Poetry," 3; "On the Relations between Analytical Psychology and Literature," 59, 65; *Psychological Types*, 80, 120, 127, 169; *Psychology and Alchemy*, 25, 29, 32, 35; "Psychology and Literature," 59; "Relations between the Ego and the

Unconscious," 63; *The Secret of the Garden Flower*, 169; *Symbols of Transformation (The Psychology of the Unconscious)*, 26–27, 29, 159, 264; *Two Essays on Analytical Psychology*, 25
Jung, Emma, 157, 368, 372, 377
Jung Institute, San Francisco, 181
Jung Institute, Zurich, 59, 129, 239
Jung-and-literature, ix. *See also* Jungian literary criticism
Jungian literary criticism: and aesthetics, 222–27; and literary character, 315–27, 335–36; contribution to revisioning psychological theory by, xi; issues in, x; and evaluation, 72–74; and modern literature, 318–19; overview of, ix–xii; practices typical of, x; psychology's contributions to critical theory in, x–xi; and cultural periods, 50–52, 79–80, 165–66; and terminology of, 94, 120–21; theoretical topics in, 38–53, 224–27; and tradition, 45
Jungian literary critics: three groupings of, 1–5; frequent topics of, 5–6

Kafka, Franz, 68
Kant, Immanuel, 216
Kaspar, 386
Kaufman, Sue, 161
Keaton, Buster, 275, 280–81
Keats, John, 112, 113, 269
Kekule, Friedrich, 333
Kenner, Hugh, 252–53
Kerényi, Karl, 132, 201, 203, 204
Kinnell, Galway, 94
Kirk, G. S., 203
Kluckhohn, Clyde, 182
Krishna, 308
Kroetsch, Robert, 287
Kundalini, 242–44

Lady Gregory, 122
Laing, R. D., 317
Lawrence, D. H., 139–52, 193, 318, 320, 323, 325, 381
Laurence, Margaret, 163, 287
Layard, John, 252
Lazarus, 96
Lear, Martha Weinman, 359
Leitch, Vincent, 3
Leonardo da Vinci, 308
Lessing, Doris, 139, 161, 162, 197, 317, 323, 370